D1364695

7th edition

The Price System and Resource Allocation

Richard H. Leftwich
Oklahoma State University

The Dryden Press
Hinsdale, Illinois

Copyright © 1979 by The Dryden Press
A division of Holt, Rinehart and Winston

All rights reserved
Library of Congress Catalog Card Number: 78-56200

ISBN: 0-03-045421-2
Printed in the United States of America
   039 9 8 7 6 5 4 3

Text and cover design by Jim Buddenbaum

To Maxine D. Leftwich

Preface

The objectives sought in this seventh edition of *The Price System and Resource Allocation* are the same as in previous editions. The book is intended basically for third-year undergraduates who have had no more than a principles course. In it a logical, consistent framework of microeconomic principles is constructed step-by-step. There are sufficient applications to demonstrate the usefulness of microeconomic theory to students. I believe that the theory core of the book provides an adequate foundation for advanced study of economics. Calculus is not used in the argument of the text, but a complete set of mathematical footnotes will help students make the transition to more advanced mathematical treatments of microeconomics.

As well as trying to improve my organization and exposition, I have added a few items in this edition. Corner solutions are discussed in the chapter on consumer choice. Lorenz curves and the negative income tax are introduced in the chapter on income distribution. Greater emphasis is given to the modern theory of consumer choice. Closer ties are made between the theory of production and the theory of costs. A chapter outline and a list of key concepts have been placed at the beginning of each chapter. Empirical material has been updated. In general, I have attempted to make the book more useful to students.

I am indebted to many for help with the revision. I appreciate especially the comments I receive from users of the book. The mathematical footnotes have been made intelligible and consistent by Ms. Shiu-fang Yu of Merck Sharp & Dohme. Many useful suggestions have come from Professor Joan M. McCrea, The University of Texas at Arlington; Professor Errol Glustoff, The University of Tennessee at Knoxville; Professor Alvin Cohen, Lehigh University; Professor T. Dudley Wallace, Duke University; Professor James B. Hagerbaumer, University of Wisconsin at Oshkosh; Professor Joe Gallo, University of Cincinnati; Professor Walter E. Mullendore, The University of Texas at Arlington; Professor E. Warren Shows, University of South

Florida; Professor John P. Henderson, Michigan State University, and Mr. David Harrison, Oklahoma State University graduate student and instructor. The secretarial work was ably handled by Ms. Gaye Trivitt and Ms. Diana Mnich.

Richard H. Leftwich

Contents

Part 1   **A review of basic economic analysis**

Chapter 1   **Economic activity and economic theory**   3

     Economic activity   3
     Methodology   8
     Price theory and economic theory   11
     Welfare   12
     Summary   13
     Suggested readings   14
     Questions and exercises   14

Chapter 2   **The organization of an economic system**   17

     A simplified model   18
     The functions of an economic system   20
     Summary   26
     Suggested readings   27
     Questions and exercises   27

Chapter 3   **The purely competitive market model**   29

     Pure competition   29
     Demand   32
     Supply   37
     Market price   39
     Price elasticity of demand   43
     Summary   56
     Suggested readings   57
     Questions and exercises   58

Chapter 4   **Basic applications of the model**   61

     Minimum price policies   61
     Maximum price policies   66
     Excise tax incidence   71
     Summary   73
     Suggested readings   73
     Questions and exercises   74

Part 2   **The underpinnings of demand**

Chapter 5   **The modern theory of consumer choice and demand**   77

The consumer's preferences   77
Constraints on the consumer   85
Maximization of consumer satisfaction   88
Demand curves and Engel curves   90
Income effects and substitution effects   98
Market demand curves   101
Exchange and welfare   102
Some applications of indifference curve analysis   104
Index numbers   109
Summary   113
Suggested readings   115
Questions and exercises   115

Chapter 6   **The utility approach to consumer choice and demand —
                   a special case**   119

The utility concept   119
Indifference curves   125
Consumer choice   128
Demand curves   132
Exchange and welfare   135
Some applications of utility analysis   138
Summary   140
Suggested readings   141
Questions and exercises   141

Chapter 7   **Market classifications and demand as viewed by the seller**   145

Pure competition   145
Pure monopoly   147
Oligopoly   148
Monopolistic competition   151
Summary   154
Suggested readings   154
Questions and exercises   155

Part 3   **The foundations of costs and supply**

Chapter 8   **The principles of production**   159

The production function   159
The law of diminishing returns   168

Product curves and technical efficiency 169
Production possibilities for the economy 182
Natural gas versus coal in power generation 186
Summary 187
Suggested readings 188
Questions and exercises 189

Chapter 9   **Costs of production** 193

The concept of costs 193
The short-run and long-run viewpoints 196
Short-run cost curves 197
Long-run cost curves 209
Some applications of cost analysis 220
Summary 223
Suggested readings 224
Questions and exercises 224

Appendix: The geometry of short-run per unit cost curves 225

Part 4   **Prices and output levels of goods and services**

Chapter 10   **Pricing and output under pure competition** 231

The very short run 231
The short run 235
The long run 244
The welfare effects of pure competition 253
Summary 257
Suggested readings 258
Questions and exercises 258

Chapter 11   **Pricing and output under pure monopoly** 261

Costs and revenues under monopoly 261
The short run 265
The long run 269
Price discrimination 273
The welfare effects of pure monopoly 277
Regulation of monopoly 280
Summary 283
Suggested readings 285
Questions and exercises 285

Appendix I: Derivation of the marginal revenue curve 286
Appendix II: Price, marginal revenue, and elasticity of demand 291

Chapter 12	**Pricing and output under oligopoly**	295
	Costs and demand	295
	Pure and differentiated oligopoly	296
	Collusion versus independent action	297
	The short run	299
	The long run	311
	Nonprice competition	318
	The welfare effects of oligopoly	320
	Summary	323
	Suggested readings	324
	Questions and exercises	324
Chapter 13	**Pricing and output under monopolistic competition**	327
	Some special characteristics	327
	The short run	328
	The long run	329
	Welfare effects of monopolistic competition	333
	Summary	335
	Suggested readings	336
	Questions and exercises	336
Part 5	**The determination of and the functions of resource prices**	
Chapter 14	**Pricing and employment of resources: Pure competition**	341
	Simultaneous employment of several variable resources	341
	Pricing and employment of a given variable resource	344
	Economic rent	354
	Summary	356
	Suggested readings	357
	Questions and exercises	357
Chapter 15	**Pricing and employment of resources: Monopoly and monopsony**	361
	Monopoly in the selling of products	361
	Monopsony in the buying of resources	368
	Summary	379
	Suggested readings	380
	Questions and exercises	380
Chapter 16	**Resource allocation**	383
	The conditions of maximum welfare	383
	Resource markets	384
	Resource allocation under pure competition	385

	Conditions preventing correct allocation	389
	Summary	397
	Suggested readings	398
	Questions and exercises	398

Chapter 17	**Distribution of income and product**	401
	Individual income determination	401
	Personal distribution of income	402
	Causes of income differences	405
	Movements toward less inequality	415
	Summary	420
	Suggested readings	420
	Questions and exercises	421

| **Part 6** | **How the pieces fit together** | |

Chapter 18	**Equilibrium and welfare**	425
	The concepts of equilibrium and welfare	425
	The conditions of optimum welfare	429
	Private enterprise and general equilibrium	436
	Summary	443
	Suggested readings	443
	Questions and exercises	443

	Appendix: Linear programming	447
	Glossary	469
	Index	481

Part 1

A review of basic economic analysis

The level of economic sophistication that students bring to the intermediate microeconomics course varies greatly from university to university, and from student to student within any one university. The first four chapters, which comprise Part 1, provide a review of the nature and purpose of microeconomic analysis. They also review the fundamentals of demand, supply, and price determination. In some universities in which students have been uniformly well trained in principles courses, Part 1 may be omitted at no great cost to the students. But in most universities it will provide and/or reinforce the foundations on which microeconomic analysis is built.

Chapter 1

Chapter contents

Economic activity

    Human wants
    Origins of wants
    Want satisfaction and levels of living

    Resources
    Classification of resources
    Characteristics of resources

    Techniques

Methodology

    The construction of economic theory
    The functions of economic theory

**Price theory and
economic theory**

Welfare

Summary

    Suggested readings
    Questions and exercises

Key concepts

Economic activity
Wants
Living standards
Resources
Techniques
Theory
Postulates or premises
Hypotheses
Principles
Positive economics
Normative economics
Microeconomics
Macroeconomics
Welfare
Pareto optimum

Economic activity and economic theory

Our economic, political, and social systems are experiencing troubled times. There has been an unparalleled period of prolonged inflation coupled with relatively high rates of unemployment. We are experiencing an "energy crisis." A system of price controls in the early 1970s not only failed to stop inflation but also generated serious economic dislocations and imbalances while it was failing. Social values and social institutions are being subjected to scrutiny and questioning more intense than any we have seen since the Great Depression. Severe criticism is being leveled at the operation of the capitalist or private enterprise system—some of it pinpoints weaknesses and some of it reveals much ignorance about the nature and performance of such a system.

This book is intended to provide background for the debate. Its purpose is twofold: (1) to spell out the conditions that must be met in *any* economic system if it is to be efficient and (2) to show the operation of the price system, with its strengths and weaknesses, as a means of moving the economy toward those conditions. We should recognize at the outset that there are alternative ways of organizing economic activity; this book, however, is concerned predominantly with the price mechanism.

In this introductory chapter we shall survey the nature of economic activity, the basic methodology of economics, and the relation of price theory to the general body of economic theory. The next three chapters will set the stage for the detailed exposition of price theory that begins in Chapter 5.

Economic activity

While the boundaries marking off economics from other disciplines or fields of knowledge are hard to draw, general agreement does exist with regard to its main contents. Economics is concerned with humanity's well-being or welfare. It encompasses the social relationships or social organization involved in allocating scarce resources among alternative human wants and in using those resouces toward the end of satisfying wants as fully as possible. The key elements of economic activity are (1) human wants, (2) resources, and (3) techniques of production. These will be discussed in turn.

Human wants

Economic activity is directed toward the satisfaction of human wants. These provide the driving, motivating force; their fulfillment may be thought of as the end or goal of economic activity. The wants that are important in any economic system may be those of the general public, those of powerful special interest groups, those of government leaders, and others. Different societies are likely to attach different relative weights to whose wants are the most important.

Wants have two characteristics—they are varied, and in the aggregate over time they are insatiable. Insatiability does not necessarily imply that any one individual's desire for a particular commodity is unlimited. The quantity of a good consumed each week that contributes to one's well-being may well be finite. It is commodities in the aggregate for which wants are unlimited, partly because of the wide variety of wants that individuals can conjure up.

Origins of wants   The insatiability of wants in the aggregate becomes evident when we consider some of the ways in which wants arise. First, they arise for what the human organism must have in order to continue functioning. The desire for food is the most obvious case in point. In intemperate climates two other desires usually arise from necessity—the desires for shelter and for clothing. One or the other, or both of these, must be fulfilled in some degree if the human organism is to survive the rigors of low temperatures or the extreme heat of the tropics.

Wants arise, too, from the culture in which we live, for every society dictates certain requisites for "the good life"—certain standards of housing and food consumption; patronizing of the arts; and possession and consumption of such items as automobiles, charcoal broilers, television sets, and stereo sound systems. The status of individuals in society is thought to depend to a considerable extent upon their levels of consumption. Consequently, many wants are generated in the process of attempting to improve one's status.

The satisfying of our biological and cultural needs requires a wide variety of goods. Individual tastes vary. Some people like roast beef, some like ham, and others like mutton. Over time these same individuals seek to satisfy their hunger with different foods. Tastes in clothing differ, and different social occasions call for different modes of dress. Age differences, climatic differences, social differences, educational differences, and a host of other differences give rise to variety in the goods desired by society in general.

Finally, wants are generated by the activity necessary to satisfy other wants, or want-satisfying activity may be said to create new wants. No better illustration can be found than that of a student pursuing higher education. The process of attending a college or university opens new vistas of potential desires that heretofore the student had not known existed—intellectual and cultural desires and many others. The generation of new wants in the process of endeavoring to satisfy old wants plays an important role in multiplying human desires.

These sources from which wants arise do not represent an exhaustive classification. This list, however, illustrates the possibility of the infinite expansion of wants over time and the impossibility of an economy's ever satiating all the wants of all its people.

Want satisfaction and levels of living The level of want satisfaction achieved in a given economic society is hard to measure. Ordinarily it is expressed in terms of per capita income—sometimes gross and sometimes net, depending on the availability of data. There may be a great dispersion around the average; and the average income figure may be misleading. Nevertheless, per capita income appears to be one of the best measures available of the performance of an economy.

Sometimes people judge the performance of an economy on the basis of whether per capita incomes are at a "satisfactory" level. The implication is that if the level is below "satisfactory," something ought to be done about it—that everyone is entitled to a "satisfactory" level of living. Judgments of these kinds are not very valuable from the point of view of economic analysis.

In the first place, the level of living "satisfactory" to a society is entirely relative to the historical time under consideration. A level of living with which most people in the United States would have been quite happy 50 years ago would not be satisfactory today. What is satisfactory today will probably not be satisfactory 50 years from now. As the economy's capacity to produce increases, the concept of what constitutes a "satisfactory" level of living shifts upward. The insatiability of human wants, together with increases over time in productive capacity, leads to an ever changing concept of what constitutes a "satisfactory" level.

In the second place, the concept of what constitutes a "satisfactory" level varies among different geographic areas. A level of living high enough to make most Asians content for the present will not be high enough for most Europeans or Americans. People become accustomed to certain living levels, and a "satisfactory" one for them becomes just a little higher than what they currently have.

For most purposes it is not relevant to judge the performance of an economy on the basis of whether it provides a "satisfactory" level of living. Rather, it is more relevant to ask whether it provides the highest level of living that its resources and techniques will permit at a given time, making due allowance for some part of current production to be set aside to augment future productive capacity. One can ask no more of an economy. It should not provide much less. To the extent that some part of current production is used to augment future productive capacity, the level of living that the economy can provide will grow continuously.

Resources

The level of want satisfaction that an economy can achieve is limited partly by the quantities and qualities of its known resources. Resources are the means available for producing goods that are used to satisfy wants. Hundreds of different kinds of resources exist in the economy. Among these are labor of all kinds, raw materials of all kinds, land, machinery, buildings, semifinished materials, fuel, power, transportation, and the like.

Classification of resources   Resources can be classified conveniently into two categories: (1) labor or human resources and (2) capital or nonhuman resources. *Labor resources* consist of labor power or the capacity for human effort, both of mind and of muscle, used in producing goods. The term *capital* can be misleading since it is used in several different ways not only by noneconomists but by economists as well. We use the term to include all nonhuman resources that can contribute toward placing goods in the hands of the ultimate consumer. Specific examples are buildings, machinery, land, available mineral resources, raw materials, semifinished materials, business inventories, and any other nonhuman tangible items used in the productive process.[1] We need particularly to guard against confusing capital and money. Money is not capital as the term is used in this book. Money as such produces nothing. It is a technique[2] facilitating the exchange of goods and services and resources. By and large the use of monetary techniques enables us to obtain higher satisfaction levels than we can reach with barter techniques.

The significance of this classification of resources should not be overstated. It is more descriptive than analytical. Within each category there are many different kinds of resources, and the differences between two

[1] In a basic sense inventories of goods in the hands of ultimate consumers also constitute capital, since it is the satisfaction yielded by goods rather than the goods themselves that consumers desire. Thus, such goods are still means of satisfying ultimate ends or desires of consumers; that is, they have yet to produce the want satisfaction they are supposed to produce. We shall not cut it this fine. Goods in the hands of the ultimate consumer will be called consumer goods rather than capital, and this will avoid some complexities.

[2] See p. 8.

kinds falling within the same classification may be more significant analytically then the differences between two kinds in separate classifications.
Consider, for example, a human ditch digger and an accountant. Both fall
under the descriptive classification of labor. However, from an analytical
point of view, the human ditch digger is more closely related to a mechanical ditch digger, which would fall under the descriptive classification
of capital, than the human ditch digger is to the accountant.

Characteristics of resources   Resources have three important characteristics: (1) most resources are limited in quantity; (2) they are versatile;
and (3) they can be combined in varying proportions to produce a given
commodity. These will be considered in turn.

Most resources are scarce in the sense that they are limited in quantity
relative to desires for the products that they can produce. These are called
economic resources. Some resources, such as the air used in internal-
combustion engines, are so abundant that they can be had for the taking.
These are called *free resources* since they command no price. If all resources were free, there would be no limitation on the extent to which
wants could be satisfied and no economic problem. Levels of living could
soar to infinite heights. Free resources are of no significance for economic
analysis and will be disregarded.

We are interested in economic resources. The scarcity of economic resources makes necessary the picking and choosing of which wants are to be
satisfied and to what degree. This is the economic problem in a nutshell.

The population of an economy sets an upper limit on the quantities of
labor resources available. Various factors—education, custom, general
state of health, age distribution—determine the actual proportion of the
population that can be considered as the labor force. Over a short period of
time—say, one year—the total labor force cannot be expanded very much,
but over a longer period it may be variable as population has time to change
and as changes occur in the factors determining the quantity and the quality
of the actual labor force.

Generally, the total capital equipment of the economy is expanding over
time, but this expansion occurs slowly. The amount that an economy can
add to its total stock of capital equipment in a year's time without seriously
restricting current consumption is a fairly small proportion of its existing
capital. Therefore, over a short period of time the quantity of capital available to produce goods is limited.

The versatility of resources refers to their capacity to be put to different
uses. Almost any kind of resource can be used in the production of a wide
variety of goods. Common labor can be used in the production of almost
every conceivable good. The more highly skilled or specialized a resource
becomes, however, the more limited are its uses. There are fewer alternative jobs for skilled machinists than for common laborers. There are still

fewer alternative jobs for the brain surgeon, the ballet dancer, or the professional athlete. Even with a high degree of resource specialization, supplies of one kind of specialized resource can be developed over time at the expense of supplies of other kinds. Individuals can be trained as physicians rather than as dentists. More bricklayers can be developed at the expense of the quantity of carpenters. More tractors and fewer combines can be produced. The resources of the economy are quite fluid with respect to the forms that they can take and the kinds of goods that they can produce. The longer the period of time under consideration, the greater their fluidity or versatility.

Possibilities of combining resources in various proportions to produce a given good usually exist. Few, if any, goods require rigid proportions of resources. Generally, the possibility exists of substituting some kinds of labor for capital, or for other kinds of labor, and vice-versa. This characteristic of resources is closely related to the characteristic of versatility. Substitution possibilities and versatility generate the potential for the economy to switch productive capacity from one line of production to another; they enable the economy to adjust to the changing character of human wants. Resources can be transferred into industries producing goods for which wants are expanding and out of industries producing goods for which wants are diminishing.

Techniques

Techniques of production and exchange, together with quantities and qualities of resources in existence, set limits on the level of want satisfaction that an economy can achieve. *Techniques* are the know-how and the physical means of transforming resources into want-satisfying form. The nature of techniques available to enterprisers is generally considered to lie largely outside the province of economic theory and in the province of engineering. However, the simultaneous choices of goods to be produced, quantities to be produced, and techniques to be used fall within the scope of economics. Economists usually assume that for the production of any commodity a given range of techniques is available and that for any quantity of the commodity produced the least-cost techniques will be used.

Methodology

In order to make a useful, systematic study of economic activity, we must learn and apply economic theory to it. But what is economic theory? Like the theory of any other science it consists of sets of principles or causal relationships among the important "facts" or variables that surround economic activity. We shall look first at the construction and functions of sets of economic principles; then we shall turn to the place of price theory within the overall scheme of the discipline.

The construction of economic theory

Any set of principles (a theory) must have a bedrock starting point consisting of propositions or conditions that are taken as given or as being so without further investigation. These we call the *postulates* or the *premises* upon which the theory is erected. In aerodynamics the forces of gravity, the operation of centrifugal force, and air resistance may be among the postulates of a theory involving lift, thrust, and drag. In economics we may build a theory of consumer behavior on the postulate of consumer rationality, defined as the general desire of consumers to secure as much satisfaction as they can in spending their incomes. The first step, then, in the construction of a theory is the specification and definition of its postulates.

The second step is the observation of "facts" concerning the activity about which we want to theorize. For example, if the activity in question is the exchange of groceries between supermarkets and consumers, the activity should be looked into as thoroughly as possible. As facts emerge from continued and repeated observation, it will become apparent that some are irrelevant and can be discarded; others will obviously be of significant value. In the grocery exchange case the hair color of consumers is not likely to be important, but the weekly amounts of money that consumers have to spend, the number of supermarkets available to them, and the weekly quantities of groceries available to be purchased will most certainly be important.

The third step—and this one will frequently be taken concurrently with the second—is the application of the rules of logic to the observed facts in an attempt to establish causal relationships among them and in order to eliminate as many irrelevant and insignificant facts as possible. *Deductive* chains of logic may lead us to believe that certain effects follow certain causes in a regular manner. We may reason that consumers with larger incomes are willing to pay higher prices for specific goods. Therefore, an increase in consumer incomes is likely to lead to higher prices. Or, on the other hand, we may reason *inductively*. Repeated observations may indicate that increases in consumer incomes and increases in prices occur simultaneously. So, putting two and two together, we reach the tentative conclusion that higher incomes cause prices to rise. Such tentative statements of cause-and-effect relationships are called *hypotheses*.

The fourth step in the process of establishing a set of principles is a crucial one. Once hypotheses have been formulated, they must be thoroughly tested to determine the degree to which they are valid, that is, the extent to which they give good results. The tools of statistics and econometrics are of particular value in this respect. Some hypotheses will not withstand the rigors of repeated testing and, consequently, must be rejected. The testing process may suggest modifications in others; then the modified hypotheses must be tested. Still other hypotheses may be found to hold up most of the time in most of the circumstances to which they are relevant. These we usually refer to as *principles*.

It would be foolish to regard a set of principles as absolute truth. The testing process in economics and in other sciences never ends. At any given point in time we think of principles as the best available statements of causal relations; however, additional data and better testing techniques may enable us to improve on them over time. Economic theory is not a once-and-for-all set of principles. It is viable—evolving and continually growing.

The functions of economic theory

The principal functions of economic theory fall into two categories: (1) to explain the nature of economic activity and (2) to predict what will happen to the economy. The explanation of the nature of economic activity enables us to understand the economic environment in which we live—how one part relates to others and what causes what. We also want to be able to predict with some degree of accuracy what is likely to happen to the key variables that affect our well-being and to be able to do something about it if we dislike the predicted consequences.

Economists differentiate between *positive economics* and *normative economics* on the basis of whether the users of theory are concerned with causal relations only or whether they desire some kind of intervention in economic activity intended to alter the course of that activity. Positive economics is supposed to be completely objective, limited to the cause-and-effect relationships of economic activity. It is concerned with the way economic relations *are*. By way of contrast, normative economics is concerned with what *ought* to be. Value judgments must necessarily be made; that is, possible objectives to be achieved must be ranked, and choices must be made among those objectives. Economic policy making—conscious intervention in economic activity with the intent of altering the course that it will take—is essentially normative in character. But if economic policy making is to be effective in improving economic well-being, it must obviously be rooted in sound positive economic analysis. Policy makers should be cognizant of the full range of consequences of the policies that they recommend.

Price theory and economic theory

Price theory (*microeconomic theory*) and the theory of the economy as a whole (*macroeconomic theory*) constitute the basic analytical tool kit of the discipline of economics. The principles of both are used in special subject areas, such as monetary economics, international trade and finance, public finance, manpower economics, agricultural economics, regional economics, and so on. The concentration on microeconomics in this book should in no way be interpreted as minimizing the importance of macroeconomics. Both parts of the kit are essential to a thorough understanding of economic activity.

Microeconomics is concerned with the economic activities of such individual economic units as consumers, resource owners, and business firms. It is concerned with the flow of goods and services from business firms to consumers, the composition of the flow, and the evaluation or pricing of the component parts of the flow. It is concerned, too, with the flow of productive resources (or their services) from resource owners to business firms, with their evaluation, and with their allocation among alternative uses.

Macroeconomics treats the economic system as a whole rather than treating the individual economic units of which it is composed. The particular goods and services making up the flow from business firms to consumers are not integral parts of the analysis, nor are the individual productive resources or services flowing from resource owners to business firms. The value of the overall flow of goods (net national product) and the value of the overall flow of resources (national income) will receive the focus of attention.

Price index numbers or general price level concepts in macroeconomics replace the individual prices of microeconomics. Macroeconomics concentrates on the causes of change in aggregate money flows, the aggregate flow of goods and services, and the general employment level of resources. Prescription of cures for economic fluctuations and for unemployment of resources follows logically from the determination of their causes. Macroeconomics has much to say about the nature of economic growth and the conditions necessary for the expansion of productive capacity and national income over time.

Price theory is somewhat abstract. We may as well face this point at the outset. Difficulties will be encountered in this respect, but if we recognize the nature of the difficulties, they will seem less formidable. Primarily, we shall find that price theory does not give a complete description of the real world. It will not tell us why a price differential of 5 cents per gallon for gasoline exists between Oklahoma City and Cleveland on any given date. However, it should help us understand the real world. It should show us in general how the price(s) of gasoline is established and the role that gasoline prices play in the overall operation of the economy.

Price theory is abstract because it does not and cannot encompass all the economic data of the real world. To take all of the data and factors that influence economic decisions of consumers, resource owners, and business firms into consideration would involve minute descriptions and analyses of every economic unit in existence, and that would be an impossible task. The function of theory is to single out what appear to be the most relevant data and to build an overall conceptual framework of the price system in operation from these. We concentrate on the data and principles that seem to be most important in motivating most economic units. In eliminating less important data and in building up a logical theoretical structure, we lose some contact with reality. However, we gain in our understanding of the overall operation of the economy because we reduce the factors to be considered to manageable proportions. We may lose sight of some individual trees, but we gain more understanding and a better view of the forest.

The sets of principles comprising price theory should show the directions in which economic units tend to move and should explain the more important reasons why they tend to move in those directions. It should be a set of logically consistent approximations of how the economy operates. The abstraction and precision of theory is essential to clear thinking and to policy making in the real world, but we should guard against the notion that it provides an unqualified description of the real world. We should·make theory our tool—not our master.

Welfare

The central theme of this book is economic *welfare,* defined as the economic well-being of those who live in the economy. The welfare or well-being of individuals presents no great conceptual difficulties. The simplest case is one in which individuals (or family units) are thought to be the best judges of what does or does not contribute to their own well-being. An individual's welfare is increased or decreased according to the individual's evaluation of the impact of events that affect her or him. As outside observers, we simply ask how events affect individuals and accept their answers at face value.

The welfare of a group is much more difficult to handle. As a starting point we can say that events that increase the well-being of every individual in the group increase the welfare of the group as a whole. But very often an event that increases the well-being of one person decreases that of another. When such is the case, the gain in the welfare of the first must be compared with the loss in the welfare of the second if any conclusions are to be drawn about the welfare of the group as a whole. Comparisons of this sort raise serious problems. How can changes in the well-being of different persons be compared? In some specific cases rough subjective judgments can be made. Taking a Rembrandt away from a connoisseur of art and giving it to a person who does not understand or value art would surely reduce group welfare. But, in general, we have no objective means of measuring and comparing the gain of one person or group of persons with the loss suffered by another individual or group when an event causes both.

We are left with a group welfare concept known as a *Pareto optimum*.[3] A Pareto optimum is said to exist when no event can increase the well-being of one person without decreasing the well-being of someone else. If we consider the matter another way, a Pareto optimum does not exist if one or more persons can be made better off without making anyone else worse off. If a Pareto optimum does not exist, a movement toward it—making at least one person better off without making anyone else worse off—increases group welfare.

There is no unique Pareto optimal situation in an economy. Suppose that all production and all exchanges that bestow advantage on anyone without disadvantaging anyone else have taken place. If any redistribution of purchasing power now occurs—for example, the imposition of taxes on the rich and the granting of subsidies to the poor—the conditions of the original Pareto optimum are violated. But a new Pareto optimum, given the new distribution of income, is possible. In fact, there will be a different set of Pareto optimal conditions for every different pattern of purchasing power distribution. If the economy moves from one Pareto optimum to another in this fashion, can we say that the welfare of the group has increased or decreased? There are no objective measures that will provide the answer. We can discuss objectively the conditions that lead to Pareto optimality, given the distribution of income, but if we want to discuss the impact of income redistribution on welfare, we must fall back on subjective value judgments to support whatever stand we take.

Summary

Economic activity revolves around three key elements: (1) human wants that are varied and insatiable; (2) resources that are limited, versatile, and capable of being combined in varying proportions to produce a given commodity; (3) techniques for utilizing resources to produce goods and services that satisfy wants. The achievement of a level of want satisfaction (level of living) as high as the economy can provide is a primary goal of economic

---

[3] Originated by the early twentieth-century Italian economist Vilfredo Pareto.

activity in most economies. To approach this end, resources and techniques are not merely used to produce goods and services that satisfy wants; they must be used to produce the items that contribute most to aggregate want satisfaction. The best possible techniques must be used; resources must be fully employed and properly allocated or distributed among the alternative wants of consumers.

The methodology of economics is like that of other sciences. Sets of principles are developed through the formulation and testing of hypotheses. These, in turn, are outgrowths of logic applied to basic premises and observations of facts.

At the outset the relationship of price theory to the overall discipline of economics and the relationship of price theory to the real world should be understood. Price theory is an essential part of the economist's tool kit and is used, together with national income theory, in the special subject areas of economics. Rather than explaining in detail the activities of economic units in the real world, it establishes general principles concerning activities on the basis of what appear to be the most important economic data. Activities of economic units in the real world approximate or tend toward those of theory. But this loss in the way of detailed contact with the real world means gain in the understanding of the main forces at work.

This book is concerned with welfare in the Pareto optimum sense; that is, it will have much to say about the conditions of economic efficiency for any given income distribution, but it will not have much to say about whether one income distribution is more efficient than another.

Suggested readings

Friedman, Milton. "The Methodology of Positive Economics," *Essays in Positive Economics*. Chicago: University of Chicago Press, 1953. Pp. 3–43.

Koopmans, Tjalling C. *Three Essays on the State of Economic Science*. New York: McGraw-Hill, Inc., 1957. Pp. 129–149.

Lange, Oscar. "The Scope and Method of Economics." *Review of Economic Studies* XIII (1945–1946): 19–32.

Marshall, Alfred. *Principles of Economics*. 8th ed. London: Macmillan & Co., Ltd., 1920. Bk. III, Chap. 2.

Questions and exercises

1. Make a list of the wants that you have developed as a direct result of attending your college or university. How have these changed since your freshman year?

2. Evaluate the following statement: "The primary cause of poverty in the United States is that people have too little money to spend." Consider in your evaluation the factors limiting the attainable living standard.

3. Explain the effects on the per capita income of an economy of each of the following:
   a. a 10 percent increase in the population
   b. restrictions on the importation of crude oil
   c. development of a substantially improved process for recovery of shale oil deposits
   d. large gifts of food to foreign populations experiencing serious nutrition problems.

4. Evaluate the following statement: "The most important test of a set of economic principles is whether or not it describes realistically the economic activity to which it is applied."

5. Will income redistribution from the rich toward the poor increase the welfare of a society? Explain why or why not.

6. Distinguish carefully between *positive economics* and *normative economics*. Discuss the interrelationships between these two concepts.

Chapter 2

Chapter contents

A simplified model

The functions of an economic system
Determination of what to produce
Organization of production
Output distribution
Rationing in very short run
Economic maintenance and growth

Summary
Suggested readings
Questions and exercises

Key concepts

Economic system
Private enterprise system
Socialistic system
Households
Firm
Economic efficiency

The organization of an economic system

Any given society or country develops an institutional framework within which its economic activity is carried on. We call such a framework an *economic system.* Economic systems of the modern world fall somewhere along a continuum between pure private enterprise at the one extreme and pure socialism at the other. The pure private enterprise system is characterized by private ownership of resources as well as goods and services. Private individuals, business enterprises, and associations of various kinds can engage in whatever voluntary production and exchange activities they desire. In the pure socialistic system there is no private property. Resources, goods, and services are owned and/or controlled by the government. Production takes place in government enterprises and the government specifies the conditions under which exchanges can occur. Whereas the private enterprise system is decentralized, the socialistic system is highly centralized.

Present-day economies are a mixture of the two systems. Some part of an economy's output will be produced socialistically; that is, by the government, or the *public sector,* of the economy. The other part will be produced by private enterprise, or the *private sector,* of the economy. Countries are referred to as socialistic or as private enterprise depending on which sector is predominant.

This chapter is an overview of an economic system with primary emphasis on private enterprise or the private sector of a mixed economy. An overview of the entire system will enable us to fit its details, as we come to them throughout the book, into their proper places and to put them in proper perspective. First, we construct a simple model of a private enterprise system. Next, we discuss the functions of an economic system with special reference to prices as the mechanism for performing those functions. Yet much of what we have to say is relevant to socialistic systems or to the public sector of mixed systems. We cannot—and should not—avoid the many points at which the private sector and the public sector of an economy affect each other.

A simplified model

The widely used "circular flow" diagram of Figure 2–1 furnishes a highly simplified model of a private enterprise economic system. Economic units are classified into two groups: (1) households and (2) business firms. These interact in two sets of markets: (1) markets for consumer goods and services and (2) resource markets. Households, business firms, consumer goods markets, and resource markets are the component parts of a private enterprise economy, and they form the core around which price theory is built.

Households include all individual and family units of the economy. They are the consumers of the economy's output of goods and services. With minor exceptions—for example, the indigent—they also own the economy's resources.

Business firms constitute a more limited group engaged in the buying and hiring of resources and the production and sale of goods and services. They include single proprietorships, partnerships, and corporations at all levels of the productive process. In some cases the same economic unit functions both as a firm and as a household, the family farm being a case in point. We shall assume that the unit's activities as a firm can be clearly separated from its activities as a household and that each activity is classified under the appropriate heading.

The upper half of Figure 2–1 represents the markets for consumer goods and services. Households as consumers and business firms as sellers interact within the markets. Goods and services flow from business firms to consumers; a *reverse* flow of money from consumers to business firms also takes place. Prices of goods and services form the connecting link between the two flows. The value of the flow of goods and services will be equal to the reverse money flow.

The lower half of Figure 2–1 represents the markets for resources. The services of labor and capital in their many forms flow from resource owners (households) to business firms. The reverse flow of money in payment for these resources occurs in such forms as wages, salaries, rents, dividends, interest, and so on, depending on the contractual arrangements under which they are delivered. These are resource prices valuing the services of resources and forming the connecting link between the two flows. In terms of money the two flows are equal.

Money circulates continuously from households to business firms and back to households again. The sale of goods and services places money at the disposal of business firms for the purchase of resource services to continue production. The sale or hire of the services of resources places money at the disposal of resource owners for the purchase of goods and

Figure 2–1   The circular flow model

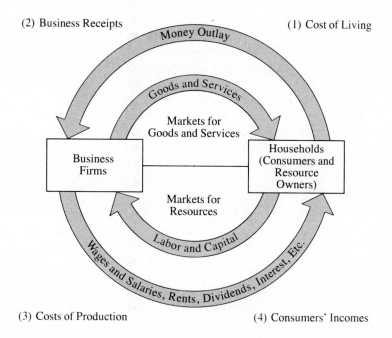

(2) Business Receipts   (1) Cost of Living

(3) Costs of Production   (4) Consumers' Incomes

services.[1] The money flow takes on four familiar aspects as it makes a complete circuit. It is consumers' costs of living at point (1) in Figure 2–1 as it leaves consumers' hands. It is business receipts for business firms at point (2). At point (3) the money flow becomes costs of production; while at point (4) it is consumers' incomes.

If the economy is stationary—neither expanding nor contracting—the flow of money of the upper half of Figure 2–1 will equal the flow of money of the lower half. The aggregate value of goods and services will equal the aggregate value of resource services. Consumers spend all their incomes; no saving occurs. Likewise, business firms pay out all money received to resource owners and there is no business saving.[2] No net investment oc-

---

[1] In some instances the money flow may be circumvented completely by direct exchange of resource services for goods or for ''income in kind'' to resource owners. To the extent that this type of transaction occurs, the money flows in each half of the diagram will be less than the value of goods and services and the value of resource services. However, since the bulk of exchange in a free enterprise economy will involve money and prices, we shall leave barter exchanges out of consideration.

[2] Profits made by business firms flow into the hands of resource owners in the form of higher-than-average dividends to stockholders or higher-than-average prices paid to owners of other resources.

curs. In the production of goods and services capital equipment wears out or depreciates. Some resource services are used to take care of replacement or depreciation, but costs of replacement or depreciation are a part of the cost of producing the goods that caused the depreciation to occur in the first place.

Expanded and more complex circular flow models are frequently used in macroeconomics. Leakages and injections into the income stream help explain growth or contraction of the economy as well as the equilibrium level of economic activity. Leakages include such things as savings, tax collections of the government, and imports of goods from abroad. Injections include investment, government expenditures, and exports.

We shall be concerned with the two sets of markets and the interactions that occur within each of them. In product markets the composition of the flow of goods and services, the prices of each, and the outputs of each will be of interest to us. Similarly, in resource markets, the prices, the employment levels, and the allocations of resources among different uses will be considered.

The functions of an economic system

Every economic system, whatever its form, must somehow perform five closely related functions. It must determine (1) what is to be produced, (2) how production is to be organized, (3) how the output is to be distributed, (4) how goods are to be rationed over very-short-run periods during which their supplies are fixed, and (5) how the productive capacity of the economy is to be maintained and expanded.

Determination of what to produce

The determination of what is to be produced in an economy is a problem of determining what wants in the aggregate are most important and in what degree they are to be satisfied. Should the amount of steel currently available be used for the production of automobiles or tanks or refrigerators or for the erection of sports arenas? Or should it be used to provide some of each? Since the resources of the economy are scarce, all wants cannot be fully satisfied. The problem is one of picking and choosing from the unlimited scope of wants those that are most important to the society as a whole. The economy must have some method of establishing values for different goods and services that is acceptable to the group and reflects the relative desires of the group for goods and services that the economy can produce.

The value of an item to society is measured by its price in a private enterprise economy, and the valuation process is accomplished by buyers as they spend their incomes. Consumers, for example, are confronted with a wide range of choices with regard to the goods that they can buy. The dollar values that they place on each of the various goods depend on how urgently they desire each good relative to other goods, their willingness and ability to back up desire with dollars, and the supplies of the goods available. The more urgently certain goods are desired, and the more willing consumers are to back up desire with dollars, the higher their prices. The less strong the desire for certain goods, the lower their prices. The greater the available supply of any particular good, the lower its price. Any one unit of the good will be of less importance to the consumer when the supply is great than when the supply is small. The more bread available to eat per week, the smaller the value each loaf will have to consumers. Conversely, the smaller the supply of any particular commodity, the higher consumers will value any one unit of it. Thus, the ways in which consumers spend their incomes establish an array of prices or a price structure in the economy that reflects the comparative values of different goods and services to the consuming public as a whole.

Changes in tastes and preferences modify the ways in which consumers spend their incomes. These changes in spending change the structure of prices in turn. Goods that consumers begin to desire more go up in price relatively, while those becoming less desirable to consumers decline in price relatively. The price structure of goods and services changes to reflect changes in consumers' tastes and preferences.

This analysis is positive in nature, telling us how goods are actually valued by means of a system of prices. It does not tell us how goods *ought* to be valued. The latter problem is an ethical one and lies largely outside the scope of price theory. A consumer with a larger income will exert more influence on the price structure than a consumer with a lower income. Conceivably, biscuits for rich people's dogs may be placed higher in the scale of values than milk for poor people's children, provided that there are enough rich people casting their dollar votes in this direction and that there are not enough poor people able to spend dollars for milk. The price system, though working perfectly in this case, may lead to social consequences that the public considers undesirable and which it attempts to modify through the political process. Income redistribution, price fixing, and progressive income taxes are examples of such political processes.

Organization of production

Concurrent with the determination of what is to be produced, an economic system must determine how its resources are to be organized to produce the desired goods in the proper quantities. The organization of production involves (1) drawing resources from industries producing goods that consumers value less and channeling them into the industries producing goods that consumers value more and (2) efficient use of resources by individual firms. These will be considered in turn.

The price system in a free enterprise economy organizes production. Firms producing goods and services that consumers want most urgently receive higher prices relative to costs and will be more profitable than those producing goods and services that consumers want less urgently. The more profitable firms can, and do, offer higher prices for resources in order to expand. Those making less profit or incurring losses are unwilling to pay as much for resources. Resource owners, in the interest of increasing their incomes, want to sell their resources to firms offering the higher prices. Therefore, there is a constant channeling of resources away from firms producing goods and services that consumers want least into the firms producing goods and services that consumers want most. Resources are moving constantly from lower-paying to higher-paying uses, or out of less important into more important uses.

The term *efficiency* in economics differs slightly from the use of the term in physics or mechanics. However, in both contexts it involves the ratio of an output to an input. With regard to mechanical efficiency we know that a steam engine is inefficient because it fails to transform a large part of the heat energy of its fuel into power. Mechanically, an internal-combustion engine is more efficient. However, if fuel for steam engines is cheap and fuel for internal-combustion engines is expensive, cheaper power may be obtained from the steam engine.

The concept of *economic efficiency* is also a ratio of output to input. The economic efficiency of a particular productive process is the ratio of useful product output to useful input of resources. The usefulness of product output, or its value to society, is measured in dollar terms. Similarly, the usefulness or value of resource input is measured in terms of dollars. Thus, the steam engine, which is less efficient mechanically, will be more efficient economically than an internal-combustion engine if it furnishes *cheaper* power for a particular productive process.

The quest for profits provides the incentive for efficient production. The more efficient the firm, given the price of the product, the greater its profits will be. To rephrase the definition of efficiency, it is the value of product output per unit input of resource value. The greater the dollar value of product output per dollar's worth of resource input, the greater economic efficiency is. Likewise, the less the dollar value of resource input needed per dollar's worth of product output, the greater economic efficiency is. Measurement of economic efficiency requires that values be placed on resources of different types and on the same type of resource in different uses. Resources are valued in the market according to their contributions to the production of goods and services.

Economic efficiency within a firm requires that the firm make choices among the different combinations of resources and techniques that can be used in the production process. The choice of techniques to use will depend on relative resource prices and the quantity of product to be produced. The aim of the profit-oriented firm is to produce whatever output it produces as cheaply (efficiently) as it can. Thus, if labor is relatively expensive and capital is relatively cheap, the firm will want to use techniques making use of much capital and little labor. If capital is relatively expensive and labor is relatively cheap, the most efficient techniques are those using little capital and much labor. The techniques to use for most efficient operation will differ at differing levels of output, also. Mass production methods and complicated machines cannot be used efficiently for small outputs, but for large outputs they can be very efficient.

Output distribution

Distribution of the product output in a private enterprise economy is accomplished by the price system simultaneously with the determination of what is to be produced and the organization of production. Product distribution depends on personal income distribution. Those with larger incomes obtain larger shares of the economy's output than do those with smaller incomes.

The income of an individual depends on two things: (1) the quantities of different resources that can be put into the productive process and (2) the prices received for them. If labor power is the only resource owned by the individual, monthly income is determined by the number of hours worked per month multiplied by the hourly wage rate received. If, in addition, the individual owns and rents land to others, the amount of land so rented multiplied by the monthly rental per acre will be income from the land. Income from labor added to income from land is total monthly income. The example can be expanded to as many different resources as the individual owns.

Income distribution, thus, depends on the distribution of resource ownership in the economy and whether or not individuals place their resources in employments producing goods that consumers want most—that is, where the highest prices are offered for resources. Low individual incomes result from small quantities of resources owned and/or the placing of resources owned in employments contributing little to consumer satisfaction. High individual incomes result from large quantities of resources owned and/or the placing of resources owned in employments where they contribute much to consumer satisfaction. Thus, income differences may result from improper channeling of certain resources into the productive process by certain individuals and from differences in resource ownership among individuals.

Income differences that arise from improper channeling of certain resources into the productive process tend to be self-correcting. Suppose that a number of individuals are capable of doing the same amount of labor per week in a certain skill category, and suppose that two groups are employed in the making of two different products. The value of the product turned out by a worker in the first group is much higher than the value of the product turned out by a worker in the second. Since society values the first group higher than it values the second, the first group of workers will receive greater individual incomes. When workers of the second group perceive the income differential, some move to the higher-paying employment. The increased supply of the first commodity lowers consumers' valuation of it, while the decreased supply of the second commodity raises consumers' valuation of it. This, in turn, lowers the incomes of the first (but now larger) group of workers and raises the incomes of the second (but now smaller) group of workers. When the income differential between workers in the two groups disappears, worker movements from the second to the first group cease. The self-correcting mechanism requires time to work and may, in some cases, be prevented from accomplishing its task by ignorance on the part of the workers of the second group or by institutional barriers that prevent them from moving. In such cases the income differentials become chronic.

A large part of the income differentials arising from differences in resource ownership will not be self-correcting. The major sources of differences in resource ownership are discussed later in Chapter 17. They can be classified under differences in labor power owned and differences in kinds and quantities of capital owned. Differences in labor power owned by different individuals stem from differences in physical and mental inheritance and from differences in opportunities to acquire specific types of training. Differences in kinds and quantities of capital owned come from many sources. These include initial differences in labor resources owned, differences in material inheritance, fortuitous circumstances, fraud, and differences in propensities to accumulate.

If society believes that income differences should be smaller, modifications can be imposed on the private enterprise economy without materially affecting the operation of the price system. Society, through the government, may levy progressive income taxes and make expenditures for welfare purposes. It may subsidize low-income groups in various ways. Redistribution of income will, however, affect the wants to be satisfied by economic activity by changing the effective pattern of social desires for goods and services. Reduction of high incomes makes the individuals who are deprived become less effective in the market place. Augmentation of low incomes makes those who are helped become more effective in the market place. The price system will reorganize production to conform with the new pattern of effective desires for goods and services.

Rationing in the very short run

An economic system must make some provision for rationing commodities over the time period during which the supplies of these cannot be changed. This time period is called the *very short run* by some and the *market period* by others. Suppose that wheat was harvested throughout the country in the same month each year. From one year to the next the supply of wheat available for consumption would be fixed, assuming there is no carry-over from one year to the next. The very short run for wheat in such a case would be one year. The economy must ration the fixed supply in two ways: (1) it must allocate the supply among the different consumers of the economy; (2) it must stretch the given supply over the time period from one harvest to the next.

In a private enterprise economy price will be the device that allocates the fixed supply among different consumers. Shortages will cause the price to increase, decreasing the amount that each consumer is willing to buy. The price will continue to increase until all consumers together are just willing to take the fixed supply. Surpluses will cause price to decrease, increasing the amount consumers are willing to buy until they take the entire supply off the market.

Price will also be the device for rationing the good over time. If the entire supply were to be dumped in consumers' hands immediately after harvest, price would be driven low. At the low price consumption would proceed at a rapid pace. As the next harvest approaches, the disappearance of most of the commodity in the first part of the period leaves very small supplies for the latter part of the period. Consequently, price would be high in the latter part of the very-short-run period.

Speculation plays an important role in smoothing out the consumption of the good over time. Knowing that the price will tend to be low early in the period and high late in the period, speculators will buy up a large part of the supply early in the period, expecting to sell it later at higher prices and thus realize a net gain on their investment in the product. Their purchases will raise the price in the early part of the period above what it would otherwise have been, thus slowing the rate at which the product is consumed at that time. Their sales in the latter period will reduce price below what it would otherwise have been and will provide greater quantities of the product for consumption in the latter part of the period. The actions of speculators modify the price rise that would have taken place over the very-short-run period and bring about a more even flow of the product to consumers over time.

Economic maintenance and growth

Every economy is expected to maintain and expand its productive capacity. *Maintenance* refers to keeping the productive power of the economic machine intact through provision for depreciation. *Expansion* refers to continuous increase in the kinds and quantities of the economy's resources, together with continuous improvement in techniques of production.

Labor power can be increased through population increases and through the development and improvement of skills by means of training and education. Development and improvement of skills in a private enterprise economy are motivated largely through the price mechanism—the prospects of higher pay for more highly skilled and more productive work. The extent to which skills can be developed and improved is conditioned by training and educational opportunities, together with physical and mental abilities.

Capital accumulation depends on a variety of complex economic motives, and much debate centers about their relative importances. For capital accumulation to occur, some resources must be diverted from the production of current consumer goods and put to work producing capital goods in excess of the amount needed to offset depreciation.

Improvements in productive techniques make possible the production of greater outputs with given quantities of resources. The motives behind the search for and the discovery of inventions and improvements are not always easy to determine. The inventor may invent because that type of activity is interesting. Frequently, improvements in techniques are the by-product of scholarship intended primarily to advance knowledge. However, a large part of the improvements in productive techniques is a direct result of the quest for profits, as is well illustrated by the increasing flow of fruitful results coming from the growing research and development departments of large corporations.

The role of the price mechanism and its degree of importance in providing for economic maintenance and growth are not clear. Certainly prices and profit prospects are an important element in determining whether or not maintenance and growth occur. But the area of economic maintenance and growth is virtually an applied subject area in itself. Consequently, we shall be concerned mainly with the first four functions as they are performed by the price system in a private enterprise economy.

Summary

The purpose of this chapter has been to obtain a picture of the economic system as a whole and to gain some appreciation of how the price mechanism guides and directs a private enterprise economy. Initially a simple economic model of a private enterprise economy was set up. Economic units were classified into two groups: (1) households and (2) business firms. They interact in the markets for consumer goods and services and in resource markets. Households as resource owners sell the services of their resources to business firms. Incomes received are used to buy goods from business firms. Business firms receive income from the sale of goods to consumers. Business incomes, in turn, are used to buy resources from resource owners.

We listed five basic functions of an economic system and discussed the ways in which a private enterprise economy performs those functions. A system of prices is the main organizing force. Prices determine what is to be produced. Prices organize production, and they play a major role in the distribution of the product. They serve to ration a particular good over its very-short-run period during which the supply of the good is fixed. They are also an element in providing for economic maintenance and growth.

Suggested readings

Friedman, Milton. *Price Theory*. Chicago: Aldine Publishing Co., 1976. Chap. 1.

Knight, Frank H. "Social Economic Organization." In Harry D. Gideonse and others, eds., *Contemporary Society: Syllabus and Selected Readings*. 4th ed. Chicago: University of Chicago Press, 1935. Pp. 125–137.

Stigler, George J. *The Theory of Price*. 3rd ed. New York: Crowell-Collier and Macmillan, Inc., 1966. Chap. 2.

Questions and exercises

1. Use the circular flow model to explain each of the following:
   a. inflation
   b. unemployment.

2. Explain the impact of a set of price controls on
   a. the determination of what is to be produced
   b. the organization of production
   c. the distribution of output.

3. Consider one of the world's underdeveloped countries in which the quantities of capital available are small and the quantities of unskilled labor are large. What kinds of technology would you expect to find in agriculture and in industry?

4. As minority groups attain improved access to educational opportunities, what will be the effects on their incomes? Why?

5. Why do you suppose it is so difficult for economic growth to be generated in the poor countries of the world?

6. Is profit-making an evil or a beneficial kind of behavior in a private enterprise economic system? Explain your answer carefully.

Chapter 3

Chapter contents   **Key concepts**

Pure competition	**The necessary conditions for pure competition**	Pure competition
	Homogeneity of the product	Perfect competition
	Smallness of each buyer or seller relative to the market	Mobility
		Demand
	Absence of artificial restraints	Complementary goods
	Mobility	Competitive or substitute goods
	"Pure" and "perfect" competition	Supply
	Pure competition in economic analysis	Equilibrium price
Demand	**Demand schedules and demand curves**	Surplus
	A change in demand versus a movement along a given demand curve	Shortage
		Price elasticity of demand
Supply		Arc elasticity of demand
		Point elasticity of demand
Market price	**Market price determination**	Cross elasticity of demand
	Changes in demand and supply	Elastic demand
Price elasticity of demand	**Measurement of price elasticity**	Inelastic demand
	Arc elasticity	Unitary elasticity of demand
	Point elasticity	
	Elasticity and total money outlays	
	Factors influencing price elasticity of demand	
	Cross elasticity of demand	
Summary	**Suggested readings**	
	Questions and exercises	

The purely competitive market model

A working knowledge of the operations of the price system as it guides and directs the economic activity of a private enterprise economy rests on the foundations of *demand, supply, markets,* and *competition.* Most people have come in contact with these concepts, and not being sophisticated in economic analysis, they toss them around loosely. But these are precise concepts to economists and are the main elements of the market models used so extensively in modern microeconomic theory. We shall first discuss the concept of competition and then turn to the concepts of demand and supply. The analysis of price determination that emerges when the demand and the supply for a particular item are brought together is the essence of the market model and is considered next. Finally, we examine the concept of price elasticity of demand.

Pure competition

The term *competition* is used ambiguously not only in ordinary conversation but in economic literature as well. Its common meaning is rivalry, but in economics when used along with the word *pure,* it carries a different meaning. In our discussion we shall begin by examining the conditions necessary for the existence of pure competition and then shall consider its role in economic analysis.

The necessary conditions for pure competition

Homogeneity of the product For competition to exist in a market all sellers of the product being exchanged sell homogeneous units of the product, or at least the buyers of that product believe that this is so. Buyers think, for example, that the bushels of No. 1 hard winter wheat sold by Farmer Brown are identical to those sold by Farmer Smith. Thus they have no reason for preferring the output of Farmer Brown to that of Farmer Smith or any other seller of No. 1 hard winter wheat.

Smallness of each buyer or seller relative to the market   Each buyer and each seller of the product under consideration is too small in relation to the entire market for the product to influence significantly the price of the product that is being bought or sold. On the selling side the individual seller supplies such a small proportion of the total supply that if the seller drops out of the market altogether, total supply will not be decreased enough to cause any rise in price. Or, if the individual seller sells the maximum amount that it can supply, the total supply will not be increased enough to cause price to fall. The individual sellers of most farm products are in this position. On the buying side any single buyer takes such a small proportion of the total amount placed on the market that that particular buyer is unable to influence its price. As consumers we are in this position with respect to most of the items that we buy. As individuals we have no impact on the price of bread, meat, milk, safety pins, and so on. Therefore, the influence in a purely competitive market of any one individual buyer or seller of a product is virtually nonexistent.

Absence of artificial restraints   Another condition necessary for the existence of pure competition is that there be no artificial restrictions on the demands for, the supplies of, and the prices of whatever is being exchanged. Prices are free to move wherever they will in response to changing conditions of demand and supply. There is no governmental price fixing nor any institutional fixing or administering of price by producers' associations, labor unions, or other private agencies. There is no supply restriction enforced by the government or by organized producer groups. Control of demand through governmental rationing is nonexistent.

Mobility   An additional requirement for pure competition is that there be mobility of goods and services and of resources in the economy. New firms are free to enter any desired industry, and resources are free to move among alternative uses to those where they desire employment. Sellers are able to dispose of their goods and services wherever the price is highest. Resources are able to secure employment in their highest paid uses.

"Pure" and "perfect" competition

Economists sometimes distinguish between "pure" and "perfect" competition. The distinction is one of degree. The four conditions just discussed are usually considered necessary for the existence of pure competition; whereas perfect competition requires that one more condition be met—that all economic units possess complete knowledge of the economy.

All discrepancies in prices quoted by sellers will be known immediately, and buyers will buy at the lowest prices. This forces sellers charging higher prices to lower their prices immediately. If different purchasers offer different prices for whatever they purchase, sellers will know it immediately and will sell to the highest bidders. The low bidders must, of necessity, raise their price offers. In the market for any particular product or resource a single price will prevail. Examples of perfect competition are very rare, but stock transactions on the New York Stock Exchange may approximate these conditions. The terms of stock transactions are flashed on the Exchange Board as they are concluded. The information is distributed immediately to interested parties all over the country. Under conditions of perfect competition adjustments of the economy to disturbances in the conditions of demand and supply will be instantaneous. Under conditions of pure competition it will take some time for adjustments to occur because of incomplete knowledge on the part of individual economic units.

Pure competition in economic analysis

Competition in economics is impersonal in its nature. There is no reason for enmity to develop between two wheat farmers over the effect that either one has on the market, since neither has any effect whatsoever. One simply does the best that is possible with what is available. Farmer Brown is not out to get or defeat Farmer Smith. By way of contrast, intense rivalry may exist between two automobile agencies or between two filling stations in the same city. One seller's actions influence the market of the other; consequently, in these cases there is rivalry but not pure competition.

No economist insists that pure competition characterizes any economy, nor does anyone claim that it ever has. The question arises, then, as to why study the principles of pure competition at all. Three important answers may be given. First, the principles of pure competition furnish a simple and logical starting point for economic analysis. Second, a large measure of competition does exist in the United States today, although perhaps not in pure form. Third, the theory of pure competition provides a sort of ''norm'' against which the actual performance of the economy can be checked or evaluated.

With regard to the first answer, an analogy can be drawn to the study of mechanics. No one questions the procedure of starting a study of mechanics leaving friction out of consideration. This omission is unrealistic since friction inevitably occurs in the real world, but the temporary postponement of its consideration allows a clear statement of mechanical principles. Friction is later introduced and taken into account. Competitive economic theory principles occupy about the same role in economic analysis as do frictionless principles in the study of mechanics. Once we understand how the frictionless (competitive) economy works, we can observe the effects of friction (imperfect competition and restraints of various sorts) and take them into account. To study the theory of pure competition does not mean that one must believe that the real world is one of pure competition, nor does it preclude the very legitimate study of imperfect competition. It brings out fundamental cause-and-effect relationships that are also important in imperfect competition. It is simply the logical place to start if one is to understand the principles of imperfect competition and their applications as well as those of pure competition.

With regard to the second answer, studies indicate that there is substantial competition in the United States economy.[1] Enough competition exists and enough economic units buy or sell under conditions approaching pure competition to give us valid answers to a great many economic problems.

Third, in the theory of a market economy pure competition tends to lead toward the set of conditions defining maximum economic welfare or well-being, given the distribution of income. The actual performance of the economy can then be appraised against its potential "best" performance. Imperfectly competitive or monopolistic forces are important in preventing the attainment of the "best" allocation and use of economic resources. Thus, the purely competitive model frequently is used as the basis for public regulation of imperfectly competitive situations. Presumably it underlies the philosophy and enforcement of the Sherman Antitrust Act of 1890 as amended, government regulation of public utilities, and many other public policy measures.

Demand

Turning now to the development of a market model we define *demand* for a good as the various quantities of it per unit of time that consumers will take off the market at all possible alternative prices, other things being equal or constant. The quantity that consumers will take will be affected by a number of circumstances, such as (1) the price of the good, (2) consumers' tastes and preferences, (3) the number of consumers under consideration, (4) consumers' income, (5) the prices of related goods, (6) the range or number of goods available to consumers, and (7) consumers' expectations regarding future prices of the product.[2] Additional circumstances could be listed, but these seem to be the most important ones.

---

[1] See F. M. Scherer, *Industrial Market Structure and Economic Performance* (Chicago: Rand McNally and Company, 1971), Chap. 3; and G. Warren Nutter and Henry A. Einhorn, *Enterprise Monopoly in the United States, 1899–1958* (New York: Columbia University Press, 1969).

[2] In functional form we can represent the demand relationship as

$$x = f(p_x, T, C, I, p_n, R, E),$$

in which

x is the quantity of good or service X
p_x is the price of X
T represents consumers' tastes and preferences
C is the number of consumers under consideration

I represents total consumers' income and its distribution
p_n represents the prices of related goods
R represents the range of goods and services available to consumers
E represents consumers' expectations.

Demand schedules and demand curves

The definition of demand singles out the relationship between possible alternative prices of the good and the quantities of it that consumers will take. Circumstances (2) through (7) are held constant in defining a given state of demand. Usually we think of quantity taken as varying inversely with price. The higher the price of the good, the less that consumers will take; and the lower the price of the good, the greater the quantity that consumers will take—other things being equal or constant. Some exceptions may occur, in which quantity taken varies directly with price, but these must be few.

Note that the term *demand* is used to refer to an entire demand schedule or demand curve.[3] A demand schedule lists the different quantities of the commodity that consumers will take opposite the various alternative prices of the good. A hypothetical demand schedule is shown in Table 3–1. Product X is the commodity; prices are listed as are quantities per unit of time. A demand curve is a demand schedule plotted on an ordinary graph. A demand curve is shown in Figure 3–1. The vertical axis of the graph measures price per unit, and the horizontal axis measures quantity of the good per unit of time. Note that the inverse relationship between price and quantity sold makes the demand curve slope downward to the right.

The quantities referred to in Table 3–1 and in Figure 3–1 have no consistent meaning unless they are put in terms of flows per time period. They may be set up on a weekly, monthly, or yearly basis, or whatever time period seems appropriate. It means nothing to say, "At a price of $4 per unit, 8 units of product will be taken by consumers." The statement becomes meaningful when we say, "At a price of $4 per unit, 8 units of product per week (or month, or whatever the time period happens to be) will be taken by consumers." Hence, we must always remember that we are dealing not merely with quantities but with quantities per unit of time. They are rates of purchase, such as 500,000 cars per month or 60 million bushels of wheat per month.

The demand curve separates the purchases that consumers are willing to make from those that they are not willing to make. It shows the maximum prices that consumers can be induced to pay for the various quantities

---

[3] The equation of the demand curve for X can be written as

$$x = f(p_x),$$

in which the other variables listed in Footnote 2 are parameters. Or, we can reverse the dependency relationship and write

$$p_x = g(x),$$

thus expressing the demand equation in the form in which it is usually shown graphically.

Although the demand equations and curves are represented in this section as being linear, this need not be the case. Linear demand curves are simply easier to draw and explain than are curvilinear ones. The equation for a linear demand curve takes the form

$$p_x = a - bx.$$

Table 3–1   Demand schedule for product X

Price	Quantity per Unit of Time (Hundreds)
$10.00	0
9.25	1
8.50	2
7.75	3
7.00	4
6.25	5
5.50	6
4.75	7
4.00	8
3.25	9
2.50	10
1.75	11
1.00	12
0.25	13

indicated on the scale of the horizontal axis, that is, the maximum price at which each of those total quantities can be sold. Or, it can be viewed as showing the maximum quantities that consumers can be induced to take at the price levels indicated on the vertical scale. Any quantity and price shown by a point on or to the left of and below the demand curve is a possible or feasible price-quantity combination to consumers. No point to

Figure 3–1   Demand curve for product X

X per Unit of Time (Hundreds)

the right of and above the demand curve is a possible or feasible combination.

A change in demand versus a movement along a given demand curve

A clear distinction must be drawn between a *movement along* a given demand curve and a *change* in demand. A movement along a given demand curve represents a change in quantity taken resulting from a change in price of the good itself when all the other circumstances influencing the quantity taken remain unchanged. In Figure 3–2 a decrease in price from p to p_1 increases the quantity taken from X to X_1. This is not called a change in demand since it occurs on a single demand curve, and the term *demand* refers to that entire demand curve. In defining demand we assume that the underlying demand circumstances remain constant while we change the price of the commodity and observe what happens to the quantity taken.[4]

When any of the circumstances held constant in defining a given state of demand are changed, the demand curve itself will change. Thus, in Figure 3–3 an increase in consumer incomes will shift the demand curve to the right from DD to D_1D_1. With higher incomes consumers will usually be

Figure 3–2   Movement along a demand curve

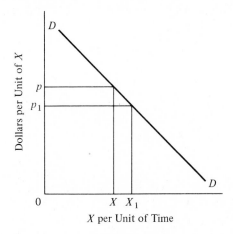

[4] In the equation

$$p_x = a - bx$$

the coordinates of p_x and x trace out a unique demand curve as long as the parameters a and b remain constant. A change in the value of p_x results in a movement along the curve to the corresponding value of x.

Figure 3–3 Changes in demand

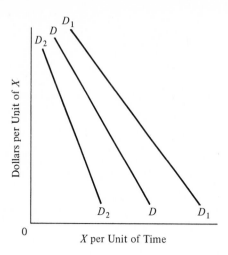

willing to increase their rate of purchase at each alternative price. A shift in consumers' tastes and preferences toward commodity X will have the same results. So, also, will an increase in the number of consumers in the group. An increase in the range of goods available to consumers may cause them to allocate less of their incomes to commodity X, thus shifting the demand curve to the left to position D_2D_2 in Figure 3–3.[5]

The effects on the demand for X of changes in the prices of goods related to X define the nature of the relationships. A related good is a *competitive* or *substitute* good if an increase in its price causes the demand curve for X to shift to the right. The shift results from consumers turning away from the now relatively higher-priced substitute to X. Suppose, for example, that X is beef and that the price of pork rises. Consumers shift away from pork toward beef, thus increasing the demand for beef.

A related good is a *complementary* good if an increase in its price causes a shift to the left in the demand curve for X. The higher price of the related good induces consumers to take less of it. If in taking less of it they have less desire for X, there is an indication of complementarity. In this case suppose that X is milk and that the price of cereal rises enough to curtail cereal consumption. The smaller quantity of cereal consumed reduces the desire for milk—the demand curve for milk then shifts to the left.

---

[5] In the equation

$$p_x = a - bx$$

a change in a will shift the price-axis intercept of the curve and a change in b will alter its slope.

Supply

The supply of a good is defined as the various quantities of it that sellers will place on the market at all possible alternative prices, other things being equal. It is the relationship between prices and quantities per unit of time that sellers are willing to sell. The same distinction is made between a supply schedule and a supply curve that is made between a demand schedule and a demand curve. A supply curve is a supply schedule plotted on a graph. Usually the supply curve will be upward sloping to the right, since a higher price will induce sellers to place more of the good on the market and may induce additional sellers to come into the field. A hypothetical supply schedule is listed in Table 3–2 and the corresponding supply curve is shown in Figure 3–4.

The "other things" that are held constant in defining a given supply curve are basically (1) the set of prices of the resources used to produce the product and (2) the range of production techniques available.[6]

Table 3–2   Supply schedule for product X

Price	Quantity per Unit of Time (Hundreds)
$4.00	0
4.25	1
4.50	2
4.75	3
5.00	4
5.25	5
5.50	6
5.75	7
6.00	8
6.25	9
6.50	10
6.75	11
7.00	12
7.25	13

[6] The supply function can be written as

$$x = s(p_x, p_r, K),$$

in which

x is the quantity of good or service X
p_x is the price of X
p_r is the set of prices of resources used in producing X
K is the range of production techniques available.

For a short-run supply function we would add M to the list of independent variables, with M representing the number of firms supplying X.

Figure 3–4   Supply curve for product X

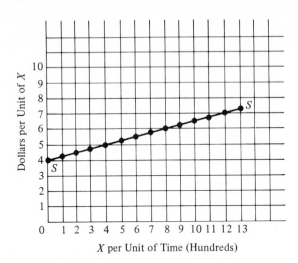

Like the demand curve, the supply curve is a boundary line between what sellers will and will not do. At any given price sellers would be willing to supply less than the quantity shown by the supply curve at that price, but they cannot be induced to supply more. To be induced to supply any given quantity, sellers must receive at least the price shown by the supply curve at that quantity. They would supply that quantity for a higher price per unit, but they will not supply it for less. Any point on, or above and to the left of, the supply curve represents a possible or feasible quantity supplied at the indicated price. Any point below and to the right of it is not possible or feasible.[7]

For consistency and accuracy in definitions it is necessary to distinguish between a movement along a given supply curve and a change in supply. In Figure 3–5 a change in the price of X from p_1 to p_2 increases the quantity

---

[7] We can express the supply equation as

$$x = h\,(p_x),$$

or, alternatively, as

$$p_x = s\,(x),$$

treating the other independent variables of Footnote 6 as parameters. Movements along the supply curve are movements from one set of coordinates to another, with the parameters of the equation remaining constant. A change in supply means a change in the supply equation parameters. Again, linear functions are used because of their simplicity, not because they are more representative of actual supply conditions. The equation for a linear supply function is

$$p_x = c + dx.$$

Figure 3–5   A change in supply versus a movement along a supply curve

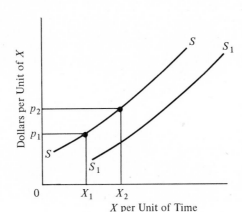

supplied from X_1 to X_2. This represents a movement along a supply curve—not a change in supply. A change in supply is defined as a shift in the supply curve (for example, from SS to S_1S_1) and results from a change in one of the "other things."[8]

Market price

Placing the demand curve and the supply curve for any given good or service on a single diagram highlights the forces determining its market price. The demand curve indicates what consumers are willing to do, while the supply curve shows what sellers are willing to do. Consumer demand is assumed to be independent of the activities of sellers. Similarly, the supply curve is assumed to be in no way dependent on consumers' activities. Consumers are assumed to operate independently of one another, and so are sellers.

Market price determination

In Figure 3–6 market price determination is illustrated. At price level p_1 consumers are willing to take quantity X_1 per unit of time. However,

---

[8] In the equation

$$p_x = c + dx$$

the coordinates of p_x and x trace out a unique supply curve as long as the parameters c and d are constant. A change in c shifts the price-axis intercept of the curve while a change in d alters its slope.

Figure 3-6 Equilibrium price determination

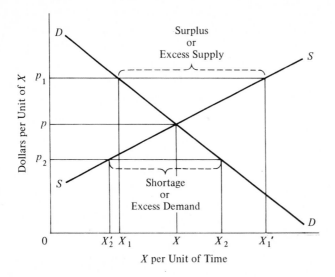

suppliers will bring quantity X_1' per unit of time to the market; thus, *surpluses* or excess supplies of $X_1 X_1'$ per unit of time accumulate. Any seller with a surplus believes that by undercutting other sellers a little, surpluses can be disposed of. Thus, an incentive exists for individual sellers to lower their prices and cut back the quantity supplied. The price will be driven down by the sellers; quantities supplied will decrease; and quantities consumed will increase. Eventually, when the price has dropped to p, consumers will be willing to take exactly the amount that sellers want to place on the market at that price.

Suppose, alternatively, that sellers initially establish the price at p_2. At this price level consumers want quantity X_2 per unit of time, but sellers will place only X_2' per unit of time on the market. Therefore, *shortages* or excess demand equal to the difference between X_2 and X_2' per time period occur. Faced by the shortages, consumers bid against each other for the available supply and will continue to do so as long as shortages exist. When the price has been driven up to p by consumers, the shortages will have disappeared and buyers will be taking the quantity that sellers want to sell.

Price p is called the *equilibrium price.* Given the conditions of demand and supply for commodity X, it is the price that, if attained, will be maintained. If the price deviates from p, forces are set in motion to bring it back to that level. A price above the equilibrium price brings about surpluses that induce sellers to undercut each other, driving the price back down to the equilibrium level. A price below the equilibrium level results in shortages that cause consumers to bid the price back up to equilibrium. At a price level of p_1 to suppliers so much of the good is placed on the market that the value that consumers place on any one unit of it is less than the supply price. At price p_2 to suppliers the quantity placed on the market is so small that the value of a unit of it to consumers is greater than the supply price. At the equilibrium price p the quantity that suppliers place on the market is such that the supply price and consumers' valuation of a unit of the good are the same.[9]

Changes in demand and supply

What happens to the equilibrium price and the quantity exchanged of a good when the demand for it changes? Suppose that DD and SS in Figure 3–7 represent the demand for and supply of apartment units in a given community. Suppose that a private college is established in the community and that its enrollment expands rapidly. The greater number of apartment consumers in the group brings about an increase in demand to D_1D_1. At the original price or rental rate p there will be a shortage equal to XX' apartments, and consumers will bid up the price to p_1. The quantity placed on the market and rented out will increase to X_1 as the higher rental rate induces some property owners and builders in the community to construct apartments. After the increase in demand the new equilibrium price and quantity are thus p_1 and X_1, respectively.

The same diagram can be used to illustrate the effects of a decrease in demand on the price and the quantity exchanged of a product. Let D_1D_1 be the initial demand curve for apartments, while SS is the supply curve. Now suppose that the state university, located in a city 30 miles away, cuts its tuition rates substantially, drawing students away from the private college community. Demand for apartments in the community drops to DD, and at the initial equilibrium price p_1 there is a surplus of $X_1'X_1$. Rental rates will decrease, and fewer apartments will be rented out as property owners find

---

[9] The equilibrium price and quantity are determined mathematically by solving the demand and supply equations simultaneously. If these are, respectively,

$$p_x = g(x)$$

and

$$p_x = s(x),$$

we have two equations, two unknowns, and a determinate solution.

More specifically, representing demand and supply as lines or curves, let the demand and supply equations be

$$p_x = 10 - \tfrac{3}{4}x \quad \text{(Demand)}$$
$$p_x = 4 + \tfrac{1}{4}x \quad \text{(Supply)}.$$

Solving these simultaneously, we find that $x = 6$ and $p_x = 5.50$.

Figure 3-7   Effects of a change in demand

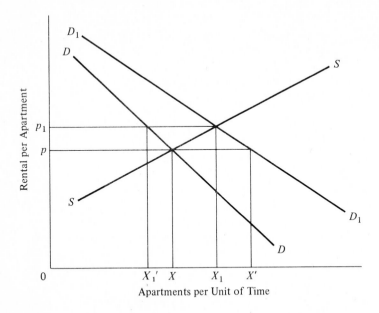

Apartments per Unit of Time

Figure 3-8   Effects of a change in supply

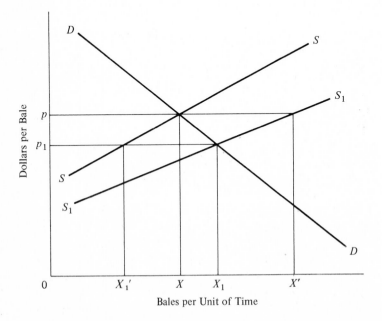

Bales per Unit of Time

it less worthwhile to make available and maintain some of their apartments. The new equilibrium price and quantity will be p and X, respectively.

Similarly, changes in supply, given the demand curve for a good, will bring about changes in the equilibrium price and quantity exchanged. In Figure 3–8 let DD and SS represent the initial demand curve and initial supply curve for bales of cotton. Suppose that growing conditions become much better than was initially expected, causing supply to increase to S_1S_1. At the initial equilibrium price p there will be a surplus of XX', causing the price to fall to p_1 and the quantity exchanged to increase to X_1. On the other hand, if S_1S_1 were the initial supply curve and a drought reduced the supply of cotton to SS, a shortage amounting to $X_1'X_1$ bales per unit of time would occur at the equilibrium price p_1. The price would rise to p, and the quantity exchanged would fall to X.

Price elasticity of demand

The concept of *elasticity* is very useful in economic analysis, as we shall see throughout the rest of this book. Price elasticity of demand measures the responsiveness of the quantity that will be taken to changes in the price of a good or service, given the demand curve for it. If the quantity taken is highly responsive to a small price change, a price increase will cause the total expenditures on the good to decrease; and a price decrease will cause them to rise. If the quantity is not very responsive to price changes, an increase in the price will increase total expenditures on the good, whereas a price decrease will cause them to fall. These points are of such importance that we shall develop them at some length below. However, first, we shall examine the technical aspects of elasticity measurement.

Measurement of price elasticity

Intuitively it appears that the slope of a demand curve is a sufficient measure of the responsiveness of quantity taken to price changes. The slope of a small segment of such a curve can be obtained by observing how much quantity taken changes when the price goes up or down by a certain amount. For example, if a decrease of 10 cents in the price of potatoes causes a 100-bushel increase in quantity taken, the slope of that portion of the curve is $-10/100$ or $-1/10$. However, if we redraw the demand curve, measuring the price in dollars instead of cents, the slope of the same segment of the demand curve becomes $(-1/10)/100$, or $-1/1000$. The shift from cents to dollars in measuring the price causes a drastic decrease in the measurement of the downward slope of the demand curve, even though there has been no real change in the demand curve itself. If we draw the demand curve again, measuring the price in dollars and the quantity taken in pecks, the slope of the same segment of the curve becomes $(-1/10)/400$, or $-1/4000$. Obviously, the slope of the demand curve is a very unreliable indicator of how responsive quantity taken is to changes in price.

The comparative slopes of demand curves for different goods are also useless as measures of the comparative responsiveness of quantities taken to changes in prices. In comparing the demand curve for wheat with the demand curve for automobiles, suppose that we want to know in which case quantity taken is more responsive to a change in price. The comparative slopes of the two demand curves tell us nothing. A $1 drop in the price of wheat may increase quantity taken by 20 million bushels per month. A $1 decrease in the price of automobiles may increase quantity taken by 5 automobiles per month. This situation, however, does not mean that the quantity taken of wheat is more responsive to changes in its price than is the quantity taken of automobiles to changes in the automobile price. A $1 change in the price of wheat is a very large relative change. A $1 change in the price of automobiles is of little relative consequence. Further, a unit of wheat and a unit of automobile are completely different concepts, and there is no basis for comparing a unit of one with a unit of the other.

The great British economist, Alfred Marshall, in response to this difficulty, defined the price elasticity of demand as the percentage change in quantity taken divided by the percentage change in price, *when the price change is small.*[10] In terms of algebra, the basic definition becomes

$$\epsilon = \frac{\Delta x/x}{\Delta p/p}$$

Consider the movement from A to B in Figure 3–9. The change in quantity from x to x_1 is Δx. The change in price from p to p_1 is Δp. The number or coefficient denoting elasticity is obtained by dividing a percentage by a percentage; it is a pure number independent of such units of measurement as bushels, pecks, or dollars. Elasticity will be the same between two given points on a demand curve for wheat, regardless of whether the price is measured in dollars or cents and regardless of whether the quantity is measured in bushels or pecks. The elasticity computed between two separate points on the demand curve is called *arc elasticity*. The elasticity computed at a single point on the curve for an infinitesimal change in price is called *point elasticity*. We shall discuss the two concepts in turn.

---

[10] Alfred Marshall, *Principles of Economics*, 8th ed. (London: Macmillan & Co., Ltd., 1920), Bk. III, Chap. IV.

Figure 3–9   Measurement of arc elasticity

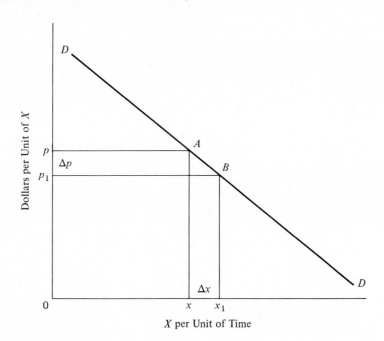

Arc elasticity

Suppose that we want to compute the elasticity of demand between A and B in Figure 3–9, and the coordinates of the two points are as follows:

	p (Cents)	x (Bushels)
At point A	100	1,000,000
At point B	90	1,200,000

If we move from point A to point B, substituting the appropriate numbers in the elasticity formula, we find that:

$$\epsilon = \frac{\dfrac{200,000}{1,000,000}}{\dfrac{-10}{100}} = \frac{200,000}{1,000,000} \times \frac{100}{-10} = -2. \qquad (3.1)$$

However, if we move in the opposite direction from point B to point A, then

$$\epsilon = \frac{\dfrac{-200,000}{1,200,000}}{\dfrac{10}{90}} = \frac{-200,000}{1,200,000} \times \frac{90}{10} = -1.5. \tag{3.2}$$

The percentage changes in quantity and price are different, depending on the price and quantity from which we start. The difference in the starting point leads us to different values of the elasticity coefficient.

These computations show that arc elasticity between any two points on a demand curve must be an approximation. The farther apart the points between which arc elasticity is calculated, the greater will be the discrepancy between the two coefficients obtained, and the less reliable either will be. If arc elasticity is to be meaningful, it must be computed between points on the demand curve that are close together.

To avoid these discrepancies a modification of the basic elasticity formula can be used. With reference to Figure 3–9, suppose that elasticity is calculated as

$$\epsilon = \frac{\Delta x/x}{\Delta p/p_1} \tag{3.3}$$

where p_1 is the lower of the two prices and x is the lower of the two quantities. Using this to compute elasticity between A and B, we find that

$$\epsilon = \frac{200,000}{1,000,000} \div -\frac{10}{90} = \frac{200,000}{1,000,000} \times -\frac{90}{10} = -1.8. \tag{3.4}$$

The modified formula provides a very usable average between the two coefficients obtained with the basic formula.[11]

The demand elasticity coefficient shows the approximate percentage change in quantity for a 1 percent change in price and will be negative in sign since the price and the quantity change in opposite directions. However, when economists speak of the magnitude of elasticity, they mean the absolute value of the coefficient, ignoring the minus sign. Thus, they say that an elasticity of minus one is greater than an elasticity of minus one-half; and an elasticity of minus two is greater than an elasticity of minus one.

---

[11] Another arc elasticity formula frequently used is:

$$\epsilon = \frac{x - x_1}{x + x_1} \div \frac{p - p_1}{p + p_1}.$$

Elasticity computed with this formula between points A and B in Figure 3–9 is -1.7. This formula, too, strikes an average between the coefficients arrived at by means of the basic formula when we work first from A to B and then work in reverse from B to A. See George J. Stigler, *The Theory of Price*, 3rd ed. (New York: Crowell-Collier and Macmillan, Inc., 1966), pp. 331–333.

Figure 3–10   Measurement of point elasticity

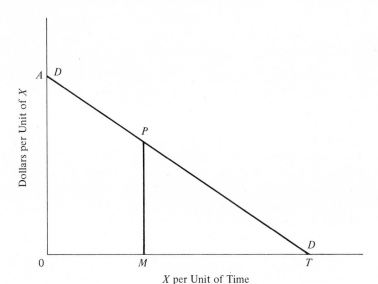

X per Unit of Time

Point elasticity

The point elasticity concept is more precise than that of arc elasticity. If the two points between which arc elasticity is measured are moved closer and closer together, arc elasticity becomes point elasticity as the distance between the points approaches zero.

Elasticity at a point can be measured by a simple geometric method. Figure 3–10 shows a straight line (linear) demand curve. To measure elasticity at point P, we start with the basic formula:

$$\epsilon = \frac{\Delta x/x}{\Delta p/p} = \frac{\Delta x}{x} \times \frac{p}{\Delta p}. \tag{3.5}$$

This can be rearranged to read[12]

$$\epsilon = \frac{\Delta x}{\Delta p} \times \frac{p}{x}. \tag{3.6}$$

On the demand curve $\Delta p/\Delta x$ is the algebraic expression of the slope of the curve for small price changes from point P. Geometrically, the slope of the

---

[12] In terms of calculus:

$$\epsilon = \frac{\lim}{\Delta p \to o} \frac{\Delta x}{\Delta p} \times \frac{p}{x} = \frac{dx}{dp} \times \frac{p}{x}.$$

demand curve is *MP/MT.* Therefore, $\Delta p/\Delta x = MP/MT,$ or, inverting both fractions, $\Delta x/\Delta p = MT/MP.$ Price at point *P* is *MP* and quantity at that point is $0M.$ Thus, at point *P*

$$\epsilon = \frac{MT}{MP} \times \frac{MP}{0M} = \frac{MT}{0M}.$$

Price elasticity coefficients are separated into three absolute value classifications. When elasticity is greater than one, demand is said to be *elastic.* When elasticity equals one, it is said to be of *unitary* elasticity. When elasticity is less than one, demand is said to be *inelastic.* These classifications are illustrated on the linear demand curve of Figure 3–11. Assume point *P* is located so that $0M = MT.$ Since elasticity of demand at point *P* equals $MT/0M,$ elasticity is unitary at that point. Consider any point farther up the demand curve—point $P_1,$ for example. Since M_1T is greater than $0M_1,$ elasticity at point P_1 is greater than one. The farther up the demand curve we move, the greater elasticity becomes, until, as we approach point A, elasticity approaches infinity (∞). Moving down the demand curve to the right from point *P*, elasticity is less than one and becomes progressively smaller the farther we move. As we approach point *T*, elasticity approaches zero.[13]

This technique for measuring point elasticity can also be used on a non-linear curve. Suppose that elasticity is to be measured at point *P* on the demand curve in Figure 3–12. First, draw a tangent to the demand curve at point *P* and extend it so that it cuts the quantity axis at point *T*. At point *P* the demand curve and the tangent coincide and have the same slopes; therefore, their elasticities must be the same at that point. Measurement of elasticity can proceed as before. Drop a perpendicular from *P* to $0T$ and call its intersection with the quantity axis point *M*. Elasticity of demand at point *P* is equal to $MT/0M.$

Elasticity and total money outlays

One of the most important aspects of demand elasticity is the relationship that exists among price changes, elasticity, and total amount of money spent for the good. The total amount spent can be viewed either as total buyers' outlay (*TO*) or total sellers' receipts (*TR*) for the item. This amount is found by multiplying the quantity sold by the price per unit at which it is sold.

---

[13] Mathematically, consider that

$$\epsilon = \frac{dx}{dp} \times \frac{p}{x}.$$

For the linear demand curve of Figure 3–11 the dx/dp term of the elasticity coefficient is constant. As $x \to 0,$ then the term $p/x \to \infty$ and $\epsilon \to \infty.$ As $p \to 0,$ then $p/x \to 0$ and $\epsilon \to 0.$

Figure 3– 11   Elasticity measurements on a linear demand curve

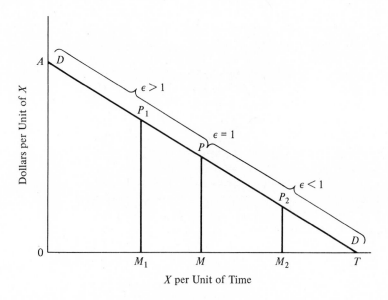

Figure 3– 12   Elasticity measurement on a nonlinear demand curve

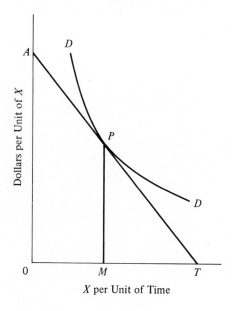

Suppose that for a certain small price decrease demand is elastic—the percentage increase in quantity sold exceeds the percentage decrease in price. Since the increase in quantity sold is proportionally greater than the decrease in price, such a price decrease increases sellers' total receipts. Similarly, if demand were inelastic for such a price decrease, the increase in quantity sold would be proportionally less than the price decrease, and sellers' total receipts would decline. If elasticity were unitary, the proportional increase in quantity sold would equal the proportional decrease in price, and total receipts would remain unchanged. For price increases the effects on total receipts will be just the opposite.[14]

These results are summarized on the linear demand curve of Figure 3–13(a) and the total receipts curve of Figure 3–13(b). Moving down the demand curve from A toward J, the elasticity of demand is decreasing but exceeds one; and TR will be increasing. For example, at price B and quantity S, TR is equal to the area of rectangle $0BGS$ in Figure 3–13(a), and the vertical distance SN in Figure 3–13(b); while at price C and quantity M, TR is the area of rectangle $0CJM$ in the upper diagram and the vertical distance MQ in the lower one.

By inspection it is apparent that $0CJM$ is larger in area than $0BGS$. As we move down the demand curve from J toward T, elasticity continues to decrease and is now less than one, and TR decreases. At price F and quantity V, TR is the area of rectangle $0FRV$ and the vertical distance VW.

---

[14] The total receipts equation is

$$TR = p \times x.$$

Differentiating with respect to x

$$\frac{dTR}{dx} = p + x \frac{dp}{dx} = p + p \left(\frac{x}{p} \times \frac{dp}{dx} \right) = p + \frac{p}{\dfrac{p}{x} \times \dfrac{dx}{dp}}.$$

Since

$$\epsilon = \frac{p}{x} \times \frac{dx}{dp},$$

then

$$\frac{dTR}{dx} = p + \frac{p}{\epsilon}.$$

The sign of ϵ is negative since dx/dp is negative; however, in terms of the absolute value of ϵ,

$$\frac{dTR}{dx} = p - \frac{p}{|\epsilon|}.$$

Therefore, for any increase in x, if

1. $|\epsilon| > 1$, then $dTR/dx > 0$ and TR increases.
2. $|\epsilon| = 1$, then $dTR/dx = 0$ and TR is unchanged.
3. $|\epsilon| < 1$, then $dTR/dx < 0$ and TR decreases.

Figure 3–13   Elasticity, price changes, and *TR*

(a)

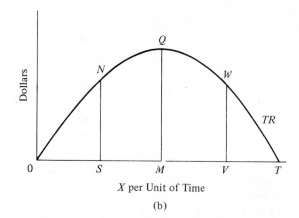

(b)

It is evident that this area is smaller than that of $0CJM$. It follows that at point J, where elasticity is unitary, TR is maximum.

When a demand curve is a rectangular hyperbola, the elasticity of demand at all points on it is unitary. Such a curve is illustrated in Figure 3–14. Its basic characteristic is that the price multiplied by the quantity taken results in the same total receipts, regardless of what price is charged. For

Figure 3-14   Unitary elasticity, price changes, and *TR*

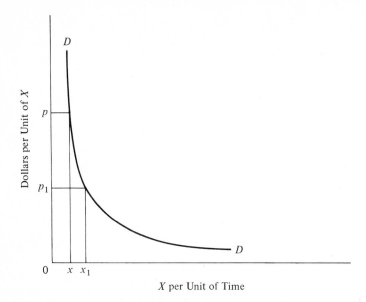

price increases or for price decreases total receipts remain unchanged; that is, $x \times p = x_1 \times p_1 = \cdots = x_n \times p_n$.[15]

A seller, contemplating changes in the price of what he sells, needs to know the elasticity of demand for the price change. If demand is inelastic, a price increase is advisable, but a price decrease is not. The former would increase the seller's total receipts, while at the same time it would cut sales. The latter would increase the seller's sales but would cut total receipts.

---

[15] If the demand curve is a rectangular hyperbola, then

$$x \times p = TR = k,$$

in which k is a constant. Therefore,

$$x = \frac{k}{p}.$$

Differentiating with respect to p,

$$\frac{dx}{dp} = -\frac{k}{p^2}.$$

Thus,

$$\epsilon = -\frac{k}{p^2} \times \frac{p}{x} = -1$$

for all values of x and p.

Factors influencing price elasticity of demand

The major factors influencing elasticity remain to be considered. These are (1) the availability of good substitutes for the item under consideration, (2) the number of uses to which it can be put, (3) its price relative to buyers' purchasing power, and (4) whether the price established is toward the upper end of the demand curve or toward the lower end of the curve. These should be thought of as points to look for in trying to determine whether demand will be more or less elastic in the neighborhood of the ruling price.

The availability of substitutes is the most important of the factors listed. If good substitutes are available, demand for a given product or resource will tend to be elastic. If the price of whole-wheat bread is decreased while the prices of other kinds remain constant, consumers will shift rapidly from the other kinds to whole-wheat bread. Conversely, increases in the price of whole-wheat bread while the prices of other kinds remain constant will cause consumers to shift rapidly away from it to the now relatively lower-priced substitutes.

The wider the range of uses for a product or resource, the more elastic demand for it will tend to be. The greater the number of uses, the greater the possibility there is for variation in quantity taken as its price varies. Suppose that aluminum could be used only in the making of airframes for aircraft. Not much possibility would exist for variation in quantity taken as its price varies, and demand for it would likely be inelastic. In reality, aluminum can be put to hundreds of uses requiring a lightweight metal. The possible variation in quantity taken is quite large. Increases in its price subtract from and decreases in its price add to the list of its economically desirable uses. These possibilities tend to make demand for aluminum more elastic.

Demand for goods that take a large amount of the buyers' purchasing power is more likely to be elastic than demand for goods that are relatively unimportant in this respect. Goods such as deep freezers, which require large outlays, make consumers price-conscious and substitute-conscious. An increase in the price of deep freezers causes shifts toward the use of commercial lockers. Quantity taken, therefore, is likely to vary considerably in response to price changes. For goods such as spices, which take a negligible part of consumers' incomes, changes in price are likely to have little effect on the quantity taken. Consumers are likely to be much less substitute-conscious.

If the ruling price is toward the upper end of the demand curve, demand is more likely to be elastic than if it were toward the lower end. This is a mathematical determinant of elasticity, and its validity depends on the shape of the curve. It rests on a different footing from that of the other three

Figure 3–15   Dependency of elasticity on comparative percentage changes

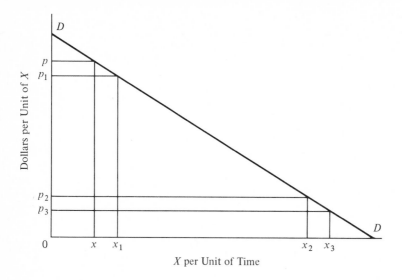

determinants. Figure 3–15 shows a linear demand curve.[16] If the original price is p and changes to p_1, and the original quantity is x and changes to x_1, the percentage change in quantity is large because the original quantity is small compared with the quantity change. The percentage change in price is small because the original price is large compared with the change in price. A large percentage change in quantity divided by a small percentage change in price means that demand is elastic.

   If the original price is p_2 and changes to p_3, and the original quantity is x_2 and changes to x_3, the reverse is the case. The percentage change in quantity is small because the original quantity is large. The percentage change in price is large because the original price is small. A small percentage change in quantity divided by a large percentage change in price means that demand is inelastic.

   With the possible exception of the first point, concerning availability of substitutes, these are not infallible criteria of elasticity of demand but simply express the nature of the forces affecting it. Additionally, they need not all work in the same direction at the same time. One or more may be working against the others, and the magnitude of elasticity will depend on the relative strengths of the opposing forces.

---

[16] The argument of this paragraph does not apply to a demand curve that is a rectangular hyperbola or to one that has greater convexity to the origin than has a rectangular hyperbola. It applies only to those with less convexity.

Cross elasticity of demand

Another elasticity concept that is useful in economic analysis is the cross elasticity of demand. It provides a measure of the extent to which commodities are related to each other. If we consider commodities X and Y, the cross elasticity of X with respect to Y is defined as the percentage change in the quantity of X taken divided by the percentage change in the price of Y. This is expressed mathematically by[17]

$$\Theta_{xy} = \frac{\Delta x/x}{\Delta p_y/p_y}. \tag{3.8}$$

Goods and services, or resources for that matter, may be related as substitutes or as complements.

When goods are substitutes for each other, the sign of the cross-elasticity coefficient between them will be positive. Frankfurters and hamburger provide an illustration. An increase in the price of frankfurters will increase hamburger consumption. Changes in the price of frankfurters and in the consumption of hamburger are in the same direction, whether price moves up or down; the cross elasticity is positive.

Goods that are complementary have negative cross-elasticity coefficients. Notebook paper and pencils serve as an illustration. An increase in the price of notebook paper cuts paper consumption and, consequently, the consumption of pencils. A decrease in the price of paper will increase its consumption and, also, the consumption of pencils. The change in the price of notebook paper is accompanied by a change in the consumption of pencils in the opposite direction. Therefore, the cross-elasticity coefficient will be negative.

Cross elasticity of demand is frequently used in attempts to define the boundaries of an industry; however, its use for this purpose has certain complications. High cross elasticities indicate close relationships or goods in the same industry. Low cross elasticities indicate remote relationships or goods in different industries. A commodity whose cross elasticity is low with respect to all other commodities is sometimes considered to be in an industry by itself. A commodity group with high cross elasticities within the group but with low cross elasticities with respect to other commodities is often said to constitute an industry. Various kinds of women's shoes will have high cross elasticities among each other but low cross elasticities with regard to other articles of women's clothing. Thus, we have a basis for separating out a women's shoe industry.

---

[17] Or, in terms of calculus,

$$\Theta_{xy} = \lim_{\Delta p_y \to 0} \frac{\Delta x}{\Delta p_y} \times \frac{p_y}{x} = \frac{\delta x}{\delta p_y} \times \frac{p_y}{x}.$$

One difficulty with cross elasticity as a means of determining industry boundaries is that of establishing how high the coefficients among commodities must be if they are to be considered in the same industry. Cross elasticities among some foods are quite high—those among frozen peas, frozen green beans, frozen asparagus spears, and the like. Others, such as those between frozen vegetables and frozen meat, are likely to be quite low. Is there a frozen food industry? Answers cannot be given unequivocally. Some general economic problems can best be solved by considering all frozen foods in the same industry. More narrow or more specific economic problems will require more narrow industry groupings—a frozen-vegetable industry or, perhaps, even a frozen-pea industry. Cross elasticities furnish a guide to, but not a hard and fast determination of, industry boundaries.

Another complication is that of chains of cross relationships. Cross elasticities may be high between passenger cars and station wagons, and between station wagons and pick-up trucks. But passenger cars and pick-up trucks may have low cross elasticities. Are they in separate industries or in the same industry? Again, the nature of the problem we want to attack must be the guide to the proper definition of industry boundaries.

Summary

The nature of pure competition and its role in economic analysis should be clearly understood. Pure competition is essentially the idea of smallness of the individual economic unit in relation to the markets in which it operates, the idea of freedom of prices to move in response to changes in demand and supply, and the idea that a considerable degree of mobility for both goods and resources exists in the economy.

The concept of pure competition does not provide an accurate description of the real world, but its usefulness is not negated thereby. It supplies the logical starting point for economic analysis. Enough competition does exist so as to give us valid answers to many economic problems. Additionally, competition provides "norms" for evaluation of the actual performance of the economy.

Demand shows the quantities per unit of time that consumers will take of a commodity at alternative prices, other things being equal. It can be represented as a demand schedule or a demand curve. We must distinguish carefully between changes in demand and movements along a given demand curve. Changes in demand result from changes in one or more of the "other things." Movements along a given demand curve assume that the "other things" do not change.

Supply shows the different quantities per unit of time of a commodity that sellers will place on the market at all possible prices, other things being equal, and, together with demand, determines the equilibrium price of the commodity. The equilibrium price of a commodity is that price that, if attained, will be maintained. Actions of sellers attempting to dispose of surpluses will push a higher-than-equilibrium price toward the equilibrium level. Actions of buyers attempting to buy short supplies will drive a lower-than-equilibrium price toward equilibrium. An increase in demand, given the supply, ordinarily causes an increase in both the price and the quantity exchanged of a good, while a decrease in demand has the opposite effect. An increase in supply, given the demand for a good, ordinarily decreases the price and increases the quantity exchanged. A decrease in supply usually increases the price and decreases the quantity exchanged.

Price elasticity of demand measures the responsiveness of quantity taken of a commodity to changes in its price. Price elasticity of demand is defined as the percentage change in quantity divided by the percentage change in price when the price change is small. Arc elasticity is an approximate measure of elasticity between two separate points. Point elasticity measures elasticity at one single point on the demand curve. Price elasticity of demand is the key element in determining what happens to total business receipts for a commodity when the price of the commodity changes, given demand. When demand is inelastic, increases in price increase total receipts, while decreases in price decrease total receipts. When demand is elastic, the opposite results occur when price is increased or decreased. The degree of demand elasticity for a certain good depends on the availability of substitutes, the number of uses for the good, the importance of the good in consumers' budgets, and the region of the demand curve within which price moves.

The cross elasticity of demand among products is also an important microconcept. High positive cross elasticities indicate a high degree of substitutability between products and are frequently used to mark off the boundaries of particular industries. High negative cross elasticities indicate a high degree of complementarity between products.

Suggested readings

Baumol, William J. *Economic Theory and Operations Analysis.* 4th ed. Englewood Cliffs, N.J.: Prentice-Hall, Inc., 1977. Chapter 9, pp. 179–190.

Knight, Frank H. *Risk, Uncertainty, and Profit.* Boston: Houghton Mifflin Company, 1921. Chap. 1.

Marshall, Alfred. *Principles of Economics.* 8th ed. London: Macmillan & Co., Ltd., 1920. Bk. III, Chap. IV; Bk. V, Chaps. I–III.

Questions and exercises

1. Draw hypothetical demand and supply curves for beef.
   a. Show and explain the equilibrium quantity and price. Show and explain the effects of (1) a support price and (2) a price ceiling.
   b. What would be the effects on price and quantity exchanged of an epidemic of hoof-and-mouth disease?
   c. Show and explain the effects of a beef boycott on the price and quantity exchanged.
   d. How would a prohibition of beef imports affect demand, supply, price, and quantity exchanged?

2. Suppose that the carpenters in a large city are unorganized and that there are many employers of carpenters' labor.
   a. Under what circumstances would unionization and an increase in wage rates result in an increase in total wages paid to carpenters?
   b. Would all carpenters who want to work be able to find employment? Explain.
   c. Will a wage-rate increase always raise the total wage bill of the carpenters?

3. In 1973 and 1974 the economy entered a state that Paul Samuelson has dubbed "stagflation," characterized by rising prices and falling outputs (increasing unemployment). With demand and supply curves for a representative product, illustrate and provide a reasonable explanation of this phenomenon.

4. In economic analysis what does the term *shortage* mean? In the United States is there a shortage of (a) crude oil, (b) milk, (c) automobiles, (d) sugar, (e) blue jeans? Explain why or why not in each case.

5. Suppose that a ceiling price of $2.00 per thousand cubic feet is placed on natural gas by the government and that the equilibrium price is above that level. Who is helped and who is hurt by the price ceiling? Would you advocate continuing the ceiling over time? Why or why not?

Chapter 4

Chapter contents   **Key concepts**

Minimum price policies	**Agricultural price supports**	Price floor
	Minimum wages	Price ceiling
	Supply restrictions	Surplus
		Shortage
Maximum price policies	**Price ceilings for "necessities"**	Excise tax
	Price ceilings to stop inflation	Tax incidence
Excise tax incidence		
Summary	**Suggested readings**	
	Questions and exercises	

Basic applications of the model

We conclude the Part 1 review of basic economic concepts and principles with some important current policy applications of those principles. The demand-supply-price model is applicable most directly to price-fixing arrangements and to certain tax policies. Many such economic policies are devised and promulgated with the express aim of correcting inequities in income distribution. However, using the model as an analytical tool, we find that the results of the arrangements are not always what they are expected to be. We shall look first at policies that fix minimum prices, or *price floors*, for specific goods. Then we shall consider maximum pricing, or *price-ceiling*, policies. Finally, we shall examine a *tax-incidence* problem.

Minimum price policies

Agricultural price supports

The outstanding example of minimum price policies by government is undoubtedly the agricultural price-support program developed by the federal government during and since the Great Depression of the 1930s. Prices of farm products sold were thought by proponents of support programs to be too low relative to the prices of products that farmers buy; that is, they were considered to be inequitable or unfair. These relatively low farm prices were thought to be an important factor in causing per capita farm income to be lower than the average per capita income in the United States. Consequently, price supports have been authorized by Congress to be used as a partial answer to the farm-income problem.

The essential price theory features of a support program are illustrated in Figure 4–1 with respect to wheat. In an uncontrolled market with the price free to move, the equilibrium price level is p per bushel and the quantity exchanged is X bushels per year. Suppose that price p is thought to be relatively too low, and a support price is set at p_1. The government supports the price by purchasing the wheat that farmers cannot sell at price p.[1] In Figure 4–1 consumers will buy X_1 bushels per year, leaving a surplus of X_1X_1' for the government to acquire.

A support price will be effective only if it is above the equilibrium level; and if it is effective, surpluses will occur. If it were below p, shortages would induce buyers to bid the price up to the equilibrium level so that the support price would not be effective. Thus, it will be effective only at price levels above p. Yet congressmen, government officials, farmers, and most of the rest of the general public profess amazement that surpluses accumulate from a price-support program and deduce from the existence of surpluses that something about the program is not being handled properly.

What does the government do in the face of the accumulating surplus? We know from the market model that if demand can be increased or supply

---

Figure 4–1   Effects of agricultural price supports

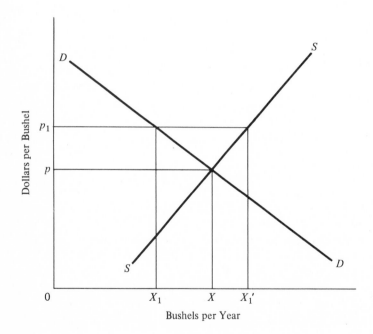

_{Bushels per Year}

---

[1] Under the various Agricultural Adjustment Acts the support price is set by means of a storage-and-loan program. A farmer, instead of selling wheat in the market at price p, can obtain a loan on the wheat from the government at price p_1 per bushel, provided the farmer puts the wheat in storage in government-approved facilities. When the loan is due to be repaid, the farmer can either sell his wheat and repay it or turn the wheat over to the government as repayment in full. What would be done if the market price of wheat were above p_1 when repayment is due? What would the farmer do if it were below p_1? In effect, the government is guaranteeing that the price will not fall below p_1. Farmers sell what they can in the market at the price, and, in essence, the government buys the surplus.

can be decreased, there will be smaller surpluses; consequently, we can predict logically that the government would pursue policies to accomplish both. To increase demand, it may stress the virtues of greater wheat consumption. It may try to sell more wheat abroad. To decrease supply, it may place restrictions on the acreage that farmers can plant. It may seek to hold land out of cultivation through a "soil bank." It may establish marketing quotas. It may also seek ways and means of disposing of the surpluses. Expanding school lunch programs and increasing foreign aid in kind furnish examples.

Interesting questions can be raised as to whether or not agricultural price supports actually contribute to greater equity in the economy. Do they reduce income inequalities? Since it is the unit price of the product that is increased, a farmer who raises and sells ten times as much wheat as another will receive ten times the amount of supplemental income that the other receives. The costs of the support program must come from tax revenues. Before the transfer of income from taxpayers to farmers occurs, are the taxpayers richer or poorer than those who are to receive the support payments? What can we say about the overall efficiency of the economy in a situation where farmers are induced either to use resources to produce more than they would have produced at an equilibrium price level or, in the event of supply restrictions, to leave some of the scarce resources of the economy idle?

Minimum wages

The simple market model is as applicable to resource markets as it is to markets for goods and services. Labor markets provide an excellent example of the minimum wage rate fixing that is so generally accepted in this country. The fixing of minimum wage rates is done in two ways: (1) by minimum wage legislation and (2) by collective bargaining contracts arrived at through union-management negotiations.

Suppose that we concentrate on a market for common unskilled labor. This provides a good example for two reasons: (1) it is purchased competitively in most cases—there are enough users, each taking a small enough proportion of the total supply, so that no one user by itself can influence the wage rate; and (2) the legal minimum wage rates set under the Fair Labor Standards Act of 1938, as amended, are effective primarily in unskilled labor markets, especially those in which minority groups and teenagers participate.

What will be the effects of a minimum wage rate set above the equilibrium level? The obvious answer is illustrated in Figure 4–2. At the equilibrium wage rate w, workers want to place h hours in employment, and this is precisely the quantity that employers are willing to use. A minimum wage rate set below w will have no effect; the equilibrium rate will prevail. But if

Figure 4–2   Effects of minimum wage rates

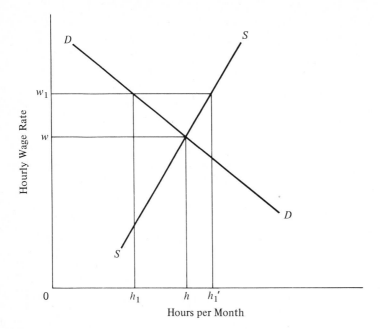

a minimum wage rate of w_1 is established by either a minimum wage law or a collective agreement of some kind, employers are willing to employ only h_1 hours, while the labor force wants to place h_1' in employment. The result will be unemployment amounting to h_1h_1' hours per month.

Many people either do not understand this conclusion or find it unpalatable; consequently, they reject the analysis that leads to it. Witness, for example, the wide support given the grape pickers of California over the last several years in their attempts to unionize and obtain higher wage rates from the grape growers. Witness also the almost complete absence of opposition to recently enacted increases in the federal minimum wage level at a time when unemployment rates exceeded 6 percent of the labor force. Union leaders are almost unanimous in expressing the opinion that there is no relationship between negotiated wage levels and the rate of unemployment.

What are the effects of the minimum wage on the incomes of workers? In Figure 4–2 the h_1 workers who remain employed at the higher wage rates clearly gain. The h_1h_1' workers who are unemployed just as clearly lose. What about the entire group of the kind of labor under consideration; that is, what happens to the total wage bill? The answer turns on the elasticity of demand. If the labor demand curve is elastic, the total wage bill decreases as the wage rate is increased. If demand is inelastic, the total wage bill rises; and if it is of unitary elasticity, the total wage bill will not change.

Supply restrictions

Groups of sellers of a good or of a resource often resort to supply restrictions in order to raise the prices of what they have to sell, with the expectation that the use of this stratagem will increase their incomes. Unions have been accused of limiting their memberships in order to hold wage rates higher than they would otherwise be. In the middle 1930s the Agricultural Adjustment Act was intended to raise the prices of certain farm products by directly curtailing the supplies. The American Medical Association and state medical associations have been said to limit medical school enrollments for the same purpose. University professors are said to induce their universities to hire only those with Ph.D. degrees to accomplish the same end.

Figure 4 – 3   Effects of supply restriction

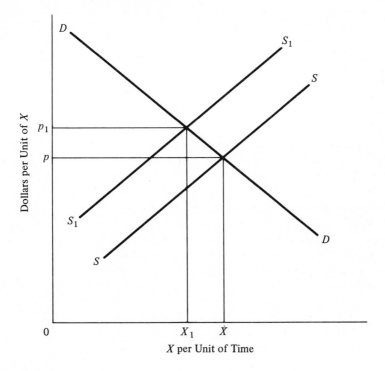

The mechanics of all these cases are the same. In Figure 4–3 with demand curve *DD* and supply curve *SS* the equilibrium price of whatever is being exchanged is *p* and the quantity bought and sold is *X*. If the supply restriction activities of the sellers of *X* are successful, the supply curve shifts to the left to S_1S_1, raising the price to p_1 and reducing the quantity sold to X_1. Do sellers as individuals gain? Do sellers as a group gain?

Individual sellers who are able to sell as much after the supply restriction as before obviously gain. If some are cut out of the market altogether, they just as obviously lose. If some must now place smaller quantities on the market at higher prices, we cannot say whether they gain or lose without further investigation. Whether sellers as a group gain or lose as a result of the higher price depends again on whether demand is elastic, inelastic, or of unitary elasticity for the price increase.

Maximum price policies

Maximum prices, or price ceilings set by governments, seem to have broad appeal for the general public under at least two sets of circumstances. First, when certain items that the public believes are necessities—for example, housing, medical care, and natural gas—are available in quantities thought to be inadequate at prices thought to be too high, there will be sentiment for price controls to keep the items within the buying reach of poor people. Second, during the periods of rising price levels that we call *inflation,* price controls are often thought to be the appropriate remedial measure.

Price ceilings for "necessities"

The so-called energy crisis provided an outstanding case study of price controls on a "necessity"—gasoline. Growing affluence (rising incomes) in the United States has caused the demand for gasoline to increase over time. Supply, too, has been increasing but not as fast in recent years as demand. Under these circumstances the price per gallon of gasoline would be expected to rise.

Gasoline, like many other products, was subjected to some degree of price controls from August 1971 through March 1974. During 1973 there were some spot shortages before the fall of the year, but with the Arab embargo on crude oil shipments to the United States in the fall and winter of 1973–74, shortages of gasoline suddenly became acute. These triggered great public and congressional pressure on the Federal Energy Office and the Cost of Living Council to hold the line on the price of gasoline so that the poor as well as the rich could have access to available supplies.

Actually, effective price ceilings insure that shortages will persist as long as the controlled price is below the equilibrium market price. In Figure 4–4 *DD* and *SS* represent the demand and supply curves for gasoline in July 1971, with *p* as the equilibrium price. By October 1973 suppose that demand has increased to D_1D_1 and supply has become S_1S_1. If the price is controlled at *p* cents per gallon, a monthly shortage of X_2X_1 gallons occurs. Suppose that the Arab embargo on shipments of crude oil to the United States shifts the supply curve of gasoline back to *SS*. The shortage becomes XX_1 gallons per month.

When the available supplies of a commodity fall short of the quantities that demanders want, a rationing problem emerges. If the price of gasoline had been permitted to rise to p_3, the quantity available per month would have been X_3. At that price consumers would have limited themselves *voluntarily* to that amount, and no rationing problem would have been evident. An equilibrium market price induces consumers to limit themselves to the supplies available. With the price controlled at *p*, however, the price of gasoline could no longer perform its rationing function. The government

Figure 4 – 4   Price controls on "necessities"

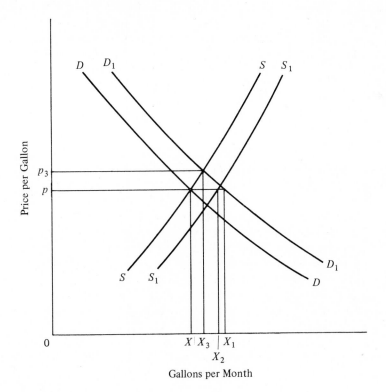

attempted to meet this problem by banning Sunday sales of gasoline and by leaving gasoline retailers with broad discretionary powers to determine how they would ration the supplies available to customers. Gasoline buyers were subjected to all sorts of arbitrary, and often wasteful, practices. Some retailers saw to it that their regular customers were taken care of first. Others limited customers to fixed amounts—for example, 5 gallons—for each trip to the pump, thus making more trips to the station necessary and in many cases inducing consumers to drive around the block to establish eligibility for another 5 gallons. Most sold their available supplies on a first-come first-served basis. In general there was frustration and discontent among the ranks of consumers. From time to time irate customers attacked station attendants. On one occasion a customer pulled out a pistol and shot an empty gas pump.

Did controls help people obtain this "necessity" at "reasonable" prices? All over the country customers were forced to wait in lines of varying lengths for their turns at the pumps. Some people got up early to be near the head of the line when the station opened. Many had to take time off from work to get to the service station during its operating hours. If the controlled price of gasoline were $0.50 per gallon and the average purchase of a customer is 10 gallons, the total purchase amounts to $5. But if the customer's time is worth $5 an hour and it is necessary to wait in line an hour to make the purchase, the total cost to the consumer becomes $10, and the actual cost per gallon becomes $1 instead of $0.50. Under these circumstances, the advantages of a controlled price are illusory. Consumers would be better off without them.

Price ceilings to stop inflation

Many people believe that price ceilings provide the appropriate mechanism for stopping inflation. Thus, in August 1971 the Nixon Administration inaugurated a set of across-the-board price controls to stop the inflation that had been rampant since the middle 1960s. The rate of inflation had increased from slightly more than 3 percent per year in early 1968 to about 6 percent in early 1970. Tight monetary and fiscal policies had brought the rate down to just under 5 percent by August 1971—but at a cost of rising unemployment. The general public, businessmen, and the Congress pressed the administration hard enough to secure the enactment of controls even though the President's economic advisors argued persistently against them. What were the results?

As the preceding subsection indicates, in markets where prices are not controlled prices serve to ration the available supplies of goods among consumers who want them. Suppose that X in Figure 4–5 is one of many goods produced and sold in the economy. Demand and supply are DD and SS, respectively. The price moves to the equilibrium level p_0, where it

Figure 4–5 Price controls to stop inflation

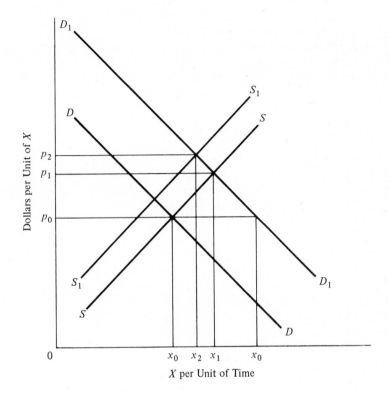

rations the available supply among consumers. Each consumer in the economy gets as much as he or she wants at the equilibrium price level; there is neither a shortage nor a surplus.

If a substantial increase in consumers' money incomes now occurs, what happens in the absence of price controls? Demand for X increases to some such level as D_1D_1, and in the absence of price controls consumers bid the price up toward p_1. As this occurs and as it becomes more profitable to produce X, producers seek larger quantities of the resources needed to make the product. The same thing is happening in the production of other goods and services; and as producers bid for resources, resource prices rise. If there were some unemployed resources initially available in the economy, unemployed units may be drawn into production, permitting expansion of the outputs of some goods and services. But when unemployment has been eliminated, this source of general expansion is no longer possible. Increases in demand when full employment prevails must be reflected in price increases, with no increases on the average in the economy's outputs.

Increases in the prices of resources used in producing any one good or service shift the supply curve for that item to the left. In Figure 4–5 resource price increases move the supply curve of X to S_1S_1. The new equilibrium price is p_2, and the new equilibrium quantity is x_2. Industry X, as we show it, has been able to increase slightly the quantities of the resources it uses and also its product output, but most of the increase in demand is reflected in an increase in the price of the product. The new equilibrium price p_2 induces consumers to ration themselves to the quantity made available at that price.

Effective price controls will change the picture. Consider once more the initial equilibrium situation for X, in which demand and supply are respectively DD and SS. Suppose again that an increase in consumer incomes shifts demand to D_1D_1. This time, however, assume that the price of X is controlled—is not permitted to rise above p_0—and that resource prices as well are not permitted to rise. The immediate impact is a shortage amounting to x_0x_0'. Consumers want more at the controlled price than suppliers will place on the market; they no longer want to limit their consumption to the quantity available. Since the price cannot operate to ration the available quantities, how is the rationing to be done? By a first-come first-served policy, with its accompanying queues or waiting in line for the product? By suppliers' whims favoring certain customers? By government-imposed rationing schemes? Or by some other method?

Maximum price policies have an additional impact on the operation of a market system—they make it impossible for relative prices of different products to reflect changes in consumers' relative valuations of different goods and for the price system to reorganize production to accommodate such changes. Figure 4–5 reflects a situation in which an increase in consumers' incomes makes product X more valuable to consumers relative to all other available goods than it was before. In the absence of controls some additional quantities of resources flow into the production of X, raising the equilibrium quantity produced from x_0 to x_2. With the price of X controlled at p_0 and with resources' prices controlled at whatever their initial levels were, this reallocation will not take place.

The actual results of wage-price controls were very much along these lines during the Nixon control period. Shortages of specific goods and services and disruptions of production cropped up in all sectors of the economy. Some refineries, unable to get crude oil, could not run at capacity. There were shortages of baling wire and fertilizer. Ironically, oil producers encountered shortages of steel casing for newly drilled oil wells and were thus handicapped in increasing the quantities of crude oil available. These are but a few examples of the effects of controls.

As Milton Friedman has aptly put it, placing a set of price controls on a market economy is like locking the rudder on a ship. It does away with the means of steering it along the paths desired by consumers.[2] Prices cannot perform their functions of reflecting the relative values of different goods and services and of organizing production according to consumer desires. Some other mechanism—for example, some kind of government rationing program and some kind of arbitrary allocation of resources among producers—must be substituted for it.

Inflation was not halted. At the end of the price control experiment in early 1974 the rate of inflation was higher than it was in 1971. Apparently the system of price controls induced a false sense of security in governmental circles. In 1971, 1972, and 1973 there were large deficits in the federal budgets and large increases in the money supply, both of which increased consumer demands for goods and services, causing continuing inflationary pressure. The system of price controls failed to accomplish what it was supposed to do.

Excise tax incidence

A classic application of the model is its use to analyze the incidence of an excise tax placed on a good or service. An excise tax may be a given amount per unit of product, such as a state gasoline tax, or it may be a percentage of the selling price of the product, such as a state sales tax. The former is called a *specific tax;* the latter is termed an *ad valorem* tax. The analysis is essentially the same for either type, but since the specific tax is a little easier to manipulate graphically, we shall focus the discussion on it.

Cigarettes will be the product to be taxed. Suppose that the equilibrium price of cigarettes is p per pack in Figure 4–6 and that the quantity exchanged is x packs per week. A tax of t per pack is placed on the product. How much of the tax is passed forward to buyers? How much of it must be paid by sellers? Does the incidence depend on whom the tax is collected from? Many people think so.

Consider first the case in which the tax is collected from cigarette sellers—retail stores. In Figure 4–6(a) the supply curve SS shows the amounts per pack that sellers as a group must receive to induce them to place on the market the various quantities that comprise the horizontal axis of the diagram. Thus, imposition of the tax t simply shifts the supply curve upward by the amount of the tax. If sellers are to be induced to place x packs per week on the market, they must receive an amount p per pack for themselves; that makes it necessary for them to collect $p + t$ from buyers.

---

[2] Milton Friedman, ''Why the Freeze Is a Mistake,'' *Newsweek,* vol. 78 (August 30, 1971), p. 23.

Buyers will not take x packs per week at a price, including tax, of $p + t$ per pack. At this level of expenditure per pack the demand curve shows that they will take x_t' only, leaving a surplus of $x_t'x$ per week on sellers' hands. Undercutting by individual sellers will move the price plus tax down to level $p_1 + t$, at which buyers will take the entire quantity x_1 that sellers will offer at a price, not including the tax, of p_1. The difference between p and $p_1 + t$ shows the amount of the tax that is passed along to buyers. The difference between p_1 and p shows the amount of the tax that must be borne by sellers.

The incidence will be exactly the same if the tax is collected from buyers instead of from sellers. The demand curve and the supply curve, DD and SS, in Figure 4–6(b) are identical to those of Figure 4–6(a). Consider next that DD represents the outlays per pack that consumers are willing to pay for each of the various quantities per week, measured along the horizontal axis. The demand curve from the consumers' viewpoint is not affected by the imposition of a tax t, but from the sellers' viewpoint the tax shifts the demand curve they face downward by the amount of the tax to D_tD_t. Consumers will buy x packs per week only if they are required to pay p per pack. After the imposition of the tax only $p - t$ per pack would be left for sellers; consequently, sellers' offerings would be reduced to x_t, leaving a shortage of x_tx. Bidding for the short supply by buyers will increase the price received by sellers to p_1. Quantity exchanged will be x_1, and buyers will be paying a total of $p_1 + t$ per pack. The incidence of the tax is the same as in the previous case. Buyers now pay $(p_1 + t) - p$ per pack more than they did before the tax. Sellers receive $p - p_1$ less.

Figure 4–6   The incidence of an excise tax

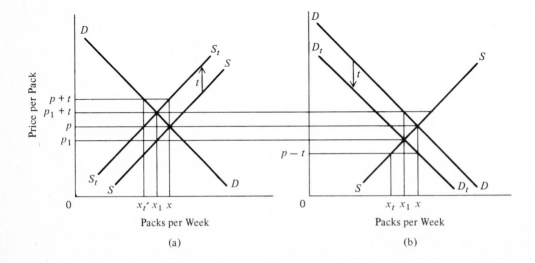

Packs per Week

(a)   (b)

Given the initial demand curve and the initial supply curve for the product, the elasticity of demand and the elasticity of supply have an important bearing on the relative shares of the tax borne by buyers and by sellers. Suppose, for example, that, given *DD,* the elasticity of supply were greater at all prices than we have shown in Figure 4–6. What happens to the incidence of the tax? Or, given *SS,* suppose that the elasticity of demand were greater at all prices. Again, what would be the impact on the incidence of the tax?

Payroll (social security) taxes are really excise taxes of an *ad valorem* type. Does it really matter whether the employer and the employee are each billed for half the tax? Would the incidence of the tax be different if it were all charged against the employer? The employee?

Summary

The market price model provides useful insights into the effects of certain governmental and private-group economic policy making. It shows that effective agricultural price supports of the storage-and-loan type will result in the accumulation of surpluses of the supported products, and that effective minimum wages will usually cause unemployment. Policies of supply restriction used in order to increase prices may or may not increase the total income of all sellers, although they will certainly increase the incomes of some sellers at the expense of those cut out of the market.

Price ceilings are sometimes placed on products in order (1) to protect consumers from high prices of some items thought to be necessities and (2) to control inflation. The model shows that effective price controls used for the first purpose will insure that a shortage comes into being and persists over time, creating a rationing problem. When price controls are used to control inflation, prices can neither serve the purpose of rationing the available supplies among consumers nor reflect the relative values that consumers as a group place on different goods and services.

Application of the model to the problem of excise tax incidence shows that there is no difference if the tax is levied on buyers or on sellers. Additionally, the incidence of the tax will vary, depending on the elasticities of demand and supply.

Suggested readings

Brozen, Yale, "The Effect of Statutory Minimum Wage Increases on Teenage Unemployment." *Journal of Law and Economics,* Vol. 12 (April 1969), pp. 109–122.

Knight, Wyllis R., "Agriculture," in Walter Adams, ed., *Structure of American Industry*, 4th ed. New York: The Macmillan Company, 1971.

Miller, James C., III, "Short-run Solutions to Airport Congestions." *Atlanta Economic Review* (October 1969), pp. 28–29.

Radford, R. A., "The Economic Organization of a P.O.W. Camp." *Economica*, Vol. XII (November 1945), pp. 189–201.

Questions and exercises

1. Consider the market for fluid milk. Illustrate with diagrams and explain the effects on price and quantity exchanged of
   a. a decline in the birth rate
   b. the discovery of a superior breed of milk cow
   c. a rise in the price of beef
   d. the imposition of substantial taxes on processed milk products.

2. Airline fares are set by the Civil Aeronautics Board. If airlines insist on providing beautiful stewardesses, handsome stewards, gourmet meals, and free movies, what do you know about the level of the fares? What would happen if fares were decontrolled?

3. What has the legalization of abortion done to the demand for, supply of, price of, quantity of, and quality of the service?

4. Many people seem to believe that the enactment and enforcement of minimum housing standards in a given city will be in the best interests of slum dwellers. What effects will the adoption of such standards have on the quality of, quantity of, and price of available housing?

5. Consider the payroll tax levied on both employers and employees to pay Social Security benefits. What would be the effect on a typical employee's take-home pay if the tax were collected entirely from employers? Entirely from employees?

6. In 1978 farmers were quite concerned about their incomes and the prices they received for their products. Through lobbying efforts, public demonstrations, and threats to "strike" they tried to get Congress to increase price supports for farm products. If they were to succeed in getting a support price (say, for wheat) substantially above the equilibrium price, what would be the effects on (1) total farm income, (2) the distribution of income, and (3) shortages or surpluses of wheat? In answering the question suppose that the support price is enforced through
   a. a storage-and-loan type program
   b. a subsidy paid to wheat farmers equal to the difference between the equilibrium price of wheat and the support price.

The demand curves for goods and services that were used in Chapters 3 and 4 are rooted in choices made by individuals or households. The more we know about how those choices are made and what affects them the better we can understand the nuances of demands. In Part 2 we develop the theory of choice and demand. In Chapters 5 and 6 the analysis is focused on the individual consumer unit, but to complete the demand picture we look at it from the point of view of the individual business concern in Chapter 7.

The modern theory of demand is presented in Chapter 5. The indifference curve analysis, which forms the core of the modern theory, evolved from the utility approach to demand developed in the latter part of the nineteenth century; however, it is not dependent on the utility approach. Many economists shun the utility approach, or at least relegate it to a secondary position. Because we believe that it contains much of interest and importance we have developed it in Chapter 6. It can, however, be omitted without loss of continuity by those who prefer to do so.

Chapter 5

Chapter contents

		Key concepts
The consumer's preferences	The consumer's indifference map Indifference curve characteristics Complementary and substitute relations	Indifference curve Indifference map Marginal rate of substitution
Constraints on the consumer	The budget line Shifts in the budget line	Indifference surface Substitute goods and services
Maximization of consumer satisfaction		Complementary goods and services
Demand curves and Engel curves	The demand curve Corner solutions Elasticity of demand and the price consumption curve Engel curves Income elasticity of demand	Budget line Maximization of satisfaction Price consumption curve Individual consumer demand curve Corner solutions
Income effects and substitution effects		Price elasticity of demand Income-consumption curve
Market demand curves		Engel curve Superior goods Inferior goods
Exchange and welfare		Income elasticity of demand Income effects
Some applications of indifference curve analysis	Economics of fringe benefits Labor supply	Substitution effects Compensating variation in income
Index numbers	The Laspeyres price index The Paasche price index	Market demand curve Edgeworth box Pareto optimum
Summary	Suggested readings Questions and exercises	Contract curve Fringe benefits Labor supply Laspeyres price index Paasche price index

The modern theory of consumer choice and demand

The theory of consumer choice provides a logical starting point for the systematic development of microeconomic principles. In this chapter we shall focus on indifference curve analysis, the general theory of consumer choice. Although indifference curve techniques date from the 1880s, they were not integrated into the main body of economic thought until the 1930s. A British economist, Francis Y. Edgeworth, introduced the concept in 1881.[1] Edgeworth's techniques, with some modifications, were adopted by an Italian economist, Vilfredo Pareto, in 1906.[2] It remained for two British economists, John R. Hicks and R. G. D. Allen, to popularize and extend the use of indifference curve analysis in the 1930s,[3] and it has since become the central core of choice and demand theory.

The consumer's preferences

We begin the study of an individual consumer's behavior by examining preferences.[4] These are summed up in graphic form as the consumer's *indifference map*. We then examine the main characteristics of the *indifference curves* that make up the indifference map.

The consumer's indifference map

In the modern world a consumer has a large number of goods and services among which preferences can be expressed. The number of possible combinations of goods confronting a consumer approaches infinity. What can

---

[1] Francis Y. Edgeworth, *Mathematical Psychics* (London: C. K. Paul & Co., 1881).

[2] Vilfredo Pareto, *Manuel d'économie politique* (Paris: V. Giard & E. Briere, 1909). The work was first published in Italian in 1906.

[3] John R. Hicks and R. G. D. Allen, "A Reconsideration of the Theory of Value," *Economica.* New Series, No. 1 (February, May 1934), pp. 52–76, 196–219.

[4] The basic consuming unit in an economy is more often a family than a single individual. The term "individual consumer" is used broadly to cover both families and unattached individuals.

be said in an analytical way about the consumer's behavior with respect to this wide range of possibilities?

In order to say much of anything it is necessary to make certain assumptions about the basic nature of the consumer's preferences. We assume *first, that the consumer is able to set up a preference ranking of the combinations available.* He or she can determine which combinations are preferred to others and among which combinations he or she is indifferent. *Second,* we assume *that the preferences of the consumer are consistent or transitive.* If combination *A* is preferred to combination *B* and combination *B* is preferred to combination *C*, then combination *A* must be preferred to combination *C*. Again, if combination *D* is equivalent to combination *E* and combination *E* is equivalent to combination *F*, then combination *D* is equivalent to combination *F*. *Third,* we assume *that the consumer prefers more of any good or service to less of it;* that is, the consumer is not satiated with any specific one.[5]

These assumptions enable us to construct an individual consumer's indifference map. To simplify matters, we shall act as though the world contains only two goods—*X* and *Y*. The consumer is asked to rank the many possible available combinations, showing those that are preferred over others as well as those among which he or she is indifferent.

A set of combinations among which the consumer is indifferent forms an *indifference schedule* or an *indifference curve.* If, for example, the consumer considers all the combinations listed in Table 5–1 as equivalent to one another, these constitute an indifference schedule. Plotting these combinations (and all those intermediate to the ones in the schedule) in Figure 5–1, we have indifference curve *I*.

Table 5–1   An indifference schedule

X (Bushels)	Y (Pints)
3	7
4	4
5	2
6	1
7	½

[5] Satiation with any one good is not impossible. We have all seen it occur temporarily with food, liquor, and other items. As we shall see, however, rational economic behavior usually rules out satiation with items that are not abundant enough to be had for the taking.

Also, there are items in the economy, like polluted water and garbage, of which the consumer desires less rather than more. These items are sometimes referred to as "bads" rather than "goods." Control over them, such as purification and disposal services, become goods and services which we can assume the consumer prefers in greater rather than lesser amounts, up to their saturation levels.

Although Figure 5–1 contains only two indifference curves, an infinite number can be drawn. The commodity space enclosed by the X and Y axes contains all possible combinations of the two goods. A combination such as C, containing 5 bushels of X and 5 pints of Y, will be preferred to combination A, containing 4 bushels of X and 4 pints of Y. (Remember the third assumption.) Other combinations equivalent to C can be located, and these trace out indifference curve *II*. In this manner we can draw as many indifference curves as we wish. All combinations on higher indifference curves—those farther from the origin—are preferable to those lying on lower indifference curves. The whole set of indifference curves constitutes the *indifference map* of the consumer.[6]

Indifference curve characteristics

A set of indifference curves exhibits three basic characteristics: (1) *the individual curves slope downward to the right;* (2) *they are nonintersecting;* and (3) *they are convex to the origin of the diagram.* These features will be considered in turn.

The downward slope to the right of indifference curves is assured by the assumption that a consumer prefers more of a good to less of it. If an indifference curve were horizontal, this would mean that the consumer is indifferent between two combinations, both of which contain the same amount of Y but one of which contains a greater amount of X than the other. A curve could be horizontal only if the consumer were receiving enough X to be saturated with it; that is, additional units of X alone would add nothing to the person's total satisfaction. Similarly, if an indifference curve were vertical, this would mean that the two combinations of X and Y, both with the same amount of X but with one containing more Y than the other, yield equivalent satisfaction to the consumer. Again, this would be the case only if the consumer had reached a saturation point for Y. For the consumer to remain indifferent among combinations after giving up units of one commodity, the loss must be compensated for with additional units of another commodity. The result, shown graphically, is a curve that is downward-sloping to the right.

---

[6] The consumer's preference function or indifference map can be represented by

$$U = f(x, y),$$

in which U represents levels of preference expressed in ordinal terms only. The equation for one indifference curve is

$$U_1 = f(x, y),$$

in which U_1 is a constant; that is, it represents a given level of preference. Other values assigned to U define other indifference curves, all of these making up the consumer's indifference map. These assigned values show the order of preference magnitudes, not absolute (measurable) magnitudes.

Figure 5–1   Indifference curves

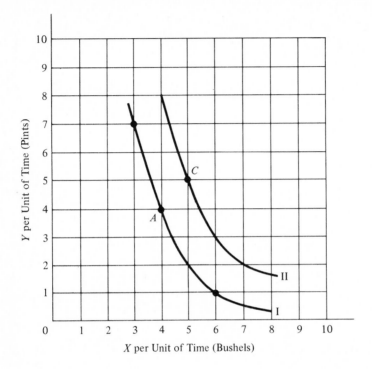

Indifference curves are nonintersecting if the transitivity assumption holds. In Figure 5–2 we see the logical contradiction of intersecting curves. Combination C is preferred to combination A. Combination A is equivalent to combination B. But combination C is also equivalent to combination B. According to the transitivity assumption, C should be *preferred* to B. Thus, the intersection of indifference curves violates the transitivity assumption. To say that indifference curves are nonintersecting is not to say that they are parallel or that they are equidistant from each other. They may run further apart at some points and closer together at others. The only restriction placed on them here is that they do not intersect.

We cannot prove conclusively at this point that indifference curves are convex to the origin, but we can show that it is likely that they are. To get at the issue, we introduce the *marginal rate of substitution* concept.

The marginal rate of substitution of one product for another, say of X for Y, is abbreviated as MRS_{xy}, and is defined as the maximum amount of Y the consumer is willing to give up to get an additional unit of X—the trade-off between bundles of goods among which he is indifferent. In Figure 5–!

Figure 5–2   Consequences of indifference curve intersection

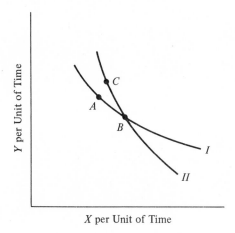

suppose that the consumer is initially taking 7 pints of Y and 3 bushels of X. To move to a consumption rate of 4 bushels of X, she would be just willing to give up the consumption of 3 pints of Y per unit of time. The marginal rate of substitution for this move is 3.

The more Y and the less X the consumer has, the more important a unit of X is to her compared with a unit of Y. For example, at point A in Figure 5–3 she would be willing to give up a relatively large amount of Y to get an additional unit of X. At point B she has much more X and much less Y than at A; hence, a unit of Y would be more important to her as compared with a unit of X than it was at point A, and she would be willing to give up less of Y to get an additional unit of X. The X axis is marked off in equal quantity units between A and B. At point A the indifference curve shows that the consumer is just willing to give up CD of Y to get an additional unit of X. As the consumer acquires more of X per unit of time and less of Y, the importance of a unit of Y becomes progressively greater as compared with the importance of a unit of X. The amounts of Y she is just willing to give up to get additional units of X become progressively smaller; that is, the marginal rate of substitution of X for Y is decreasing.[7]

If the marginal rate of substitution of X for Y is decreasing, the indifference curve must be convex toward the origin. If it were constant, the amounts of Y the consumer would give up to get additional units of X would be constant instead of decreasing; the indifference curve would be a straight

---

[7] It may be helpful to work out the MRS_{xy} arithmetically between different points on indifference curve I of Figure 5–1 before proceeding to the more abstract geometric representation of it in Figure 5–3.

Figure 5–3   Diminishing marginal rate of substitution

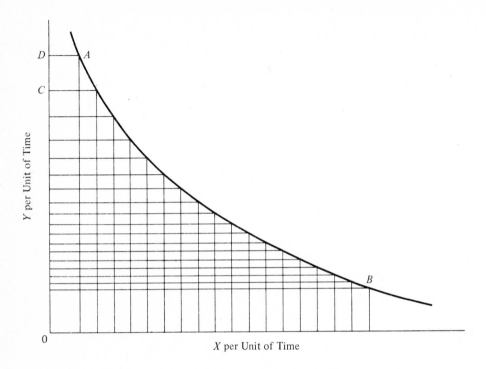

line sloping downward to the right. If the marginal rate of substitution were increasing, the indifference curve would be concave to the origin.[8]

[8] The total differential of the preference function of Footnote 6 is

$$dU = f_x dx + f_y dy.$$

For a given indifference curve $dU = 0$, so

$$0 = f_x dx + f_y dy$$

and

$$-\frac{dy}{dx} = \frac{f_x}{f_y} = MRS_{xy}.$$

To determine the shape of an indifference curve, we look at the derivative of the MRS_{xy} with respect to x. Since

$$MRS_{xy} = -\frac{dy}{dx},$$

then

$$\frac{d}{dx}(MRS_{xy}) = \frac{d}{dx}\left(-\frac{dy}{dx}\right) = -\frac{d^2y}{dx^2}.$$

If

$$\frac{d^2y}{dx^2} > 0,$$

Complementary and substitute relations

If the consumer thinks of goods and services as being related to one another, the relationship may be either one of complementarity or one of substitutability. Generally speaking, two goods are complements if an increase (decrease) in the consumption level of one increases (decreases) the relative desirability to the consumer of the other. Goods are substitutes for each other if an increase (decrease) in the consumption level of one decreases (increases) the relative desirability of the other.

These definitions can be made more explicit with the aid of indifference curve concepts. Suppose that the consumer is no longer confined to a two-commodity world but that there are choices among X, Y, and a host of other goods and services. Let the quantities of the other goods and services be measured in terms of monetary units, while X and Y are measured in bushels and pints as before. In Figure 5–4 monetary units M are measured on the vertical axis while the axes of the horizontal plane show units of Y and X. The consumer now has the options of substituting X for M, Y for M, and X for Y. If the consumption level of Y is zero, indifference curve AB represents combinations of M and X that yield the consumer a given level of satisfaction. If the consumption level of X is zero, indifference curve BC shows combinations of M and Y that yield the *same level* of satisfaction as do those of AB. If the consumption level of Y is y_1, indifference curve A_1B_1 shows combinations of M and X that, together with y_1 of Y, yield the *same level* of satisfaction as do those of AB and BC. A family of curves such as A_1B_1, one for each level of consumption of Y, can be drawn tracing out an *indifference surface* bounded by ABC that is convex toward the origin of the diagram.

To determine whether X and Y are complements or substitutes we hold the consumer's satisfaction level constant; that is, we stay on a given indifference surface. Suppose that initially the consumer is using no Y and has a

---

then $$-\frac{d^2y}{dx^2} < 0, \quad \text{or} \quad \frac{d}{dx}(MRS_{xy}) < 0,$$

and the indifference curve is convex to the origin. If

$$\frac{d^2y}{dx^2} < 0,$$

then $$-\frac{d^2y}{dx^2} > 0, \quad \text{or} \quad \frac{d}{dx}(MRS_{xy}) > 0,$$

and the indifference curve is concave to the origin. If

$$\frac{d^2y}{dx^2} = 0,$$

then $$-\frac{d^2y}{dx^2} = 0, \quad \text{or} \quad \frac{d}{dx}(MRS_{xy}) = 0,$$

and the indifference curve is linear.

Figure 5–4 Substitutes and complements

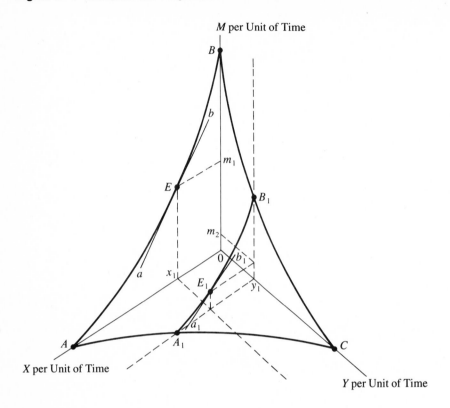

combination of x_1 units of X and m_1 of M. The MRS_{xm} at point E as measured by the slope of line ab shows the amount of money the consumer is just willing to give up for a unit of X at that point; that is, it shows the *money value* to the consumer of a unit of X. Now, holding the consumption level of X and the consumer's satisfaction level constant, we increase the amount of Y used to y_1. To compensate for the increased consumption of Y the amount of money in the new combination has been reduced to m_2. Has the increase in the consumption of Y increased or reduced the money value of a unit of X? The MRS_{xm} at point E_1 as measured by the slope of line a_1b_1 provides the answer. The MRS_{xm} at E_1 is less than the MRS_{xm} at E, meaning that the increase in the consumption of Y has caused a decrease in the *money value* of a unit of X to the consumer. Therefore, good Y is a *substitute* for good X. If the MRS_{xm} at E_1 had been greater than the MRS_{xm} at E (and this will be the case for many goods), then good Y would be a *complement* to good X.

Examples of complementary and substitute goods abound in the world around us. Tennis rackets and tennis balls, bread and jelly, coffee and doughnuts, automobiles and gasoline are among the many sets of complementary goods. Sets of substitute goods include ham and steak, automobile travel and airplane travel, electric razors and safety razors, and many others.

Constraints on the consumer

What the consumer is able to do has thus far been left to one side; we have presented a picture of tastes and preferences only. The constraints on the individual's consumption activities are shown by *budget lines*, sometimes called *lines of attainable combinations*.

The budget line

The consumer's purchasing power and the prices of what the consumer wants to buy determine his or her budget line. Purchasing power is usually referred to as income. The term is not limited to current earnings but is used broadly to include any supplements to or deletions from whatever those earnings may be. We think of the consumer's income, defined in this way, as a weekly, monthly, or yearly average. The prices faced by the consumer are the market prices of the items that the individual purchases.

To show how the budget line is established, we again limit the consumer

Figure 5–5 The budget line

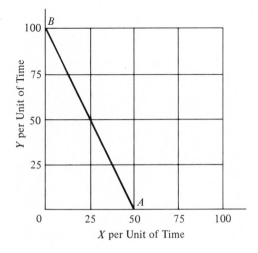

to a two-good world. Suppose that Mary Smith has an income of $100 per week and prices of X and Y are $2 and $1, respectively. If she were to spend her entire income on X, she could consume 50 units per week—she would be at point A in Figure 5–5. On the other hand, if she were to buy Y and no X, she could consume 100 units of Y and would be at point B. If she is at point B and desires to include X in her consumption pattern, she must decrease her consumption of Y to do so. A decrease of 2 units in her consumption of Y releases $2 that can be used to purchase a unit of X. Every 1-unit increase in the quantity of X consumed requires a 2-unit decrease in her consumption of Y, as long as p_y remains at $1 and p_x is $2. Thus, her budget line is a straight line joining points B and A.

The slope of the budget line is determined by the ratio of p_x to p_y. Suppose that Thomas Green's income is I, the price of X is p_{x1}, and the price of Y is p_{y1}. If he should spend all of his income on Y, I_1/p_{y1} in Figure 5–6 shows the total number of units of Y that he could purchase. If he were to spend all of his income on X, I_1/p_{x1} shows the number of units of X that he could purchase. The budget line BA joins the two extreme points.[9]

The slope of the budget line is

$$- \frac{I_1/p_{y1}}{I_1/p_{x1}} = - \frac{I_1}{p_{y1}} \times \frac{p_{x1}}{I_1} = - \frac{p_{x1}}{p_{y1}}$$

or, in more general terms, the slope of any budget line is

$$- \frac{I/p_y}{I/p_x} = - \frac{I}{p_y} \times \frac{p_x}{I} = - \frac{p_x}{p_y}. \tag{5.1}$$

Note that the consumer can obtain any combination of goods within or on the boundaries of the triangle $B0A$ in Figures 5–5 or 5–6. All of these constitute his set of *feasible* combinations. The budget line BA separates the feasible combinations—what the consumer is able to purchase—from those combinations beyond his financial reach.

Shifts in the budget line

Changes in a consumer's income and changes in the prices of the goods and services available will shift an individual's budget line. Suppose that Thomas Green is again the consumer, that his income is I_1 initially, and that the prices of X and Y are p_{x1} and p_{y1}, respectively. His budget line is BA in

---

[9] The budget-line equation for the two-commodity example of the text is

$$xp_x + yp_y = I.$$

Solving for y, we obtain

$$y = \frac{I}{p_y} - \frac{p_x}{p_y} \cdot x,$$

indicating that the Y-axis intercept is I/p_y and that the slope of the line is $-p_x/p_y$.

Figure 5–6   Changes in the budget line

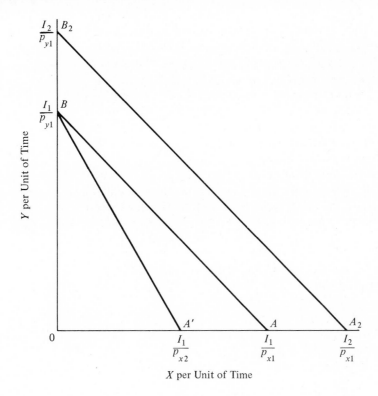

X per Unit of Time

Figure 5–6. If the price of X now increases to p_{x2}, while his income and the price of Y remain constant, the budget line becomes BA'. There is no change in the amount of Y that his income will purchase if it is all spent on Y; however, the higher price of X reduces from $0A$ to $0A'$ the amount of X that he could purchase if his money were all spent on X. The new budget line therefore joins B and A'.

Returning to the initial budget line BA, suppose now that Green's income rises from I_1 to I_2 while the prices of X and Y remain constant. The budget line shifts to the right parallel to itself to B_2A_2. The larger income enables him to purchase greater amounts of X, if X alone is purchased, or greater amounts of Y, if Y alone is purchased, so that A_2 lies to the right of A and B_2 lies above B. Since the prices of X and Y have not changed, both budget lines have a slope of $-p_{x1}/p_{y1}$ and are therefore parallel.[10]

---

[10] Note that in Footnote 9 changes in p_x change the slope of the budget line but not its Y-axis intercept. Changes in I shift the budget line up or down without changing its slope.

Maximization of consumer satisfaction

The theory of consumer behavior is built on the premise that individual consumers attempt to move toward those combinations of goods and services available to them that are most preferred; that is, they seek to maximize satisfaction. To show the conditions under which a consumer can attain this goal, the consumer's preference factors (the indifference map) and the factors restraining him (the budget line) are brought together in Figure 5–7. Any combination such as A, B, C, D, or E on the budget line is available. So is any combination, such as G, lying to the left of or below the budget line. Because of the budget restraint, combinations lying to the right of or above the budget line are not available.

The most preferred combination must lie on the budget line. A consumer who takes combination G violates the assumption that more of a good is always preferred to less. By moving from G to C the consumer obtains more X without sacrificing any Y and consequently gets on a higher indifference curve. This sort of move is always possible for a combination below the budget line. Of the combinations on the budget line, the consumer chooses the one that is on the highest indifference curve touched by the budget line. This will be combination C. Combinations A, B, D, and E all lie

Figure 5 – 7   The consumer's preferred combination

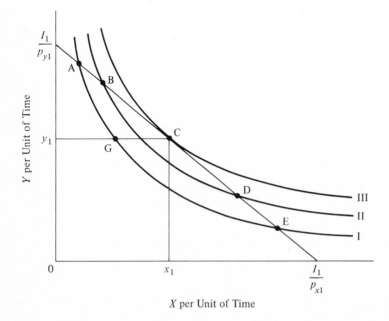

X per Unit of Time

on lower indifference curves. Combination C is on the highest indifference curve that the consumer can reach and, further, is the only combination available on that indifference curve. Thus, the consumer's preferred combination is always that at which the person's budget line is tangent to an indifference curve. In Figure 5–7 it contains x_1 of X and y_1 of Y.

Tangency of the budget line to an indifference curve means that the rate at which the consumer is *willing* to give up Y to obtain X is equal to the rate at which he would be *required* by the market to give up Y to obtain X—that is, his $MRS_{xy} = p_x/p_y$.[11] The slope of an indifference curve at any point on it is his MRS_{xy} at that point. The slope of a budget line at any point on it is p_x/p_y. At the point of tangency—that is, at C—the slopes of the two curves are necessarily the same.

Consider point A in Figure 5–7. The slope of indifference curve I is greater than the slope of the line of attainable combinations. In other words, the amount of Y that the consumer *is willing* to give up to get an additional unit of X is greater than the amount of Y that he *would have* to give up to get an additional unit of X (that is, $MRS_{xy} > p_x/p_y$). The consumer would give up units of Y for additional units of X because it is possible to move to a peferred position by doing so. The same would be the case at point B. At point D the slope of indifference curve II is less than the slope of the line of attainable combinations, meaning that the amount of Y that the consumer is willing to give up to get an additional unit of X is less than the amount that would have to be given up (that is, $MRS_{xy} < p_x/p_y$). Therefore, the consumer would not move beyond point C to such a point as D, for such a movement is toward a less-preferred position. The consumer is in equilibrium, or is in his most preferred position at point C, where the marginal rate of substitution of X for Y is equal to the ratio of their respective prices and he is disposing of his entire income.[12]

---

[11] Since the indifference curves and the budget lines both have negative slopes, we shall disregard the minus signs of the slope measurements and consider the absolute values only. This practice is conventional and avoids problems arising from mathematical semantics.

[12] To solve the consumer's maximization problem mathematically, let his preference function be

$$U = f(x, y). \tag{1}$$

The budget restraint is

$$xp_x + yp_y = I$$

or

$$xp_x + yp_y - I = 0. \tag{2}$$

To maximize (1) subject to (2) we use the Lagrange multiplier method, forming a new function in which V is a function of x, y, and λ such that

$$V = g(x, y, \lambda) = f(x, y) - \lambda(xp_x + yp_y - I). \tag{3}$$

For maximization of V,

$$\frac{\delta V}{\delta x} = f_x - \lambda p_x = 0, \text{ or: } f_x = \lambda p_x \tag{4}$$

Suppose in Figure 5–7 that Y is milk and X is honey and that the consumer's budget for the two is fixed. The consumer is initially at point A, and we shall assume that MRS_{xy} at this point is 4. Thus, he is just *willing* to give up 4 pints of milk for an additional pound of honey. Let the price of milk p_y be \$1 per pint and the price of honey p_x be \$2 per pound. At these prices the market requires that he give up only 2 pints of milk to increase his consumption of honey by 1 pound. Under this set of conditions the consumer can do what the market requires—he can give up 2 pints of milk for 1 pound of honey. Since he still has 2 pints of milk that he would have been willing to give up, he clearly is in a preferred position.

Demand curves and Engel curves

The analytical devices just developed enable us to get at the forces underlying a consumer's demand curve and Engel curve for any given good or service. For an individual consumer the demand curve for an item shows the quantities per unit of time that the consumer will take at various possible prices, other things being equal. An Engel curve[13] shows the quantities of an item per unit of time that a consumer will take at *various levels of income,* other things being equal.

The demand curve

Consider first the demand curve for some product X. The consumer's income, the price of Y, and the consumer's tastes and preferences (the indifference curves) are held constant. We vary the price of X and observe the quantities of X taken when the consumer is maximizing satisfaction at each different price.

$$\frac{\delta V}{\delta y} = f_y - \lambda p_y = 0, \text{ or: } f_y = \lambda p_y \tag{5}$$

$$\frac{\delta V}{\delta \lambda} = xp_x + yp_y - I = 0, \text{ or: } xp_x + yp_y = I. \tag{6}$$

Dividing (4) by (5) and letting (6) stand as it is, the conditions for maximum satisfaction become

$$\frac{f_x}{f_y} = \frac{p_x}{p_y}; \text{ that is } MRS_{xy} = \frac{p_x}{p_y} \tag{7}$$

with

$$xp_x + yp_y = I. \tag{8}$$

[13] Engel curves are named after Ernst Engel, a German pioneer of the last half of the 1800s in the field of budget studies. See George J. Stigler, "The Early History of Empirical Studies of Consumer Behavior," *The Journal of Political Economy,* Vol. LXII (April 1954), pp. 98–100.

Figure 5 – 8   The consumer's demand curve for one good

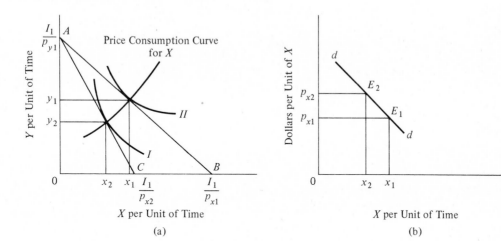

(a)   (b)

Changes in the price of X cause shifts in the consumer's budget line. Let the budget line be AB in Figure 5–8(a). An increase in the price of X to p_{x2} decreases the total number of units of X the consumer can buy to some quantity I_1/p_{x2} if the entire income is spent on that product, and the new budget line becomes AC. It lies below line AB and has a steeper slope.[14]

Line AC will necessarily be tangent to a lower indifference curve than was line AB, and the new combination of X and Y preferred by the consumer will differ from the original one. Initially, the consumer preferred the combination x_1 of X and y_1 of Y. The new preferred combination will be x_2 of X and y_2 of Y. Different prices of X cause the budget line to assume different positions, with its focal point always remaining at A. Higher prices of X rotate it clockwise, making it tangent to lower indifference curves. Lower prices of X rotate it counterclockwise, making it tangent to higher indifference curves.

The line joining satisfaction-maximizing combinations of goods at the various prices of X is called the *price consumption curve* for X and is illustrated in Figure 5–8(a). Note that in reality it shows no prices. It is traced out by preferred combinations of X and Y when the consumer's tastes and preferences, income, and the price of one commodity are held constant and the price of the other commodity is varied.

The necessary information for establishing the consumer's demand schedule and demand curve for X is obtained from Figure 5–8(a). When the

---

[14] The slope of AB is p_{x1}/p_{y1}. The slope of AC is p_{x2}/p_{y1}. Since $p_{x2} > p_{x1}$, then $p_{x2}/p_{y1} > p_{x1}/p_{y1}$.

price of X is p_{x1}, the consumer will take quantity x_1 of X. This choice establishes one point on the demand schedule or demand curve. At the higher price p_{x2}, the consumer will take the smaller quantity x_2 of X, establishing a second point on the demand schedule or demand curve for X. These points are plotted as E_1 and E_2 in Figure 5–8(b). Additional price-quantity points can be found in a similar manner and plotted on a conventional demand diagram in the usual way. Most such demand schedules or demand curves show an inverse relationship between price and quantity—the higher the price of X, the lower the quantity taken, and vice-versa.[15]

Corner solutions

Among the wide array of goods and services from which a consumer can choose there will be items that the consumer does not buy. The consumer's tastes and preferences may be such that some of these are not desired under any circumstances, even if their prices were zero. As such they simply do not enter into an analysis of that consumer's choices. But others may or may not be purchased, depending upon their prices.

Consider an item such as champagne. In Figure 5–9 quantities per unit of time are measured along the horizontal axis. The vertical axis shows quantities, say identical baskets, of a composite of all other goods and services that enter into the consumer's field of choice. Let the price of each basket of the composite be p_{y1}, and let the consumer's income be I_1. Representative indifference curves are shown by I, II, III, and IV. At any champagne price below p_{c3}, champagne enters the consumer's budget. If the price is p_{c2} the quantity taken is c_2. If the price is still lower, say p_{c1}, the quantity taken increases to c_1. But if the price is p_{c3} or higher, champagne is ruled out of the consumer's purchases; the quantity taken becomes zero. The consumer will be on the highest possible indifference curve—indifference curve II—with combination A which contains no champagne. Combination A is called a *corner solution* to the consumer's maximization problem.

A corner solution occurs only if $MRS_{cy} \leq p_c/p_y$ at a point such as A where the consumer's budget line intersects the Y axis. At such a point if $MRS_{cy} > p_c/p_y$, the consumer is willing to give up more Y to obtain a unit of champagne than the market requires and will thus maximize satisfaction by

---

[15] Mathematically, the demand curve for X is obtained from the solution of equations (4), (5), and (6) of Footnote 12 for x, y, and λ in terms of p_x, p_y, and I; thus, for good X

$$x = x(p_x, p_y, I). \tag{9}$$

Then, treating p_y and I as given parameters, the demand equation can be expressed as

$$x = D(p_x). \tag{10}$$

The demand curve for Y can be derived similarly.

Figure 5-9   A corner solution

Champagne per Unit of Time

moving down the budget line. This would be the case if the price of champagne were p_{c2} or p_{c3}. Translating prices and corresponding quantities of champagne into demand curve form, price p_{c3} is the price at which the consumer's demand curve for champagne intersects the price axis.

Elasticity of demand and the price consumption curve

If the X axis represents units of any good X and the Y axis represents purchasing power not spent on X,[16] the slope of the price consumption curve indicates whether elasticity of demand for the good is unitary, greater than one, or less than one.

---

[16] A given indifference curve thus shows combinations of purchasing power and X among which the consumer is indifferent. The budget line is drawn in the usual way. The price of purchasing power, or p_{y1}, in dollars is \$1 a unit. Hence, I_1/p_{y1} is the consumer's income. Since the slope of the budget line is p_{x1}/p_{y1} and p_{y1} equals \$1, that slope is p_{x1}.

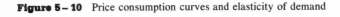

Figure 5–10   Price consumption curves and elasticity of demand

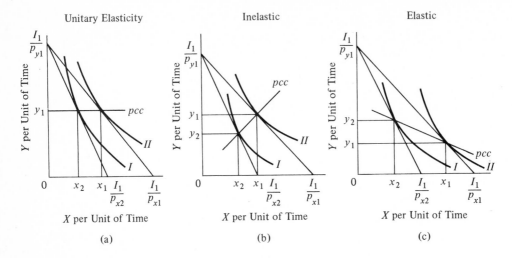

In Figure 5–10(a) the indifference curves are such that the price consumption curve is parallel to the X axis, or has a slope of zero. As the price of X rises from p_{x1} to p_{x2}, the portion of the consumer's income *not* spent on X remains constant at $0y_1$. Thus, the amount spent on X must remain constant also. If a rise in the price of X causes no change in the consumer's spending on X, then the consumer's demand for X must have unitary elasticity for the price increase.

The upward slope of the price consumption curve in Figure 5–10(b) means that demand for X is inelastic. A rise in the price of X from p_{x1} to p_{x2} brings about a decrease in the portion of income not spent on X from $0y_1$ to $0y_2$. In other words, more income is spent on X at the higher price. An increase in expenditures on X as the price of X rises can result only when demand for X is inelastic for the price increases.

Figure 5–10(c) shows a downward-sloping price consumption curve, meaning that demand for X is elastic. The rise in the price of X increases the portion of income not spent on X from $0y_1$ to $0y_2$. Therefore, less is spent on X. An increase in the price of X that decreases total expenditure on X results from an elastic demand curve for X between two prices.

Engel curves

To obtain the Engel curves for good X or good Y, the prices of the goods, along with the consumer's tastes and preferences, are held constant and income is allowed to vary. In Figure 5–11 an increase in income from I_1 to I_2

Figure 5 – 11   The consumer's Engel curve for one good

(a)

(b)

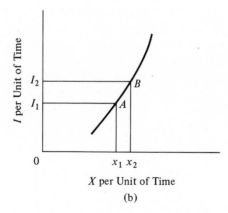

(c)

shifts the consumer's budget line to the right parallel to the original one. The points of tangency of the budget lines with indifference curves of the consumer show the combinations of X and Y that will be taken at each income level. These combinations, together with the corresponding income levels, provide the data for the construction of the consumer's Engel curves. At an income level of I_1, the consumer will take quantity x_1 of X. This choice is plotted as point A in Figure 5–11(b). At income level I_2 quantity x_2 will be taken. This choice is plotted as point B. If budget lines corresponding to other levels of income were shown in Figure 5–11(a), corresponding quantities of X could be determined and plotted against those income levels on Figure 5–11(b).[17]

Goods and services are sometimes classified as *superior* or *inferior* depending upon how the consumption of them varies as income changes. A *superior* good is one for which the consumption level increases as consumer income increases. The Engel curves of Figure 5–11(a) and 5–11(b) indicate that product X is superior. The distinguishing characteristic of *inferior* goods is that as the consumer's income increases, the consumption level of them decreases. Hamburger is a case in point, since at high income levels consumers tend to substitute more expensive meat cuts—prime rib and steak—for it. A graphic picture of the income consumption curve and the Engel curve for such a good is presented in Figure 5–12. At income level I_1 Figure 5–12(a) shows that the consumer takes x_1 of X in his most preferred position. This is plotted as point A in Figure 5–12(b). Similarly, at income level I_2 the consumer takes x_2, and point B on his Engel curve is located. Note that both the income consumption curve with respect to X and the Engel curve slope upward to the *left*.

Engel curves provide valuable information regarding consumption patterns for different commodities and for different individuals. For certain basic commodities, such as food, as the consumer's income increases from very low levels, consumption may increase considerably at first; then, as income continues to increase, the increases in consumption may become smaller and smaller relative to income increases. A pattern of this type is illustrated in Figure 5–11(b). For certain other items, such as housing, as the consumer's income increases the quantity purchased per unit of time may increase in greater proportion than income does. Figure 5–11(c) reflects a situation of this type. It is also quite possible that an item is a superior good at low-income levels and becomes an inferior good at high-income levels.

---

[17] Mathematically, the Engel curve for good X comes from equation (9) of Footnote 15. The prices of X and Y, p_x and p_y, are held constant and the Engel curve equation becomes

$$x = E\,(I). \tag{11}$$

The Engel curve for Y is obtained similarly from the good Y counterpart of equation (9).

Figure 5-12   Engel curve for an inferior good

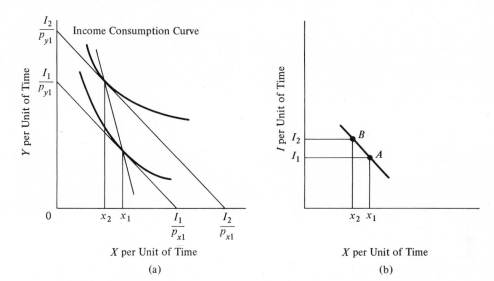

(a)

(b)

Income elasticity of demand

The responsiveness to the quantity taken of an item to income changes is called the *income elasticity of demand* for that item. The elasticity concept is not a new one at this point, so we need only to spell it out in this particular context. It is defined as

$$\Theta = \frac{\Delta x/x}{\Delta I/I},\tag{5.2}$$

that is, the percentage change in quantity divided by the percentage change in the level of income, when the change in the level of income is small.[18] For an arc such as *EF* in Figure 5–13(a) the appropriate data can be fed into the elasticity formula to determine the magnitude of elasticity. In Figure 5–13(b) income elasticity at point *A* will be *MT/0M*. The derivation of the point income elasticity measurement is exactly the same as it is for a point price elasticity measurement. At point *B* would the income elasticity of *CC* be greater than or less than one? What would an Engel curve with an income elasticity of one at all points look like?

---

[18] In terms of calculus it becomes

$$\Theta = \lim_{\Delta I \to 0} \frac{\Delta x/x}{\Delta I/I} = \frac{dx/x}{dI/I} = \frac{dx}{dI} \times \frac{I}{x}.$$

Figure 5–13 Income elasticity of demand

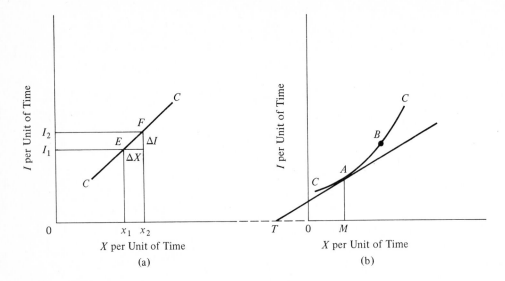

(a)

(b)

Income effects and substitution effects

The inverse relationship that most demand curves show between the price
of an item and the quantity per unit of time that a consumer will take is the
combined result of a *substitution effect* and an *income effect* of a price
change. When the price of an item rises and consumers turn away from it
toward now relatively lower-priced substitutes, a decrease in quantity
occurs because of the substitution. Additionally, the rise in the price of
the item lowers the consumer's real income, or purchasing power, causing
the consumer to reduce purchases of all superior goods. To the extent that the
reduction in real income affects that individual's consumption of the item
under consideration, we have an income effect.

The separation of income and substitution effects is illustrated in Figure
5–14. The consumer's income is I_1 and the prices of X and Y are p_{x1} and p_{yq},
respectively. Combination A, containing x_1 of X and y_1 of Y, is the consumer's preferred combination. Suppose that the price of X now rises to
p_{x2}, rotating the budget line clockwise with I_1/p_{y1} as its focal point until it
cuts the X axis at I_1/p_{x2}. Note that because of the increase in the price of X
the slope of the new budget line is greater than that of the old one. The
slope of the original budget line is p_{x1}/p_{y1}, while that of the new one is
p_{x2}/p_{y1}. Combination B, containing x_2 of X and y_2 of Y is the consumer's
preferred combination after the rise in the price of X.

Figure 5–14   Income and substitution effects

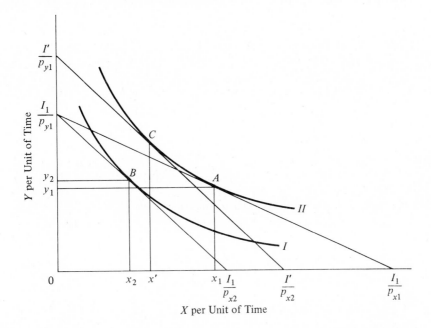

That the consumer's real income has been decreased by the increase in the price of X is illustrated graphically by the fact that combination B lies on a lower indifference curve than combination A does. The movement from combination A to combination B, and the reduction in the quantity of X taken from x_1 to x_2, shows the combined income and substitution effects of the price change.

To isolate the substitution effect and determine its magnitude, we increase the consumer's money income enough to compensate for the loss in purchasing power. The additional purchasing power, or the "compensating increase in income," will move the budget line to the right, parallel to itself; and when just enough has been given the consumer to offset the loss in real income, it will lie tangent to indifference curve II at point C. Combination C is at the same level of preference for the consumer as combination A is; but, because of the now higher price of X, combination A is not available to him. He has been induced to substitute the relatively cheaper Y for the relatively more expensive X in order to avoid a less-preferred position. The income effect of the increase in the price of X has been eliminated by the compensating variation in the consumer's income; hence, the movement from A to C, or the decrease in X taken from x_1 to x', is the pure substitution effect. It results solely from the change in the price of X relative to the price of Y.

The income effect, apart from the substitution effect, can be determined by taking the compensating variation in income away from the consumer. The budget line shifts to the left, and the highest indifference curve to which it is tangent is indifference curve I. Combination B, y_2 of Y and x_2 of X, is the preferred position. The movement from C to B is the income effect and reduces the quantity of X taken from x' to x_2.

The movement of the consumer from combination A to combination B, with the increase of the price of X from p_{x1} to p_{x2} is thus broken down into two steps, one showing the substitution effect and the other showing the income effect. Usually they operate in the same direction. If X is an inferior good, however, the income effect will work in the opposite direction from the substitution effect. In such a case the increase in the price of X causes a tendency on the part of the consumer to substitute relatively lower-priced goods for X, but at the same time the lower real income of the consumer induces an increase in the consumption of X.[19] Try redrawing Figure 5–14 on the assumption that X is an inferior good.

[19] To show the separation of substitution effects and income effects for good X mathematically, we return to equations (4), (5), and (6) of Footnote 12. The total differentials of these equations are, respectively:

$$f_{xx}dx + f_{xy}dy - \lambda dp_x - p_x d\lambda = 0 \tag{12}$$
$$f_{yx}dx + f_{yy}dy - \lambda dp_y - p_y d\lambda = 0 \tag{13}$$
$$dI - xdp_x - p_x dx - ydp_y - p_y dy = 0 \tag{14}$$

or

$$f_{xx}dx + f_{xy}dy - p_x d\lambda = \lambda dp_x \tag{12}$$
$$f_{yx}dx + f_{yy}dy - p_y d\lambda = \lambda dp_y \tag{13}$$
$$-p_x dx - p_y dy = -dI + xdp_x + ydp_y. \tag{14}$$

Regarding the right-hand terms as constants, we obtain the determinant

$$D = \begin{vmatrix} f_{xx} & f_{xy} & -p_x \\ f_{yx} & f_{yy} & -p_y \\ -p_x & -p_y & 0 \end{vmatrix}, \tag{15}$$

in which D_{ij} represents the cofactor of the element in the ith row and jth column. Then Cramer's rule is used to solve for dx, dy, and $d\lambda$. With respect to good X:

$$dx = \frac{\lambda D_{11}dp_x + \lambda D_{21}dp_y + D_{31}(-dI + xdp_x + ydp_y)}{D}. \tag{16}$$

Now, from equation (16), assuming that p_y and I remain constant and dividing through by dp_x, we obtain the total response in the quantity taken of X to a change in its price:

$$\frac{dx}{dp_x} = \frac{\lambda D_{11}}{D} + x\frac{D_{31}}{D}. \tag{17}$$

If, in equation (16), p_x and p_y are held constant, then

$$\frac{dx}{dI}\bigg|_{dp_x = dp_y = 0} = -\frac{D_{31}}{D}. \tag{18}$$

If a change in the price of good X is compensated for by an income change such that the consumer remains on the same indifference curve when the price of X changes—that is, $dU = 0$—then (from Footnote 6) $f_x dx + f_y dy = 0$.

The substitution effect is usually much stronger than the income effect. A consumer who purchases a great many goods will not ordinarily experience a large drop in real income when the price of one of the goods rises. There may be a large substitution effect, however, when good substitutes are available for the commodity in question.

Market demand curves

The market demand curve for a commodity is composed of the individual consumer's demand curves for that commodity. We defined the demand curve of an individual consumer in much the same way as we defined a market demand curve. It shows the different quantities that the consumer will take at all possible prices, other things being equal. Thus, by summing the quantities that all consumers in the market will take at each possible price, we arrive at the market demand curve.

The process of summing individual consumer demand curves to obtain the market demand curve is illustrated in Figure 5–15. Suppose that there are two consumers only—G and H—who buy commodity X. Their individual demand curves are d_1d_1 and d_2d_2, respectively. At a price of p_1 consumer G will be willing to take x_1 per unit of time while consumer H will be willing to take x_1' per unit of time. Together they will be willing to take quantity $X_1 = (x_1 + x_1')$ at that price, and A is located as a point on the market demand curve. Likewise, at price p_2 consumer G will be willing to take x_2 units per unit of time while consumer H will be willing to take x_2'. Together they will be willing to take $X_2 = (x_2 + x_2')$ at that price, and B is located as a point on the market demand curve. Additional points can be

---

Since, for the consumer to be in equilibrium,

$$\frac{f_x}{f_y} = \frac{p_x}{p_y},$$

then $p_x dx + p_y dy = 0$. This expression is the left-hand side of equation (14); therefore, that equation becomes $0 = -dI + x dp_x + y dp_y$, and from equation (16)

$$\left. \frac{\partial x}{\partial p_x} \right|_{dU=0} = \frac{\lambda D_{11}}{D}. \tag{19}$$

Substituting the equalities of equations (18) and (19) in equation (17), we obtain

$$\frac{dx}{dp_x} = \left. \frac{\partial x}{\partial p_x} \right|_{dU=0} - x \times \left. \frac{\partial x}{\partial I} \right|_{dp_x = dp_y = 0}, \tag{20}$$

or

Total effect   The   The
of a change = substitution − income.
in p_x effect   effect

Figure 5–15   Construction of a market demand curve

located similarly and the market demand curve DD is drawn through them. The market demand curve for a commodity, then, is the horizontal summation of the individual consumer demand curves for the commodity.

Exchange and welfare

The forces giving rise to voluntary exchange of items among individuals and the impact of voluntary exchange on welfare can be readily explained in terms of indifference curve analysis. Suppose that we consider two consumers, A and B, each of whom receives and consumes quantities of two commodities, X and Y, per unit of time.

Individual A's tastes and preferences for X and Y are shown on the conventional part of Figure 5–16. The indifference map of B is rotated 180 degrees and is superimposed on that of A so that the axes of the two diagrams form what is called an *Edgeworth box*. The diagram for B can be placed so that $0M$ represents the entire amount of Y received by the two individuals and $0N$ represents the entire amount of X received. The indifference curves of A are convex to 0, while those of B are convex to $0'$. Any point on or in the rectangle represents a possible distribution of the goods between the two individuals.

The initial distribution of X and Y can be represented by any point such as F, lying within the rectangle formed by the two sets of axes. Individual A gets $0y_1$ of Y per unit of time, and B gets y_1M. The amount of X received per unit of time by A is $0X_1$ and that by B is x_1N. Individual A is on indifference curve I_1. Individual B is on indifference curve I'. For A the marginal rate of substitution of X for Y at point F is greater than it is for B. Individual A

Figure 5–16   The basis of exchange

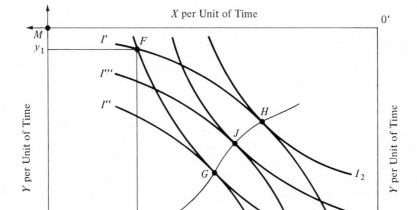

would be willing to give up more Y to get an additional unit of X than B would require to induce him to part with a unit of X. Thus, the stage is set for exchange.

Whenever the initial distribution of the two commodities is such that the MRS_{xy} for one party is not equal to the MRS_{xy} for another party, either or both may gain from exchange. If F is the initial distribution of X and Y, exchanges of Y by individual A to individual B for X could take place in such a way that indifference curve I_1 is followed downward to the right. Individual A would be made no worse off and individual B would be made progressively better off until the distribution of goods between the two is that represented by point G, at which indifference curve I_1 is tangent to indifference curve I''. No further exchange can occur without making one or both parties worse off than they are at G. Similarly, individual A could exchange Y to individual B for X in such a way that indifference curve I' is followed downward to the right. Such exchanges would leave B no worse off than before but would place A on successively higher indifference curves, or in more preferred positions, until the distribution of goods is that represented by point H, at which indifference curve I' is tangent to indifference curve I_2. Any further exchanges will result in a decrease in well-being for one or both parties.

Again, starting at F, both parties could gain from exchanges that follow a path from F to J, falling somewhere within the area bounded by FG and FH. Both parties would reach higher preference levels until some point J, at which an indifference curve of A is tangent to an indifference curve of B, is reached. Further exchanges would result in one or both parties being made worse off.

Exchanges that alter the distribution of goods from one at which an indifference curve of one consumer intersects an indifference curve of another consumer, toward a distribution within the area bounded by the two indifference curves and within which tangency occurs, lead toward a *Pareto optimum* or an *efficient* distribution of the goods.

In Chapter 1 we defined a Pareto optimum condition as one in which no one can be made better off without making someone else worse off, and it is this condition that occurs at G or J or H or at any other point at which an indifference curve of A is tangent to an indifference curve of B. A line joining all of these tangency points, GJH as extended in Figure 5–16, is called a *contract curve*.

For an efficient distribution of goods between the two parties to exist, or for a Pareto optimum in distribution to exist, the MRS_{xy} for one must be equal to the MRS_{xy} for the other. That is, if the maximum amount of Y that individual A is willing to give up to get an additional unit of X is equal to the minimum amount of Y that B would accept in exchange for a unit of X, then no gain from such an exchange would occur for either party. These conditions are fulfilled at every point along the contract curve. At each such point an indifference curve of A is tangent to an indifference curve of B; that is, individual A's indifference curve has the same slope as does individual B's or MRS_{xy} is the same for A as it is for B.

This analysis shows that some redistributions of goods (income) among consumers will increase welfare, but we are left in the dark with respect to others. With the initial distribution F any point on the contract curve from G to H inclusive is a Pareto optimum, and a movement from F to any such point increases the welfare of the community. However, there are any number of efficient or Pareto optimum distributions of X and Y between consumers A and B; there is one for every point on the contract curve. If a redistribution from J to H is effected, for example, consumer B is made worse off and consumer A is made better off. Who knows whether the increase in A's welfare is just offset, more than offset, or less than offset by the decrease in the welfare of B?

Some applications of indifference curve analysis

Indifference curve analysis is useful in analyzing most problems of choices among alternatives. Two common problems—choices between pay in the form of money or in the form of fringe benefits and choices between work and leisure—provide excellent illustrations of its applications. Also, it can supply useful information about index numbers.

Economics of fringe benefits

Fringe benefits—such as guarantees of retirement pay, some free medical services, life insurance, the use of company recreational facilities, and many others—have become commonplace as part of an employee's pay package. These are costs to employers, just as wages and salaries are costs, and these benefits constitute a part of what employees earn. The question that we consider here is whether employees would be better or worse off if employers were to pay them the money value (cost) of the fringe benefits instead of providing the fringe benefits in kind. To keep the choice problem as simple as possible, we assume that there are no tax advantages to employers or employees in paying employees in the form of fringe benefits rather than money.[20]

Suppose initially that an individual's income with no fringe benefits is $0I_1$ dollars, measured along the vertical axis of Figure 5–17 (a). Units of medical service are measured along the horizontal axis, and the amount that the person's total income will purchase at price p_{m1} per unit is $0D$. With the indifference map shown and budget line I_1D, the individual spends I_1C_1 of income for $0M_1$ units of medical service.

The employer decides to give the individual a pay increase in the form of "free" medical service amounting to $0M_1'$ units per month. The fringe benefit obviously increases the welfare of the individual, but if the pay increase were given in the form of money rather than in the specific form of the good or service, would the individual's welfare be increased by more, by less, or by the same amount?

Figure 5–17(a) illustrates a case in which welfare is increased less by the fringe benefit than it would be by an equivalent amount of money paid to the individual. Free medical services of $0M_1'$ combined with a money income of $0I_1$ shift the budget line to I_1BE. The I_1B segment is determined by the money income $0I_1$—which has not been increased—and the $0M_1'$ (which $= I_1B$) units of medical service that can now be obtained without the use of any of the money income available to the individual.

If, however, more than $0M_1'$ units of medical service per month were consumed, the individual would be required to pay p_{m1} for each unit in excess of $0M_1$. These circumstances are shown by the BE segment of the

[20] The institutional arrangements that exist in any society obviously affect the choices that are made. The basic "pure" choice, however, is that between pay in the form of, say, medical services versus pay in the form of money, keeping the choice free of such institutional arrangements as tax laws. Then one can, if so desired, introduce institutional arrangements and examine the impact of these on the choices made.

Figure 5 – 17   Fringe benefits versus money income

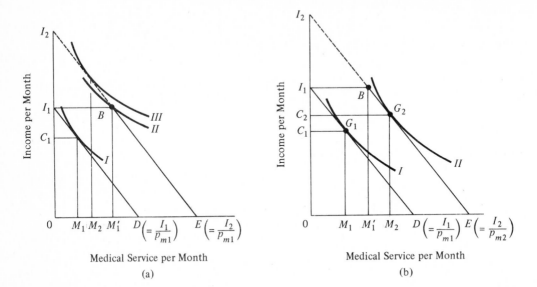

(a)

(b)

budget line. Note that BE is parallel to I_1D since the slope of both curves is equal to p_{m1}. Note also that $DE = 0M_1'$. The new budget line is "kinked" or has a corner in it at B. Indifference curve II is the highest that the individual can reach so that in this case the entire amount of free medical services is consumed, leaving $0I_1$ dollars to spend on other goods and services.

If the individual receives the increase in pay in money equal to the value of the fringe-benefit medical services, the budget line becomes I_2E. The increase in money income, I_1I_2, is $0M_1' \times p_{m1}$, that is, what the value of the fringe benefit medical services would be in the market. The BE segment of the budget line is the same as it is in the fringe-benefit case since the individual would, if at point B, be spending I_1I_2 dollars for $0M_1'$ of medical services, leaving $0I_1$ dollars to be spent as desired. The segment of I_2E above point B is the significant one. It represents opportunities open to the consumer that were not available under the fringe-benefit arrangement. The consumption of medical services can be reduced below $0M_1'$ units, and for each unit that it is so reduced the consumer will have p_{m1} more dollars to spend on other things. Given the indifference map of 5–17(a), the individual would indeed reduce consumption of medical services to $0M_2$ per month—where indifference curve III is tangent to the I_2E segment of the budget line. This segment was not available under the fringe-benefit arrangement. In this case the individual's welfare would be greater if the employee's pay increase were in the form of money rather than "free" medical services.

If an individual's preferences are such that after a pay increase more medical services per month are desired than the pay increase would buy or provide, the person's welfare will not be affected by the form of the increase. This situation is illustrated in Figure 5–17(b). Prior to the pay increase the individual has an income of $0I$ and is in equilibrium at G_1, taking $0M_1$ units of medical services per month. Suppose that a pay increase in the form of medical services amounting to $0M_1'$ is given, changing the employee's budget line to I_1BE. The new equilibrium position is G_2, and $0M_2$ units of medical services per month are purchased.

If the pay increase were in the form of money equivalent to the value of the fringe-benefit medical services, the employee's new equilibrium position would also be G_2. The budget line becomes I_2E rather than I_1BE, but since the tangency to an indifference curve occurs in the BE segment common to both budget lines, the results are the same either way.

Labor supply

Indifference curve techniques provide some insights into an individual's choice between leisure and income, or, put the other way around, the choice of the amount of labor time the individual is willing to supply at different wage rates. Suppose, for example, that the indifference map in Figure 5–18(a) shows a person's preference structure for combinations of daily income and leisure. Income is measured on the vertical axis, and leisure is measured on the horizontal axis. Any one indifference curve shows combinations of income and leisure that are equivalent to the individual. Higher indifference curves show preferred sets of income-leisure combinations.

A budget line, or income line, shows the income level that can be obtained by working (giving up leisure) different numbers of hours at a given wage rate. The distance $0H$ represents the maximum number of hours of leisure per day that it would be possible for the individual to trade for work. Some minimum number of hours is required for eating and sleeping. If this number were 10 hours per day, then $0H$ would be 14 hours. At a wage rate of w_1, the individual can earn an income of $I_1 (= 0H \times w_1)$ by working $0H$ hours per day, keeping his or her tradable leisure at zero. If h_1H hours per day are worked, income earned is $I_1' (= h_1H \times w_1)$ and the tradable leisure time is $0h_1$ hours. Note that the slope of the income line is the wage rate w_1.

The individual would be expected to seek out the most preferred combination of income and leisure from all of the combinations that the income line will permit. Given the wage rate w_1, combination A is preferred over all of the others available; this is the highest indifference curve that can be

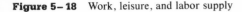

Figure 5–18   Work, leisure, and labor supply

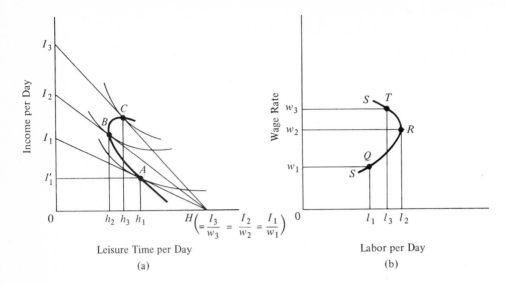

Leisure Time per Day

(a)

Labor per Day

(b)

reached. The person will work h_1H hours earning an income of I_1' dollars per day. At this point the marginal rate of substitution of leisure for income is equal to the wage rate—the amount of income that the individual would be willing to sacrifice to obtain an additional hour of leisure is the amount that he or she would be required to sacrifice in the labor market.

By considering the income lines generated for different wage rates, points on the individual's labor supply curve can be determined. At wage rate w_1, the amount of labor supply will be h_1H ($= 0l_1$) per day, and this point is plotted as point Q in Figure 5–18(b). A higher wage rate w_2 will shift the income line clockwise to I_2H, increasing the amount of labor supplied to h_2H ($= 0l_2$). In Figure 5–18(b) this is plotted as point R. A still higher wage rate w_3 generates income line I_3H and induces the individual to supply h_3H ($= 0l_3$) hours of labor per day, giving rise to point T. These and other points located in a similar fashion trace out the labor supply curve SS.

The total impact of a wage rate change on the amount of labor supplied (or leisure demanded) is the combined result of an income effect and a substitution effect. For the increase in the wage rate from w_1 to w_2, we show the substitution effect outweighing the income effect; the higher cost of an hour of leisure induces the individual to substitute income for leisure by working more hours per day. The income effect of the wage rate increase would be expected in and of itself to increase the amount of leisure desired and to decrease the amount of work that the individual wants to do. The increase in the wage rate from w_2 to w_3 illustrates a situation in which the income effect of a wage increase outweighs the substitution effect. If and when this situation occurs for an individual, it makes the labor supply curve bend upward and to the left, as Figure 5–18(b) illustrates. Can you separate the income and substitution effects diagrammatically?

Index numbers*

The inflation that has been occurring over the last decade has brought to the foreground two questions on which indifference curve analysis can shed light. First, how is the rate of inflation measured? Second, what impact does inflation have on the welfare of a consumer? The Laspeyres price index and the Paasche price index are commonly used to provide partial answers.

The Laspeyres price index

In Figure 5–19 the Laspeyres price index is illustrated. The diagram is for one individual and covers a two-year time series composed of year 0 and year 1.

In year 0, suppose that the individual exercises free choice in the spending of income. Let the income level be I_0^L and the prices of X and Y be p_{x0} and p_{y0}, respectively. The most preferred position is combination B_0 containing x_0 of X and y_0 of Y. Total expenditures are described by

$$I_0^L = x_0 p_{x0} + y_0 p_{y0}. \tag{5.3}$$

Next consider how much money bundle B_0 would cost in year 1. If the prices of X and Y in that year are p_{x1} and p_{y1}, respectively, and we let I_1^L be the cost of the bundle, then

$$I_1^L = x_0 p_{x1} + y_0 p_{y1}. \tag{5.4}$$

The Laspeyres price index is, in turn,

$$L = \frac{I_1^L}{I_0^L} \times 100 = \frac{x_0 p_{x1} + y_0 p_{y1}}{x_0 p_{x0} + y_0 p_{y0}} \times 100. \tag{5.5}$$

It measures the expenditure that the consumer must make in year 1 as a percentage of the expenditure in year 0, in order to obtain in year 1 the same bundle of goods that maximized satisfaction in year 0.

---

* This section may be omitted without loss of continuity.

Figure 5–19 The Laspeyres price index

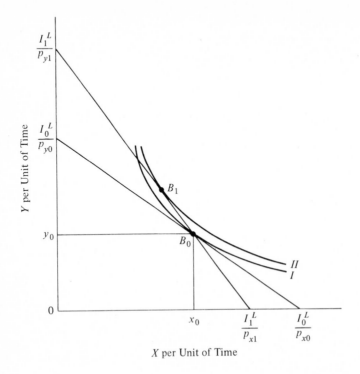

X per Unit of Time

The Laspeyres index is the *maximum* estimate of the increase in the individual's cost of living since it presumes that with expenditure I_1^L the consumer would be at the same level of satisfaction—with bundle B_0 on indifference curve *I*—in year 1 as in year zero. It is a maximum because in actuality, with an expenditure level of I_1^L in year 1 at prices p_{x1} and p_{y1}, the consumer would not want to stay at bundle B_0. By giving up some of the now relatively higher-priced *X* for some of the now relatively lower-priced *Y*, she can move to B_1 and to the higher preference level shown by indifference curve *II*. Thus, the change in the expenditure level that must occur to enable the consumer to continue to purchase in year 1 the same combination that was purchased in year 0 overstates the increase in the cost of maintaining a given level of consumer welfare—unless it should happen that the prices of *X* and *Y* increase in the same direction and in the same proportion. In this case B_1 will coincide with B_0, and the index measures accurately the change in the cost of living.

What happens to the consumer's welfare from year 0 to year 1? Note that while I_0^L is the actual expenditure in year 0, I_1^L is *not* the actual expenditure in year 1. Rather $I_1{}^L$ is the expenditure that would be necessary in that year to purchase the year-0 satisfaction-maximizing bundle of goods. Let the consumer's *actual* expenditure be $I_a{}^L$ in year 1.

We can be sure that the consumer's welfare is greater in year 1 than in year 0 if

$$\frac{I_a{}^L}{I_0{}^L} > \frac{I_1{}^L}{I_0{}^L}. \tag{5.6}$$

This means that the percentage increase in the consumer's income exceeds the maximum estimate of the percentage increase in the cost of living. In Figure 5–19 the *actual* budget line for year 1 would lie to the right of *NM* and would be parallel to it. It would thus be tangent to an indifference curve even higher than *II*. However, if

$$\frac{I_a{}^L}{I_0{}^L} \le \frac{I_1{}^L}{I_0{}^L}, \tag{5.7}$$

we cannot be certain that the consumer's welfare is the same as or less than it was in year 0. It may be greater. The *actual* budget line for year 1 would lie to the left of *NM* and would be parallel to it. If it is tangent to an indifference curve *between I* and *II*, the consumer is better off in year 1 than in year 0. If it is tangent to indifference curve *I*, there is no change in the consumer's welfare. If it lies far enough to the left of *NM* to be tangent to an indifference curve below *I*, the consumer is worse off in year 0. The fly in the ointment is, of course, the fact that the real increase in the cost of living may be less than

$$\frac{I_1{}^L}{I_0{}^L}.$$

The Paasche price index

A slightly different estimate of changes in the cost of living over time is provided by the Paasche price index. Whereas the Laspeyres index shows the relative change in the cost of purchasing a *year-0* bundle of goods between year 0 and year 1, the Paasche index shows the relative change in purchasing a *year-1* bundle of goods between year 0 and year 1.

Suppose the consumer exercises free choice in spending year-1 income. In Figure 5–20, with an income level of $I_1{}^P$ and at prices p_{x1} and p_{y1} for goods X and Y, combination B_1 is the preferred set of purchases. Combination B_1 contains x_1 of X and y_1 of Y, and the consumer's total expenditures are described by

$$I_1{}^P = x_1 p_{x1} + y_1 p_{y1}. \tag{5.8}$$

Figure 5–20   The Paasche price index

The same bundle of goods in year 0 at year-0 prices p_{x0} and p_{y0} would have cost

$$I_0^P = x_1 p_{x0} + y_1 p_{y0}. \tag{5.9}$$

The Paasche price index, then, is

$$\frac{I_1^P}{I_0^P} \times 100 = \frac{x_1 p_{x1} + y_1 p_{y1}}{x_1 p_{x0} + y_1 p_{y0}} \cdot 100. \tag{5.10}$$

The Paasche index represents the *minimum* estimate of the increase in the cost of living from year 0 to year 1. It reflects the increase from I_0^P to I_1^P in the cost of combination B_1. However, with an expenditure level of I_0^P the consumer would have purchased combination B_0 in year 0 and would have been on indifference curve *II* in that year. The expenditure level of I_1^P in year 1 yields a lower level of satisfaction than did I_0^P in year 0. The actual increase in the cost of living thus exceeds $I_1^P - I_0^P$ by whatever money value the consumer attaches to the reduction in satisfaction represented by the movement from indifference curve *II* to indifference curve *I*. However, if p_x and p_y change by the same proportional amount and in the same direction between year 0 and year 1, then B_0 and B_1 coincide, and the index correctly measures the change in the cost of living.

Consider again the change in a consumer's welfare between year 0 and year 1. Let the actual income in year 0 be $I_a{}^P$. If

$$\frac{I_1{}^P}{I_a{}^P} \leq \frac{I_1{}^P}{I_0{}^P}, \tag{5.11}$$

we can be sure that her welfare has decreased between year 0 and year 1, because the increase in actual income is less than the minimum estimate of the increase in the cost of living. In Figure 5–20 the budget line for *actual* income in year 0 would lie on or to the right of *NM* and would be parallel to it. It would be tangent either to indifference curve *II* at B_0 or to a higher indifference curve. Thus, the welfare loss to the consumer from year 0 to year 1 would be that involved in dropping back from indifference curve *II* or a higher indifference curve to indifference curve *I*.

If

$$\frac{I_1{}^P}{I_a{}^P} > \frac{I_1{}^P}{I_0{}^P}, \tag{5.12}$$

we cannot be certain whether or not the consumer's welfare has decreased, increased, or remained constant. The budget line for *actual* income in year 0 will lie to the left of *NM* and will be parallel to it. If it is tangent to an indifference curve *between I* and *II*, the consumer's welfare decreases between year 0 and year 1 since the consumer must drop back from that indifference curve to combination B_1 on indifference curve *I*. If the year-0 actual budget line is tangent to indifference curve *I*, there is no change in the consumer's welfare between year 0 and year 1, although there would be a change in the combination of goods purchased (a movement up and around indifference curve *I*). If the actual budget line of year 0 is tangent to an indifference curve lower than *I*, then the consumer's welfare does indeed increase between year 0 and year 1.

Summary

The indifference curve apparatus provides a useful framework for the theory of consumer choice and exchange. A consumer's tastes and preferences are represented by her or his indifference map. The consumer's opportunity factors—income and the prices of goods purchased—are represented by her or his budget line. The point at which the budget line is tangent to an indifference curve represents the combination of goods that the consumer prefers of those available.

The consumer's demand curve for one good is obtained by varying the price of the good while holding constant tastes and preferences, income, and prices of other goods. The resulting points of consumer equilibrium trace out the price consumption curve for the commodity. Information for the demand curve can be taken from the indifference curve diagram.

The slope of the price consumption curve for a commodity indicates the elasticity of demand when the commodity under consideration is measured on the X axis and money is measured on the Y axis. A horizontal price consumption curve means that demand has unitary elasticity. When the price consumption curve slopes upward to the right, demand is inelastic. When it slopes downward to the right, demand is elastic.

Engel curves for commodities are derived by varying the consumer's income, and holding tastes and preferences and the prices of all goods constant. The points of consumer equilibrium form the income consumption curve. The indifference curve diagram furnishes the necessary data for setting up Engel curves.

The change in quantity taken as a result of a price change, as shown by the demand curve for an item, is the combined result of two forces—an income effect and a substitution effect. For normal goods these work in the same direction to produce a decrease in quantity for an increase in price, or an increase in quantity for a decrease in price. For inferior goods the two effects work in opposite directions, but the substitution effect is usually the much stronger of the two.

By means of an Edgeworth box the conditions for an efficient or Pareto optimum distribution of goods among consumers can be established. These are that the MRS_{xy} of one consumer for any two goods, X and Y, must be the same as the MRS_{xy} of any other consumer for the same two goods. Distributions of goods satisfying these conditions form the contract curve. For any distribution of goods not on the contract curve a redistribution can occur that moves to the contract curve and increases community welfare. No conclusions regarding community welfare can be drawn from redistributions that occur along the contract curve.

Among the applications of indifference curve techniques is the analysis of fringe benefits in lieu of money as a part of an employee's total compensation. If an employee voluntarily takes as much or larger quantities of fringe-benefit items than are provided as a part of the employee's compensation, it makes no difference whether that part of the compensation is paid in fringe benefits or in money. Otherwise, the individual is better off if payment is entirely in money.

Another application of indifference curve techniques is the analysis of labor-leisure choices of an individual. Higher wage rates raise the price of leisure and induce the individual to substitute income for leisure, that is, to work more. This substitution effect ordinarily has an income effect working against it.

Through the use of indifference curve analysis it can be shown that a Laspeyres price index provides a maximum estimate of increases in the cost of living over time while a Paasche price index provides a minimum estimate of such increases.

Suggested readings

Baumol, William J., *Economic Theory and Operations Analysis*, 4th ed. Englewood Cliffs, N.J.: Prentice-Hall, Inc., 1977. Pp. 193–213.
Hicks, John R., *Value and Capital*, 2nd ed. Oxford, Eng.: The Clarendon Press, 1946. Chaps. 1–2.

Questions and exercises

1. Consider an indigent family on relief rolls. Let food and housing be the only items making up the family's budget. Using indifference curve analysis, discuss whether relief payments should be made in (1) kind (that is, a monthly allotment of food and clothing) or (2) money (that is, a monthly welfare check).

2. With regard to an individual's labor-leisure choices, show and explain with indifference curve techniques
   a. the number of hours per day that she would work when the maximum possible hours of work is H_0 and the age rate is w_0 per hour
   b. the effects on hours worked if she were given a wage subsidy of s_0 per hour
   c. the effects on hours worked, compared with 2b if she were given a cash subsidy (with the wage rate remaining at w_0) equal to the total amount of subsidy paid in equilibrium under 2b.

3. a. Consider the following model:
      (1) There are two consumers—Mr. A and Mr. B.
      (2) They consume two products—gasoline (G) and other (O)—and the total supplies available of these are fixed.
      (3) Mr. A is much richer than Mr. B.
      (4) The greater the amount of G consumed by Mr. A, given the amount of O that he consumes, the smaller is his MRS_{go}.
      (5) The greater the amount of G consumed by Mr. B, given the amount of O he consumes, the smaller is his MRS_{go}.
      Show with a diagram and explain an equilibrium distribution of the goods between the consumers. Can you say anything about p_g and p_o?
   b. Suppose that
      (1) The supply of gasoline available to A and B is reduced but that all of the reduction is initially borne by Mr. A—Mr. B's consumption bundle remains fixed.

(2) Through price controls both p_g and p_o are prevented from rising. Show diagrammatically and explain the welfare effects of the price controls. Now let the price controls be removed. Show and explain the impact on welfare.

4. a. Draw an individual's indifference curve map and line of attainable combinations on the same diagram.
   b. Explain the *economic meaning* of the point of tangency between the line of attainable combinations and an indifference curve.
   c. Explain what happens when the price of one product falls.
   d. Explain what happens when the consumer's income rises but product prices remain the same.
   e. Explain what happens when both the consumer's income and the prices of products rise.

Chapter 6

Chapter contents

The utility concept	**Nonrelated goods and services**
	Total utility
	Marginal utility
	Related goods and services
Indifference curves	
Consumer choice	**Objectives and constraints**
	Maximization of utility
Demand curves	**The demand curve for _X_**
	Quantities taken of other goods
Exchange and welfare	
Some applications of utility analysis	**Value in use and value in exchange**
	Energy conservation
Summary	**Suggested readings**
	Questions and exercises

Key concepts

Utility
Marginal utility
Saturation point
Substitute goods and services
Complementary goods and services
Utility surface
Indifference curves
Marginal rate of substitution
Maximization of utility
Individual consumer demand curve
Price elasticity of demand
Pareto optimum
Value in use
Value in exchange

The utility approach to consumer choice and demand—a special case*

The general theory of consumer choice and demand discussed in the last chapter evolved from an older utility approach that has subsequently come to be recognized as a special case of the general theory. The general theory—indifference curve analysis—is self-contained; it does not depend on the utility analysis from which it grew. However, there is much in the utility approach that provides additional insight into consumer behavior. There is also much that is repetitive as one compares this chapter with the preceding one. We try to present the utility approach in a reasonably complete form.

Utility theory, or subjective value theory, came on the scene in the 1870s with the almost simultaneous publication of its basic aspects by three economists working independently—William Stanley Jevons of Great Britain, Karl Menger of Austria, and Léon Walras of France. Present-day utility theory owes much to all three of these economists.

The utility concept

The term *utility* means the satisfaction that a consumer receives from whatever goods and services the individual consumes. It is useful analytically to distinguish between total utility concepts and marginal utility concepts under circumstances in which goods are not related to one another and under those in which relatedness occurs.

Nonrelated goods and services

Different kinds of items are unrelated, insofar as their consumption is concerned, if the utility or satisfaction obtained from one is in no way dependent upon the amount that the consumer consumes of the others. It is unlikely, for example, that the utility obtained from consuming nails has any significant bearing on that obtained from the consumption of gasoline.

Total utility The *total utility* attained from a commodity refers to the entire amount of satisfaction a consumer receives from consuming it at

* This chapter may be omitted without loss of continuity.

Figure 6–1   Total and marginal utility

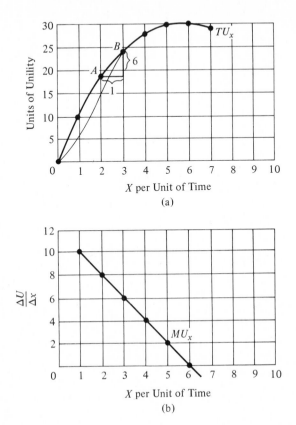

various rates. The more of an item a consumer consumes per unit of time, the greater will be the total utility or satisfaction received from it up to a point. At some rate of consumption total utility will reach a maximum. No greater satisfaction from it is forthcoming even though more of it is thrust upon the consumer. This state is called the *saturation point* for that commodity.[1]

A hypothetical total utility curve showing these properties is drawn in Figure 6–1(a). In plotting the curve we assume that utility can be quantified and measured, and that different quantities of utility to the consumer can be

---

[1] Conceivably, still more units of the good forced upon the consumer can cause total utility to decrease if for no other reason than storage problems. However, the possibility of decreases in total utility beyond the saturation point is of no importance for our purposes.

added to arrive at a meaningful total; that is, utility is assumed to be *cardinal* in nature.[2]

The saturation point is reached at a consumption level of 6 units of X per unit of time. Up to that level total utility is increasing as consumption increases. Beyond that level, total utility decreases.[3]

Marginal utility   The change in total utility resulting from a 1-unit change in consumption per unit of time is the *marginal utility* of a good. In Figure 6–1(a) if the consumer were consuming 2 units per unit of time and increased the consumption level to 3, the individual's total utility would increase from 18 to 24 units and the marginal utility would be 6.

The slope of the total utility curve between points A and B shows the increase in utility resulting from the increase in consumption from 2 to 3 units of X and is equal to 6/1 if that segment of the curve is considered to be a straight line. The total utility curve is not necessarily a straight line between A and B, but the error involved in considering it linear is not significant and becomes progressively less the smaller the distance between points. If the distance on the X axis that measures 1 unit of X is infinitesimal, marginal utility at any given level of consumption is measured by the slope of the total utility curve at that point.[4]

Marginal utility is reflected in the shape of the total utility curve as the rate of consumption is increased or decreased. In Figure 6–1(a) marginal utility decreases as consumption per unit of time increases between 0 and 6. This statement can be rephrased by saying that each additional unit of consumption per unit of time adds less and less to total utility, until finally the sixth unit adds nothing at all. Note also that as consumption per unit of time increases, the average slope of the total utility curve between any two consecutive consumption levels becomes smaller and smaller until, between 5 and 6 units of X, it becomes 0. The concept of diminishing marginal utility and the concavity of the total utility curve, when viewed from below, are the same thing.

---

[2] Whether utility can be measured cardinally or whether its measurement has ordinal meaning only has been an historical source of controversy in the development of economic thought. The theory presented here does not really require measurability but requires only that the consumer be able to distinguish between greater and lesser amounts of utility. For expositional purposes we shall treat utility as though it were cardinal.

[3] This paragraph assumes that the rate of consumption is increased by discrete units. Total utility is maximum at 5 as well as at 6 units of X per unit of time. However, there are pedagogical advantages to considering the maximum as occurring at 6 units.

[4] In terms of differential calculus, if the total utility curve were

$$U = f(x) = 12x - x^2,$$

then

$$MU = \frac{dU}{dx} = f'(x) = 12 - 2x.$$

Marginal utility at 2 units of X is 8 units of utility; at 3 units of X it is 6 units of utility.

Diminishing marginal utility need not be the case for all levels of consumption between 0 and 6 units of X. The lighter curve in Figure 6–1(a) could conceivably be the total utility curve between 0 and 3. Suppose, for example, that a single television set in a home with several children causes so much friction over program selection that it adds little to the satisfaction of the family. Two sets—one for the parents and one for the children—may yield more than twice the satisfaction of one. But the successive increases in total utility yielded by three, four, and five sets will surely be successively smaller. Thus, through some range of consumption levels, marginal utility may increase as the consumption increases, and the total utility curve will be convex downward for that range. Beyond that range marginal utility decreases. If a saturation point for a commodity exists for a given consumer, as the person's consumption level approaches that point, marginal utility must be decreasing even though it may have been increasing at lower levels of consumption.

The marginal utility curve of Figure 6–1(b) is constructed from the total utility curve of Figure 6–1(a). In Figure 6–1(b) the utility axis is stretched so that the vertical distance measuring one unit is greater than it is in Figure 6–1(a). The X axis is the same for the two diagrams. Marginal utility is plotted as a vertical distance above the X axis at each level of consumption. At a consumption level of 6 in Figure 6–1(a) the average slope of the total utility curve between 5 and 6 is 0. Hence, marginal utility is 0; in Figure 6–1(b) the marginal utility curve intersects the X axis at that consumption level. In Figure 6–1(b) a line MU_x joining the plotted marginal utilities at each level of consumption is the marginal utility curve for X.

A set of a consumer's marginal utility curves for the different commodities consumed provides a graphic picture of the consumer's tastes and preferences at any given time. For those commodities with which the consumer is easily satiated the marginal utility curves will slope off very rapidly, reaching zero at relatively low levels of consumption. For other commodities with which the consumer is not easily satiated the marginal utility curves will slope off gradually and will reach zero at relatively high levels of consumption.[5] Changes in the consumer's tastes and preferences will change the shapes and positions of the marginal utility curves for different commodities.

Related goods and services

A great many of the goods and services that an individual consumes are related to each other in some way; that is, the quantity that the person takes

[5] As a practical matter, no consumer will reach the saturation point for any good that commands a price, except by accident. The reason for this statement will become apparent in the next section of the chapter.

of one affects the utility that is obtained from others. These may be complementary relationships, or they may be substitute relationships. In general, goods that are consumed together, such as bread and butter or tennis rackets and tennis balls, are complementary goods; while those that compete with each other in the consumer's scale of preferences, such as beef and pork, are substitute goods.

The nature of relatedness is illustrated in the three-dimensional diagram of Figure 6–2(a). The X and Y axes define a horizontal plane, and total utility is measured as a vertical distance above it. For example, if the individual consumes combination A_1 per week, containing x_1 units of X and y_1 units of Y, the total utility for that consumer from both will be A_1B_1. Points such as B_1, B_2, B_4, F_1, F_2, and F_5—showing total utility for different combinations of X and Y—trace out a *total utility surface* lying above the XY plane.

The utility surface pictured in Figure 6–2(a) shows not only the total utility obtained by the consumer from the consumption of X and Y in various combinations, but also how total utility changes as the rate of consumption of one good is changed, given the rate of consumption of the other.

Consider, for example, variations in the consumption of X at each of three different levels of consumption of Y. If no Y is consumed, the total utility of the consumer, as is shown in Figure 6–2(a), is TU_x^0 for different rates of consumption of X. The same curve is also pictured on the two-dimensional diagram of Figure 6–2(b). If the amount of Y consumed per week is y_1, total utility is y_1B_0 if no X is taken. Changes in quantity of X with the consumption level of Y held constant at y_1 trace out the total utility curve TU_x^1. We can visualize the consumer as starting from point B_0 on the utility surface and moving up over the surface directly above the dotted line $y_1A_1A_2A_4$. Again the resulting TU_x^1 curve is plotted in two dimensions in Figure 6–2(b). The meaning of the third total utility curve for X, TU_x^2, is now obvious. If no X is consumed, total utility from y_2 of Y alone is y_2F_0. If Y is held constant at y_2, increasing levels of consumption of X will yield the total utility curve TU_x^2 on the utility surface and in the two-dimensional diagram Figure 6–2(b). The curves TU_y^0, TU_y^1, and TU_y^2 are derived in a similar fashion.[6]

Taking the interrelatedness of goods X and Y into account undoubtedly makes utility theory more realistic, but it makes it more complex, too. For one thing, there are innumerable possible total utility curves for each prod-

---

[6] If all goods consumed are related, the consumer's utility function is of the general form

$$U = f(x, y. . . n).$$

If all goods consumed are independent of one another, it takes the form

$$U = f(x) + g(y) + \cdots + n(n).$$

Figure 6–2   The utility surface

(a)

(b)

(c)

uct. There is a different total utility curve for X associated with each different quantity of Y that the consumer might consume. Similarly there is a different total utility curve for Y for each different level of consumption of X. There are also innumerable marginal utility curves for each product. Since the total utility curves for X differ at each different level of consumption of Y, so do the corresponding marginal utility curves for X. For example, in Figure 6–2(c) MU_x^0, MU_x^1, and MU_x^2 are derived from TU_x^0, TU_x^1, and TU_x^2, respectively. Here we see that at a consumption level of x_1 of X the marginal utility of X depends on the amount of Y consumed as well as on the quantity x_1 of X. If no Y is consumed, it is M_0 or the slope of TU_x^0 at point D_1. If y_1 of Y is consumed, it is M_1 or the slope of TU_x^1 at B_1. If y_2 of Y is consumed, it is M_2 or the slope of TU_x^2 at F_1. Similar reasoning applies to Y. If diminishing marginal utility occurs with any increase in the consumption of either X or Y, the utility surface will have the inverted bowl shape exhibited in Figure 6–2(a); that is, any total utility curve drawn for either X or Y will be convex upward.

Indifference curves

We take a side trip at this point to show how indifference curve analysis evolved from utility theory. However, utility theory itself was a self-contained theory of consumer choice and demand—albeit a special case. In the next section we get back on the main utility theory road, which depends in no way on this section.

In Figure 6–3(a) suppose that a consumer initially consumes good Y only and that she consumes it at a rate of y_1 per unit of time. Her total utility is y_1A_1 or $0U_1$. Is it not possible that by giving up the consumption of a small amount of Y and by increasing the consumption of X in some amount, she can maintain her level of utility constant? Reducing consumption of Y and increasing consumption of X in the manner described, she moves around the indifference surface at a constant distance about the XY plane. Her path traces out the curve A_1B_2. Projected vertically downward on the XY plane, the A_1B_2 curve becomes the dashed line y_1x_2. This curve is redrawn with respect only to the XY plane in Figure 6–3(b).

The curve y_1x_2 shows all combinations of X and Y that yield levels of utility equal to $0U_1$ or y_1A_1. For example, in Figure 6–3(a) at point E the consumer is taking y_0 of Y and x_1 of X; this combination yields a total utility of EF ($= y_1A_1$). Similarly, if she consumes X alone at level x_2, her total utility is x_2B_2 ($= y_1A_1$). Curve y_1x_2 is in every sense an indifference curve like those of the preceding chapter. Since all combinations of X and Y shown by this curve yield the same total utility to the consumer, she is indifferent as to which of them that she consumes.

Figure 6-3   Indifference curves from a utility surface

(a)

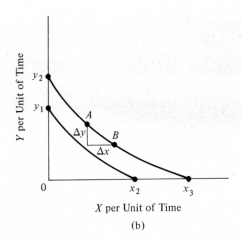

(b)

Higher levels of utility are shown by contour lines higher up on the surface, while lower contour lines show lower levels of utility. Projected on the XY plane, the indifference curves corresponding to higher contour lines lie farther from the origin, as does y_2x_3 in Figure 6-3(b). The projections of lower contour lines lie closer to the origin. These observations are based on the assumption that the utility surface tapers toward a summit as we move up. It is usually thought of as having an inverted bowl shape, although this restrictive shape is not really necessary for the foregoing observations to hold.

The marginal rate of substitution of X for Y is measured by the *ratio* of the marginal utility of X to the marginal utility of Y, or $MRS_{xy} = MU_x/MU_y$. In Figure 6–3(b) suppose that the consumer is originally consuming combination A. If she were to move from combination A to combination B, she would give up Δy of Y and acquire Δx of X with *no change* in her total utility level. The loss in utility from giving up Y is $\Delta y \times MU_y$. The gain from acquiring X is $\Delta x \times MU_x$. Therefore,

$$\Delta y \times MU_y = \Delta x \times MU_x \qquad (6.1)$$

$$\frac{\Delta y}{\Delta x} = \frac{MU_x}{MU_y} = MRS_{xy}. \qquad (6.2)$$

In this discussion we have continued to assume that utility is measurable. For example, in Figure 6–3(a) the distance $0U_1$ is a definite measurable magnitude, say 8 units of utility, while $0U_2$ is 10 units of utility. Accordingly, in Figure 6–3(b) we would attach the number 8 to the y_1x_2 indifference curve and 10 to the y_2x_3 curve. However, is it essential that we attach absolute utility *magnitudes* to each indifference curve? Would it not be possible, once we have an indifference map, to attach a utility *ranking* to each curve instead?

If we do so, the 8 and the 10 have no significance as absolute measures. They would show only the order of utility magnitudes; that is, 10 is greater than 8. We could accomplish the same thing by attaching the number 1 to y_1x_2 and the number 2 to y_2x_3.[7]

If the order, but not the absolute measure, of utility magnitudes is all that is required, we can forget about how high the utility surface rises above the XY plane. Only its general shape is important. Suppose that we think of it as being collapsible from the top down in such a way that contour lines from bottom to top retain their original shapes. If we do so, we are free of the assumption that utility is measurable. The indifference map is the same in all essential respects as those developed earlier in Chapter 5.

---

[7] If the consumer's utility function is represented by

$$U = f(x, y),$$

then the equation for one indifference curve is

$$U_1 = f(x, y),$$

in which U_1 is a constant. Other values assigned to U define other indifference curves, all of these making up the consumer's indifference map. It is necessary only that the assigned values show the order of utility magnitudes; it is not necessary that they show absolute (measurable) utility magnitudes.

Consumer choice

Returning now to the main road, the utility concepts provide a basis for determining how a consumer will allocate income among the various goods and services that confront the individual. They are more awkward to use than the more general indifference curve analysis. To keep the discussion as simple as possible, we assume (1) that the goods and services contemplated by the consumer are nonrelated; (2) that utility is cardinal; and (3) that the marginal utility of each item consumed is diminishing.[8] None of these do any violence to the conclusions reached, but they do much to smooth the path toward those conclusions.

Objectives and constraints

The objective usually postulated for a rational consumer is the maximization of satisfaction or utility. The consumer's preferences are described by his utility curves for the various goods and services that confront him. His choice problem is to select from these the kinds and amounts that will yield him the greatest total amount of utility.

The consumer is constrained by his income (the dollars per unit of time that he has to spend) and the prices of the goods and services available to him. Typically, his income per unit of time is a more or less fixed amount, as are the prices he faces (since he is a pure competitor in the purchase of most things). Subject to these constraints the consumer makes his choices.

Maximization of utility

To avoid unnecessary complexity, we limit the consumer to two goods, X and Y, priced at p_x and p_y, respectively. If p_x and p_y are given and constant, we can measure quantities of these goods in terms of dollars' worths. For example, if a bushel of X costs \$2, we can record that physical quantity as two dollars' worths; a half-bushel is equivalent to one dollar's worth. Table 6–1(a) records a consumer's hypothetical marginal utility schedules for X and Y, measuring quantities in dollars' worths and assuming independence between the two goods.[9]

---

[8] Actually, all that we need to assume is that the marginal utility of one good decreases relative to the marginal utilities of other goods as consumption of the one is increased in proportion to the consumption of the others. The marginal utility of X could be increasing. However, if the additional consumption of X raises the marginal utilities of other goods, that of X has decreased *relative* to those of the other goods.

[9] Assuming that the marginal utility schedule of each commodity is independent of the level of consumption of the other commodity, we can go directly and quickly to the conditions necessary for maximization of satisfaction. If X and Y were substitutes, the more of X consumed, the lower the marginal utility of Y would be at various consumption levels of Y. If they were complements, the more of X consumed, the higher the marginal utility of Y would be at various consumption levels of Y. These possibilities do not change the conditions necessary for maximization of satisfaction, but they make numerical exposition of these conditions virtually impossible.

Table 6–1   Marginal utility schedules

(a)

Product X		Product Y	
Quantity (Dollars' Worths)	MU_x (Units of Utility)	Quantity (Dollars' Worths)	MU_y (Units of Utility)
1	40	1	30
2	36	2	29
3	32	3	28
4	28	4	27
5	24	5	26
6	20	6	25
7	12	7	24
8	4	8	20

(b)

Product X		Product Y	
Quantity (Bushels)	MU_x (Units of Utility)	Quantity (Pints)	MU_y (Units of Utility)
1	50	1	30
2	44	2	28
3	38	3	26
4	32	4	24
5	26	5	22
6	20	6	20
7	12	7	16
8	4	8	10

If the consumer has an income of $12 per unit of time, what is the allocation of it between X and Y that will maximize his utility? Suppose that he spends only $1 per unit of time. Spent on Y, it will yield only 30 units of satisfaction; whereas if it is spent on X, it will yield 40. Thus, the dollar will be allocated to X. If the consumer increases his expenditure level to $2, where should the second dollar go? Spent on X, it will increase his total utility by 36 (the marginal utility of a second dollar's worth of X); but spent on Y, it adds only 30 units. The second dollar will be spent on X and so will the third dollar. The situation changes when the total expenditure increases from $3 to $4. A fourth dollar spent on X will increase the total utility by 28 units; but if the fourth dollar is spent on the first dollar's worth of Y, the increase is 30 units. The fourth dollar will go for Y. As expenditure per unit of time is increased dollar by dollar, the fifth should go for Y; the sixth and seventh, one each on X and Y; the eighth, ninth, and tenth on Y; and the eleventh and twelfth, one each on X and Y. The consumer is now taking five dollars' worths of X and seven dollars' worths of Y. The marginal utility per dollar's worth of X is equal to that of a dollar's worth of Y—both are 24 units of utility.

We know that the consumer's utility for the $12 expenditure is maximum because it was placed dollar by dollar where each dollar made its greatest contribution to total utility.

Generalizing, we can say that a consumer maximizes utility by allocating income among the goods and services (including savings) available in such a way that (1) the marginal utility per dollar's worth of any one is equal to the marginal utility per dollar's worth of any other and (2) all of the income is spent. Savings, which may appear to pose a problem, are simply treated as any other good. A consumer obtains utility from savings. Presumably, the marginal utility of savings, like that of other goods and services, diminishes as its quantity is increased.

Suppose we look at the problem again with data arranged a little differently. Consider another consumer whose marginal utility schedules are based on bushels and pints like those of Table 6–1(b). The price of X is $2 per bushel and that of Y is $1 per pint. This consumer's income is $15 per unit of time. How should it be allocated between X and Y?

Since the marginal utility schedules are in terms of physical measurements of X and Y, rather than in terms of dollars' worths, we need a means of converting the information that they contain into marginal utilities per dollar's worth. To obtain it, consider the fourth bushel of X. If the consumer were taking 4 bushels of X, the fourth bushel has a marginal utility of 32 units. The fourth bushel (like any other bushel) costs $2. At this consumption level the marginal utility per bushel of X divided by the price of X, or MU_x/p_x, is the marginal utility per dollar's worth of X. Thus, the marginal utility per dollar's worth of X is 16 units at this point. Likewise, the marginal utility per pint of Y at any consumption level divided by the price of Y, or MU_y/p_y, can be read as the marginal utility per dollar's worth of Y at that consumption level. The first condition for maximizing satisfaction becomes

$$\frac{MU_x}{p_x} = \frac{MU_y}{p_y} = \frac{MU_z}{p_z} = \cdots . \tag{6.3}$$

The requirement that the consumer be spending all of her income—no more and no less—is expressed as

$$x \times p_x + y \times p_y + z \times p_z + \cdots = I. \tag{6.4}$$

The total expenditure on X is the price of X times the amount of X purchased. The same holds for the expenditure on each other good or service, including savings. The total of these must equal the income I.

Since the price of X is $2 per bushel and the price of Y is $1 per pint, we must find some combination of X and Y at which the marginal utility per bushel of X is twice the marginal utility per pint of Y. This combination occurs at 6 bushels of X and 8 pints of Y. However, the total amount spent on X would be $12, and the total amount spent on Y would be $8. The consumer is exceeding her income. Thus, the second condition for maximization of total utility is not met, although the first one is satisfied. Another possible combination is the one containing 4 bushels of X and 7 pints of Y. The first condition is met since 32/\$2 = 16/\$1. The second condition is met also since 4 bushels × \$2 + 7 pints × \$1 = \$15. Thus, the consumer should take 4 bushels of X and 7 pints of Y to maximize her total utility.

To demonstrate that utility is maximized, transfer a dollar from X to Y. Giving up a dollar's worth of X, or half of the fourth bushel, reduces total utility by 16 units. Spending the dollar for an eighth pint of Y increases total utility by 10. There is a net loss of 6 units. If the dollar were transferred in the opposite direction, there would also be a net loss of utility—3 units in this case.[10]

The data confronting the consumer may not yield the neat solution of this example. Suppose the consumer's income were \$14 per unit of time instead of \$15. How should it be allocated? She could give up either a half-bushel of X or a pint of Y. In either case total utility would be decreased by 16 units. Or if her income were \$16 instead of \$15, she would take half of the fifth bushel of X. The increase in total utility would be 13 units. If she had taken the eighth pint of Y, her total utility would have increased by 10 units only. Thus, the consumer seeking maximum satisfaction should allocate income among various goods so as to approach as nearly as possible the condition that the marginal utility of a dollar's worth of one good equals the marginal utility of a dollar's worth of any other good purchased.

How would the theory work for a typical family? Suppose that the family budget is composed of the following items: food, clothing, housing, automobile, medical care, recreation, and education. Over a short period of time expenditures in some of the classifications are more or less fixed in amount. The mortgage payments, for example, are a fixed monthly amount. The grocery bill and medical expenditures are sometimes thought to be dictated by necessity rather than choice. The other categories are likely to be more variable, but habit may be influential in determining them in the short run.

Over a longer period of time, however, expenditures on any or all of the budgeted items are subject to change. The family seeking to get the greatest

---

[10] The mathematical problem is that of maximizing the consumer's utility function subject to the budget restraint. Using the symbols of the text, the utility function is

$$U = f(x, y).$$

The budget restraint is

$$xp_x + yp_y = I \quad \text{or} \quad xp_x + yp_y - I = 0.$$

The maximization problem is identical to that shown in Footnote 12, Chapter 5. From that footnote

$$f_x = MU_x = \lambda p_x \quad \text{and} \quad f_y = MU_y = \lambda p_y.$$

Therefore,

$$\frac{MU_x}{MU_y} = \frac{\lambda p_x}{\lambda p_y}, \quad \text{or} \quad \frac{MU_x}{p_x} = \frac{MU_y}{p_y}.$$

possible satisfaction from its limited income will reappraise its budget from time to time. The family car begins to rattle a little, and at the same time it appears desirable to add a new bedroom to the house for Junior. It is out of the question to purchase both a new car and a new room, and a choice must be made regarding the direction of expenditure. Still, if either is to be gotten, it will be necessary to cut down on educational expenses for the older daughter, who has been attending a private university. Should she be transferred to the state university where expenses are less? Food and clothing budgeting will also be required in order to make the new car or the new room possible. Likewise, the family will need to economize on recreation, and even on medical expenses. When Junior has a minor illness, he will have to get over it without a visit to the doctor. A whole chain of decisions will be made on the basis of marginal utility principles if maximum satisfaction for the family is to be attained.

The family subjectively estimates the marginal utilities of dollars spent in each of the various directions. Transfers of expenditures from the items where marginal utility per dollar's worth is less toward items where marginal utility per dollar's worth is greater serve to increase total satisfaction.

Demand curves

The utility approach to consumer choice can be extended to explain the establishment of individual consumer demand curves for goods and services. Again, we limit the consumer to a two-commodity world in which X and Y are independent goods. The consumer's utility curves are given and remain constant throughout the analysis. The marginal utility of each good is assumed to be diminishing.

The demand curve for X[11]

To establish the consumer's demand curve for X, suppose that initially the price of X is p_{x1} and the price of Y is p_{y1}. We shall assume that at all times

[11] The analysis presented here is essentially that of Walras. See Léon Walras, *Abrégé des eléments d'économie politique pure* (Paris: R. Pichon et R. Durand-Auzias, 1938), pp. 131–133. The transition from the theory of consumer behavior to demand curves set out in the text differs from the usual Marshallian treatment, which considers the marginal utility of money constant and simply converts the marginal utility curve for a commodity into the demand curve for it. See Kenneth E. Boulding, *Economic Analysis*, 4th ed., Vol. 1 (New York: Harper & Row, Publishers, Inc., 1966), pp. 520–527.

The Marshallian approach ignores the income effects of price changes. The approach used in the text includes income effects as well as substitution effects. This approach in turn makes the utility analysis of the present chapter more nearly parallel to the indifference curve analysis of the last chapter.

Figure 6–4   Determination of quantities demanded

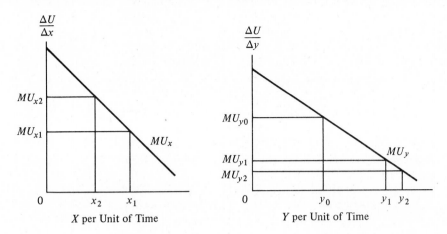

Figure 6–4   Determination of quantities demanded

the consumer is operating at the limit of the income restraint. The consumer will maximize satisfaction or be in equilibrium when taking the quantity of X and that quantity of Y at which

$$\frac{MU_{x1}}{p_{x1}} = \frac{MU_{y1}}{p_{y1}}. \tag{6.5}$$

Thus, at price p_{x1} the consumer is taking a definite quantity of X—that quantity which makes the marginal utility of a dollar's worth of X equal to the marginal utility of a dollar's worth of Y. We shall call this quantity x_1.[12]

The consumer's initial position of equilibrium is shown graphically in Figure 6–4. Assuming that p_{x1} is twice p_{y1}, the consumer takes quantity x_1 of X and y_1 of Y. These quantities are such that MU_{x1} is twice MU_{y1}.[13] One point on the consumer's demand schedule or demand curve for X has now been established. At price p_{x1} the consumer will take quantity x_1.

The problem is to establish the quantities of X that will be taken at other prices of X when the consumer is in equilibrium at each of those prices with the price of Y remaining constant at p_{y1}, the consumer's marginal utility curves or tastes and preferences remaining constant, and the income remaining constant.

Suppose that the price of X rises to p_{x2} and that the consumer continues to take the same amount of X as before. The marginal utility per bushel of X

---

[12] The consumer will also be taking some definite quantity y_1 of Y; however, we are primarily concerned with the quantity of X that is taken.

[13] For any given ratio of p_x and p_y, quantities of X and Y taken must be such that

$$p_x/p_y = MU_x/MU_y, \text{ or } MU_x/p_x = MU_y/p_y.$$

will remain unchanged, but the marginal utility per dollar's worth of X, MU_{x1}/p_{x2}, will be less. At the higher price p_{x2} the consumer spends more income on X than before, leaving less to be spent on Y. Since p_{y1} is the given price of Y, the consumer will necessarily cut purchases of Y to some quantity y_0. The decrease in the number of pints of Y consumed raises the marginal utility per pint of Y to MU_{y0} (see Figure 6–4). The marginal utility per dollar's worth of Y is increased to MU_{y0}/p_{y1} and

$$\frac{MU_{x1}}{p_{x2}} < \frac{MU_{y0}}{p_{y1}} ; \tag{6.6}$$

that is, the marginal utility of a dollar's worth of X is now less than the marginal utility of a dollar's worth of Y. The consumer is not maximizing satisfaction.

The consumer clearly will not continue to take quantity x_1 of X after the price has gone up to p_{x2}. Satisfaction can be increased by transferring dollars from X to Y. The loss from taking a dollar away from X is the marginal utility of a dollar's worth of X. The gain from buying an additional dollar's worth of Y is the marginal utility of a dollar's worth of Y. Since $MU_{x1}/p_{x2} < MU_{y0}/p_{y1}$, such a transfer will yield a net gain in total utility.

The transfer of dollars from X to Y will continue as long as the marginal utility of a dollar's worth of X is less than the marginal utility of a dollar's worth of Y. However, as the consumer gives up units of X, the marginal utility per bushel of X increases, causing the marginal utility per dollar's worth of X to increase since its price remains at p_{x2}. As the consumer buys additional units of Y, the marginal utility per pint of Y declines, as does the marginal utility per dollar's worth of Y. The transfer will stop when the consumer has again equalized the marginal utility per dollar's worth of X with the marginal utility per dollar's worth of Y and is thus maximizing satisfaction. The quantity of Y taken will have increased from y_0 to some quantity y_2. The quantity of X taken will have decreased from x_1 to x_2. Quantities x_2 and y_2 must be such that

$$\frac{MU_{x2}}{p_{x2}} = \frac{MU_{y2}}{p_{y1}} . \tag{6.7}$$

The quantities of X and Y that bring MU_x and MU_y into the proper relationship are shown in Figure 6–4 as x_2 and y_2. We now have another point on the consumer's demand curve for X. At price p_{x2} the consumer takes x_2 of X. The analysis has shown that an increase in the price of X causes a decrease in the quantity taken.

Using $MU_{x2}/p_{x2} = MU_{y2}/p_{y1}$ as a new starting point, we can change the price of X again and repeat this process. In the resulting new equilibrium position the quantity of X taken at the new price is established. Through continued repetition of the process we can determine a series of price-

Figure 6–5   Individual consumer demand curve

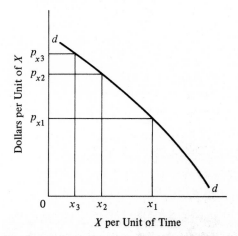

quantity combinations that represent the demand schedule and that can be plotted as the demand curve. Such a curve is shown in Figure 6–5.

Quantities taken of other goods

As a corollary it may be instructive to take a closer view of what happens to the quantity of Y taken. When the price of X increases to p_{x2}, is the quantity of Y at the new equilibrium position greater than the original quantity? The answer is, "not necessarily," even though we show it to be greater in Figure 6–4. The crucial factor is the elasticity of demand for X. If demand for X is elastic, the increase in the price of X must decrease total spending on X, leaving more of the consumer's income to spend on Y. In this case quantity y_2 would indeed be greater than quantity y_1, as we depict it in Figure 6–4. However, if elasticity of demand for X is unitary, total spending on X and total spending on Y will each remain constant, and there will be no change in the quantity of Y taken. Should demand for X be inelastic, the price increase for X would increase total spending on X and decrease total spending on Y. The new equilibrium quantity of Y taken would be smaller than y_1.

Exchange and welfare

In any voluntary exchange of goods among individuals all parties to the exchange expect to increase their satisfaction or welfare. It is this prospect

of gain that causes voluntary exchange to occur. The point can be illustrated clearly by means of utility analysis. We limit ourselves to two consumers, A and B, each of whom receives constant quantities per unit of
time of two goods, X and Y. Marginal utility schedules for the two goods for
each consumer are shown in Table 6–2.

Table 6–2   The basis of exchange

Individual A				Individual B			
Product X		Product Y		Product X		Product Y	
Quantity (Bushels)	MU_x (Units of Utility)	Quantity (Pints)	MU_y (Units of Utility)	Quantity (Bushels)	MU_x (Units of Utility)	Quantity (Pints)	MU_y (Units of Utility)
1	14	1	10	1	20	1	18
2	13	2	9	2	19	2	17
3	12	3	8	3	18	3	16
4	11	4	7	4	17	4	14
5	10	5	6	5	16	5	12
6	9	6	"5	6	15	6	10
7	8	7	4	7	14	7	8
8	7	8	3	8	13	8	6
9	6	9	2	9	12	9	4
10	5	10	1	10	10	10	2

Comparative marginal utilities of the goods indicate their comparative
worths or values to a consumer. Suppose consumer A has 5 bushels of X
and 6 pints of Y. A bushel of X at this point contributes 10 units of utility to
A's total satisfaction. A pint of Y contributes 5 units of utility. If A were to
lose a bushel of X, the loss in satisfaction would be 10 units of utility; or if A
were to lose a pint of Y, the loss would be 5 units of utility. Thus, a bushel of
X to A is worth 2 pints of Y. Alternatively, we can say that a pint of Y is
worth one-half bushel of X.

Suppose that the supplies of goods X and Y are fixed at 12 bushels of X
and 12 pints of Y per week and that these are initially distributed between
the two consumers so that A has 9 bushels of X and 3 pints of Y, while B has
3 bushels of X and 9 pints of Y. Since for A the marginal utility of a bushel of
X is 6 units of utility and a pint of Y is 8 units of utility, a pint of Y is worth
1-1/3 bushels of X to A. For B the marginal utility of a bushel of X is 18
units of utility and that of a pint of Y is 4 units of utility. Thus, for consumer
B a pint of Y is worth only 2/9 of a bushel of X.

Under these circumstances both parties will gladly do some exchanging,
and exchange will increase community welfare. Individual A will be willing
to trade a bushel of X to individual B for a pint of Y, and individual B will be

willing to trade a pint of Y for a bushel of X. For individual A the pint of Y gained would be worth 1-1/3 times the bushel of X given up. For individual B the pint of Y given up would be worth only 2/9 of the bushel of X gained. To put it another way, in trading a bushel of X for a pint of Y, individual A would give up 6 units of utility in exchange for 7 units, experiencing a net gain of 1 unit of utility. Individual B would give up 4 units of utility in exchange for 17 units, experiencing a net gain of 13 units of utility.[14] The welfare of both is increased by the exchange, and no one's welfare is decreased.

Once this exchange has been consummated, an additional exchange could result in a further gain for both parties. Individual A, with 8 bushels of X and 4 pints of Y, will no longer be willing to exchange on a bushel-for-a-pint basis since the loss from such a transaction would be greater than the gain. However, individual B can still gain from trading pints of Y for bushels of X. Since trade is no longer attractive to A on a bushel-for-a-pint basis, B will alter the terms of the trade. If B, who now has 4 bushels of X and 8 pints of Y, were to give up 2 pints of Y for a bushel of X, then B would give up 14 units of utility, would gain 16 units, and would still experience a 2-unit net gain in utility. Individual A would find this offer attractive, for 11 units of utility would be received in exchange for 7.

Once the second exchange has occurred, no further gains are available from trade between the two parties; a Pareto optimum has been reached and exchange will cease. Individual A has 7 bushels of X and 6 pints of Y with marginal utilities of 8 and 5 units of utility, respectively. Individual B has 5 bushels of X and 6 pints of Y with marginal utilities of 16 and 10 units of utility, respectively. For A the unit of X is worth 1-3/5 units of Y. Individual B's relative valuations of X and Y are exactly the same; hence, neither can gain from further exchange.

The general principle underlying the discussion is that for exchange to occur, two or more individuals must place different relative valuations on the goods involved. Relative valuations of goods by a single party depend on relative marginal utilities of the goods. Thus, for all consumers to be in equilibrium—that is, for there to be no incentives to exchange—each individual's holdings of goods must be such that the ratio of the marginal utilities of the goods for him is the same as it is for everyone else. In our simple example for A and B to be in equilibrium, MU_x/MU_y for A must equal MU_x/MU_y for B. When these conditions do not hold, it becomes worthwhile for the parties to engage in exchange until they do.

---

[14] The one-for-one exchange ratio used here is not the only one at which the initial exchange could occur. Both parties can gain from any exchange ratio at which the amount of X that A is willing to give up to get a pint of Y exceeds the amount of X that B would require to give up a pint of Y.

Some applications of utility analysis

Value in use and value in exchange

The development of a utility theory of choice and exchange enabled economists to explain what the early classical economists of the late eighteenth and early nineteenth centuries called the diamond-water paradox. The paradox was that some goods, like diamonds, have a limited total use value to any one person; yet in markets they have a very high exchange value. Other goods, like water, have a very great total use value to any one person; yet in markets they have a very low exchange value. Early economists were unable to provide a satisfactory explanation of this phenomenon.

The subjective value, or marginal utility, economists of the late nineteenth century used a device like Table 6–3 to provide the answer. Measuring water in 100-gallon units and diamonds in 5-carat units, suppose that when consumer A is maximizing satisfaction, 900 gallons of water and 2 5-carat units of diamonds are purchased per year. The total utility of water to A is 196 units of utility. But how does A value any of the 100-unit increments of the total supply? The definition of marginal utility informs us that, at the 900-gallon consumption level, 100 gallons contribute 12 units of utility to A's satisfaction level. Consumer A would be willing to trade 100 gallons of water for units of any other good that provides a marginal utility of 12 or more utility units.

Diamonds, on the other hand, provide a total of 76 units of utility at the 2-unit level of consumption. But the marginal utility of a unit of diamonds is 36 units. Consumer A would not be willing to trade a unit of diamonds for

Table 6–3   The diamond-water paradox

Water				Diamonds		
Gallons per Year	MU per 100 Gallons	TU		Units per Year	MU per Units	TU
100	30	30		1	40	40
200	28	58		2	36	76
300	26	84		3	24	100
400	24	108		4	10	110
500	22	130		5	0	110
600	20	150				
700	18	168				
800	16	184				
900	12	196				
1000	8	204				

units of any other good unless the marginal utility of such a good were 36 utility units or more.

The water, which has great use value to A, has a low exchange value because to A its supply is large and its marginal utility is low. The diamonds, which have a much lower use value to A, have a high exchange value because their supply to A is small and their marginal utility is high. Exchange value of a good, then, is really determined by the use value to the consumer of the marginal unit—that is, by the marginal utility of a unit of the good at the current rate of consumption.

Energy conservation

Since the energy "crisis" of 1973–1974, great national concern for energy conservation has been evidenced. To most people conservation means (1) voluntary restraints by individuals on the amounts of gasoline, electricity, and other energy-providing goods that they consume and/or (2) mandatory curbs by the government on the amounts individuals are allowed to consume. Both types of measures imply that prices are fixed below their equilibrium levels. If X represents nonenergy goods and E represents energy goods, at least some persons will be in disequilibrium positions with

$$\frac{MU_x}{p_x} < \frac{MU_e}{p_e}.$$

This means simply that energy goods are undervalued—that consumers want more at current prices than they get.

The disequilibrium positions make the exercise of voluntary restraints on consumption virtually impossible to sustain over time. The temptation is always there to turn the thermostat up to 74 degrees in the winter or down to 76 degrees in the summer. In addition, attempts to secure voluntary restraints promote ill will between those who feel "patriotic" and those who do not. The former will be very upset with the actions of those who do not comply.

Disequilibrium of individuals also creates problems in the enforcement of mandatory curbs on consumption. Users will be divided into a number of special-interest groups. In the case of motor fuel, for example, truckers and farmers represent two such groups. Individuals in each, faced with short supplies, believe that they are being discriminated against. Group is set against group. And how can those people responsible for allocations determine for whom the fuel is most important?

The obvious way to avoid the problems just posed is to utilize energy prices to do the rationing. We shall assume that the annual (or monthly) supplies to be made available are fixed and that consumers bid for the available supplies. As p_e rises, MU_e/p_e for individuals will fall and so will the amounts of energy that consumers want to consume. *Positive incentives* will exist to turn the thermostat down in the winter and up in the summer. *All* users of motor fuel will have incentives to conserve its use. No one needs to make decisions concerning who gets the available supplies. Energy prices will rise until all consumers together are just willing to take the available supplies. The amount of energy consumed by each consumer will be that at which

$$\frac{MU_x}{p_x} = \frac{MU_e}{p_e}.$$

Summary

The utility approach to the theory of individual consumer choice and demand is a special case of the indifference curve approach. It can be used to explain, among other things, the consumer's allocation of income among the goods that he or she buys, the consumer's demand curve for any given product, and the exchange of goods among individuals. The conclusions reached depend on the principle of *relatively* diminishing marginal utility of any one good or service as the consumption of it is increased relative to that of other goods and services.

A consumer seeks to maximize the satisfaction derived from the goods and services obtainable with one's given income. Maximization requires that the individual allocate income in such a way that when he or she is spending the entire income, the marginal utility per dollar's worth of one is equal to the marginal utility per dollar's worth of every other good or service.

To establish the consumer's demand curve for any one good, we vary its price, holding constant the prices of other goods, the consumer's income, and tastes and preferences as shown by the individual's utility schedules or curves. At each of the prices the consumer maximizes satisfaction, thus determining the quantity that will be taken at each price. The resulting price-quantity combinations form the consumer's demand schedule and can be plotted as that person's demand curve.

Voluntary exchange of goods among individuals increases the welfare of both parties to the exchange. Incentives for voluntary exchange occur wherever the ratios of the marginal utilities of goods for one consumer differ from the corresponding ratios for another. The condition for simultaneous equilibrium for all consumers is that the ratios of marginal utilities of all goods be the same for all individuals.

Suggested readings

Boulding, Kenneth E., *Economic Analysis,* 4th ed., Vol. 1. New York: Harper & Row, Publishers, Inc. 1966. Chap. 24.

Marshall, Alfred, *Principles of Economics,* 8th ed. London: Macmillan & Co., Ltd., 1920. Bk. III, Chaps. V–VI.

Stigler, George J., "The Development of Utility Theory, I." *The Journal of Political Economy,* Vol. LVIII (August 1950), pp. 307–324.

Questions and exercises

1. Tom Jones has an income of $50 per day, which he spends on food and clothing. His total utility schedules for each are listed below. The price of food is $2 per pound, and the price of clothing is $4 per yard.

Food		Clothing	
Pounds	TU_f	Yards	TU_c
1	50	1	120
2	95	2	230
3	135	3	330
4	170	4	420
5	200	5	500
6	225	6	570
7	245	7	630
8	260	8	680
9	270	9	720
10	275	10	750

   a. How much of each should he purchase to maximize satisfaction? Why?

   b. What will happen to his satisfaction level if he transfers a dollar from food to clothing?

   c. If a dollar is added to his income, on which item should he spend it? Why?

   d. If the price of food rises to $3 and his income remains at $50, how should he allocate it between food and clothing?

2. If the marginal utility of a person's income decreases as the person's income increases, would you expect that the individual would be willing to make a bet in which the chance of winning $100 is exactly the same as the chance of losing $100? Why or why not?

3. Suppose a consumer can allocate income among any number of goods and services. Does it make sense for the consumer to purchase that

quantity of any one good that will maximize her total utility for that good?

4. Evaluate this quotation: "The observation that the marginal rate of substitution between any two goods is ordinarily decreasing for a consumer rests on the older observation that the marginal utilities of the goods to the consumer are decreasing."

5. Suppose that two children of primary school age engage in voluntary exchange—one trades a sack of marbles to the other for a pocket knife. Explain the effects of the trade on the welfare of the community.

6. A 1913 Liberty nickel sells for over $50,000 while a nickel of recent mintage is worth only five cents. Only five such 1913 nickels were minted. Explain the difference in price. What can you say about the total utility of 1913 nickels as compared with that of nickels currently in circulation? What about the comparative marginal utilities?

Chapter 7

Chapter contents

Pure competition	**The demand curve**	
	Influence of the firm on demand, price, and output	
Pure monopoly	**The demand curve**	
	Influence of the firm on demand, price, and output	
Oligopoly	**The demand curve**	
	Influence of the firm on demand, price, and output	
Monopolistic competition	**The demand curve**	
	Influence of the firm on demand, price, and output	
Summary	**Suggested readings**	
	Questions and exercises	

Key concepts

Demand curve facing the firm
Pure competition
Infinite elasticity of demand
Pure monopoly
Cross elasticity of demand
Oligopoly
Pure oligopoly
Differentiated oligopoly
Interdependence of firms
Monopolistic competition
Elastic demand

Market classifications and demand as viewed by the seller

Three demand perspectives are important in microeconomics. First, demand can be viewed from the perspective of the individual consumer—the *individual consumer's demand curve* for the product. Second, individual consumer demand curves for a product can be aggregated into the *market demand curve* for it. Third, we must consider how demand looks to the individual seller of a product. It is this *demand curve faced by the firm* that we consider in this chapter. The other two were developed in Chapter 5.

No special definition of a firm is necessary at this point. It is an individual business concern; it may be a single proprietorship, a partnership, or a corporation. To simplify exposition, we shall assume that it produces one product only.

The demand curve faced by a firm for its product *shows the amounts that it can sell at different possible prices, other things being equal;* and this curve could appropriately be called a *sales curve*. Its nature depends on the type of market in which the firm sells. Selling markets are usually classified into four different types based on (1) the importance of individual firms in relation to the entire market in which they sell and (2) whether or not the products sold in a particular market are homogeneous. The market types are (1) pure competition, (2) pure monopoly, (3) oligopoly, and (4) monopolistic competition. Markets of the real world do not always fall neatly into one classification or another; they may be a mixture of two or more. However, it is useful in establishing a frame of reference to analyze the demand curve faced by the firm in each of the four theoretical or pure classifications. Detailed analysis of pricing and output under each will follow in Chapters 10–13.

Pure competition

The conditions necessary for pure competition to exist in a market were outlined in Chapter 3. In *pure competition* there are many firms selling the identical product with no one firm large enough relative to the entire market to influence the market price. If one firm drops out of the market, supply is

not decreased enough to cause the price to increase perceptibly. Neither is
it feasible for one firm to expand output enough to cause any perceptible
decrease in market price. No single seller believes that it affects or is
affected by other sellers in the market. No rivalries arise. There will be no
reactions of other firms to actions taken by any one firm. Relationships
among firms will be impersonal.

The demand curve

In pure competition the demand curve facing the firm is horizontal at the
prevailing market or equilibrium price. At any price above the prevailing
market price it can sell nothing. Since all firms of the industry sell the
identical product, consumers will turn to firms charging the market price if
one firm raises its selling price above that level. The proportion of the total
market filled by one seller is so small that the firm can dispose of its entire
output at the prevailing market price; hence, there is no necessity for lowering the price below that of the other sellers. Any firm attempting to do so
will find itself swamped with buyers who promptly bid it back to the equilibrium level.

A firm producing potatoes faces this sort of demand curve. When it hauls
its potatoes to market, it receives the going market price. On the one hand,
if it asks for more than the market price and sticks to its request, it will
undoubtedly haul the potatoes home again. On the other hand, no amount
of potatoes that it alone can bring to market will drive the price down. It can
sell all it desires to sell at the going market price.

Diagrammatically, the nature of the demand curve faced by the firm is
illustrated by *dd* on the left-hand side of Figure 7–1. The market demand
curve and the market supply curve are *DD* and *SS*, respectively. The
market price is *p;* it determines the horizontal *infinitely elastic* demand
curve faced by the firm. The price axes of the two diagrams are identical;
however, quantity measurements of the market diagram are compressed
considerably as compared with those of the firm diagram. For example, if x_0
measures 10 units of X for the firm, suppose that X_0 measures 10,000 units
of X for the total market.

In reality the demand curve faced by the firm is an infinitesimal segment
of the market demand curve in the neighborhood of quantity X stretched
out over the firm diagram. Any one firm can be thought of as supplying the
last small portion of quantity X. Stretching this small segment out over the
firm diagram makes the demand curve faced by the firm appear to be
horizontal.

Influence of the firm on demand, price, and output

Any forces that change market demand or market supply will change the
market price of the product and, consequently, the demand curve faced by

Figure 7–1   The demand curve facing the firm—pure competition

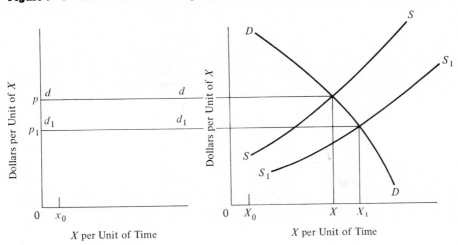

the firm. The firm by itself can do nothing about either the demand curve it faces or the market price. It must accept both as given data. If market supply increases to S_1S_1, the market price decreases to p_1; and the demand curve faced by the firm shifts downward to d_1d_1. Any such change is beyond the control of the individual firm. The firm can only adjust its output, and it will gear its output to the prevailing market price.

Pure monopoly

A market situation in which a single firm sells a product for which there are no good substitutes is called *pure monopoly*. The firm has the market for the product all to itself. There are no similar products whose price or sales will influence the monopolist's price or sales perceptibly, and vice versa. Cross elasticity of demand between the monopolist's product and other products will either be zero or small enough to be neglected by all firms in the economy. The monopolistic firm does not believe that its actions will evoke retaliation of any kind from firms in other industries. Similarly, the monopolist does not consider actions taken by firms in other industries to be of sufficient importance to warrant taking them into account. The monopolist *is* the industry from the selling point of view. A case in point is the supplier of telephone service to a particular community.

The demand curve

The market demand curve for the product is also the demand curve faced by the monopolist. Figure 7–2 shows the market demand curve for the

Figure 7–2   The demand curve facing the firm—pure monopoly

product that is produced and sold by a monopolist. It shows the different quantities that buyers will take off the market at all possible prices. Since the monopolist is the only seller of the product, it is possible to sell at different possible prices exactly the amounts that buyers will take at those prices.

Influence of the firm on demand, price, and output

The monopolist is able to exert some influence on the price, output, and demand for its product. The market demand curve delineates the limits of the monopolist's market. Faced by a given demand curve, the firm can increase sales if it is willing to lower its price, or it can increase its price if it is willing to restrict its sales volume. Additionally, the firm may be able to affect the demand curve itself through sales promotion activities of various kinds. The firm may be able to induce more people to want its product, thus increasing demand; and the firm may be able to make demand less elastic if it can convince enough people that they cannot afford to be without the product. It follows that if the monopolist is able to increase demand, it can increase sales to some extent without lowering the price or, alternatively, it can increase the price to some extent without restricting its sales volume.

Oligopoly

An *oligopolistic* industry is one in which the number of sellers is small enough for the activities of a single seller to affect other firms and for the activities of other firms to affect that firm in turn. Changes in the output and the price charged by one firm will affect the amounts that other sellers can sell and the prices that they can charge. Hence, other firms will react in one way or another to price-output changes on the part of a single firm. Individual sellers are *interdependent*—not independent as they are under pure competition or pure monopoly.

Oligopolistic industries are frequently classified as (1) *differentiated* or (2) *pure*. A differentiated oligopolistic industry is one in which the firms produce and sell *differentiated products*. The products of all firms in the industry are very good substitutes for each other—they have high cross elasticities of demand—but the product of each firm has its own distinguishing characteristics. The differences may be real or fancied. They may consist of differences in quality and design, as is the case in the automobile industry; or they may consist merely of differences in brand names, as is the case in the sale of aspirin tablets.

A pure oligopolistic industry is one in which the firms all produce an identical product. Purchasers have no cause for preferring the product of one firm to that of another on any basis except price. Examples of industries approaching the pure oligopoly category are the cement, aluminum, and steel industries.

The demand curve

There is no typical demand situation facing an oligopolistic firm. The interdependence of sellers in an oligopolistic market makes the determination of the single seller's demand curve difficult. In some situations the demand curve faced by the firm is indeterminate. In others it can be located with some degree of accuracy.

The oligopolistic seller's demand curve will be indeterminate when the firm cannot predict what the reactions of its rivals will be to price and output changes on its part. The output that the one firm can sell if it changes its price depends on the manner in which other firms react to this price change.

The range of possible reactions is fairly broad. Rivals may just meet the price change; they may change price in the same direction but by less than the change of the original seller; they may exceed the price change; they may improve the quality of their products; they may engage in extensive advertising campaigns; or they may react in other ways. Inability of the individual seller to predict which reactions will occur and in what degree they will occur amounts to inability to determine the demand curve that particular firm faces.

When the single seller knows with some accuracy how its rivals will react to price changes on its part, the demand curve the firm faces becomes correspondingly more determinate. If reliable judgments with regard to the probable effect on rivals' reactions to its own sales can be formed, the firm can take these into account. However, each different reaction by each different rival will result in different quantities that the single seller can market. Consequently, ascertaining the effects of rivals' reactions to the quantities that can be sold at different prices is at best a complex process for the individual firm. A few examples should improve our grasp of the problems involved.

Suppose that there are two producers in a particular industry and that price changes by either will be just matched by the other. Suppose also that the producers are of approximately equal size and prestige and produce virtually identical products. The market demand curve is DD in Figure 7–3.

Figure 7– 3   The demand curve facing the firm—oligopoly

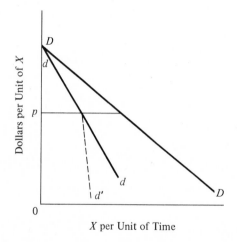

If each firm knows that the other will just match its price changes, at any given price each will expect to get approximately half the market. Each will face a fairly determinate demand curve dd for its output, and such a demand curve will lie about halfway between DD and the price axis.

Suppose next that one producer does not behave in the way just described. With an initial price of p suppose that when firm A cuts the price, firm B cuts the price still further. Firm B will take some of firm A's customers away. The demand curve faced by firm A will not then follow dd but will follow some path such as the broken line d'. Firm A, since its rival reacts by cutting its price still more, will lose a part of its share of the market when it cuts its price. Firm A will not take this situation lying down. It may undercut B's price again, and the situation may develop into a price war—an indeterminate situation.

Suppose that the producers in a given oligopolistic industry form a cartel.

Under the cartel arrangement the firms of the industry act as a single unit, each having some voice in the setting of price, output, and other industry policies. When all firms act as a unit, the amount that one firm can sell at different possible prices becomes irrelevant. The cartel is concerned with how much the industry as a whole can sell at different possible prices. Thus, the cartel is in much the same position as a pure monopolist is, and it is the cartel that faces the market demand curve. The demand curve faced by a single firm fails to be a consideration.

These examples provide a small sample of the possible demand situations faced by an oligopolistic seller. Additional illustrations will be presented in Chapter 12. Our goal at this point is to show that when the demand curve faced by one seller is determinate, the curve's position and its shape will depend on what the reactions of rivals will be to price changes on the part of the single firm.

Influence of the firm on demand, price, and output

Generally, the oligopolistic firm is able to influence in some degree the demand curve faced by it, its price, and its output. Through sales promotion efforts the firm may be able to shift the demand curve for what it sells to the right—partly by increasing consumer demand for this type of product, but mostly by inducing consumers to desert its rivals and buy its brand. The firm may be able to accomplish this through advertising or through design and quality changes, provided such changes give its brand more customer appeal. Rivals will not be sitting idly by in such cases and may retaliate by vigorous campaigns of their own. The firms with the most successful campaigns will be the ones that succeed in increasing demand for their brands.

Whether the firm does or does not face a determinate demand curve, it knows that in general its demand curve slopes downward to the right. To increase sales, it must usually lower price—unless the sales increase is made possible by a shift to the right of the demand curve. Higher prices can be obtained at the expense of sales, unless they are obtained through or in conjunction with increases in demand. Generally, the demand curve faced by an individual oligopolist will be fairly elastic because of the existence of good substitutes produced by other firms in the industry. Elasticity of demand, however, as well as the position of the demand curve, will depend on rivals' reactions to the price and output changes of the single seller.

Monopolistic competition

Monopolistic competition is a market situation in which there are many sellers of a particular product, but the product of each seller is in some way differentiated, in the minds of consumers, from the product of every other seller. As in pure competition there are enough sellers, and each is small enough relative to the entire market so that the activities of one will have no effects on the others. Relationships among firms are impersonal. Product differentiation may take the form of brand names, trademarks, quality difference, or differences in conveniences or services offered to consumers. The products are good substitutes for each other—their cross-elasticities are high. Examples of industries approaching monopolistic competition include the women's hosiery industry, various textile products, and service trades in large cities.

The demand curve

The shape of the demand curve faced by the firm under monopolistic competition stems from product differentiation. The influence of product differentiation can be seen readily if at first we assume its absence. This assumption leaves us with the case of pure competition and a horizontal demand curve such as dd in Figure 7–4. Suppose that we introduce the concept of product differentiation and observe how dd is affected. When products are differentiated, consumers become more or less attached to particular brand names. At any given price for commodity X some consumers will be on the margin of switching to other brands, while others are attached to X at that price with varying degrees of tightness.

Figure 7–4   The demand curve facing the firm—monopolistic competition

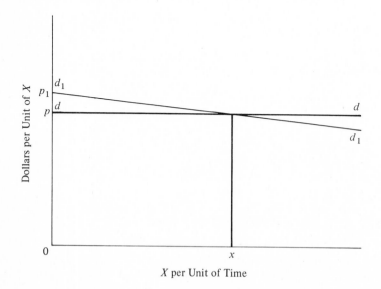

Suppose that for the monopolistic competitor quantity x will be taken at price p. If the firm raises the price, those consumers on the verge of switching to other brands will make the switch, since the other brands are now relatively lower in price. The higher the firm raises its price, the more customers it will lose to relatively lower-priced brands. Since other brands will usually be very good substitutes for that of the firm under consideration, the rise in price necessary for the firm to lose all its customers (pp_1) will not be large. For price increases above p the demand curve faced by the firm will be the lighter line in the diagram. Similarly, if the firm lowers the price below p, it will pick up marginal customers of other sellers, since its price is now relatively lower as compared with other firms' prices. It will not have to lower price much to pick up all the additional customers it can handle. Thus, for decreases in price below p the lighter line in the diagram shows the demand curve faced by the one firm. The entire demand curve faced by the monopolistic competitor is one such as d_1d_1.

It may be thought that price reductions by one firm that attract customers away from the other firms in the industry will evoke some kind of retaliatory action on the part of the other firms, as in the case of oligopoly. Such is not the case, however, because there are many firms in a monopolistically competitive industry. The firm that reduces its price will attract so few customers from each of the others that the other firms will not notice or feel the loss. Nevertheless, for the one firm the total increase in customers will be substantial.

Likewise, it may seem that the price increases by one firm that drive customers away would increase demand for the products of the other firms. The customers shifting to other firms, however, will be widely scattered among those firms. Not enough will go to any other single firm to cause any perceptible increase in demand for its product, even though the loss of customers to the price-raising firm is substantial.

Influence of the firm on demand, price, and output

The individual firm in a monopolistically competitive industry may be able to influence demand for its own product to some perceptible degree through advertising. However, the existence of many good substitutes will preclude much success in this direction.

The firm is subjected to highly competitive forces, yet it is to a small extent a sort of monopolist since it has some discretion in setting price and output. However, if the firm raises price very much, it loses all its customers, and it does not have to lower price very far to secure all the customers it can handle. Within that limited price range the firm has price-setting discretion. Outside that price range it is subject to competitive forces. The demand curve faced by a firm under monopolistic competition will be highly elastic throughout its relevant range. The cause is not hard to find.

The products of all firms in the industry, even though differentiated, are very good substitutes for each other.

Summary

Analysis of the demand situation facing the individual business firm is organized around four market classifications. The conditions of demand facing the individual firm differ from classification to classification, these differences stemming from two sources: (1) the importance of the individual firm in the market in which it sells and (2) product differentiation or product homogeneity.

Pure competition stands at one extreme of the classification, and pure monopoly stands at the other. Purely competitive firms sell homogeneous products, and each is so small relative to the entire market that by itself it cannot influence market price. Hence, the demand curve faced by the firm is horizontal at the equilibrium market price. A monopolist firm is a single seller of a product not closely related to any other product. It faces the market demand curve for its product.

Oligopoly and monopolistic competition fill the gap between these two extremes. Monopolistic competition differs from pure competition in one respect only—products of different sellers are differentiated. This fact gives the monopolistic competitor a small amount of control over its price; however, each firm is so small relative to the entire market that by itself it cannot affect other firms in the industry. It faces a downward-sloping, highly elastic demand curve.

With regard to the number of firms in the industry, oligopoly lies between the extremes of pure competition and monopolistic competition on the one hand, and pure monopoly on the other. Its primary characteristic is that there are few enough firms in the industry for the activities of one firm to have repercussions on the price and sales of the other firms. Hence, rivalries develop under oligopoly. The demand curve faced by a single seller depends on what the reactions of rivals will be to market activities on the part of the one firm. If the reactions of rivals cannot be predicted, the demand curve faced by the firm cannot be determined.

Suggested readings

Fellner, William, *Modern Economic Analysis*. New York: McGraw-Hill, Inc., 1960. Chap. 17.

Machlup, Fritz, "Monopoly and Competition: A Classification of Market Positions." *American Economic Review,* Vol. XXVII (September 1937), pp. 445–451.

Questions and exercises

1. Draw and explain the demand curve facing an oligopolistic firm if other firms in the market will match any price decreases but will not follow any price increases by the firm. Is this a plausible situation? Why?

2. Evaluate the following statement: For an industry to be one of monopolistic competition it is not important that there be *actual differences* in the items sold by the various sellers; it is only necessary that consumers *think* that differences exist.

3. How would you classify firms that sell aspirin? Haircuts? Wheat? Oil? Automobiles? Steel? Panty hose? In each case state the reasons for your classification.

4. In which of the four market classifications would you expect firms to advertise their products? Why? Do you think such advertising is in the best interests of consumers? Explain.

5. How would you classify the General Store in Dodge City in 1900?

Part 3   The foundations of costs and supply

We do for costs of production in Part 3 what we did for
demand in Part 2. We examine the individual firm—its
production possibilities, its motivations, and its behavior—
to see what determines its costs of producing goods and
services. These costs in turn form the basis of supply.

   The type of selling market in which the firm operates is
not important in Part 3. The principles of production and the
cost curves of the firm do not depend on the type of market
in which it sells its product. Market structure becomes
an important consideration again in Part 4.

Chapter 8

Chapter contents

The production function
- **The concept**
- **The production surface**
- Isoquants
- Isoquant characteristics
- **Product curves**

The law of diminishing returns

Product curves and technical efficiency
- **The three stages for labor**
- **The three stages for capital**
- The product schedules
- The product curves
- **Stage II combinations**
- **A generalized Stage II**
- **The least cost combination**

Production possibilities for the economy
- **Resource allocation among products**
- **Transformation curves**

Natural gas versus coal in power generation

Summary
- **Suggested readings**
- **Questions and exercises**

Key concepts

Production function
Production surface
Isoquants
Marginal rate of technical substitution
Marginal physical product of a resource
Law of diminishing returns
Technical efficiency
Linearly homogeneous production functions
Ridge lines
Isocosts
Least-cost resource combination
Expansion path
Efficient allocation of resources
Transformation curve

The principles of production

In order to understand costs and supply, one must first understand the principles of production. The principles of production in microeconomic theory extend beyond costs and supply; they also provide the basis of resource pricing and employment, resource allocation, and product distribution. Production theory, like the theory of consumer behavior, is basically a theory of choice among alternatives. The key economic unit is the individual firm rather than the individual consumer. Whereas the individual consumer attempts to maximize satisfaction by the way in which he or she spends income on consumer goods, the individual firm attempts to maximize the product output it can obtain with any given cost outlay by the way in which it secures and combines resource inputs. A fundamental difference between the two theories is that the purchasing power of the consumer is more or less fixed, while the possible outlays of the firm are variable. This difference will not be of much concern in the present chapter, but it will be important later on.

In this chapter the concept of a firm's production function is first explained, and then the law of diminishing returns is considered. Finally, resource product curves and the comparative efficiencies of different resource combinations are analyzed.

The production function

The concept

The term *production function* refers to the physical relationships between a firm's inputs of resources and its output of goods or services per unit of time, leaving prices aside. It can be expressed in general mathematical terms as

$$x = f(a, b, c). \tag{8.1}$$

The firm's output is represented by x, and its inputs are represented by a, b, and c. The equation can be expanded readily to include as many different resources as are used in the production of any given good. It furnishes a convenient way of relating product output to resource inputs.

Firms can usually vary the proportions in which resources are combined in production processes. This flexibility brings about several possible types of relations among inputs, among inputs and outputs, and among outputs. Where inputs can be substituted for one another in the production of a product, there will be a number of alternative sets of input quantities that will produce a given level of product output, and the firm must make choices among them. By increasing or decreasing the quantities of all resource inputs used, the firm can increase or decrease its output level. It can also increase or decrease output within limits by increasing or decreasing the quantity used of one or more resource inputs, holding the quantities of other resource inputs constant. And, given the bundle of resources available to it, a firm that produces more than one product can increase its output level of one product by reducing its output level of another, transferring the resources thus released to the production of the first.

The input-input, input-output, and output-output relationships that characterize a firm's production function depend on the techniques of production used. Of the range of techniques available, we assume that the firm will use those that are most efficient—that is, the ones that will provide the greatest value of output for a given value of input. Generally speaking, an improvement in techniques will increase the output that can be produced from given quantities of resources.

The production surface

In many ways a firm's production function is analogous to the preference function or the utility function of an individual consumer, although one must be careful not to confuse the two. A firm uses resource inputs to generate product or service outputs. Usually these quantities have cardinal properties—the product output can be measured, added, and, in most cases, seen. An individual consumer purchases and uses products and services to generate a much more nebulous kind of output—satisfaction—which cannot be measured, added, or seen. It has ordinal properties but not cardinal properties.

Suppose, then, that a firm uses two resource inputs, A and B, to obtain outputs of product X. In the three-dimensional diagram of Figure 8–1(a) the coordinates in the horizontal AB plane show input combinations. Product output associated with each input combination is measured vertically above the plane. If no resource A is used, total product curve TP_b^0 is generated by varying the quantity of resource B used. An output of $b_3E_3(= 0x_3)$ is produced with b_3 of B alone. Similarly, if no resource B is used, TP_a^0 is generated by varying the quantity of resource A used. With a_3 of A the output level is $a_3F_3(= 0x_3)$. A combination of b_1 of B and a_1 of A yields an

Figure 8–1   A production surface and its isoquants

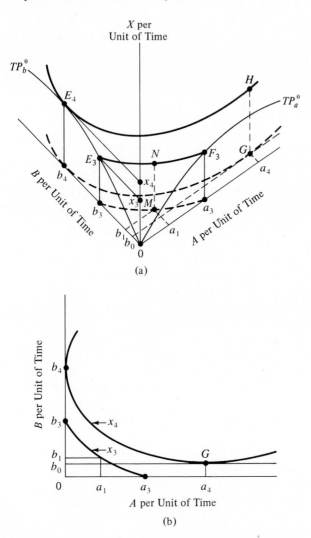

(a)

(b)

output level of $MN = 0x_3$. The whole range of input combinations generates an inverted bowl-shaped production surface, showing the output associated with every possible input combination.

Isoquants   Contour lines can be drawn around the production surface of
Figure 8–1(a) at each possible level of output. All points on a given contour
line are equidistant from the AB plane; that is, any one contour line represents a constant or given level of production. These contour lines can be

projected downward onto the AB plane, forming a set of *isoquants,* or product indifference curves. Any one isoquant, say b_3a_3 in Figure 8–1, shows the different combinations of A and B with which the firm can obtain a product output of x_3. If the production surface has an inverted bowl shape, higher contour lines like E_4H, when projected to the AB plane, become isoquants like b_4G lying farther from the origin of the diagram. A complete set of isoquants for the firm is called its isoquant map.[1]

Isoquant characteristics   The general characteristics of isoquants are the same as those of indifference curves. First, they slope downward to the right for those combinations of resources that firms will want to use. Second, they do not intersect. Third, they are convex to the origin of the diagram.

Isoquants slope downward to the right for the resources that can be substituted for one another in the production process. For example, usually there are possibilities of substitutions between capital resources and labor resources used. If less of one is used, more of the other must be used to compensate for the decrease in the first, if the level of output is to remain constant. Exceptions will occur where resources cannot be substituted for one another in production processes.[2] There are no substitutes for raw milk as an input in the production of the pasteurized product. In other cases, in the short run, fixed proportions of resources may be required.

An intersection of isoquants is not logical. An intersection point would mean that a single combination of resources produces two different maximum outputs, thereby implying that an increase in the level of output can be accomplished with no increase in the amount of any resource used. To the right of the intersection point the implication is that by decreasing the quantities of all resources used, product output can be increased. Thus, isoquant intersections are economic nonsense.

Convexity to the origin reflects the fact that different resources are not ordinarily perfect substitutes. Consider labor and capital used in digging a ditch of a certain length, width, and depth. Within limits they can be substituted for each other. But the more labor and the less capital used to dig the ditch, the more difficult it becomes to substitute additional labor for capital.

---

[1] Let the production function be

$$x = f(a, b),$$

in which x is the quantity produced of the good or service and a and b are quantities of resource inputs. An isoquant is the locus of all combinations of resources A and B that yield a given output level; that is,

$$x_3 = f(a, b)$$

defines an isoquant. A family of isoquants, or an isoquant map, is described by treating x as a parameter and assigning different values to it.

[2] For a discussion of irregularly shaped isoquants, see Sidney Weintraub, *Intermediate Price Theory* (Philadelphia: Chilton Company, 1964), pp. 34, 40–42.

Additional units of labor will just compensate for smaller and smaller amounts of capital given up. The same reasoning applies to other resources.

The more of resource A and the less of resource B the firm uses to produce a constant amount of product X, the more difficult it becomes to substitute additional units of A for B; that is, additional units of A will just compensate for smaller and smaller amounts of B given up. This principle is called the principle of *diminishing marginal rate of technical substitution of A for B* ($MRTS_{ab}$). The $MRTS_{ab}$ is measured at any point on an isoquant by the slope of the isoquant at that point. It is defined as the amount of B lost that will be just compensated for by an additional unit of A with no change in product output occurring.

Product curves

Product schedules and product curves for either resource A or resource B can be derived from the firm's system of isoquants. With reference to Figure 8–2, suppose that the firm considers the employment of alternative

Figure 8–2 · Effects on total product of quantity changes in one resource

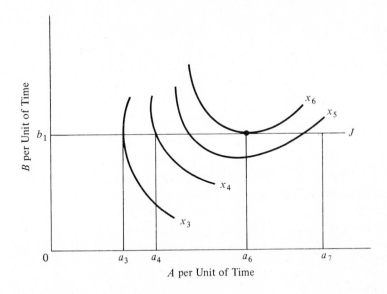

quantities of A per unit of time with a fixed amount b_1 of B. A movement to the right along the line b_1J reflects the use of larger quantities of A. Each isoquant intersected by line b_1J shows the product output obtained with each quantity of A. Thus, when a_4 of A is used with b_1 of B, total product will be x_4. The greater the amount of A used, the greater will be the total product until the firm is using a_6 of the resource. With greater quantities of A, line b_1J intersects lower and lower isoquants, showing that the total product decreases. Thus, the firm would never use more than a_6 of A with b_1 of B, even if A were free. The total product curve for larger and larger quantities of A used with the fixed amount of B increases, reaches a maximum at a_6 of A, and then decreases. This curve is shown in Figure 8–3.

Figure 8–3   Total product curve for one resource

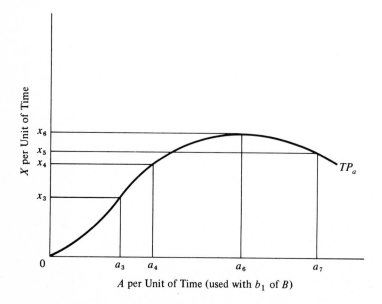

A per Unit of Time (used with b_1 of B)

The average product and marginal physical product schedules or curves of a resource are derived from its total product schedule or curve. Suppose that a firm conducts a series of experiments to determine the total product output it can get from various quantities of labor per unit of time used with a unit of capital. The results are listed in column (3) of Table 8–1 as the *total product* of labor. As the amount of labor is increased up to 7 units, output increases. At 7 and 8 units of labor the maximum total product that a unit of capital will produce is obtained.

The *average product* of labor, computed from columns (2) and (3), is the total product of labor at each level of employment divided by that quantity of labor. Note that in column (4) average product rises as the quantity of labor is increased, reaches a maximum at 3 and 4 units of labor per unit of capital, and then decreases as the employment of labor is increased further.

The change in total product per unit change in the quantity of labor employed, holding the quantity of capital constant, is called the *marginal physical product* of labor. In Table 8–1 an increase in the employment of labor from zero to 1 unit increases total product from zero to 3; thus, the

Table 8–1   Product schedules for labor

(1) Capital	(2) Labor	(3) Total Product (Labor)	(4) Average Product (Labor)	(5) Marginal Physical Product (Labor)	
1	1	3	3	3	
1	2	7	$3^1/_2$	4	Stage I
1	3	12	4	5	
1	4	16	4	4	
1	5	19	$3^4/_5$	3	Stage II
1	6	21	$3^1/_2$	2	
1	7	22	$3^1/_7$	1	
1	8	22	$2^3/_4$	0	
1	9	21	$2^1/_3$	−1	Stage III
1	10	15	$1^1/_2$	−6	

marginal physical product of labor at the 1-unit level of employment is 3 units of product. Two units of labor employed rather than 1 unit increase total product to 7 units, and the marginal physical product of labor at the 2-unit level of employment is 4 units of product. The rest of column (5) is computed in a similar fashion.

The total, average, and marginal product concepts are shown graphically in Figure 8–4. The vertical axis of Figure 8–4(a) measures product produced per unit of capital (Product/Capital); and the horizontal axis measures labor used per unit of capital (Labor/Capital). The total product curve (TP_l) is in all essential respects like that of Figure 8–3.[3] When l_1 units of labor are used on the unit of capital, total product reaches a maximum. In the illustration additional units of labor per unit of capital cause total product to decrease.

---

[3] The total product curve of Figure 8–4 begins at the origin of the diagram, but it is not necessary that it do so. For some resources not absolutely essential in the production of the product, it may begin above the origin—cottonseed meal fed to cows to increase milk production is a case in point. In other cases no product may be obtained until several units of the variable resource are applied to the fixed complex of other resources. For example, one worker in a steel mill will produce nothing. Two workers can do no better. A certain minimum complement of labor is necessary before any production can be obtained. In this case the total product curve of labor begins to the right of the origin.

The average product curve for labor (AP_l) of Figure 8–4(b) is derived from the total product curve (TP_l) of Figure 8–4(a). The vertical axis of Figure 8–4(b) measures product per unit of labor (Product/Labor). The horizontal axis is the same as that of Figure 8–4(a). Since average product is total product divided by the number of units of labor used, average product in Figure 8–4(a) at l' units of labor is $l'A'/0l'$, which measures the slope of the line $0A'$—this ratio is plotted in Figure 8–4(b). As the quantity of labor

Figure 8–4   Product curves for labor

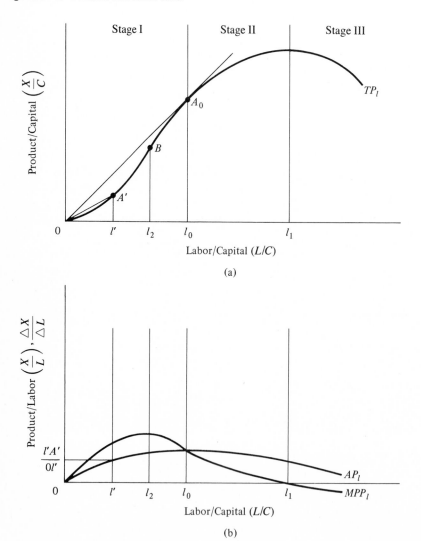

(a)

(b)

is increased from zero to l_0, in Figure 8–4(a), the slopes of the corresponding $0A$ lines increase; that is, the average product of labor increases. At l_0 units of labor the slope of line $0A_0$ is greater than that of any other $0A$ line drawn from the origin to the total product curve. Thus, the average product of labor is maximum at this point. Beyond l_0 units of labor the average product decreases, but it remains positive as long as total product is positive. The slopes of the $0A$ lines corresponding to the various quantities of labor in Figure 8–4(a) are plotted as the AP_l curve in Figure 8–4(b).

The slope of the total product curve at any given quantity of labor measures the marginal physical product of labor at that point. Both the slope of TP_l and the marginal physical product of labor (MPP_l) are defined as the change in total product per unit change in the quantity of labor used. Marginal physical product reaches a maximum at point B, where the total product curve turns from concave upward to concave downward. At quantity l_1 of labor the total product is maximum; hence, marginal physical product is zero. Beyond l_1 additional units of labor cause the total product to decrease, meaning that the marginal physical product is negative.[4] The slopes of TP_l at the various quantities of labor in Figure 8–4(a) are plotted as MPP_l in Figure 8–4(b).

An additional guide to the proper location of the marginal physical product curve is its relation to the average product curve. When average product is increasing, marginal physical product is greater than average product. When average product is maximum, marginal physical product equals average product. When average product is decreasing, marginal physical product is less than average product.[5] These relationships are verified by columns (4) and (5) of Table 8–1.

---

[4] Let the production function be

$$x = g(k, l).$$

Total product of labor can be expressed as

$$TP_l = x = g(\bar{k}, l) = f(l),$$

in which $\bar{k}$ represents a fixed amount of capital.

The average product of labor becomes

$$AP_l = \frac{TP_l}{l} = \frac{f(l)}{l},$$

and

$$MPP_l = \frac{dTP_l}{dl} = f'(l).$$

[5] To illustrate these relationships, consider a succession of men entering a room, each taller than the one who preceded him. As each man enters, the average height of the men in the room increases; however, except for the first man, average height will be less than that of the man currently entering. The height of each man as he enters is marginal height and is analogous to marginal physical product. Average height is analogous to average product. Thus, for average product (height) to be increasing, marginal physical product (height) must exceed the average.

Suppose that additional men enter, each successively shorter than the one preceding him and all shorter than the average height before they entered. Average height will decrease but will not be as low

The law of diminishing returns

The product schedules of Table 8–1 and the product curves of Figure 8–4 illustrate the celebrated *law of diminishing returns,* which describes the direction and the rate of change that the firm's output takes when the input of only one resource is varied. It states that *if the input of one resource is increased by equal increments per unit of time while the inputs of other resources are held constant, total product output will increase; but beyond some point the resulting output increases will become smaller and smaller.*[6] If the increases in the variable resource are carried far enough, total product will reach a maximum and may then decrease. The law is consistent with observations that there are limits to the output that can be obtained by increasing the quantity of a single resource applied to constant quantities of other resources.

Diminishing returns may or may not occur for the first few one-unit increases in the variable resource used with the fixed quantities of other resources. It is possible for diminishing returns or diminishing increases in total product to occur for all such increments. This is frequently the case with the application of fertilizer to given complexes of seed, land, labor, and machinery.

But a stage of increasing returns may also characterize the initial increases in the variable resource before diminishing returns begin. An example of this situation is the amount of labor used to operate a factory of a given size. Smaller quantities of labor than that for which the factory is designed tend to operate inefficiently because of the multiplicity of jobs to

---

as marginal height. When average height is maximum, the height of the last man who entered must have been equal to average height, since he caused neither an increase nor a decrease in average height.

Mathematically, if AP_l is increasing, then

$$\frac{d\,(AP_l)}{dl} = \frac{d\left(\frac{f\,(l)}{l}\right)}{dl} > 0,$$

so

$$\frac{l \times f'\,(l) - f\,(l)}{l^2} > 0$$

or

$$f'\,(l) - \frac{f\,(l)}{l} > 0;$$

therefore,

$$f'\,(l) > \frac{f\,(l)}{l}\,;$$

that is, $MPP_l > AP_l$. Similarly, it can be shown that if AP_l is constant or if it is maximum, $MPP_l = AP_l$; and if AP_l is decreasing, $MPP_l < AP_l$.

[6] *The different quantities* of the variable resource refer to *alternative quantities* used with constant amounts of other resources, not to a chronological application of additional units.

be performed by each individual and because of time lost in changing from one job to another. Equal increments in labor used bring about successively greater increments in total product up to some point. In Table 8–1 through 3 units of labor, and in Figure 8–4 through l_2 units of labor, we show increasing returns.[7] Beyond these points increases in the quantity of labor used lead to diminishing returns.

Product curves and technical efficiency

The three product curves defined and described above show the *technical efficiency* of resources for various resource combinations that may be used in producing a product. The technical efficiency of any given resource is defined as the ratio of product output to the resource input; that is, it is the average product of the resource. The greater the product output per unit of resource input, the greater the technical efficiency of the resource is said to be.

Suppose that the production function of the firm shows *constant returns to size*. Changes of a given proportion in the quantities of all resources used will change product output in the same proportion. A fifty-percent increase in the quantities of all resources used to produce the product will result in a fifty-percent increase in the output of the firm. Doubling the quantities of all resource inputs will double the product output. Both capital and labor are completely divisible with respect to quantities used; and techniques of production are such that the same techniques will be used for any given ratio of labor to capital, regardless of the absolute amounts of resources used. The same techniques would be used if 2 units of labor work 1 unit of capital as are used if 1 unit of labor works ½ unit of capital or if 4 units of labor work 2 units of capital. A production function of this type is said to be *linearly homogeneous*.[8]

We are concerned with the *ratio* of the resources as we establish the firm's product curves; we are not really limited to 1 unit of capital or to a fixed amount of capital. We can think of the firm as using any amount of

---

[7] Whether or not we assume that diminishing returns occur at the outset is not important. Usually, for expository purposes we assume first increasing and then decreasing returns as the quantity of the variable resource is increased.

[8] The production function $x = g(k, l)$ is said to be homogeneous of degree n if

$$\lambda^n x = g(\lambda k, \lambda l).$$

It exhibits

1. constant returns to scale, or is linearly homogeneous, when $n = 1$
2. increasing returns to scale when $n > 1$
3. decreasing returns to scale when $n < 1$.

capital it wishes to use; but in establishing the product curves, we convert our observations into terms of product obtainable from 1 unit of the capital resource. For example, if 10 units of labor working 2 units of capital produce 38 units of product per unit of time, for purposes of establishing the product curves we would convert the data to an equivalent of 1 unit of capital—that is, 5 units of labor working 1 unit of capital produce an output of 19 units of product per unit of time.[9] An increase in the quantity of capital used, with the quantity of labor being held constant, is equivalent to a decrease in the quantity of labor, with the quantity of capital being held constant, when we think in terms of the ratio used of the two resources.

---

[9] If the production function of Footnote 8 is linearly homogeneous, it takes the form

$$\lambda x = g(\lambda k, \lambda l),$$

which exhibits the following properties:

1. AP_l and AP_k are functions of the *ratio* of capital to labor.
   Letting

   $$\lambda = \frac{1}{l} \, ,$$

   then

   $$\frac{1}{l} x = g\left(\frac{1}{l} k, \frac{1}{l} l\right) = g\left(\frac{k}{l}, 1\right) = h\left(\frac{k}{l}\right);$$

   that is,

   $$AP_l = h\left(\frac{k}{l}\right) = h(r) \text{ where } r = \frac{k}{l}$$

   and

   $$AP_k = \frac{x}{k} = \frac{x}{l} \times \frac{l}{k} = AP_l \times \frac{1}{r} = \frac{h(r)}{r} \, .$$

   Thus, both AP_l and AP_k are functions of the capital-labor ratio only. They are constant for all changes in K and L in equal proportions, since such changes do not alter the k/l ratio.

2. The MPP_k and MPP_l are also functions of the k/l ratio, only. Since

   $$AP_l = \frac{x}{l} = h(r),$$

   then

   $$x = l \times h(r).$$

   So

   $$MPP_l = \frac{\delta x}{\delta l} = h(r) + l \frac{dh(r)}{dr} \times \frac{\delta r}{\delta l} = h(r) + l \times h'(r) \times \frac{-k}{l^2}$$

   $$= h(r) - \frac{k}{l} \times h'(r) = h(r) - r \times h'(r).$$

   Also,

   $$MPP_k = \frac{\delta x}{\delta k} = l \frac{\delta h(r)}{\delta k} = l \frac{dh(r)}{dr} \times \frac{\delta r}{\delta k} = l \times h'(r) \left(\frac{1}{l}\right) = h'(r).$$

The three stages for labor

The product schedules of Table 8–1 and the product curves of Figure 8–4 can be divided into three stages. In each of the three stages the average product curve and the total product curve of labor provide information with regard to how efficiently the resources are used for various labor-capital ratios. As the ratio of labor to capital is increased—that is, as more and more labor per unit of capital is used—the average product curve provides information regarding the amount of product obtained per unit of labor for the various ratios. The total product curve provides information regarding the amount of product obtained per unit of capital.

Stage I is characterized by increases in the average product of labor as more labor per unit of capital is used. These increases mean that the technical efficiency of labor—the product per worker—increases. The total product obtained per unit of capital as larger quantities of labor are applied to it also increases in Stage I. The increases in total product show us that the technical efficiency of capital also increases in Stage I. Thus, increases in the quantity of labor applied to a unit of capital in Stage I increase the technical efficiency with which *both* labor and capital are utilized.

Stage II is characterized by decreasing average product and decreasing marginal physical product of labor. But the marginal physical product is positive since total product continues to increase. In Stage II, as larger quantities of labor per unit of capital are used, the technical efficiency of labor—product per worker—decreases. However, the technical efficiency of capital—product per unit of capital—continues to increase.

In Stage III the application of larger quantities of labor to a unit of capital decreases the average product of labor still more. Additionally, the marginal physical product of labor is negative and total product is decreasing. The efficiency of labor and the efficiency of capital both decrease when the firm pushes into Stage III combinations.

In looking over the three stages we note two things: (1) the combination of labor and capital that leads to maximum technical efficiency of labor lies at the boundary line between Stages I and II and (2) the combination of labor and capital leading to maximum technical efficiency of capital is the one at the boundary line between Stages II and III.

The three stages for capital

If the production function of the firm is linearly homogeneous, we can rework Table 8–1 and Figure 8–4, determining the product schedules and product curves for alternative quantities of capital applied to one unit of labor. We can show that Stage I for labor is Stage III for capital, that Stage III for labor is Stage I for capital, and that Stage II for labor is also Stage II for capital.

To facilitate comparison of the product curves of labor with those of capital, it will be convenient to set up the product schedules of Table 8–2 and the product curves of Figure 8–5 in an unorthodox way. Table 8–2, showing the effects of increasing the ratio of capital to labor, should be read from bottom to top. Figure 8–5, read in the conventional way from left to right, shows the effects of increasing the ratio of labor to capital, but, read from right to left, it shows the effects of increasing the ratio of capital to labor.

Table 8–2   Product schedules for capital

(1) Capital	(2) Labor	(3) Total Product (Capital)	(4) Marginal Physical Product (Capital)	(5) Average Product (Capital)	
1	1	3	$(-)1$	3	Stage III
$1/2$	1	$3^{1}/_{2}$	$(-)3$	7	
$1/3$	1	4	0	12	
$1/4$	1	4	4	16	Stage II
$1/5$	1	$3^{4}/_{5}$	9	19	
$1/6$	1	$3^{1}/_{2}$	15	21	
$1/7$	1	$3^{1}/_{7}$	22	22	
$1/8$	1	$2^{3}/_{4}$	30	22	Stage I
$1/9$	1	$2^{1}/_{3}$	75	21	
$1/10$	1	$1^{1}/_{2}$	15	15	

The product schedules   The results of the reworking of Table 8–1 are shown in Table 8–2. At the bottom of Table 8–1, 10 units of labor are used per unit of capital. In terms of a ratio this combination means the same thing as using 1/10 of a unit of capital per unit of labor. These numbers are shown in columns (1) and (2) in the last row of Table 8–2. Similarly, in terms of ratios, 9 units of labor per unit of capital are the same as 1/9 of a unit of capital per unit of labor; and so on up through the table until we reach the top, where 1 unit of capital is used with 1 unit of labor. The ratios of capital and labor are the same throughout Tables 8–1 and 8–2.

The total product schedule for various amounts of capital applied to one unit of labor is determined from column (3) of Table 8–1. Ten units of labor applied to 1 unit of capital produce 15 units of product. Obviously, then, 1/10 of a unit of capital applied to 1 unit of labor should produce a total product of 15/10 or 1½ units of product. This result is listed in the last row of column (3) in Table 8–2. Since 9 units of labor applied to 1 unit of capital

Figure 8-5   Product curves for capital

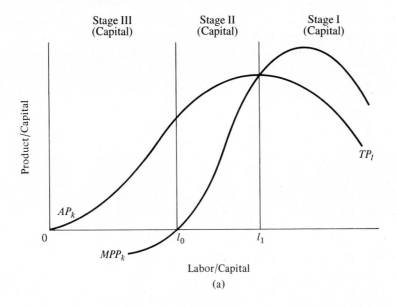

Stage III
(Capital)

Stage II
(Capital)

Stage I
(Capital)

Product/Capital

TP_l

AP_k

0

l_0

l_1

MPP_k

Labor/Capital

(a)

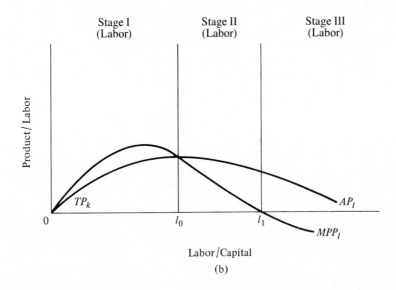

Stage I
(Labor)

Stage II
(Labor)

Stage III
(Labor)

Product/Labor

TP_k

0

l_0

l_1

AP_l

MPP_l

Labor/Capital

(b)

produce 21 units of product, 1/9 of a unit of capital applied to 1 unit of labor will produce a total product of 2⅓. Total product of the larger quantities of capital used with 1 unit of labor is computed in a similar way to complete column (3).

The marginal physical product schedule for capital should show the increments in total product per full unit increment in capital at the various ratios of capital to labor used. The first 1/10 of a unit of capital used increases total product from zero to 1½ units. Therefore, at this ratio of capital to labor the marginal physical product of a unit of capital is $1\frac{1}{2} \div 1/10 = 3/2 \times 10 = 15$ units of product. This quantity is listed in column (4) in the last row of Table 8–2.

An increase in capital from 1/10 of a unit to 1/9 of a unit increases total product from 1½ to 2⅓. The product increment is $7/3 - 3/2 = 14/6 - 9/6 = 5/6$ of a unit of product. The capital increment is $1/9 - 1/10 = 10/90 - 9/90 = 1/90$ of a unit of capital. Marginal physical product of a unit of capital at this point is $5/6 \div 1/90 = 5/6 \times 90 = 75$ units of product. Column (4) is calculated by similar computations on up through columns (1) and (3) of Table 8–2.

Column (5) of Table 8–2, read from bottom to top, presents average product per unit of capital for the various capital-to-labor ratios. The average product of capital for each ratio is obtained by dividing the total product of capital by the quantity of capital used. Since 1/10 of a unit of capital produces 1½ units of product, the average product of capital equals $1\frac{1}{2} \div 1/10 = 15$ at this point. Similarly, 2⅓ units of product divided by 1/9 of a unit of capital equals an average product of capital at this point of 21 units. The other figures of column (5) are determined by similar computations.

When Table 8–1 is compared with Table 8–2, two columns of Table 8–1 turn out to be identical with two columns in Table 8–2. First, the total product schedule of labor applied to 1 unit of capital [see Table 8–1, column (3)] has become the average product schedule of capital applied to 1 unit of labor [see Table 8–2, column (5)]. Second, the average product schedule of labor applied to 1 unit of capital [see Table 8–1, column (4)] has become the total product schedule of capital applied to 1 unit of labor [see Table 8–2, column (3)]. A little reflection will reveal that these relationships should be expected. The total product of more and more labor applied to one unit of capital is the average product of capital (or the product per unit of capital) as the ratio of labor to capital is increased. Likewise, the average product of labor (product per unit of labor) is necessarily the total product of various quantities of capital applied to one unit of labor.

A further observation can be made. Stages I, II, and III are marked off approximately for labor in Table 8–1.[10] Stages I, II, and III for capital are marked off approximately in Table 8–2. That which is Stage I for labor in Table 8–1 has become Stage III for capital in Table 8–2. That which is Stage

---

[10] The boundary lines between stages must be approximations when product schedules are set up in table form. Only on continuous graphs can the exact boundaries between the stages be established.

III for labor in Table 8–1 has become Stage I for capital in Table 8–2. Stage II for labor is also Stage II for capital in both tables.

The product curves   In Figure 8–5 product curves for capital per unit of labor, as well as those for labor per unit of capital, are shown. The product curves for both labor applied to a unit of capital and capital applied to a unit of labor are drawn in the diagram. Reading the horizontal axes from left to right, the ratio of labor to capital is increasing, giving rise to the three familiar product curves for labor [TP_l in Figure 8–5(a); AP_l and MPP_l in Figure 8–5(b)]. Reading the horizontal axes from right to left, the ratio of capital to labor is increasing. The total product curve of labor when the ratio of labor to capital is increased becomes the average product curve for capital when the ratio of capital to labor is increased. The average product curve for labor when the ratio of labor to capital is increased becomes the total product curve for capital when the ratio of capital to labor is increased. Note that the marginal physical product curve for capital, reading from right to left in Figure 8–5(a), lies above the average product curve for capital when average product is increasing, cuts the average product curve at its maximum point, and lies below the average product curve when that curve is decreasing. Note also that the marginal physical product curve for capital reaches zero at the ratio of capital to labor at which the total product of capital is maximum. The marginal physical product of capital is negative where increases in the quantity of capital per unit of labor lead to decreases in the total product of capital. The three stages for both capital and labor are shown in Figure 8–5.

Stage II combinations

Stage II contains all the relevant ratios of labor to capital for the firm. The three stages—their relationships and their characteristics—are summed up in Table 8–3. In Stage I for labor, labor is used too sparsely on the capital, and increases in the ratio of labor to capital will increase its average product. The firm should increase the ratio of labor to capital used, at least to the point at which the average product of labor will no longer increase. Such an increase will place the firm in Stage II.

Table 8–3   The three stages for labor and capital

Labor Productivity When the Ratio of Labor to Capital Is Increased		Capital Productivity When the Ratio of Capital to Labor Is Increased	
Stage I	Increasing AP_l	Negative MPP_k	Stage III
Stage II	Decreasing AP_l and MPP_l, but MPP_l is positive	Decreasing AP_k and MPP_k, but MPP_k is positive	Stage II
Stage III	Negative MPP_l	Increasing AP_k	Stage I

In Stage III for labor the marginal physical product of labor is negative, meaning that too much labor is used per unit of capital. The ratio of labor to capital should be decreased at least to the point at which the marginal physical product of labor is no longer negative. Now only Stage II ratios remain with us.

The main points emerging from the foregoing discussion are worth emphasizing. The combination of labor and capital that yields maximum efficiency of labor lies at the boundary between Stage I and Stage II for labor. The one that yields maximum efficiency for capital lies at the boundary between Stage II and Stage III for labor.

The introduction of resource costs into the picture puts the economic issues facing the firm into proper perspective. Suppose that capital is so plentiful that it costs nothing at all, while labor is scarce enough to command some price. Because whatever cost outlay the firm makes will go for labor, the firm will achieve its greatest economic efficiency (lowest cost per unit of product) at the ratio of labor to capital that maximizes product per unit of labor. This ratio occurs at the boundary between Stages I and II for labor. The output per unit expenditure will increase through Stage I and decrease through Stages II and III.

Suppose that labor can be had for the asking and that capital is a scarce resource that commands a price. In this case the entire cost outlay goes for capital, and economic efficiency is greatest when the ratio of labor to capital is such that product per unit of capital is maximum. Throughout Stage I and Stage II product per unit of capital (and per unit expenditure) increases as the ratio of labor to capital is increased. At the boundary between Stages II and III for labor, product per unit of capital and product per unit of expenditure are maximum. In Stage III it decreases.

Suppose next that both labor and capital are economic resources; that is, both are scarce enough to command a price. Increases in the ratio of labor to capital in Stage I for labor increase both the product per unit of labor and the product per unit of capital. These increases also increase the product obtained per unit of expenditure on both; hence, the firm will move at least to the boundary between Stages I and II. If the firm moves into Stage II, increasing the ratio of labor to capital, the product per unit expenditure on labor decreases while that per unit expenditure on capital increases. Which is more important, the increasing efficiency of capital or the decreasing efficiency of labor? We shall return to the question in a moment. If the firm moves into Stage III for labor, the product per unit expenditure on capital and on labor both decrease; hence, when both resources have costs, the firm should not go beyond the boundary line between Stages II and III for labor.

Labor to capital ratios of Stage I and Stage III are ruled out of the firm's consideration under all circumstances. The firm will not operate in Stage I for either resource when capital is free and when labor has costs, or when labor is free and capital has costs, or when both resources command prices. The same reasoning applies to Stage III. Stage II is left as the possible range of relevant ratios of labor to capital.

Which of the ratios of labor to capital falling within Stage II will the firm use? The answer depends on the comparative costs or prices per unit of capital and labor. We have already observed that if capital is free and labor must be paid, the firm will use the ratio at which Stage II for labor begins. If capital must be paid and labor is free, the firm will use the ratio at which Stage II for labor ends. From these points we can deduce that the less the price of capital relative to the price of labor, the closer the ratio should be to the beginning of labor's Stage II. The less the price of labor relative to the price of capital, the closer the ratios should be to the end of labor's Stage II. Thus, for any resource that a firm employs we can say that the firm should use some ratio of that resource to other resources that falls within Stage II for that resource.

A generalized Stage II

Isoquant diagrams enable us to establish a generalized Stage II—not restricted to a linearly homogeneous production function. Consider the isoquant map in Figure 8–6. From it we can read off the set of resource

Figure 8–6   Stage II on an isoquant diagram

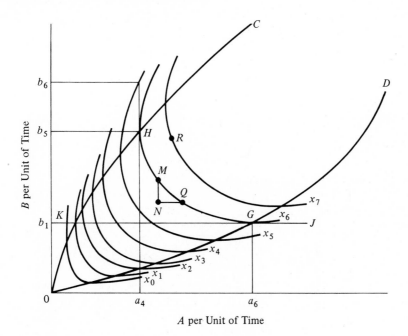

B per Unit of Time

A per Unit of Time

combinations that will produce any given level of output. In addition, we can locate the total product curves for resource A—a different one for each different level of resource B with which alternative quantities of A are used. We can also locate the total product curves for resource B—one for each different quantity of A with which alternative quantities of B are used.

On any given isoquant the marginal rate of technical substitution of A for B is measured by the ratio of the marginal physical product of A to the marginal physical product of B. In Figure 8–6 suppose that combination M of A and B is used to produce x_6 of X. In moving from combination M to combination Q, holding the output level constant at x_6, the firm gives up MN of resource B for NQ of resource A. The reduction in output from giving up MN of B is $MN \times MPP_b$. The increase in output fron NQ of A is $NQ \times MPP_a$. Since the reduction in output from giving up B must equal the increase in output from the additional A, then

$$MN \times MPP_b = NQ \times MPP_a,$$

or

$$\frac{MN}{NQ} = \frac{MPP_a}{MPP_b}.$$

Since

$$MRTS_{ab} = \frac{MN}{NQ},$$

then

$$MRTS_{ab} = \frac{MPP_a}{MPP_b}. \qquad (8.2)$$

If the $MRTS_{ab}$ is 2, then MPP_a is twice as large as MPP_b, meaning that an additional 1 unit of A will compensate for the loss of 2 units of B.[11]

---

[11] The marginal rate of technical substitution of A for B on any given isoquant is found by differentiating the isoquant equation as follows:

$$x_0 = f(a, b)$$

and

$$dx_0 = f_a da + f_b db = 0.$$

Therefore,

$$-\frac{db}{da} = \frac{f_a}{f_b} = MRTS_{ab}.$$

The partial derivatives f_a and f_b are, respectively, MPP_a and MPP_b. If an isoquant is to be convex to the origin, then

$$\frac{d^2b}{da^2} > 0;$$

that is,

$$-\frac{d^2b}{da^2} = \frac{d}{da}\left(\frac{f_a}{f_b}\right) = \frac{d}{da}(MRTS_{ab}) < 0,$$

or the $MRTS_{ab}$ is diminishing.

The line $0D$ joining the points at which isoquants become horizontal is called a *ridge line*. Consider point G on isoquant x_6. Since the slope of the isoquant, or $MRTS_{ab}$, is zero, it is apparent that MPP_a is also zero at this point. For a movement to the right from point G along line b_1J the total product of A will decline; and MPP_a is negative for such a movement. This situation means that the firm is moving into Stage III for resource A. The same thing can be said for a movement to the right from every point along $0D$; any combination of A and B to the right of $0D$ is in a generalized Stage III for resource A. The upward slopes of those portions of the isoquants lying to the right of $0D$ reflect the negative MPP_a in Stage III for A.

Line $0C$ joining the points at which isoquants become vertical is also a ridge line. At point H an increase in resource B along line a_4H as extended will decrease the total product of B; that is, MPP_b is negative for the increase. The same thing can be said for any increase in B from a point on $0C$. Consequently, any combination of A and B that lies above $0C$ is in Stage III for resource B.

The combinations comprising the area between ridge lines $0D$ and $0C$ thus constitute a generalized Stage II for both resources. These are the combinations that are relevant for the production decisions of the firm. We need not restrict our thinking to a linearly homogeneous production function or to a production function in which one resource is fixed in quantity. A change in the quantity of either resource from a combination such as R in the generalized Stage II area will show diminishing returns for that resource.

The least cost combination

Which of the Stage II combinations should a firm use in the production of its product? We assume that the firm's objective is to minimize the cost of producing any given output level; that is, the resource combination should be the one that keeps its cost outlay for that output as low as possible. Another way of stating the objective is to say that whatever cost outlay the firm makes, it should use the resource combination that will produce the greatest amount of product for that cost outlay.

The problem facing a firm is essentially the same as that facing a consumer. Isoquants show the outputs that the firm gets from "consuming" various combinations of resources. These are analogous to indifference curves, which show the "outputs" of satisfaction a consumer gets from consuming various combinations of goods and services. To complete the analogy we need the firm's counterpart of the consumer's budget line.

This counterpart is called an *isocost* or "equal cost" curve. Let the firm's total cost outlay on resources A and B be T_1 dollars, while the resource prices are p_a and p_b, respectively. In Figure 8–7 the amount of B that the firm can get if it buys no A is T_1/p_b. The amount of A that the firm can get if

Figure 8–7   Cost minimization

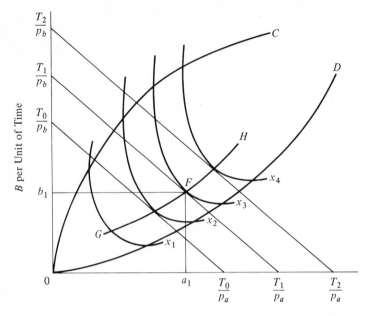

A per Unit of Time

it buys no *B* is T_1/p_a. A line joining these two points shows all combinations of the two that cost outlay T_1 will purchase. This line is the isocost curve.[12] Its slope will have an absolute value of

$$\frac{T_1/p_b}{T_1/p_a} = \frac{T_1}{p_b} \times \frac{p_a}{T_1} = \frac{p_a}{p_b}. \tag{8.3}$$

[12] An isocost curve for a firm using two resources, *A* and *B*, can be represented by the equation

$$ap_a + bp_b = T_0 \qquad \text{or} \qquad bp_b = T_0 - ap_a.$$

Dividing through by p_b we obtain

$$b = \frac{T_0}{p_b} - a\frac{p_a}{p_b}$$

in which

$$\frac{T_0}{p_b}$$

is the intercept on the *B* axis and

$$\frac{p_a}{p_b}$$

is the slope of the curve.

Treating *T* as a parameter and assigning different values to it generates a family of parallel isocost curves.

The maximum output obtainable with a given cost outlay is that of the highest isoquant touched by the isocost curve. In Figure 8–7, given the firm's production function, resource prices of p_a and p_b, and a cost outlay of T_1, the maximum amount of X that can be obtained is x_3. This is produced with a_1 of A and b_1 of B. Any other combination that will produce x_3 lies above the isocost curve generated by cost outlay T_1; and as long as p_a and p_b remain constant, other combinations could be obtained only by increasing the cost outlay.

Changes in the firm's cost outlay, given the prices of resources A and B, will shift the isocost curve parallel to itself. If the cost outlay were a smaller amount, T_0, the isocost curve would shift to the left. Thus, in Figure 8–7, T_0 would be the least possible cost of producing output x_2. If the cost outlay were a greater amount, T_2, the isocost curve would shift to the right, and T_2 would be the least possible cost of producing output x_4. The line GH joining all points of equilibrium (least cost resource combinations) for each possible cost outlay is called the *expansion path* of the firm.

For a firm to minimize the costs of producing a given output level, the marginal rate of technical substitution between any two resources must be equal to the ratio of the prices of those resources. In Figure 8–7 cost outlay T_1 is the minimum cost of producing output level x_3. However, resource combination F, containing a_1 of A and b_1 of B, is the only resource combination that will achieve this result. What are the conditions that prevail at F? The slope of the isocost curve for outlay T_1 is p_a/p_b throughout its entire length. The slope of isoquant x_3 at point F is measured by MPP_a/MPP_b. Thus, at point F:

$$\frac{p_a}{p_b} = \frac{MPP_a}{MPP_b} = MRTS_{ab}, \tag{8.4}$$

which can be rewritten as

$$\frac{MPP_a}{p_a} = \frac{MPP_b}{p_b}.$$

To secure a given output at the least possible cost the marginal physical product of a dollar's worth of one resource must be equal to the marginal physical product of a dollar's worth of every other resource used.[13]

---

[13] To minimize costs,

$$T = ap_a + bp_b, \tag{1}$$

for a given level of output,

$$x_1 = f(a, b), \tag{2}$$

differentiate (2), obtaining

$$\frac{db}{da} = -\frac{f_a}{f_b}. \tag{3}$$

Production possibilities for the economy

Once we have determined the production functions of individual firms or producing units, we can easily expand the analysis to show what constitutes efficient allocations of resources among producing units. We shall look first at the conditions leading to Pareto optimality in the allocation of resources among alternative uses. Then we shall consider the whole range of combinations of goods that an economy may produce efficiently. We shall limit ourselves to a simple economy that produces two goods, X and Y, using two resources, A and B.

Resource allocation among products

When two resources, A and B, are used to produce two products, X and Y, some distributions of the resources between the two uses will be more efficient than others. An *efficient distribution* is a Pareto optimal distribution—one from which an increase in the output of one good can take place only if the output of the other is decreased. In the discussion that follows it makes no difference whether the products are produced by the same or by different firms. We assume that the supplies of resources A and B are fixed amounts per unit of time; that is, the resource supply curves are perfectly inelastic.

The Edgeworth box in Figure 8–8 provides a convenient method of determining which distributions are most efficient. Let the quantity of resource A be $0_x a_5$ or $0_y a'_5$ and the quantity of resource B be $0_x b_5$ or $0_y b'_5$. Isoquants showing production levels of X are convex to the 0_x origin, and

---

Then take the first partial derivative of T with respect to a, obtaining

$$\frac{\delta T}{\delta a} = p_a + p_b \frac{db}{da}. \tag{4}$$

Substituting (3) in (4) and setting the derivative equal to zero, we have

$$\frac{\delta T}{\delta a} = p_a - p_b \frac{f_a}{f_b} = 0, \tag{5}$$

and the first-order minimum cost condition becomes

$$\frac{p_a}{p_b} = \frac{f_a}{f_b}; \tag{6}$$

that is,

$$MRTS_{ab} = \frac{p_a}{p_b}, \text{ or } \frac{MPP_a}{p_a} = \frac{MPP_b}{p_b}.$$

The second-order condition for minimum cost is that at the point of tangency of the isoquant curve and the isocost line, the isoquant curve be convex to the origin, or

$$\frac{d^2 b}{da^2} > 0. \tag{7}$$

Figure 8–8   Efficient resource distributions

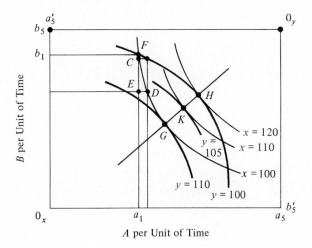

those showing production levels of Y are convex to the 0_y origin. Suppose that the initial distribution of the two resources is shown by point F with $0_x a_1$ of A and $0_x b_1$ of B used in the production of X and with $a_1 a_5$ of A and $b_1 b_5$ of B used in the production of Y.

Are these the most efficient combinations of available resources for the production of X and Y? The output levels are 100 units of each. The slope of the $x = 100$ isoquant at point F, or MPP_a/MPP_b, in the production of X is greater than the slope of the $y = 100$ isoquant, or MPP_a/MPP_b, in the production of Y. This information means that if a unit of A is transferred from the production of Y to the production of X, with the output of X held constant at 100 units, the quantity of B released from the production of X is more than enough to compensate in the production of Y for the release of the unit of A. Suppose, for example, that ED in Figure 8–8 represents the unit of A transferred from the production of Y to the production of X. If the production of X is held at the 100-unit level, EF units of B are released from the production of X. But to hold the output of Y constant at the 100-unit level, only CF units of B are needed to compensate for the unit of A transferred out. Thus, we have a surplus of EC units of B if production of X and Y is held at the original levels.

The released units of B can be used to increase one or both of the product outputs. If the output of X is held at 100 units and the surplus B is turned to the production of Y, this usage constitutes a movement downward to the right around isoquant $x = 100$ and to a Y isoquant above the 100-unit level. Transfers of A from the production of Y to the production of X and of B from the production of X to the production of Y, carried from point F to point G, increase the output of Y to 110 units *without* decreasing the amount of X produced. If the released units of B were used to increase the output of X, holding Y constant at 100 units, a movement from F to H could take place, increasing the production of X to 120 units. The released B can be used to increase the production of both X and Y, moving from point F to some point K between G and H, where an X isoquant is tangent to a Y isoquant. As we have located it, point K represents output levels of 110 units of X and 105 units of Y. Clearly, in all of these cases the efficiency with which resources are used is increased.

Any one of the points—G, H, or K—is Pareto optimal. Resource redistributions from F to any one of these points increase the output of at least one of the products without decreasing the output of the other. Once the resource distribution becomes G, H, or K, however, no further transfer of *any kind* can be made without decreasing the output of at least one of the goods. A Pareto optimal distribution of resources is said to be an *efficient* distribution.

The condition that must be met for an efficient resource distribution is that $MPP_{ax}/MPP_{bx} = MPP_{ay}/MPP_{by}$; that is, the point locating the efficient distribution in the Edgeworth box must be a point of tangency between an isoquant of one product and an isoquant of the other. In Figure 8–8 the contract curve GKH extended is the locus of all such points. Any point on it, once reached, is Pareto optimal. The analysis tells us nothing about how much X and how much Y the society wants produced. More information is needed to handle this problem. All we have learned is that any distribution of resources, like F, that is not on the contract curve is inefficient. The output of one or both products can be increased by a redistribution of the resources between the two uses to a distribution that lies on a segment of the contract curve like GH—within the arcs of the isoquants that pass through F.

Transformation curves

The information provided by the contract curve of Figure 8–8 is frequently displayed in the form of a *transformation curve* for the two products, showing the combinations of them that can be produced efficiently, given the resource supplies and techniques of production available for producing them. In Figure 8–8, if all the resources available in the economy are used to produce Y, the total output of the product is shown by the Y isoquant that passes through 0_x. If this amount of Y is y_5, we can plot the combination as point M in Figure 8–9. Product X can be produced only if some of product Y is given up, with resources being transferred from the production of Y to the production of X. In Figure 8–8 the process of giving up successively more Y to produce successively more X is represented by a movement along the contract curve from 0_x toward 0_y. Each pair of tangent isoquants provides

Figure 8-9   Transformation curve for two products

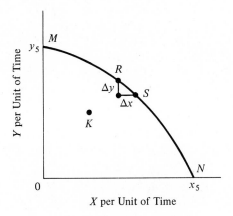

the X and Y output combinations that are plotted as the transformation curve in Figure 8–9. The larger the output of X, the smaller the amount of Y that can be produced; thus, the transformation curve must slope downward to the right. If all of the available resources are used to produce X, the total output is x_5 units per unit of time, as is shown by point N in Figure 8–9.

The average slope $\Delta y/\Delta x$ of the transformation curve between two points close together, such as R and S, measures the *marginal rate of transformation* of X for Y, or MRT_{xy}.[14] This is defined as the amount of Y that must be given up to produce an additional unit of X. The MRT_{xy} is shown as increasing in Figure 8–9, meaning that the less Y and the more X the economy chooses to produce, the more Y it must give up in order to produce an additional unit of X. The primary explanation of this relationship is that some of the economy's resources tend to be more specialized to the production of X, while others are much more useful in producing Y. When all of the economy's resources are used in producing Y, not much Y must be sacrificed to produce a unit of X, since those resources more specialized to the production of X are the ones that are transferred. However, the larger the output of X becomes, and the smaller the output of Y becomes, the more necessary it is to transfer those resources more specialized to the production of Y to production of the additional X. Consequently, larger and larger amounts of Y must be given up for one-unit increases in the output of X.

The transformation model provides an excellent summary of the production choices available to a society. If some of its resources are unemployed, the combination of goods will be one such as K lying below the transforma-

---

[14] In terms of calculus, MRT_{xy} at any given point on the transformation curve is the slope of the curve at that point, that is, dy/dx.

tion curve. The output of one or both products can be increased without decreasing the output of any other good. An inefficient distribution of resources brings about the same result. The combinations on the curve show the production possibilities or alternatives when resources are fully employed and are distributed or allocated efficiently. They are Pareto optimal production possibilities. We will return to the model in the welfare analysis of Chapter 18.

Natural gas versus coal in power generation

A number of power plants have been ordered by the Department of Energy to shift from the use of natural gas to coal in the generation of electricity. The impact of such an order on an individual firm is to (1) curtail the output attainable with a given cost outlay or (2) increase the total cost of producing a given output. The principles of production illustrate the nature of these options.

Suppose the firm prior to the order is spending T_1 dollars on resources in Figure 8–10. Let the horizontal axis measure BTUs of energy per day and let p_{e_1} be the price per BTU when the firm uses natural gas. The lower end of the isocost line is determined by T_1/p_{e_1}. On the vertical axis we measure total expenditure on other resources. Since the price of a dollar's worth of other resources is one dollar, the upper end of the isocost line is $T_1/\$1$ or T_1. The maximum output of the firm for the given cost outlay is x_2 kilowatt hours of electricity. The firm will be purchasing enough natural gas to provide e_1 BTUs of energy and will be spending o_1 dollars on other resources.

The order to shift to coal raises the price per BTU to p_{e_2}, rotating the isocost clockwise until its lower end becomes T_1/p_{e_2}. The expenditure of T_1 dollars will now produce a maximum output of only x_1 kilowatt hours of electricity. Or, if output were to be increased back to the x_2 level, an additional total expenditure on resources amounting to T_1T_2 would be required.

Several interesting points or questions are raised by this case. Since natural gas is more efficient than coal, why should firms be ordered to shift to coal? The answer usually given is that supplies of natural gas are running out and remaining reserves need to be conserved. Yet the Federal Power Commission maintains ceiling prices on natural gas that are well below the equilibrium level. Artificially low prices for natural gas encourage greater use of it relative to coal, thus providing incentives contrary to conservation and contrary to the orders to shift to coal. On the other hand, mandatory shifts from gas to coal reduce the demand for gas and make it easier for the Federal Power Commission to hold to its price ceiling for gas. And the price

Figure 8–10 Gas versus coal in power generation

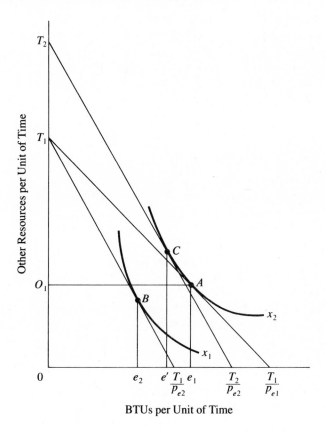

BTUs per Unit of Time

ceiling for gas inhibits the discovery and recovery of additional supplies. Obviously it is much easier to raise questions than it is to answer them.

Summary

The principles of production lay the foundation for the analyses of costs, supplies, resource pricing and employment, resource allocation, and product distribution. These topics will be considered in later chapters.

The term production function is applied to the physical relationship between resource inputs and product output of a firm. Product output is determined partly by the quantities of resource inputs and partly by the techniques of production used by the firm. The production function can be summed up graphically as a production surface and displayed in two dimensions as an isoquant map.

Holding the quantities of all other resources constant, the quantity of any one resource can be varied and the effects on product output can be observed. As the quantity of the variable resource is increased, the law of diminishing returns will become effective. We distinguished among total product, marginal physical product, and average product of the variable resource. The product schedules or product curves of the variable resource were divided into three stages. Stage I is characterized by increasing average product. In Stage II average and marginal physical products of the variable resource are decreasing, but its marginal physical product is still positive. In Stage III the marginal physical product of the variable resource is negative. We deduced that only those ratios of the variable resource to other resources lying within Stage II may be economically efficient for the firm to use.

The precise combination of variable resources that the firm should use depends on the marginal rate of technical substitution among those resources and on their respective prices. To maximize product with a given cost outlay, or to minimize cost for a given amount of product, resources should be combined in ratios such that the $MRTS_{ab} = p_a/p_b$; that is, so that the marginal physical product per dollar's worth of one equals the marginal physical product per dollar's worth of each other resource used.

An Edgeworth box is useful in showing the distributions of resources among products that are efficient in a Pareto optimal sense. The resulting contract curve provides the necessary information for establishing a transformation curve showing the optimal production possibilities for the economy.

Suggested readings

Baumol, William J., *Economic Theory and Operations Analysis,* 4th ed. Englewood Cliffs, N.J.: Prentice-Hall, Inc., 1977. Chap. 11, pp. 267–289.

Cassels, John M., "On the Law of Variable Proportions," *Explorations in Economics.* New York: McGraw-Hill, Inc., 1936. Pp. 223–236. Reprinted in *Readings in the Theory of Income Distribution.* Philadelphia: P. Blakiston's Sons & Company, 1946. Pp. 103–118.

Heady, Earl O., *Economics of Agricultural Production and Resource Use.* Englewood Cliffs, N.J.: Prentice-Hall, Inc., 1952. Chap. 2.

Knight, Frank H., *Risk, Uncertainty, and Profit.* Boston: Houghton Mifflin Company, 1921. Pp. 94–104.

Tangri, O. P., "Omissions in the Treatment of the Law of Variable Proportions." *American Economic Review,* Vol. LVI (June 1966), pp. 484–493.

Questions and exercises

1. Draw an isoquant map for a firm that uses two resources, A and B, to produce product X. Explain
   a. the downward slope of an isoquant
   b. nonintersection of any two isoquants
   c. convexity to the origin of an isoquant
   d. the ridge lines
   e. the three stages for each resource
   f. output maximization given the firm's cost outlay and the prices of the resources.

2. If a fixed amount of labor and a fixed amount of capital are available to produce tractors and airplanes, illustrate and explain
   a. the conditions for an efficient allocation of the resources between the two products
   b. how a transformation curve for the two products is developed
   c. the probable slope of the transformation curve.

3. During World War II the United States built a number of airstrips in Mainland China utilizing local labor. Both men and women sat around rock piles breaking rock up into gravel with hammers. Concrete was mixed by hand and was carried to the runway forms in baskets on the heads of long lines of workers. Would it have been more efficient to have brought in rock crushers and concrete mixers to do the job? Explain carefully.

4. The Acme Manufacturing Company has been engaged in the production of metal spools, all of a uniform type, for many years. Production schedules for labor and machinery are independent of each other and of other resources. On a monthly basis they are estimated to be as follows:

Labor Employed	Spools per Month	Machinery (Physical Units)	Spools per Month
1	200	1	300
2	370	2	430
3	500	3	500
4	600	4	545
5	675	5	570
6	740	6	586
7	800	7	600
8	855	8	612
9	900	9	622
10	940	10	630
11	970	11	635

The company is currently employing 7 workers and 7 units of machinery.

a. What is the average product of workers? Of machinery? Explain.

b. What is the marginal physical product of workers? Of machinery? Explain.

c. If one additional worker were to be employed, how many units of machinery could be given up without loss of production? Explain.

d. If a monthly cost outlay of $5,100 is to be made and the respective monthly prices of workers and units of machinery are $600 and $100, what combination of workers and machinery should be used?

e. What is the average cost of spools at this point? Explain.

Chapter 9

Chapter contents

		Key concepts
The concept of costs	**The alternative cost principle**	Alternative costs
	Explicit and implicit costs	Explicit costs
	Cost, resource prices, and efficiency	Implicit costs
		Short run
The short-run and long-run viewpoints	**The short run**	Long run
	The long run	Fixed costs
Short-run cost curves	**Total cost curves**	Variable costs
	Total fixed costs	Total costs
	Total variable costs	Average costs
	Total costs	Marginal cost
		Most efficient rate of output
	Per unit cost curves	Economies of size
	Average fixed costs	Diseconomies of size
	Average variable costs	Most efficient size of plant
	Average costs	
	Marginal cost	
	Relationship of MC to AC and to AVC	
	The most efficient rate of output	
Long-run cost curves	**Long-run total costs**	
	Long-run average costs	
	Economies of size	
	Division and specialization of labor	
	Technological factors	
	Diseconomies of size	
	The most efficient size of plant	
	Long-run marginal cost	
	Relationships between LMC and SMC	
Some applications of cost analysis	**Costs of obtaining a higher education**	
	Cost minimization by a multiple-unit firm	
Summary	**Suggested readings**	
	Questions and exercises	
Appendix to Chapter 9		
The geometry of short-run per unit cost curves	**The average fixed cost curve**	
	The average variable cost curve	
	The average cost curve	
	The relationship of AC and MC	

Costs of production

Costs of production constitute a major determinant of the quantities of a good or service that will be placed on the market. To understand supply and quantities supplied we must understand costs, which are rooted in the principles of production. We shall consider first the meaning of costs and second the short-run and long-run cost curves of the individual firm or production unit.

The concept of costs

The concept of costs of production as used in economic analysis differs somewhat from common usage of the term. Common usage ordinarily conveys some idea of the expenditures of a firm necessary in turning out a product, but it is not always clear which categories of expenditure are included and which are excluded. The economic concept is more precise and consistent. To build up the concept as it is used in economics, we shall discuss first the alternative cost principle and then the implicit and explicit aspects of costs.

The alternative cost principle

The basic idea of the alternative cost principle is contained in the transformation curve of the last chapter. Under conditions of full employment and when resources are efficiently allocated among goods and services, an increase in the output of any one product requires the sacrifice of some amounts of alternative products. If a certain kind of labor is used in making both washing machines and refrigerators, an increase in the output of refrigerators entails a reduction in the quantity of washing machines available, since labor must be withdrawn from that use. If steel is used in making automobiles and football stadiums, an increase in football stadiums leaves less steel available for making automobiles, reducing the number of automobiles that are manufactured. Thus, the production of any product requires the sacrifice of some value of alternative products.

Economists define the costs of production of a particular product as the value of the forgone alternative products that resources used in its production could have produced. This principle is called the *alternative cost principle,* or the *opportunity cost principle.* The costs of resources to a firm are their values in their best alternative uses. The firm, in order to secure the services of resources, must pay for them amounts equal to what they can earn in those alternative uses. In the earlier example of labor the cost of the labor in the manufacture of washing machines is the value of refrigerators that the labor could have produced. Unless the manufacturer of washing machines pays that amount for the labor, it will go into or remain in refrigerator production. The steel example is similar. Automobile manufacturers must pay enough for steel to attract or hold the desired amounts away from alternative employments of steel—and this value is its cost to the automobile firm from the economist's point of view.

Explicit and implicit costs

The outlays made by a firm (that we usually think of as its expenses) are the *explicit costs of production.* They consist of explicit payments for resources bought outright or hired by the firm. The firm's payroll, payments for raw and semifinished materials, payments of overhead costs of various kinds, and costs charged against sinking funds and depreciation reserves are examples of explicit costs. They are the costs that accountants list as the firm's expenses.

Implicit costs of production are the costs of self-owned, self-employed resources frequently overlooked in computing the expenses of the firm. The salary of a single proprietor who sets aside no salary for himself but who takes the firm's "profits" as payment for his services is an excellent example. A still more common implicit cost is the return to the owners of a firm on their investment in plant, equipment, and inventories.

The consideration of the firm owner's salary as a cost can be easily explained. In accordance with the alternative cost principle, the cost of the single proprietor's services in producing the firm's product is the value of the forgone alternative product that would have been produced had the owner worked for someone else in a similar capacity. We consider as a part of the firm's costs, then, a salary for the proprietor equal to the value of the owner's services in his or her best alternative employment. This cost is an implicit cost, which does not take the form of an "expense" outlay.

The consideration of a return on investment as a cost of production is more tricky. Return on investment usually is thought of as coming from the firm's profits rather than as being a cost of production. A simple case is a single proprietor who has invested in (purchased) the land, building, and equipment for the business establishment. A return on the investment equal to what the proprietor could have earned had the same amount been invested elsewhere in the economy is an implicit cost of production. Had the proprietor invested elsewhere, the investment would have purchased resources to produce other goods. What those resources could earn in those alternative uses would determine the return on investment that could have been earned had the proprietor invested there.

The same principle on a larger scale applies to a corporation. Stockholders are the real owners of the corporation's land, plant, equipment, and inventories[1]—they have invested money in resources used by the corporation. Dividends equal to what stockholders could earn had they invested elsewhere in the economy are implicit costs of production from the point of view of the economist. The costs of resources obtained by the firm with stockholders' investments are, according to the alternative cost principle, the value of the alternative products forgone by holding the investment where it is. To hold the investment where it is, the corporation must pay a return to stockholders equal to what they could earn if they should invest elsewhere in the economy.

Cost, resource prices, and efficiency

Costs of production incurred by the firm consist of both explicit and implicit obligations to resource owners. These obligations are just large enough to obtain and hold resources in the employment of the firm. Usually the firm's "expenses" include the explicit obligations only. Thus, costs of production as viewed by the economist differ somewhat from (and will usually be larger than) the firm's accounting "expenses."

Our discussion of costs will be oversimplified to some extent. We shall be concerned with a firm's costs of production at various alternative product outputs. Costs at each output depend on (1) the values of the resources the firm uses—that is, resource prices—and (2) the techniques available for combining resources to produce the output. We shall eliminate the problem of resource pricing by assuming that the firm is a pure competitor in the purchase of resources; that is, the single firm takes such a small proportion of the total amount of any given resource in existence that by itself it cannot influence the resource price. The firm can get all it wants of any one resource at a constant price per unit. Thus, differences in costs at different output levels result from differences in the efficiency of the techniques that the firm can use at each of those outputs. The effects on costs of possible changes in resource prices as a result of output changes on the part of a firm can be taken into consideration later on, after resource pricing has been discussed.

---

[1] Additionally, the corporation may have borrowed money by selling bonds to increase the amounts of its plant and equipment. Thus, bondholders, too, have invested money in the corporation. Interest payments on the bonds—the return on the bondholders' investments—are explicit payments and are recorded as costs by the corporation as well as by the economist.

The short-run and long-run viewpoints

In analyzing a firm's costs of production a distinction is made between the short-run and long-run viewpoints. These are essentially planning rather than calendar time concepts; they refer to the time horizon over which the firm's planning stretches. We shall examine them in turn.

The short run

A planning period so short that the firm is unable to consider varying the quantities of some resources used is called the *short run*. It is possible to think of a period so short that no resource can be varied in quantity. Then, as the planning period is lengthened, it becomes possible to vary the quantity of one. A progressive lengthening of the period permits more and more resources to become variable in quantity until, ultimately, they all fall into the variable category. Any period between that in which no resources can be varied in quantity and that in which all resources but one are variable can legitimately be called the short run. However, to facilitate exposition we ordinarily use a more restricting definition.

The possibilities of varying the quantities of different resources depend on their nature and the terms of hire or purchase. Some, such as land and buildings, may be leased by the firm for given time periods; or, if they are owned outright, it may take some time to acquire additional quantities or to dispose of a part of the quantities already owned. The quantity of top management is not ordinarily readily variable. Heavy machinery especially designed for the firm's use cannot be quickly increased or decreased in quantity. Typically, the period required for variation in the quantities of such resources as power, labor, transportation, raw materials, and semifinished materials will be shorter than that required for variation in the quantities of land, buildings, heavy machinery, and top management.

The usual interpretation of the short-run concept is a planning period so short that the firm does not have time to vary the quantities of such resources as land, buildings, heavy machinery, and top management. These are the firm's short-run *fixed resources*. This concept of the short run does allow variation in the quantities of such resources as labor, raw materials, and the like. These are the firm's *variable resources*.[2]

The calendar time length of the short run will vary from industry to industry. For some industries the short run may be very short indeed. Such will be the case where the quantities of fixed resources used by a firm in the

---

[2] A clear distinction between which resources are fixed and which resources are variable is not always possible. For some firms some of the resources listed here as ''variable'' may require more time for alterations in quantity taken than some listed as ''fixed.'' For example, contractual arrangements for the purchase of power or labor may be such that quantities of these cannot readily be varied. Yet it may be possible for the firm to lease out, sublease, or sell some part of its ''fixed'' resources on short notice.

industry are typically small or can be added to or subtracted from in a short space of time. Various textile industries and many service industries are cases in point. For other industries the short run may be several years. It takes time to add to the productive capacity of an automobile firm or a basic steel firm.

The quantities of fixed resources used determine the size of the firm's plant.[3] The size of plant sets the upper limit to the amount of output per unit of time that the firm is capable of producing. The firm can vary its output up to that limit, however, by increasing or decreasing the quantities of variable resources used in the fixed size of plant.

The fixed resources or the plant may be compared with a meat grinder. The variable resource will be analogous to unground meat. In this case the output of ground meat per unit of time can be varied by varying the input of unground meat. There will be some upper limit beyond which the output cannot be increased, regardless of how much unground meat is on hand to push through it.

The capital and labor example of the preceding chapter can also be viewed in a short-run context. We can think of the fixed amount of capital as the fixed size of plant and the variable quantities of labor as the variable resources used with it.

The long run

No definitional difficulties are presented by the *long run*. It is a planning period long enough for the firm to be able to vary the quantities per unit of time of all resources used. Thus, all resources are variable. No problem of classifying resources as fixed or variable exists. The firm can vary its size of plant as it desires, from very small to large or vice-versa. Infinitesimal variations in size are usually possible.

Short-run cost curves

Classification of resources in the short run as fixed and variable enables us to classify their costs as fixed costs and variable costs. *Fixed costs* are the costs of fixed resources. *Variable costs* are those of variable resources. The distinction between fixed and variable costs is basic to the discussions of total costs, average costs, and marginal costs that follow.

---

[3] The term *plant* is used here in a broad context to cover the whole scope of the firm's operations. A firm may operate several establishments at different locations; we shall view these all together as the firm's "plant."

Total cost curves

In the short run the total costs of a firm depend on the firm's size and on the output level produced. The component parts of total costs are total fixed costs and total variable costs. We shall examine these in turn.

Total fixed costs   The costs per unit of time of its fixed resources constitute the firm's *total fixed costs*. They include the salaries that must be paid top management to keep it intact over time. They include the costs of holding and maintaining its land—that is, what the land would be worth in alternative uses over time. They include the cost of keeping investment in plant and equipment from shifting away from the firm. Short-run total fixed costs are thus the alternative costs of the fixed resources. They are the obligations that the firm must incur to keep these resources from slipping away in the long run. Note that total fixed costs depend on the size of the firm's operation—its size of plant. They do not depend on the output level at which the plant is operated. So, we can say that a firm's short-run total fixed costs are constant for all possible levels of output.

A hypothetical total fixed cost schedule is presented in Table 9–1; the corresponding total fixed cost curve is plotted in Figure 9–2. Note that the

Table 9–1   Total cost schedules for a firm

Quantity of X	Total Fixed Cost	Total Variable Cost	Total Cost
1	$100	$ 40	$140
2	100	70	170
3	100	85	185
4	100	96	196
5	100	104	204
6	100	110	210
7	100	115	215
8	100	120	220
9	100	126	226
10	100	134	234
11	100	145	245
12	100	160	260
13	100	180	280
14	100	206	306
15	100	239	339
16	100	280	380
17	100	330	430
18	100	390	490
19	100	461	561
20	100	544	644

total fixed cost curve is independent of the output level, is parallel to the quantity axis, and lies above it by the amount of the total fixed costs.

Total variable costs   The alternative costs or the total obligations that a firm must incur for its variable resources constitute its *total variable costs*. Unlike its total fixed costs, the firm's total variable costs must vary directly with its output. Larger outputs require larger quantities of variable resources and, hence, larger cost obligations. For example, the larger the output of an oil refinery, the larger the quantity of crude oil inputs it must use and the larger will be its crude oil costs.

The shape of the total variable cost curve with respect to the firm's output will depend on whether increasing or diminishing returns to variable resources exist as larger and larger quantities of them are used with the firm's given size of plant. Consider the simple case in which a firm uses only one variable resource, resource A. A conventional total product curve for A is drawn on the right-hand side of Figure 9–1, showing increasing returns to

Figure 9–1   Relation between the TVC curve and the total product curve of variable resources

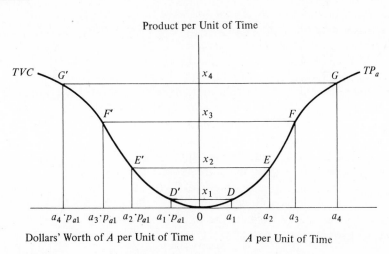

A for quantities up to a_3 and diminishing returns for larger quantities. The point of inflection on the TP_a curve is at F.

The TP_a curve is easily converted into the total variable cost curve of the firm once the price of the variable resource A is known. Let the price of A be p_{a1}, so that for any given input of A total variable cost is that quantity of A multiplied by its price. Measure total variable cost (dollars' worth of A)

on a horizontal axis stretching to the left of the origin. Total variable cost when a_1 of A is used is $a_1 \times p_{a1}$, and the corresponding output of product is x_1. On the left-hand diagram these coordinates locate point D' on the firm's total variable cost curve. Points E', F', and G' are located in a similar manner, and all such points together trace out the firm's total variable cost curve.

The TVC curve in the left-hand diagram is a mirror image of the TP_a curve in the right-hand diagram. If, for example, p_{a1} is \$1 and we let the distance on the horizontal axis that measures 1 unit of A to the right of the origin be equal to the distance that measures \$1's worth of A to the left of the origin, the reflection is exact. The point of inflection F' on TVC is the precise counterpart of F on TP_a. Both curves are concave upward from the origin to their respective inflection points and are concave downward beyond the inflection points because of increasing returns to A for quantities up to a_3 and decreasing returns for still greater quantities. If we rotate the left-hand side of the diagram 90 degrees clockwise, letting the product axis become the horizontal axis, the TVC curve is concave downward out to the inflection point and concave upward beyond that point.

In the usual case a firm uses several variable resources rather than only one, but the principles at work are the same as those of the single resource example. With a given size of plant—a given complex of fixed resources— we can think in terms of increasing the complex of variable resources used. Since we start from a very small complex, increasing returns to the variable resources may occur—equal increments in outlays on the entire complex may result in larger and larger increments in output—and the TVC curve, consequently, will be convex downward. As larger and larger outlays are made, however, diminishing returns to the complex come into play—equal increments in TVC result in smaller and smaller increments in output—and the TVC curve becomes concave upward. At some output level the fixed size of plant will have reached its absolute maximum capacity to produce. Now the total variable cost curve turns straight up. Increased obligations incurred for still larger quantities of variable resources will lead to no increases in output at all. The total variable cost schedule of Table 9–1, plotted as the TVC curve of Figure 9–2, reflects the results of increasing and diminishing returns to variable resources.

Total costs   The summation of total fixed costs and total variable costs for various output levels comprise the *total costs* of the firm for those output levels. The total cost column of Table 9–1 is obtained by adding total fixed cost and total variable cost at each level of output. Likewise, the total cost curve of Figure 9–2 is obtained by summing the TFC curve and the TVC curve vertically. The TC curve and the TVC curve must necessarily have the same shape, since each increase in output per unit of time increases total costs and total variable costs by the same amount. The output in-

Figure 9–2   Total cost curves of a firm

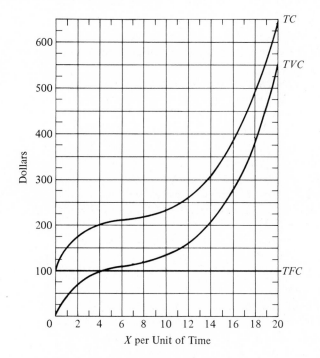

crease does not affect total fixed costs. The *TC* curve lies above the *TVC* curve by an amount equal to *TFC* at all output levels.[4]

Per unit cost curves

In price and output analysis *per unit cost curves* are used extensively—more so than total cost curves are. Per unit cost curves show the same kind of information as total cost curves, but in a different form. The per unit cost curves are the average fixed cost curve, the average variable cost curve, the average cost curve, and the marginal cost curve.

Average fixed costs   The fixed costs per unit of product at various levels of output, or the *average fixed costs,* are obtained by dividing total fixed

---

[4] The short-run total cost function can be represented mathematically as

$$C = k + f(x),$$

in which

$$TC = C$$
$$TFC = k$$
$$TVC = f(x).$$

costs by those outputs. Thus, the average fixed cost column of Table 9–2 is computed by dividing the total fixed cost column of Table 9–1 by the different quantities of X. The average fixed cost schedule is plotted in Figure 9–3 as the AFC curve.

Table 9–2   Per unit cost schedules of a firm

Quantity of X	Average Fixed Cost	Average Variable Cost	Average Cost	Marginal Cost
1	$100.00	$40.00	$140.00	—
2	50.00	35.00	85.00	30
3	33.33	28.33	61.66	15
4	25.00	24.00	49.00	11
5	20.00	20.80	40.80	8
6	16.67	18.33	35.00	6
7	14.29	16.43	30.72	5
8	12.50	15.00	27.50	5
9	11.11	14.00	25.11	6
10	10.00	13.40	23.40	8
11	9.09	13.18	22.27	11
12	8.33	13.33	21.66	15
13	7.69	13.85	21.54	20
14	7.14	14.72	21.86	26
15	6.67	15.93	22.60	33
16	6.25	17.50	23.75	41
17	5.88	19.41	25.29	50
18	5.55	21.67	27.22	60
19	5.26	24.27	29.53	71
20	5.00	27.20	32.20	83

The greater the output of the firm, the smaller average fixed costs will be. Since total fixed costs remain the same regardless of output, fixed costs are spread over more units of ouput; and each unit of output bears a smaller share. Therefore, the average fixed cost curve is downward sloping to the right throughout its entire length. As output per unit of time increases, it approaches—but never reaches—the quantity axis. Thus, it becomes apparent that firms with large fixed costs—the railroads, for example, with their tremendous fixed charges on roadbeds and rolling stock—can substantially reduce their fixed costs per unit by producing larger outputs.

Average variable costs   Variable costs per unit of output are computed in the same way as fixed costs per unit of output. The average variable cost column of Table 9–2 is obtained by dividing total variable costs in Table 9–1

Figure 9–3   Per unit cost curves of a firm

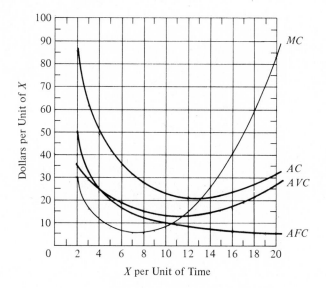

at various outputs by those outputs. Plotted graphically, the average variable cost column of Table 9–2 becomes the *AVC* curve of Figure 9–3.

The *average variable cost* curve usually will have a U shape. Its U shape can be explained in terms of the principles of production. Suppose, for example, that a factory is designed to employ approximately 100 workers. The size of plant is fixed, and labor is the only variable resource. The amount of product produced if only one worker is employed will be extremely small, but if an additional worker is employed, the two can split up the jobs to be performed and can more than double the single worker's output. In other words, the average product of labor increases with the employment of the additional worker. If a doubling of labor (variable) costs will more than double output, labor costs per unit of output (average variable costs) will decrease. Thus, throughout Stage I for labor the average product per worker increases and the average variable costs decrease. When enough workers are employed to go into Stage II, average product of labor decreases or, what amounts to the same thing, average variable costs increase. The average variable cost curve in this case is a sort of monetized mirror reflection of the average product curve for labor.

The same general principles apply when a complex of several variable resources is used by the firm. At small input levels of the complex, product per unit of cost outlay or "average product" of the complex will be increasing, meaning that average variable costs will be decreasing. As input levels are increased, "average product" reaches a maximum and then decreases. Average variable costs correspondingly reach a minimum and then increase.

When a complex of variable resources is used by the firm, combinations of ratios of the variable resources to each other must be considered also. Suppose that the firm for which the cost curves of Figure 9–3 are drawn uses three variable resources—A, B, and C—with its given size of plant. Resource prices are p_a, p_b, and p_c, respectively. If the firm's output is to be 6 units of product and if its average variable costs are to be as low as possible ($18.33) for that output, the variable resources must be combined in such proportions that

$$\frac{MPP_a}{p_a} = \frac{MPP_b}{p_b} = \frac{MPP_c}{p_c}.$$

If they are not so combined, average variable costs for that output will exceed $18.33. Similarly, each point on the average variable cost curve can be attained only if the firm combines variable resources in the proper proportions for each and every output at which those points are located. Failure to do so will result in higher costs.

Average costs   The overall costs per unit of output, the *average costs*, can be obtained in either of two ways. If total costs at various outputs in Table 9–1 are divided by the respective outputs, the result is the average cost column of Table 9–2. Alternatively, in Table 9–2 average fixed costs and average variable costs added together at each of the output levels produce the average cost column. Graphically, the AC curve in Figure 9–3 represents the average cost column of Table 9–2 plotted against outputs. The AC curve is also the vertical summation of the AFC curve and the AVC curve.

The average cost curve, too, is usually thought to be a U-shaped curve. Its U shape depends on the efficiency with which both fixed and variable resources are used. Given the size of plant, the greater the output is of the firm, the greater the efficiency of the fixed resources will be as a group; that is, the smaller average fixed costs become. In Figure 9–3 variable resources are used more and more efficiently until output reaches 11 units. Up to this level average costs must be decreasing because the efficiency of both fixed and variable resources is increasing. Between 11 and 13 units of output, average fixed costs decrease, but average variable costs increase as variable resources become less efficient. However, the decreases in average fixed costs more than offset the increases in average variable costs so that average costs continue to decrease. Beyond 13 units of output per unit of time, decreases in the efficiency of variable resources more than offset increases in the efficiency of fixed resources, and average costs rise. We should note an obvious fact in passing: The minimum point on the average variable cost curve lies at a lower output level than does the minimum point on the average cost curve.[5]

Marginal cost   The change in total costs resulting from a one-unit change in output is called *marginal cost*. It can be defined just as accurately as the change in total variable costs resulting from a one-unit change in output, since a change in output changes total variable costs and total costs by exactly the same amounts. Marginal cost depends in no way on fixed costs. The marginal cost column of Table 9–2 can be computed from either the total variable cost column or the total cost column of Table 9–1. It is plotted graphically as *MC* in Figure 9–3.

Figure 9–4 shows the relationship between a marginal cost curve and the total cost curve from which it is derived. Consider output x on the total cost diagram of Figure 9–4(a). Total costs at that output are T. Now let output be increased by one unit to x_1. Total costs increase to T_1. Marginal cost of the x_1 unit is $T_1 - T$. The marginal cost of a unit of output at any level of output can be found in the same way. The marginal cost values plotted against outputs in Figure 9–4(b) form the marginal cost curve. At any given output level marginal cost is measured by the distance from the base line up to the marginal cost curve. Thus, at x_1, marginal cost of the x_1 unit is M dollars. This represents the same number of dollars as does $T_1 - T$ on the total cost diagram.

The marginal cost curve usually is U-shaped, and its shape comes from that of the *TC* curve. Up to the x_2 level of output the *TC* curve is concave downward; or, what amounts to the same thing, each one-unit increase in output per unit of time up to that point will increase total costs by a smaller amount than did the preceding one. Hence, marginal cost is decreasing as output is increased to that level. Point E on the *TC* curve is the point of

---

[5] The average cost function is derived from Footnote 4 by dividing the total cost function by output and is

$$AC = \frac{C}{x} = \frac{k}{x} + \frac{f(x)}{x}.$$

in which

$$AFC = \frac{k}{x}$$

$$AVC = \frac{f(x)}{x}.$$

Since

$$AFC = \frac{k}{x},$$

then

$$x \times AFC = k$$

and the *AFC* curve is thus a rectangular hyperbola.

Figure 9–4   The relationship between MC and TC

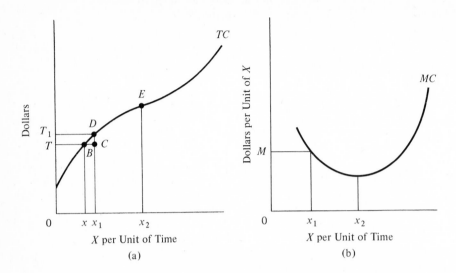

inflection. At output level x_2, at which the point of inflection occurs, marginal cost takes on its minimum value. At outputs greater than x_2 the total cost curve is concave upward, meaning that each one-unit increase in output per unit of time increases total costs by more than the preceding one did. Therefore, marginal cost will be increasing for outputs beyond that level.

Marginal cost at any given output can be thought of geometrically as the slope of the total cost curve at that output. The approximate slope of the total cost curve of Figure 9–4(a) between B and D is CD/BC. BC is equal to one unit of output, and CD is equal to $T_1 - T$, or marginal cost of the x_1 unit. The slope of the total cost curve between B and D is thus equal to marginal cost of the x_1 unit. For the typical firm one unit of output is measured by an infinitesimal distance along the quantity axis. The large size of the unit of output (x to x_1) in Figure 9–4(a) is for purposes of illustration only. If one unit of output is measured by an infinitesimal distance along the quantity axis, marginal cost at any given output is numerically equal to the slope of the total cost curve at that output. The slope of the TC curve of Figure 9–4(a) is decreasing between zero and output x_2 (although TC is rising) and is increasing beyond x_2. Thus, marginal cost first decreases and then increases as output increases.

Relationship of *MC* to *AC* and to *AVC*

The marginal cost curve bears a unique relationship to the average cost curve derived from the same total cost curve. When AC is decreasing as output increases, *MC* is less than *AC*. When *AC* is increasing as output increases, *MC* is greater than *AC*. It follows that at the output at which *AC* is minimum, *MC* is equal to *AC*. These relationships are shown in Figure 9–5.

Figure 9–5   The relationship between *MC* and *AC*

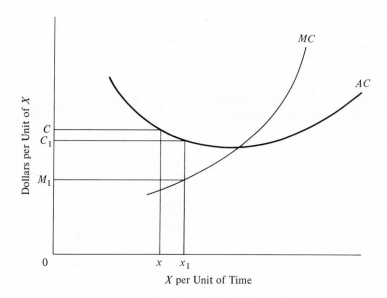

For example, suppose that the firm's output is x. Its average cost is $0C$. We know that average cost at any output equals the total cost of that output divided by the output; therefore, $0C = TC/x$ at output x. Suppose that the output is increased by one unit to x_1 and that the addition to total costs is $0M_1$, which is the marginal cost of the x_1 unit. Suppose further, as we have shown in Figure 9–5, that marginal cost of the x_1 unit is less than the average cost $0C$ of x units. Since the additional unit of output per unit of time adds a lesser amount to total costs than was the average cost of x units, the average cost of x_1 units must be less than the average cost of x units. However, the average cost of x_1 units will not be pulled down as low as the marginal cost of the x_1 unit. Thus, $0C_1 < 0C$, but $0C_1 > 0M_1$; or when average costs are decreasing, marginal cost is necessarily less than average cost. Similarly, when an additional unit of output adds an amount to total costs equal to the old average cost, the new average cost will equal the old and will also be equal to marginal cost of the additional unit of output. Also, when an additional unit of output adds a greater amount to total costs than was the original average cost, the new average cost will be greater than the original but will be less than the marginal cost of the additional unit. These relationships can be verified by reference to Table 9–2 and Figure 9–3.

The relationships between marginal cost and average variable cost will be identical with the relationships between marginal cost and average cost— and for the same reasons. When average variable cost is decreasing, marginal cost will be less than average variable cost. When average variable cost is minimum, marginal cost and average variable cost will be equal. When average variable cost is increasing, marginal cost will be greater than average variable cost. These relationships can also be verified by Table 9–2 and Figure 9–3.

The complete set of short-run per unit cost curves is pictured in Figure 9–3. The marginal cost curve cuts the average variable cost curve and the average cost curve at their respective minimum points. An increase in fixed costs would shift the average cost curve upward and to the right in such a way that the marginal cost curve would still intersect it at its minimum point. No change in the marginal cost curve would be involved, since marginal cost is independent of fixed cost.[6]

---

[6] Starting from the total cost function

$$C = k + f(x),$$

the marginal cost function becomes

$$MC = \frac{dC}{dx} = f'(x)$$

and is thus seen to depend in no way on k. Further, if average cost is decreasing, then

$$\frac{d\left(\frac{C}{x}\right)}{dx} = \frac{x\frac{dC}{dx} - C}{x^2} < 0,$$

or

$$\frac{dC}{dx} - \frac{C}{x} < 0,$$

and

$$\frac{dC}{dx} < \frac{C}{x},$$

which means that $MC < AC$. Similarly, it can be shown that if AC is increasing, then

$$\frac{d\left(\frac{C}{x}\right)}{dx} > 0,$$

or

$$\frac{dC}{dx} > \frac{C}{x};$$

or

$$MC > AC.$$

If AC is constant, then

$$\frac{d\left(\frac{C}{x}\right)}{dx} = 0,$$

or

$$\frac{dC}{dx} = \frac{C}{x},$$

or

$$MC = AC.$$

As we have presented them, the variations in the component parts of short-run costs as the firm varies output do not depend on changes in the price paid per unit for each of the various resources used by the firm. We assumed at the outset that the firm can get all it wants of any resource at a constant price per unit; that is, it buys resources under conditions of pure competition. The shapes of the short-run curves reflect the efficiency with which resources can be used at the alternative output levels obtainable with a given plant size.

In the real world we observe such things as quantity discounts on resources purchased in large amounts by the firm. This represents a departure from pure competition in the buying of resources; it is a departure from the assumptions on which our cost curves are based. Should quantity discounts occur, the total variable cost curve and the total cost curve will increase less as output is increased than they would otherwise. Correspondingly, quantity discounts would cause the average variable cost curve and the average cost curve to show greater decreases, then smaller increases, than they would otherwise show as output is increased. Further modifications of short-run cost analysis will be developed in Chapters 14 and 15.

The most efficient rate of output

The output at which its short-run average cost is lowest is the output at which any given size of plant is most efficient. Here the value of the inputs of resources per unit output of product is least. As we shall see later, the most efficient rate of output for a given plant size is not necessarily the output at which the firm makes the greatest profits. Profits depend on revenue as well as costs.

Long-run cost curves

In the long-run planning period any size of plant is a possibility for the firm. All resources are variable. The firm can change the quantities used per unit of time, of land, buildings, machinery, management, and all other resources. There will be no fixed costs. We need to concern ourselves with the long-run total cost curve, the long-run marginal cost curve, and the long-run average cost curve.

Long-run total costs

We would expect that the long-run total cost curve would look like that of Figure 9–6(b), starting at the origin of the diagram and moving upward to the right in much the same fashion as a total variable cost curve. The *LTC*

Figure 9–6   From isoquants to the *LTC* curve

(a)

(b)

curve, as we have drawn it, reflects first decreasing long-run average costs and then increasing long-run average costs.

The long-run total cost curve of Figure 9–6(b) is based on the isoquant-isocost map of Figure 9–6(a). The production function represented by the isoquant map generates a typical long-run total cost curve. Let numbers on the isoquants indicate the levels of output. The prices of resources A and B are constant at p_{a_1} and p_{b_1}, respectively, and determine the slope $(-p_{a_1}/p_{b_1})$ of the family of isocost curves. Alternative possible total cost outlays are shown as the numerators of the various fractions $(TCO/p_{b_1}$ and $TCO/p_{a_1})$ along both the B and the A axes. Note that the isocosts showing \$100 increments in total cost outlay are spaced equally from one another.

The spacing of the isoquants reflects first economies of size and then diseconomies of size as the firm's plant size is increased. To state it another way, the spacing reflects increasing efficiency and then decreasing efficiency in the use of resources as the plant size is increased. As we move along the expansion path, equal increments in the firm's output require decreasing increments in total cost outlay until point H is reached. Beyond point H increasing increments in cost outlay are required to bring about equal increments in output. The resulting total cost curve is that of Figure 9–6(b).

Long-run average costs

The long-run average cost curve is derived from the long-run total cost curve in the same way as any average curve is derived from a total curve. At each level of output we divide LTC by output to find LAC for that output. The result is the LAC curve.

It is instructive, however, to build up the LAC curve in an alternative way. Think of the long run as a set of alternative short-run situations into any one of which the firm can move. At any given time we can adopt the short-run viewpoint, considering the alternative output levels that can be produced with the size of plant in existence at that time. Yet, from the point of view of a long-run planning period the firm has opportunities to change the short-run picture. The long run may be compared with the action sequence of a motion picture. If we stop the film and look at a single picture, we have a short-run concept.

Suppose now that it is technically possible for the firm to build only three alternative sizes of plant. These are represented by SAC_1, SAC_2, and SAC_3 in Figure 9–7. Each SAC curve is the short-run average cost curve for a given plant size. In the long run the firm can build any one of these, or it can shift from one to another.

Which one should the firm build? The answer depends on, and will vary with, the long-run output per unit of time to be produced. Whatever the

Figure 9–7   The long-run average cost curve, three alternative plant sizes

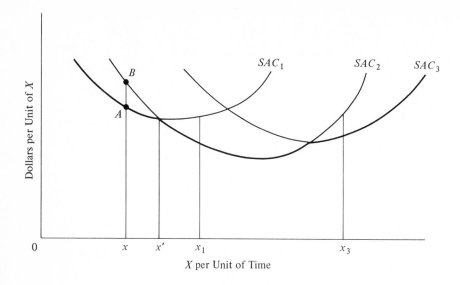

output is to be, the firm will want to produce at an average cost as low as possible for that output.

Suppose the output level is to be x. The firm should construct the plant represented by SAC_1, which will produce output x at a smaller cost per unit (xA) than will either of the other two. Costs would be xB per unit if SAC_2 were used. For output x' the firm would be indifferent between SAC_1 and SAC_2 but for output x_1 it would prefer to use SAC_2. For output x_3 the firm would construct and use the plant represented by SAC_3. We are now in a position to define the *long-run average cost curve*. It shows the least possible cost per unit of producing various outputs when the firm can plan to build any desired size of plant. In Figure 9–7 the heavy portions of the SAC curves form the long-run average cost curve. The light portions of the SAC curves are irrelevant. The firm would never operate in the light portions in the long run, because if it were to do so, it could reduce costs by changing plant size.

The possible plant sizes that a firm can build as a long-run undertaking usually are unlimited in number. For every conceivable size there will be another infinitesimally larger or infinitesimally smaller. Their SAC curves are those of Figure 9–8, and any number of additional SAC curves can be drawn between any two of those in the diagram. The outer portions of the SAC curves form a heavy line, the long-run average cost curve or the LAC curve of Figure 9–8. Since the long-run average cost curve is made up of very small segments of the various SAC curves, it can be considered as a

Figure 9−8 The long-run average cost curve, infinite alternative plant sizes

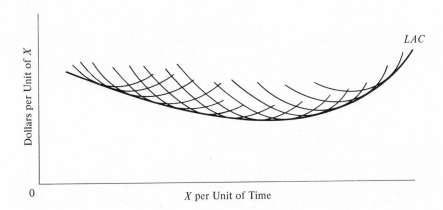

curve just tangent to all possible *SAC* curves representing the plant sizes that the firm conceivably could build. Mathematically it is an envelope curve to the *SAC* curves.

Every point on the long-run average cost curve, or the long-run total cost curve for that matter, requires that the firm be using a least cost combination of resources. For a given output long-run total cost and long-run average cost are least when *all* resources used are combined in proportions such that the marginal physical product per dollar's worth of one equals the marginal physical product per dollar's worth of every other resource used. This statement means that a dollar spent on management must add the same amount to total product as a dollar spent on raw materials. A dollar spent on labor and a dollar spent on machinery must both yield the same addition to total product, and so on for all resources. Should these conditions not be fulfilled—if a dollar spent on management adds less to total product than a dollar spent on machines—then some shifts in expenditures from management to machines will increase total product without increasing total costs; or, if we consider the matter another way, the shifts will provide a decrease in total cost or a decrease in average cost, holding total product constant. Thus, the cost levels shown by the long-run average cost curve for various outputs can be attained by the firm only if the least cost resource combination is used for each output.

Economies of size

The long-run average cost curve is usually thought to be a U-shaped curve. Such will be the case if a firm becomes successively more efficient up to some specific size or range of sizes and if it then becomes successively less efficient as the range of plant sizes from very small to very large is considered. Increasing efficiency associated with larger and larger plant sizes is reflected by SAC curves lying successively at lower levels and farther to the right. Examples are provided by SAC_1, SAC_2, and SAC_3 in Figure 9–9. Decreasing efficiency associated with still larger plant sizes would be shown by SAC curves lying successively at higher levels and farther to the right. The resulting LAC curve would thus have a general U shape.

Figure 9–9   Economies and diseconomies of size

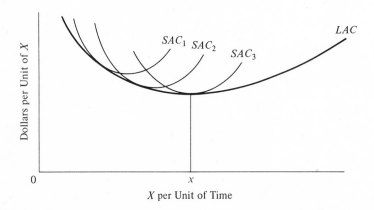

The forces causing the LAC curve to decrease for larger outputs and sizes of plant are called *economies of size*. Two important economies of size are (1) increasing possibilities of division and specialization of labor and (2) increasing possibilities of using advanced technological developments and/or larger machines. The economies will be discussed in turn.

Division and specialization of labor   The advantages of division and specialization of labor have long been known to both economists and the general public.[7] A small plant employing few workers cannot specialize the workers on particular operations as readily as can a larger plant employing a larger work force. In the small plant the typical worker performs several different operations in the process of producing the commodity and may not be particularly proficient at some of them. In addition, time may be lost in changing from one set of tools to another in performing different operations.

In a larger plant greater specialization may be possible, with the worker performing that process at which he is most adept. Specialization on a particular process eliminates the time lost in changing from one set of tools

[7] See Adam Smith, *The Wealth of Nations*, Edwin Cannan, ed. (New York: Modern Library, Inc., 1937), Bk. I, Chaps. I–III.

to another. Also, the worker performing a single type of operation develops shortcuts and speed in performing it. The efficiency of the workers is likely to be higher and cost per unit of output correspondingly lower where division and specialization of labor are possible. A word of warning may be necessary, though. In some cases it may be possible to carry specialization to the point at which the monotony of the task begins to counteract increases in the efficiency of the individual's performance.

Technological factors   The possibility of lowering costs per unit of output by mass-production technology increases as the plant size is increased. In the first place, the cheapest way of producing a small output will usually not be one that employs the most advanced technological methods. Consider, for example, the production of automobile hoods. If the output were to be two or three hoods per week, large automatic presses would not be used. The cheapest way to produce the hoods probably would be to hammer them out by hand. The cost per unit would be comparatively high. There would be no cheap way of producing the small output or of operating the small plant for the production of a small output.

For larger outputs and plant sizes mass-production technological methods can be used to effect reductions in per unit costs. In this example if output were to be several thousand units per week, then a larger plant with automatic presses could be installed, and costs per unit would be substantially lower than was possible with the small plant.

In the second place, technological considerations are usually such that in order to double the capacity of a machine to produce, a doubling of material, construction, and operating costs of the machine is not necessary. For example, it is cheaper to build and operate a 600-horsepower diesel motor than it is to build and operate two 300-horsepower diesel motors. The 600-horsepower motor has no more working parts than a single 300-horsepower motor. Additionally, the 600-horsepower motor does not require twice the amount of materials used in building a single 300-horsepower motor. The same type of example can be made for almost any machine. Technological possibilities represent a very important explanation of the increasing efficiency of larger and larger plant sizes, up to some limit.

Diseconomies of size

The question arises as to why, once the plant is large enough to take advantage of all economies of size, still larger sizes are likely to result in less efficiency. It would appear, offhand, that the firm would be able at least to maintain the economies of size. The answer usually given to this question is that there are limitations to the efficiency of management in controlling and coordinating a single firm. These limitations are called *diseconomies of size*.

As the size of the plant is increased, management, like the lower echelons of labor, may become more efficient through division of tasks and specialization in particular functions; but the argument commonly made is that beyond some certain size the difficulties of coordinating and controlling the firm multiply rapidly. The contacts of top management with the day-to-day operations of the business become more and more remote, causing operating efficiency in production departments to decrease. Decision-making responsibility must be delegated, and coordination must be established among the decision-making subordinates. The paper work, travel expenses, telephone bills, and additional employees necessary for coordination pile up. Occasionally, plans of separate decision-making subordinates fail to mesh and costly slowdowns occur. To the extent that increasing difficulties of coordination and control reduce the efficiency per dollar outlay on management as the size of the plant is increased, per unit costs of production will increase.

The discussion so far may be interpreted to mean that as the size of plant is increased, economies of size cause the long-run average cost curve to decrease, and then, when all economies of size are realized, diseconomies of size begin straightaway. Such is not necessarily the case. Once the plant is large enough to take advantage of all economies of size, there may be a range of larger plant sizes where diseconomies are not yet evident. As a result the long-run average cost curve will have a horizontal series of minimum points rather than the single minimum point of the conventional long-run average cost curve. When the plant has become sufficiently large for diseconomies of size to occur, the long-run average cost curve turns upward to the right. Another possibility is that some diseconomies begin to occur in a plant too small to realize all economies of size. If the economies of size for larger plants more than offset the diseconomies, the long-run average cost curve slopes downward to the right. Where diseconomies of size more than offset economies of size, the long-run average cost curve slopes upward to the right.

The most efficient size of plant

The most efficient size of plant is the one generating the short-run average cost curve that forms the minimum point of the long-run average cost curve. It can also be thought of as that size of plant with a short-run average cost curve tangent to the long-run average cost curve at the minimum points of both. The short-run average cost curve of the most efficient size of plant in Figure 9–10 is *SAC*.

Firms will not invariably construct plants of most efficient size and operate them at the most efficient rates of output. As we shall see, they will do so under conditions of pure competition in the long run; however, under pure monopoly, oligopoly, and monopolistic competition they are not likely

Figure 9-10   The most efficient size of plant

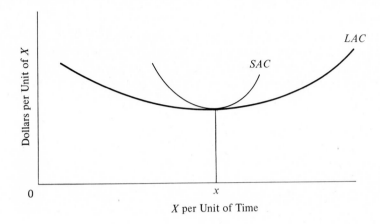

X per Unit of Time

to do so. The size of plant that will operate at the lowest cost per unit for given outputs will vary with the output to be produced. For example, in Figure 9–10 plant SAC will produce output x more cheaply than will a plant of any other size, and output x can be produced at a lower cost per unit than can any other output. But for outputs greater or less than x per unit costs will necessarily be higher. Plant sizes other than the most efficient size will produce such outputs at lower costs per unit than will the one of most efficient size.

How can we determine the size of plant to be constructed for a specific output? Consider Figure 9–11. Suppose that the firm is producing output x_1 with plant SAC_1. Plant SAC_1 is being operated at less than its most efficient rate of output. Let the output level be increased to x_2. The increase can be accomplished in either of two ways: (1) by increasing the output rate with plant SAC_1 or (2) by changing to a larger plant size. Either method will allow the firm to reduce costs per unit. Method 1 will cause SAC_1 to be used at its most efficient rate of output. Costs are lower than c_1. However, if the firm should use Method 2, economies of size from the larger plant will allow even greater per-unit cost reductions for output x_2 than will Method 1. Costs per unit will be c_2 with plant SAC_2, and this is the lowest cost at which that output can be produced. For outputs between 0 and x the firm will achieve lowest per unit costs for any given output by using a plant smaller than the most efficient size at less than the most efficient rate of output. Similarly, for any given output greater than x, the lowest cost per unit will be achieved if the firm uses a plant larger than the most efficient size at a greater than most efficient rate of output. The applicable general principle is this: To minimize cost for any given output the firm should use

Figure 9–11   Appropriate plant size for a given output

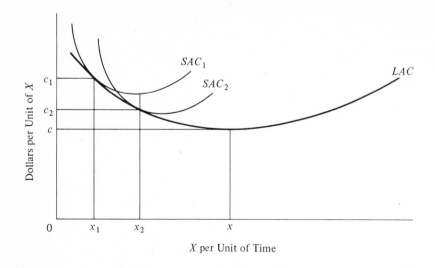

the plant size for which the short-run average cost curve is tangent to the long-run average cost curve at that output.

Long-run marginal cost

The *long-run marginal cost curve* shows the change in long-run total cost per unit change in the firm's output when the firm has ample time to accomplish the output change by making the appropriate adjustments in the quantities of all resources used, including those that constitute its plant. Or we can think of the *LMC* curve as measuring the slopes of the *LTC* curve at various output levels.

From the *LTC* curve of Figure 9–12 we can deduce that *LMC* would be less than *LAC* where *LAC* is decreasing—that is, from zero to output x—and would be greater than *LAC* for output levels beyond x where *LAC* is increasing. At output x, *LMC* and *LAC* are equal. These relationships are shown in Figure 9–13 by the *LAC* and *LMC* curves. The *LMC* curve bears the same relationship to its *LAC* curve that any given *SMC* curve bears to its *SAC* curve.

Relationships between *LMC* and *SMC*

When the firm has constructed the proper size of plant for producing a given output, short-run marginal cost will equal long-run marginal cost at that output. Suppose, for example, that the given output is x_2 in Figure

Figure 9–12   The relationship between short-run and long-run total costs

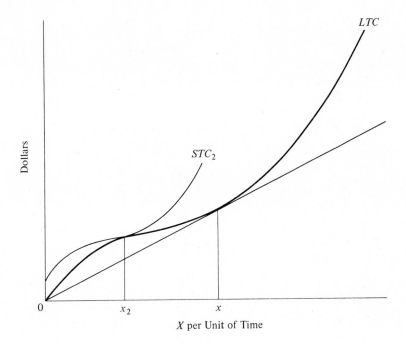

Figure 9–13   Relationship between SMC and LMC for a given SAC and LAC

9–13. The firm would use the plant represented by SAC_2, which is tangent to the LAC curve at that output. The corresponding total cost curves would be STC_2 and LTC in Figure 9–12. We can verify that STC_2 would lie above LTC at output levels below x_2 because SAC_2 is greater than LAC at those output levels. At output x_2, STC_2 would be equal to LTC because SAC_2 and LAC are equal. At outputs greater than x_2, STC_2 would again exceed LTC because SAC_2 for those outputs again lies above LAC. At output x_2, where SAC_2 is tangent to LAC, STC_2 must also be tangent to LTC. At outputs in the neighborhood of, but below x_2, the STC_2 curve must have a smaller slope than the LTC curve. At output levels greater than x_2, the STC_2 curve must have a greater slope than the LTC curve. At x_2, where STC_2 is tangent to LTC, both curves have the same slope.

Because the slope of the STC_2 curve is the short-run marginal cost for that size of plant and because the slope of LTC is the long-run marginal cost, it follows that $SMC_2 < LMC$ at outputs just smaller than x_2; $SMC_2 > LMC$ at outputs just larger than x_2; and SMC_2 equals LMC at output x_2. These relationships are shown in Figure 9–13.

Some applications of cost analysis

Costs of obtaining a higher education

What are the annual costs to a student of attending a college or university? Or, to state the question in a slightly different way, what does it cost a student to invest in human capital to the extent of 30 hours of college or university credit over the course of an academic year? Most students and their parents will underestimate the cost.

The explicit costs to the student are fairly clear. Tuition is a prime consideration. Next in importance (first at some schools) would be living expenses—room, board, and incidentals. Books and supplies round out the list. Here the calculations are likely to stop.

At least two items of an implicit nature are frequently overlooked. The most important one—and the largest cost item in a year of academic training—is the student's forgone earnings. What could the student have earned if she or he had elected to join the labor force in lieu of enrolling in the college or university and investing her or his time in studying? Another is the forgone interest on tuition payments. If tuition is paid at the beginning of each semester, the student loses interest on one-half the annual tuition for the academic year since a semester's tuition could have been kept out on loan at the going interest rate. Similar forgone interest costs may occur if room and board payments are made on a semester-by-semester basis.

However, these latter interest costs can be avoided if a student lives off the campus and/or pays room and board on a monthly basis.

Let us summarize and provide perspective. Dollar amounts that may approximate the various cost items for a student at a typical(?) college or university for an academic year (1979) are listed below:

Explicit Costs	
Tuition	$3,500
Room and board	3,000
Books and supplies	300
Subtotal	$6,800
Implicit Costs	
Forgone Earnings	$9,000
Forgone Interest	175
($1,750 @ 10%)	
Subtotal	$9,175
Total Costs	$15,975

Cost minimization by a multiple-unit firm

We have derived the cost curves for the overall operation of a firm, aggregating the costs of production of the various production units that the firm may operate if it is indeed a multiple-unit firm. An interesting problem remains, however. How should such a firm allocate its total output level among its production units in order to minimize the cost of producing the output level? Should it always seek to produce in those units that have the lowest average costs?

Suppose that a firm producing crude oil is composed of two units, Unit 1 and Unit 2. The short-run average and marginal cost curves of each unit are illustrated in Figure 9–14. Let the firm's anticipated total output level be X barrels per day.

To minimize its costs the firm should allocate the X barrels between Unit 1 and Unit 2 in such a way that the *marginal cost* of production in Unit 1 is equal to that of Unit 2; that is, Unit 1 should produce x_1 barrels and Unit 2 should produce x_2 barrels with $x_1 + x_2 = X$. Marginal cost in both Unit 1 and Unit 2 is M, or $10. Note that the average costs for Unit 1 are higher than the average costs for Unit 2 at these output levels.

Nevertheless, the firm's total costs are minimized. Suppose that the output level of Unit 1 is reduced by 1 barrel, while the output level of Unit 2 is increased by 1 barrel. Since marginal cost at the x_1 output level is $10, a 1-barrel reduction in the output of Unit 1 reduces the firm's total costs by that amount. But a 1-barrel increase in the output of Unit 2 pushes marginal cost in Unit 2 above $10—say, to $10.25. By the definition of marginal cost this amounts to a $10.25 increase in the firm's total costs. The *net* effect of a

Figure 9–14   Cost minimization by a multiple-unit firm

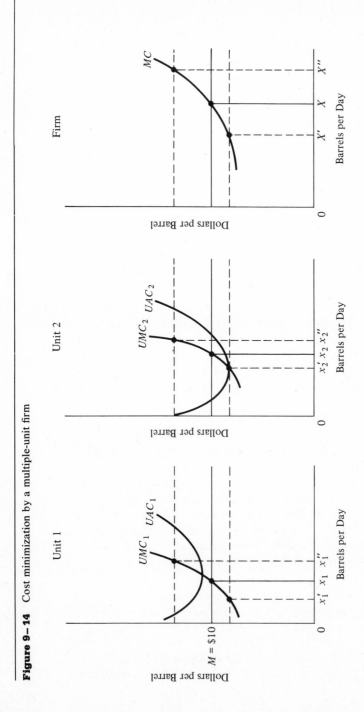

shift of a barrel of oil per day from Unit 1 to Unit 2 is a $0.25 increase in the firm's total costs. Similarly, from the original output levels, x_1 and x_2, a shift in production from Unit 2 to Unit 1 would increase the firm's total costs. Total costs are thus minimum when production is allocated so that the marginal cost is the same in each production unit.

These conditions for minimizing the firm's total costs are applicable for any total output level. If the firm were to produce X' barrels per day, x_1' should be produced by Unit 1 and x_2' should be produced by Unit 2. If the total output were to be X'', then x_1'' should be produced by Unit 1 and x_2'' should be produced by Unit 2. In each instance the total output is so allocated that marginal costs are the same for the two production units. If UMC_1 and UMC_2 are summed horizontally, we obtain the firm's overall marginal cost curve MC. This curve shows the marginal cost at alternative total output levels when each of those output levels is allocated among production units so as to minimize total costs.

Summary

Costs of production are the obligations incurred by the firm for resources used in the production of its product. The cost of any given resource is determined by its value in its best alternative use. This principle is called the alternative cost doctrine. Costs of production differ from the usual concept of the firm's "expenses," which usually coincide with explicit resource costs. In determining costs of production implicit resource costs also must be included. The analysis of costs presented in the chapter assumes that the firm by itself cannot influence the price of any resource that it buys.

In the short run resources used by the firm are classified as fixed and variable. The obligations incurred for them are fixed costs and variable costs. Total fixed costs and total variable costs for different outputs are the component parts of total costs. From the three total cost curves we derive the corresponding per unit cost curves—average fixed cost, average variable cost, and average cost. The short-run average cost curve shows the least per unit cost of producing different outputs with a given plant size and is a U-shaped curve. In addition, we derive the marginal cost curve. The output at which short-run average cost is least is called the optimum rate of output for a given size of plant.

All resources can be varied in quantity by the firm in the long run; consequently, all costs are variable. The long-run average cost curve shows the least per unit cost of producing various outputs when the firm is free to change its plant to any desired size. It is the envelope curve to the short-run average cost curves of all possible sizes of plant, and it is usually U-shaped.

The factors causing its U shape are called economies of size and diseconomies of size. The long-run marginal cost curve shows the change in total costs resulting from a one-unit change in output when the firm is free to vary the quantities used of all resources.

For whatever output the firm produces in the long run, if the least per unit cost is to be obtained for that output, the plant size must be such that its short-run average cost curve is tangent to the long-run average cost curve at that output. For such a plant size short-run marginal cost will equal long-run marginal cost at the output of tangency.

Suggested readings

Stigler, George J., *The Theory of Price,* 3rd ed. New York: Crowell-Collier and Macmillan, Inc., 1966. Chaps. 6, 9.

Viner, Jacob, "Cost Curves and Supply Curves," *Zeitschrift für Nationalökonomie,* Vol. III (1931), pp. 23–46. Reprinted in American Economic Association, *Readings in Price Theory,* George J. Stigler and Kenneth E. Boulding, eds. Homewood, Ill.: Richard D. Irwin, Inc., 1952. Pp. 198–232.

Questions and exercises

1. A steel mill uses labor and capital to produce tons of steel. The prices of labor and capital are p_{l_1} and p_{k_1}, respectively. With an isoquant-isocost diagram show how
   a. its short-run total cost curve is generated and explain the shape of the curve
   b. its long-run total cost curve is generated and explain the shape of the curve.

2. It is often argued that the reason for being of state universities is that they provide higher education at a lower cost than do private universities. Assuming that the quality of output is the same for each type of university, discuss this issue in terms of the annual costs
   a. to a student and his or her family
   b. to the society as a whole.

3. For automobiles of comparable size it would appear that General Motors produces at a lower cost per unit than does American Motors. If such is the case, what are some of the possible explanations for the cost differential?

4. The long-run average cost curve of a firm is given. Locate an output level to the left of its minimum point. What scale of plant should the firm use to produce that output? Show these points diagrammatically and draw in the long-run marginal cost and the short-run marginal cost curves. Explain your answers.

Appendix to Chapter 9
The geometry of short-run per unit cost curves

The relationships between total cost curves and per unit cost curves can be shown geometrically. Using the three total cost curves as starting points, we shall derive from them the corresponding per unit cost curves. Then we shall show geometrically the relationship between the average cost curve and the marginal cost curve.

The average fixed cost curve

In Figure 9–15(b) the average fixed cost curve is derived from the total fixed cost curve of Figure 9–15(a). The quantity scales of the two diagrams are

Figure 9–15 The geometry of *TFC* and *AFC*

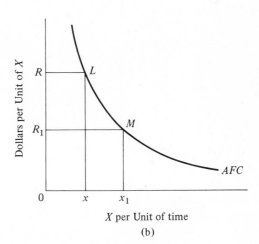

the same. The vertical axis of Figure 9–15(a) measures total fixed costs, whereas that of Figure 9–15(b) measures fixed cost per unit.

Consider output x in Figure 9–15(a). At that output total fixed cost is measured by xA. Now consider the straight line $0A$. The slope of $0A$ is $xA/0x$, which is numerically equal to average fixed cost $0R$ in Figure 9–15(b). Likewise, at output x_1 average fixed cost $0R_1$ in Figure 9–15(b) equals the slope of $0A_1$ or $x_1A_1/0x_1$.

At successively larger outputs the slopes of the corresponding $0A$ lines became smaller and smaller, showing that average fixed cost decreases as output increases; however, it can never reach zero. The numerical slopes of the $0A$ lines plotted against the respective outputs for which they are drawn comprise the average fixed cost curve of Figure 9–15(b).

Geometrically, the AFC curve is a rectangular hyperbola. It approaches but never reaches both the dollar axis and the quantity axis. It is convex to the origin of the diagram. The distinguishing feature of a rectangular hyperbola is that at any point on the curve, such as L, the values represented on each axis, when multiplied together, produce the same mathematical product as the multiplication of the corresponding values at any other point on the curve, such as M. In other words, $0x \times 0R = 0x_1 \times 0R_1$. Such must necessarily be the case for the average fixed cost curve. Becuase total fixed costs are constant and because average fixed cost at any output times that output equals total fixed cost, the mathematical product of any output times its corresponding average fixed cost must equal the mathematical product of any other output times its corresponding average fixed cost.

The average variable cost curve

In Figure 9–16(b) the average variable cost curve is derived from the total variable cost curve in Figure 9–16(a). The process of derivation is similar to that used in obtaining the AFC curve. At output x, TVC equals xB; hence, AVC at output x equals $xB/0x$, equals the slope of line $0B$. At x_1, AVC equals $x_1B_1/0x_1$, equals the slope of $0B_1$. At x_3, AVC equals $x_3B_3/0x_3$, equals the slope of $0B_3$. At x_4, AVC equals $x_4B_4/0x_4$, equals the slope of $0B_4$. The numerical slopes of the $0B$ lines plotted against their respective outputs trace out the AVC curve of Figure 9–16(b).

Figure 9–16   The geometry of TVC and AVC

(a)

(b)

The geometric derivation of the AVC curve makes it clear that the curve takes its shape from the TVC curve. Between 0 output and output x_3 the $0B$ line for each successively larger output must have a smaller slope than the one for the preceding output. Hence, between 0 and x_3 the AVC curve must be decreasing. At output x_3 line $0B_3$ is just tangent to the TVC curve and, thus, has a smaller slope than any other $0B$ line can possibly have. At x_3, AVC is as low as it can get. At outputs greater than x_3 the $0B$ lines will increase in slope, meaning that AVC is increasing. The AVC curve must have a U shape if we have correctly established the shape of the TVC curve.

The average cost curve

In Figure 9–17(b) the average cost is derived from the total cost curve in the same way that the AVC curve is derived from the TVC curve. At output x,

Figure 9–17   The geometry of TC and AC

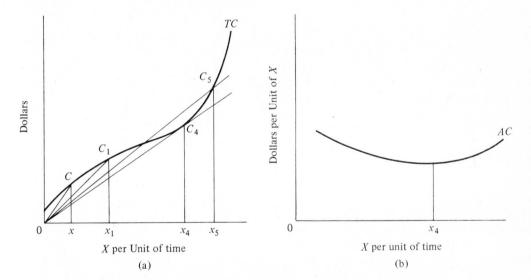

(a)   (b)

TC equals xC, so AC equals $xC/0x$, equals the slope of line $0C$. At output x_1, AC equals $x_1C_1/0x_1$, equals the slope of $0C_1$. At output x_4, AC equals $x_4C_4/0x_4$, equals the slope of $0C_4$. At output x_5, AC equals $x_5C_5/0x_5$, equals the slope of $0C_5$. The slopes of the $0C$ lines plotted against the corresponding outputs locate the AC curve in Figure 9–17(b).

If the shape of the TC curve is correct, the AC curve must be a U-shaped curve. The $0C$ lines decrease in slope as output increases up to output x_4. At output x_4, $0C_4$ is tangent to the TC curve and, consequently, is the one of least slope. Here AC is minimum. At greater outputs the slopes of the $0C$ lines are increasing; that is, AC is increasing.

The relationship of *AC* and *MC*

The relationship between AC and MC can be shown geometrically with the aid of the TC curve of Figure 9–18. Consider output x_1. Average cost at x_1 is

Figure 9–18   The geometry of AC and MC

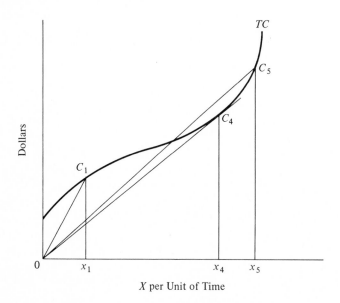

equal to the slope of line $0C_1$. Marginal cost at output x_1 is equal to the slope of the TC curve at that output. The line $0C_1$ has a greater slope than does the TC curve at output x_1; hence, average cost at x_1 is greater than marginal cost at the same output. This will be the case for any output up to x_4. At output x_4 the slope of the line $0C_4$ is equal to the slope of the total cost curve at that output, meaning that average cost and marginal cost are equal at that output. As we have seen already, average cost is minimum at output x_4. At output x_5 the slope of line $0C_5$ is less than the slope of the TC curve, meaning that marginal cost is greater than average cost at that output. This relationship will hold at any output above x_4—that is, at outputs for which average cost is increasing. Thus, when average cost is decreasing, marginal cost is less than average cost. When average cost is minimum, marginal cost equals average cost. When average cost is increasing, marginal cost is greater than average cost.

Part 4

Prices and output levels of goods and services

We bring demand and costs together in Part 4. Building on the foundations laid in Parts 2 and 3 we develop models of the market mechanism to show how prices and output levels of goods and services are determined under each of the four basic selling market structures that were introduced in Chapter 7.

Chapter 10

Chapter contents

		Key concepts
The very short run	**Rationing among consumers**	Pure competition
	Rationing over time	Very short run
	A corollary	Short run
		Profits
The short run	**The firm**	Losses
	Profits	Marginal revenue
	Profit maximization: total curves	Marginal costs
	Profit maximization: per unit curves	Shut down price
	Loss minimization	Short-run supply curve, firm
	Short-run supply curve of the firm	Short-run supply curve, market
	The market	Long run
	Short-run supply curve of the market	Most efficient size of plant
	Short-run equilibrium	Most efficient rate of output
	Supply curve modifications	Increasing cost industry
The long run	**The firm: size of plant adjustments**	Long-run supply curve, market
	The firm and the market	External diseconomies
	Long-run equilibrium	Constant cost inudstry
	Increasing costs	Decreasing cost industry
	Constant costs	External economies
	Decreasing costs	Welfare
The welfare effects of pure competition	**The very short run**	
	The short run	
	The long run	
Summary	**Suggested readings**	
	Questions and exercises	

Pricing and output under pure competition

The purely competitive model of prices and outputs is constructed in this chapter. It explains how production is organized by prices and profits in a purely competitive or frictionless private enterprise economy. Ways in which monopoly elements modify the operation and the results of the system are taken into account in the following three chapters.

Pure competition was defined in Chapter 3. Its prime characteristics are (1) product homogeneity among the sellers of an industry, (2) many buyers and sellers of the product—that is, enough of each so that no one is large enough relative to the entire market to influence product price—(3) an absence of artificial restraints on demand, supply, and product price, and (4) mobility of goods and resources.

The very short run

The *very-short-run* period, or *market* period, refers to situations in which supplies of products are already in existence. For example, demand for a product may be seasonal, with production scheduled ahead of the season in which the product is to be sold. The clothing industries are cases in point. Spring, summer, fall, and winter production are based on estimated seasonal demands and occur well in advance of the season of sales. Other examples are fresh fruit and vegetable retail markets. Retailers purchase stocks of perishable goods. Once the stocks are on hand, they must be disposed of before they spoil. Still another example is that of a product produced seasonally for a demand that continues the year around. Production of wheat and other farm crops is typical of this type of situation. Two basic problems must be solved by the economy in the very short run: (1) how are existing supplies of goods to be allocated or rationed among the many consumers who want them, and (2) how are given supplies to be rationed over their entire very-short-run periods?

Rationing among consumers

Price is the mechanism for rationing or allocating a fixed supply among the consumers who want it. Suppose that the period during which the supply is

Figure 10–1   Very-short-run rationing among consumers

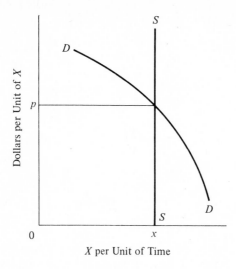

fixed is one day and that the demand curve of Figure 10–1 shows the different quantities per day that consumers will take from the market at different possible prices. The supply curve is vertical since the supply for the day is fixed. Price p will clear the market. Everyone who wants the commodity at that price will receive it in the desired amounts. At a price below p a shortage will develop, and consumers will drive the price up. At a price above p a surplus will exist, and individual sellers will lower their prices to get surpluses off their hands. At price p consumers voluntarily ration themselves to the fixed supply.

Rationing over time

Prices also serve to ration a fixed supply over time, but the rationing process is more complex. Suppose that the market period is one year. Suppose, however, that the demand curve of Figure 10–2 is based on a 4-month period only. To simplify matters, suppose further that the demand curves for each of the three 4-month periods of the year are alike. Assume that sellers more or less correctly anticipate the market for each 4-month period and sell or hold their supplies accordingly.

Since the diagram applies to a 4-month period only, the supply curve for the first 4-month period will not be vertical. Sellers have the option of selling during any of the three 4-month periods. The higher the price offered during the first period, the greater the quantity of the good they would be

Figure 10–2 Very-short-run rationing over time

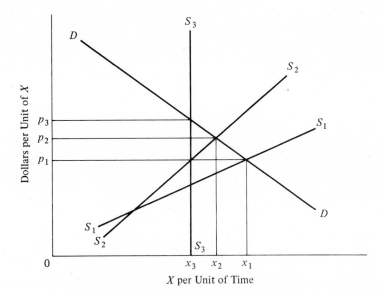

expected to place on the market during that period. Thus, the supply curve for the first 4-month period will be upward-sloping to the right as is S_1S_1. The market price will be p_1, and the quantity sold will be x_1.

The supply curve for the second 4-month period would be expected to lie above S_1S_1, except at low prices, and to be less elastic. It would lie above S_1S_1 because sellers, to be induced to hold quantities over, would require sufficiently higher prices for different quantities to cover storage costs and a normal rate of return on investment in the goods carried over. At extremely low prices, however, the second 4-month period may lie to the right of S_1S_1. The possibility of low prices in the second period would be more serious to sellers than would a similar possibility in the first period because the opportunities for disposing of supplies held over are reduced. Consequently, sellers may be induced to place more on the market than they would be willing to at those same prices in the first period. The smaller elasticity at various prices is also a result of the narrowing of opportunities for disposing of the supplies held over. The periods during which supply can be disposed of now have been reduced to two. The supply curve for the second period would look something like S_2S_2. The price would be p_2, and the quantity sold would be x_2.

The third 4-month period will be identical with the case shown in Figure 10–1. The remaining supply must be disposed of in the third period; consequently, the supply curve will be S_3S_3 in Figure 10–2. Note that S_3S_3 lies above S_2S_2 except at low prices and that it is less elastic than S_2S_2. In fact, S_3S_3 is completely inelastic. The price will be p_3, and the quantity sold will be x_3.

The successively higher prices for the 4-month periods will occur as shown only if sellers correctly anticipate demand and the amounts that should be held over. If sellers misjudge the future market and hold large quantities over to the second and third periods, the prices during those periods may fall below that of the first period. If sellers' anticipations are correct, the price for each successive period should be sufficiently higher than that of preceding periods to pay storage costs, a normal rate of return on investment in held-over supplies, and compensation for the risks involved in holding supplies over to succeeding periods.

Thus, price is the rationer of fixed supplies over time. Sellers or speculators, as the case may be, in holding supplies off the market during the early part of the overall very-short-run period cause the price to be higher during that time than it would otherwise have been. By their speculative activity they smooth out both the prices and quantities sold over the entire period. In the absence of any speculative activity relatively large quantities would be placed on the market early in the period, holding the price down. Relatively small quantities available in the latter part of the period would cause the price to be high. The speculative activity described, while not eliminating the upward price trend over time, does much to narrow the diferential between the early and late parts of the period. Activity of this type occurs regularly in the markets for those storable farm products lying outside the price-support program.

A corollary

A corollary to this discussion is that once a good is on the market in fixed quantity, costs of production play no part in the determination of its price. The price will be determined solely by the fixed supply, together with demand for the product.[1] It is futile for holders of such a product to try to recoup production costs. A purely competitive seller who cannot consume the product himself will prefer to dispose of his holdings at any price above zero rather than keep it indefinitely. Old bread and overripe bananas are cases in point. Costs of production enter the picture only when there is some possibility of varying the supply produced over the time period under consideration. Such a possibility exists in both the short and the long run, which we have yet to consider.

---

[1] Note that in the example of Figure 10–2 market supply is fixed at an absolute quantity for the third period only.

The short run

A time period in which a firm can vary its output but does not have time to change its size of plant is the *short run*. The number of firms in an industry is fixed because new firms do not have time to enter and existing firms do not have time to leave. Any changes in industry output must come from the fixed plant capacity of existing firms. Since each firm is too small, relative to the market in which it sells, to be able to affect the market price of the product, the problem facing the firm is that of determining what output to produce and sell. For the market as a whole the market price and market output must be determined.

The firm

As a starting point, we use the premise that a firm's objective is to maximize its profits or to minimize its losses if it cannot make profits. This premise can be modified to include such objectives as sales maximization with a minimum profit constraint, concern for the environment, enhancement of community cultural activities, and the like. But usually we expect a firm to make those choices that will enable it to make more profits rather than less, and such choices lead toward profit maximization.

Profits   Since the concept of profit is ambiguous enough to require explicit definition, a note on profits is in order before proceeding further. *Economic profits* are a pure surplus or an excess of total receipts over *all* costs of production incurred by the firm. Included as costs are obligations incurred for all resources used equal to what those resources could earn employed in their next best alternative uses, that is, the opportunity or alternative costs of all resources used. These costs include returns to the owners of capital used equivalent to what they could get had they invested in capital elsewhere in the economy. They include implicit returns to labor owned by the operator of the business. Thus, profits are so much "gravy" for the firm.

The contrast between the concept of economic profits as defined and the accountant's concept of a corporation's net income or "profits" should help make this definition clear. Corporation income taxes will be ignored. A corporation's "profits" are determined by the accountant as follows:

Gross income
- Expenses (including interest payments on bonds,
          amortization expenses, depreciation expenses, and so on)
= Net income or "profits"

However, from the point of view of economics certain costs have been left out of consideration. Obligations incurred to the owners of the corporation's capital (its stockholders) are as much costs of production as are those incurred for labor or for raw materials. The corporation is usually thought to make payments to capital owners in the form of dividends from the corporation's "profits," but from the point of view of economic theory such a conception is incorrect. To arrive at economic profits, dividend payments equal to what investors could earn had they invested elsewhere in the economy should be subtracted from the corporation's net income as follows:

$$\begin{array}{l} \text{Net income or ``profits''} \\ \underline{- \text{ Average dividends}} \\ = \text{Economic profits} \end{array}.$$

What happens to profits made by an individual firm? They accrue primarily to the owners of the firm in the form of (1) higher returns to investors in the business or (2) increases in the value of the owners' holdings. The former means higher-than-average dividends to stockholders in the case of the corporation or a higher income in the case of a single proprietor or partner than could have been earned had that individual invested and/or worked elsewhere. The latter means that some of the economic profits are plowed back into the firm to expand or improve it. This action increases the value of the owners' holdings. Profits may be used sometimes to pay other resource owners' returns that are more than the opportunity costs of their resources.

Profit maximization: total curves   Profit maximization involves a comparison of total costs with total receipts at various possible output levels and choice of the output at which total receipts exceed total costs by the greatest amount. Total receipts, or total revenue at different outputs, are plotted against short-run total costs at various levels of output in Figure 10–3. The total cost curve is the short-run total cost curve of the preceding chapter. The total receipts curve needs further elaboration.

Since the purely competitive firm can sell either large or small outputs at the same price per unit, its total receipts curve will be a linear upward-sloping curve starting at zero. If sales of the firm are zero, so are total receipts. If sales are one unit of output per unit of time, the firm's total receipts are equal to the price of the product. At two units of output and sales, total receipts will be twice the price of the product. Each one-unit addition to the firm's sales per unit of time will increase total receipts by a constant amount—the price per unit of product—hence, the total receipts curve is upward-sloping and linear.[2]

---

[2] The total receipts curve can be written as

$$R = f(x) = xp.$$

Figure 10–3   Short-run profit maximization: total curves

(a)

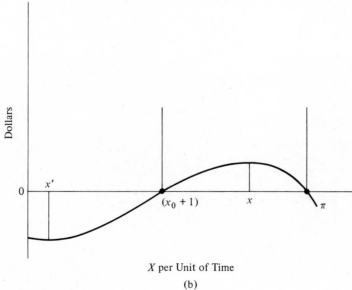

(b)

Profits of the firm are maximum at output x, where the vertical distance of TR above TC is greatest. The amount is measured by AB. At output x the slopes of the two curves are equal. At outputs just smaller than x the slope of TR exceeds that of TC; hence, the two curves spread farther and farther apart as output increases. At outputs just greater than x the slope of TC exceeds that of TR; hence, the two curves come closer and closer together as output increases.

The amount by which the firm's total receipts change when its sales are changed by one unit is called *marginal revenue*. Under conditions of pure competition, since the product price is fixed in the firm's view, the change in total receipts brought about by a one-unit change in sales is necessarily equal to the product price. Marginal revenue and the product price for the purely competitive seller are the same thing. In Figure 10–3(a) an increase in sales from x_0 to $(x_0 + 1)$ increases TR by an amount equal to p. Thus, marginal revenue and product price are equal to the slope of the TR curve.[3]

The necessary conditions for profit maximization can be restated in terms of marginal revenue and marginal cost. Since marginal cost is equal to the slope of the TC curve and marginal revenue is equal to the slope of the TR curve, profits are maximized at the output at which marginal cost equals marginal revenue.[4] At outputs between x' and x we can see that marginal revenue is greater than marginal cost. Therefore, larger outputs in this range up to x will add more to the firm's total receipts than to the firm's total costs and, consequently, will make net additions to profits or net deductions from losses. Beyond output x marginal cost is greater than marginal revenue. Thus, larger outputs beyond x add more to total costs than to total receipts and cause profits to decrease.[5]

---

[3] The relationship between marginal revenue and total revenue is the same as that between marginal utility and total utility, between marginal physical product and total product of a resource, and between marginal cost and total cost. Since

$$R = f(x) = xp,$$

in which p is a constant, then

$$MR = \frac{dR}{dx} = f'(x) = p.$$

[4] This statement must be used with caution. Consider output x' in Figure 10–3. At output x' losses are maximized rather than profits, although marginal cost equals marginal revenue. The relationship between the TR curve and the TC curve at the output of equality between MR and MC must be considered carefully.

[5] Denoting profits by π and letting the total cost function be $C = g(x)$, then

$$\pi = R - C = f(x) - g(x).$$

The first-order conditions for profit maximization are

$$\frac{d\pi}{dx} = f'(x) - g'(x) = 0,$$

or

$$f'(x) = g'(x);$$

Profit maximization: per unit curves Analysis of the firm's profit-maximizing output is usually put in terms of per unit cost and revenue curves. The basic analysis is the same as above, but the diagrammatic treatment is in a different form. The firm's short-run average cost curve and short-run marginal cost curve are shown in Figure 10–4, as is the demand

---

Figure 10-4   Short-run profit maximization: per unit curves

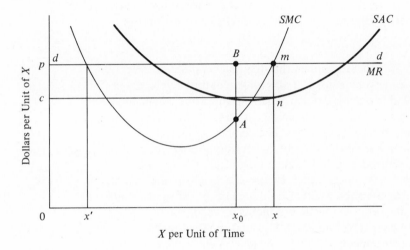

curve faced by the firm. Since marginal revenue is equal to the price per unit, the marginal revenue curve coincides with the demand curve faced by the firm. Both are horizontal at the level of the market price of the product.

Profits are maximum at the output level at which marginal cost equals marginal revenue, that is, at x, where SMC equals MR.[6] At any output less than x, say x_0, marginal revenue x_0B exceeds marginal cost x_0A. Larger

---

that is,

$$MR = MC.$$

If the second-order conditions show

$$\frac{d^2\pi}{dx^2} < 0,$$

the output is one of maximum profit—like x in Figure 10–3(b). If the second-order conditions show

$$\frac{d^2\pi}{dx^2} > 0,$$

losses are maximized. This is the case at x' in Figure 10–3(b).

[6] Note that MC equals MR at output x', but this is an output of maximum loss. For profit maximization MC must equal MR and, *additionally*, the MC curve must intersect the MR curve from below.

outputs up to x will increase total receipts more than they increase total costs; hence, profits will increase up to that point. Beyond output x, SMC is greater than MR, and movement to those larger outputs will increase total costs more than they increase total receipts, causing profits to decrease. Therefore, x is the output of maximum profits. Total profits of the firm appear in Figure 10–4 as the area of the rectangle $cpmn$. Profit per unit is the price p minus average cost c at output x. Total profit is equal to profit per unit multiplied by sales; that is, total profit equals $cp \times x$. Note that at output x profit per unit is not maximized, nor is there any reason why it should be. The concern of the firm is with total profits, not with profit per unit.

Loss minimization   If it should happen that the market price of the product is less than short-run average costs at all possible output levels, the firm will incur losses instead of making profits. Since the short run is defined as a time period so short that the firm cannot change its size of plant, liquidation of the plant in the short run is not possible. The choices open to the firm are (1) whether to produce at a loss or (2) whether to discontinue production. Fixed costs will be incurred even if the second alternative is chosen.

The firm's decision rests on whether or not the price of the product covers average variable costs (or whether total receipts cover total variable costs). Suppose the market price of the product is p_0 in Figure 10–5. If the firm produces x_0, at which SMC equals MR_0, total receipts equal $p_0 \times x_0$. Total variable costs also equal $p_0 \times x_0$; hence, total receipts just cover total variable costs. Total costs are equal to total variable costs plus total fixed

Figure 10–5   Short-run loss minimization

costs; therefore, if variable costs are just covered, the firm's loss will be equal to total fixed costs. It makes no difference whether the firm produces or not. In either case losses equal total fixed costs.

If the market price is less than minimum average variable costs, the firm will minimize losses by discontinuing production. The loss will equal total fixed costs when the firm produces nothing. If the firm should produce at a price less than p_0, average variable costs would be greater than price and total variable costs would be greater than total receipts. Losses would equal total fixed costs plus that part of total variable costs not covered by total receipts. Price p_0 is called the *shut down price*.

At a price greater than minimum average variable costs, but less than minimum SAC, it pays the firm to produce. At a price such as p_1, an output of x_1 results in losses that are less in amount than total fixed costs. Total receipts are $p_1 \times x_1$. Total variable costs are $v_1 \times x_1$. Total receipts exceed total variable costs by an amount equal to $v_1 p_1 \times x_1$. The excess of total receipts over total variable costs can be applied against total fixed costs, thus reducing losses to an amount less than total fixed costs. Loss in this case equals $p_1 c_1 \times x_1$.

Suppose, for example, that the firm under consideration is a wheat farmer who owns his farm and his machinery. The farm is mortgaged and the machinery is not yet paid for. Mortgage and machinery payments constitute fixed costs and must be met whether or not the farmer produces wheat. Outlays for seed, gasoline, fertilizer, and his own labor represent variable costs. If the farmer produces nothing, there are no outlays on variable resources.

Under what circumstances should the farmer produce nothing at all and hire his labor out to someone else? If expected receipts from the wheat crop are not sufficient to cover the costs of seed, gasoline, fertilizer, and his own labor, he should not produce. If he produces under these circumstances, his losses will equal mortgage and machinery payments plus that part of his variable costs not covered by his receipts. If he does not produce, his losses will equal mortgage and machinery payments only. Thus, he should not produce.

Under what circumstances will it be to his advantage to produce even though incurring losses? If expected receipts will more than cover the variable costs, the excess can be applied to the mortgage and machinery payments, and production should be undertaken. Under these circumstances a decision not to produce means that the loss will be the full amount of the fixed costs. If the farmer produces, the loss will be less than the total fixed costs.

At output level x_1, when the market price is p_1, equality between SMC and MR shows that losses are minimum. At a lower output MR is greater than SMC, and increases in output will add more to total receipts than to total costs, thus reducing losses. Beyond x_1, SMC is greater than MR, meaning that increases in output add more to total costs than to total receipts. The increases in output will increase the losses. Hence, losses are minimum at the output where SMC equals MR.

To summarize, the firm maximizes profits or minimizes losses by producing the output at which SMC equals MR, or the price. There is one exception. If the market price is less than the firm's average variable costs, losses will be minimized by stopping production altogether, leaving losses equal to total fixed costs.

Short-run supply curve of the firm   That part of the firm's SMC curve that lies above the AVC curve is the firm's *short-run supply curve* for the product. The SMC curve shows the different quantities that the firm will place on the market at different possible prices. At each possible price the firm will produce the amount at which SMC equals p (and MR) to maximize profits or minimize losses. Supply drops to zero at any price below AVC.

The market

The market price has been taken as given thus far, but we now have the tools necessary to see how it is determined. Market price emerges from interactions between demanders of a good, on the one hand, and suppliers of the good, on the other. We discussed the forces underlying a market demand curve in previous chapters, but we have yet to establish the market supply curve. The short-run market supply curve for a commodity is a short step beyond the individual firm supply curve. After we establish it, we shall consider short-run equilibrium for an entire market.

Short-run supply curve of the market   As a first approximation we can think of the *market short-run supply curve* as the horizontal summation of the short-run supply curves of all firms in the market. This supply curve shows the quantities of the commodity that all firms together will place on the market at various possible prices. Such a market short-run supply curve is valid if resource supplies to the group of firms in the market are perfectly elastic, that is, if changes in resource inputs and product output by all firms simultaneously have no effect on resource prices. We shall return to this point shortly.

Short-run equilibrium   Diagrammatically, Figure 10–6 shows the determination of market price, market output, and the output of one representative firm of the industry. The output axis of the market diagram is considerably compressed as compared with that of the firm diagram. The price axes of the two diagrams are identical. The market demand curve for the product is shown as DD in the market diagram. The SAC and SMC curves of the representative firm are drawn in the firm diagram. The horizontal

Figure 10–6   Short-run equilibrium: firm and industry

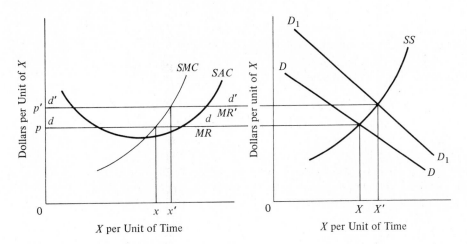

summation of all individual firm supply curves establishes the market short-run supply curve SS. The short-run equilibrium market price will be p. The demand curve and the marginal revenue curve faced by the firm will be horizontal at that level. To maximize profits, the representative firm, and each firm in the market, will produce the output at which $SMC = MR = p$. The firm output is x. The combined outputs of all firms are the market output X. The market as a whole and each individual firm in the market are in short-run equilibrium.

An increase in market demand for the product to D_1D_1 will increase the short-run equilibrium price and output. The increase in demand will cause a shortage of the good at the old price p. The price will be driven up by consumers to p'. The demand curve and marginal revenue curve faced by the firm shift up to the level of the new market price. To maximize profits, each firm will increase its output up to the level at which its SMC equals its new marginal revenue and the new market price. The new output level for the representative firm will be x', and the new market output will be X'.

Supply curve modifications   When an expansion or contraction of resource inputs by all firms acting simultaneously cause resource prices to change, the market short-run supply curve is no longer the horizontal summation of individual firm supply curves. Even though one firm cannot affect resource prices through expansion or contraction of the quantities it buys, all firms acting at the same time may be able to do so. If the expansion of the market output and resource inputs increases resource prices, individual firm cost curves will shift upward. If expansion decreases resource prices, firm cost curves will shift downward. The possibility exists, too, that some resource prices will increase and some will decrease. The effect may be to change the shape of the cost curves slightly and to cause some shift up or down, depending on whether resource price increases or resource price decreases are predominant.

The net effect of resource price increases when expansion occurs will be to make the market short-run supply curve less elastic than it would otherwise be. In Figure 10–6 the increase in demand increases price and marginal revenue, inducing firms to expand output. But suppose that the output expansion causes resource prices to increase, shifting SAC and SMC upward. The upward shift in SMC is also a shift to the left, meaning that the new SMC curve will equal marginal revenue or price at a smaller output than would be the case had the SMC curve not shifted. Similarly, resource price decreases resulting from expansion of the market output will cause the market supply curve to be more elastic than the market supply curve shown in Figure 10–6. The market short-run supply curve in this case is obtained by summing individual firm profit-maximizing outputs at each possible level of the market price.

The long run

The possibilities of output variation in a purely competitive industry are much greater in the long run than in the short run. In the *long run* output can be varied through increases or decreases in the utilization of existing plant capacity—as is the case in the short run. More important, however, in the long run firms have time to increase or decrease their plant sizes, and there is ample time and opportunity for new firms to enter or for existing firms to leave the industry. The two latter possibilities greatly increase the elasticity of the long-run market supply curve as compared with the short-run market supply curve. Long-run adjustments in the size of plant by individual firms will occur simultaneously with the entrance or exit of firms to and from the industry, but they can be more easily understood if they are considered first by themselves.

The firm: size of plant adjustments

The firm's determination of the size of plant to use can be put into proper focus by assuming that entry into the industry is blocked in some way. Suppose that the firm is faced with a certain market price, say p, in Figure 10–7. Its long-run average cost curve and long-run marginal cost curve are LAC and LMC, respectively. To maximize long-run profits, the firm should produce output x, at which long-run marginal cost equals marginal revenue. The plant size that enables the firm to produce output x at the least possible

Figure 10–7 Plant size adjustment in the long run

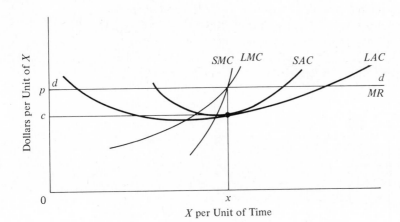

cost per unit is SAC, and for that size of plant short-run marginal cost also is equal to marginal revenue. Profits of the firm are $cp \times x$.

The firm and the market

Long-run equilibrium For a firm *long-run equilibrium* means that it has either no incentive or no opportunity to change what it is doing. If profit maximization is its objective, the firm of Figure 10–7 is in long-run equilibrium. Its $LMC = MR = p$, so that there is no incentive to change the size of its plant. Its $SMC = MR = p$, so that there is no incentive to move from an output level of x per unit of time.

Long-run equilibrium for the industry implies more than that the firms in the industry are in long-run equilibrium. In addition, there must be no incentive for new firms to enter the industry or for existing firms to leave. In other words, there must be no lure of economic profits to induce the entry of new firms, nor can there be the pain of losses to induce present firms to leave.

If entry into the industry is open—and in pure competition it is not blocked—profits like those made by the firm of Figure 10–7 will attract new firms. The industry promises a rate of return to investors greater than that they can earn on the average elsewhere in the economy. The entry of new firms increases the supply of product X and causes the price to move downward from its original level p. Each individual firm in the industry, faced with a downward-shifting demand curve and marginal revenue curve, will cut its output level below x and will reduce its size of plant below SAC. In the interest of maximizing profits, outputs will be cut to levels at which the long-run marginal cost curve cuts the successively lower marginal revenue curves.

Economic profits can be made by firms in the industry until enough firms have entered to drive the price down to p_1, as is shown in Figure 10–8. At

Figure 10–8   Long-run equilibrium

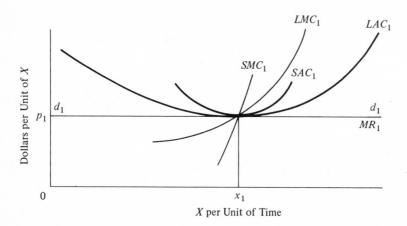

that point individual firms will have cut their plants back to the most efficient sizes as is shown by SAC_1, and they will operate at the most efficient rate of output. Economic profits have been eliminated by the entry of new firms, and there is no incentive for more firms to enter. No losses are being incurred, and, thus, there is no incentive for firms to leave the industry. The firms in the industry are doing satisfactorily; they are earning returns for all resources equal to what those resources could earn in alternative employments.[7]

---

[7] In the discussion of the long run we shall assume that for all firms, both in the industry and potentially in it, the minimum points of the *LAC* curves lie at the same level. This condition is a necessary one for defining the long-run equilibrium position of an industry.

In reality long-run equilibrium is never likely to be achieved in any industry. It is a will-o'-the-wisp that industries forever chase but never catch. Before an industry can reach equilibrium, conditions defining the equilibrium position change. Demand for the product changes, or costs of production change as a result of resource price changes, or techniques of production alter. Thus, the chase goes on toward a new equilibrium position. The long-run (and other) equilibrium concepts are important, however, because they show us the motivation for and the direction of the chase. Additionally, they show us how the chase works toward (in most cases) solution of the economic problem.

The argument usually made regarding equality of minimum long-run average costs of firms in the industry rests on the alternative cost doctrine. Initial inequalities in such costs may result from superior management of particular firms, from favorable locations of certain firms with respect to power, markets, and sources of raw and semifinished materials, or from other similar causes. According to the alternative cost doctrine these differentials will not persist. The superior manager who can make profits for the firm

The industry is in long-run equilibrium when all firms of the industry are in the position shown in Figure 10–8. For every firm $LAC = SAC = p$ at the output being produced, and at no other output can lower average costs be obtained. Also, for each firm there is no incentive to increase or decrease the size of plant or output since $LMC = SMC = MR$.

For long-run industry equilibrium to exist, individual firms must also be in long-run equilibrium. The converse of this assertion will not hold. An individual firm could be in long-run equilibrium while making profits—as in Figure 10–7, for example. But in this case the industry would not be in equilibrium. The existence of long-run industry equilibrium requires long-run individual firm equilibrium at a no-profit, no-loss level of operation.

Similarly, long-run industry and individual firm equilibrium requires that short-run equilibrium exist at the same time. Short-run individual firm and industry equilibrium can exist even though there is long-run individual firm and/or industry disequilibrium. Long-run equilibrium of an industry is a more general concept than is either long-run equilibrium for a firm or short-run equilibrium for both a firm and an industry.

Although this analysis serves to introduce the concept of long-run equilibrium in a purely competitive industry, it is by no means a complete analysis of the long-run adjustments within the industry that occur as a result of some disturbing force. Usually cost changes as well as price changes will take place as new firms, attracted by profits, enter the industry. The nature of the cost adjustments, if any, will depend on whether the industry is one of increasing costs, constant costs, or decreasing costs. Each of these will be analyzed in turn below.

Increasing costs   Consider first an industry of *increasing costs*. The nature of increasing costs will become evident as we move through the analysis. Suppose that the industry is initially in long-run equilibrium. Then suppose that the disturbing force is an increase in demand for product X. We shall trace through the short-run and long-run effects of the increase in demand. Then the long-run market supply curve for the product will be established.

Long-run equilibrium diagrams for the industry and for a representative firm of the industry are shown in Figure 10–9. The market demand curve is DD, and the market short-run supply curve is SS. The firm's long-run average cost curve and short-run average cost curve are LAC and SAC,

---

could do the same for other firms in the industry and, perhaps, in others outside the industry. The manager's prospective value to other firms becomes his or her cost to the firm in which the manager works; thus, the cost of the manager's services to the one firm increases to the point at which the manager can make pure profits for none. The same argument applies to a favorable location. The cost of the favorable location becomes its value to other firms that could use it to advantage. Its value to other firms is the capitalized value of the returns it could earn for them. Hence, the profits it can earn for any one firm disappear as its cost is correctly determined.

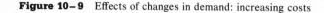

Figure 10–9 Effects of changes in demand: increasing costs

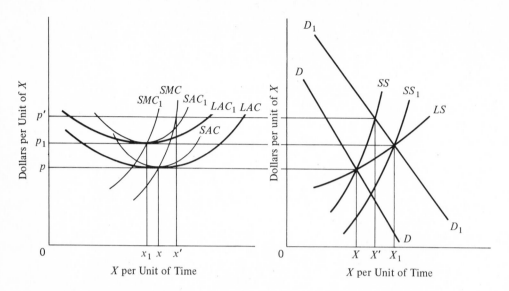

respectively. The firm's short-run marginal cost curve for size of plant SAC is SMC. The long-run marginal cost curve is omitted. It is not essential for the analysis and unduly complicates the diagram.

Since the industry and the firm are in long-run equilibrium, they are necessarily in short-run equilibrium, too. Therefore, we can think of the market demand curve and the market short-run supply curve as establishing the industry price p. The demand curve and the marginal revenue curve faced by the firm are horizontal and are equal to price p at all levels of output for the firm. The firm produces the output at which SMC (and LMC) equals marginal revenue or price. Individual firm output is x. Industry output X is the summation of individual firm outputs at price p. There are just enough firms in the industry to make the price equal to minimum short-run and long-run average costs for the firm at output x. The firm is using the most efficient size of plant at the most efficient rate of output. There are no economic profits or losses being incurred.

What will be the short-run effects of an increase in demand to $D_1 D_1$? The market price will rise to p'. In order to maximize profits, the firm will increase output to x', the output at which SMC equals the new marginal revenue. Industry output will increase to X'. The firm will be making profits equal to output x', multiplied by the difference between price p' and short-run average costs at output x'. The short-run effects of the increase in demand are (1) an increase in price and (2) some increase in output as existing plant capacity is worked with greater intensity.

Consider now the long-run effects. The existence of profits will bring new

firms into the industry. As new firms enter, increasing the industry's productive capacity, the market short-run supply curve will shift to the right.
The more firms that enter, the farther to the right the curve will move. The
increases in supply will cause price to move downward from the short-run
high of p'. As the price goes down, individual firms will reduce output from
the short-run high of x'.

In an increasing cost industry the entry of new firms causes the whole set
of cost curves for existing firms to shift upward. Such a shift will occur in
an industry that uses significant proportions of the total supplies available
of the resources necessary for making its product. Suppose, for example,
that one such resource is a special steel alloy. The entry of new firms in the
industry increases the demand for such resources, thus increasing their
prices. As resource prices rise, the set of cost curves shifts upward
accordingly.

Any given set of cost curves presupposes that the firm can get all it wants
of any one resource at a constant price per unit. No single firm causes the
prices of resources to change since it does not take a large enough amount
of any resource to be able to affect its price. It is the greater demand for
resources brought about by the entry of new firms into the industry and,
perhaps, by the simultaneous expansion of output by existing firms that
causes resource prices to rise. The forces causing resource prices to rise lie
completely outside the control of the individual firm and are said to be
external to the firm. The increases in resource prices and the consequent
upward shifts of the cost curves are thus the result of *external diseconomies*
of increasing production in the industry.

A two-way squeeze is put on profits by the entry of new firms as the price
falls and costs rise. New firms enter until the price decreases enough and
costs rise enough for the price to be equal again to minimum long-run
average costs for individual firms. All profit is squeezed out. In Figure 10–9
the new price is p_1, and the new cost curves are LAC_1, SAC_1, and SMC_1.
The entry of new firms stops and the industry is once more in long-run
equilibrium. The new long-run market price of p_1 lies between the original
long-run price of p and the short-run high of p'. The new firm output is x_1 at
which SMC_1 is equal to the new long-run marginal revenue and price.
Industry output will have increased to X_1, since the increased capacity of
the industry has moved the short-run supply curve to SS_1.[8]

---

[8] To keep an already complex exposition as simple as possible, a long-run development of a transitory
nature has been ignored in the argument of the text. The short-run high price, resulting from the increase in demand for the product, not only attracts profit-seeking new firms into the industry but also
creates an incentive for existing firms to increase their plant sizes beyond the most efficient size. This
situation will be the case since for the individual firm maximum long-run profits are obtained at the output at which long-run marginal cost equals marginal revenue and price (see Figure 10–7). Then, as the
entrance of new firms lowers price, the output at which long-run marginal cost equals price becomes
smaller. The firm is induced to reduce its plant size. When enough firms have entered to eliminate
profits, the firm once more will be building the most efficient size of plant.

Will the new long-run output of the firm be equal to, greater than, or less than the old long-run output x? The answer depends on the way in which the cost curves shift upward. Whether the cost curves shift straight up, a little to the left, or a little to the right depends on the comparative price increases of different classes of resources. If all resource prices increase proportionally, the same combinations of resources will be the least cost combinations. The cost curves will shift straight up, and the new long-run firm output will be equal to the old. Suppose, however, that short-run fixed resources go up relatively more in price than do those that are considered variable in the short run. The firm will want to economize on the now relatively more expensive fixed resources. The proportions of the relatively more expensive fixed resources to the relatively cheaper variable ones will be decreased to secure least cost combinations. The most efficient size of plant will tend to be slightly smaller in the new long-run equilibrium position than it was in the old. Hence, the new long-run equilibrium firm output will tend to be smaller than the old, as is shown in Figure 10–9. If short-run fixed resources increase proportionally less in price than do short-run variable resources, least cost combinations favor larger sizes of plant. The firm will want to economize on the now relatively more expensive resources and use larger proportions of those which constitute the plant. The new most efficient size of plant and the new output will tend to be larger than the old.

The long-run industry supply curve is *LS* in Figure 10–9. It joins all points of long-run equilibrium for the industry. Alternatively, the industry long-run supply curve can be thought of as the horizontal summation of the minimum points of all individual firm *LAC* curves as the entry of new firms shifts their cost curves upward. The industry long-run supply curve shows the industry outputs that will be forthcoming at different possible prices when there is ample time for size of plant adjustments as well as for the entry and exit of firms.

Constant costs   The pattern of analysis for an industry of constant costs is basically the same as that for an industry of increasing costs. Starting from the position of long-run equilibrium shown in Figure 10–10, suppose that an increase in demand occurs. The short-run effects are the same as before. The price will increase to p'; the firm's output will increase to x'; and the market output will increase to X'. Economic profits will be made by the individual firms of the industry.

New firms will be attracted into the industry in the long run. As before, the short-run market supply curve will shift to the right as new firms enter, causing the price to decrease.

In a *constant cost* industry the entry of new firms does not increase market demands for resources sufficiently to cause their prices to increase. Of the total supplies of resources necessary for the production of X, this industry takes a small enough part so that no influence is exerted on their

Figure 10–10   Effects of changes in demand: constant costs

prices by the new firms coming in. If the entry of new firms has no effect on resource prices, the cost curves of existing firms will remain as they were before. Profits will be made until enough firms have entered to bring the price back down to p. Price and minimum long-run average costs will be equal, and long-run equilibrium will be reestablished. The new short-run supply curve will be SS_1. Individual firm output will be that at which SMC equals marginal revenue and price p. The entry of new firms will have increased industry output substantially to X_1. The long-run supply curve will be LS and will be horizontal at the level of minimum long-run average costs.

Decreasing costs   Cases of decreasing costs are probably rather rare. Analytically, they parallel increasing and constant cost cases. As before, we start with an industry and its firms in long-run equilibrium and then assume demand increases. The short-run effects are the same as before. In Figure 10–11 the market price will increase to p'; firm output goes up to x'; and the industry output increases to X'. Pure profits equal to x' times the difference between p' and SAC at output x' will be made by the representative firm.

New firms will be attracted into the industry in the long run because of the pure profits available. The industry short-run supply curve moves to the right as new firms add to the industry's productive capacity. Price goes down as new firms enter.

In a *decreasing cost* industry the entry of new firms must cause resource prices to fall. The decrease in resource prices as new firms enter causes the cost curves to shift downward. Both the price of X and costs of production

Figure 10–11   Effects of changes in demand: decreasing costs

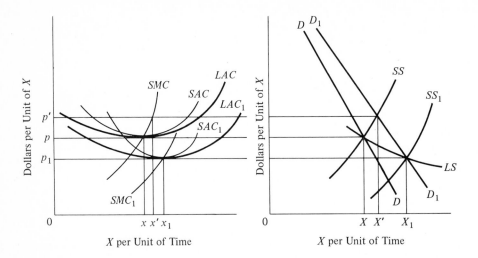

are decreasing. Eventually, the declining product price overtakes the declining cost curves, and profit is squeezed out. The new long-run equilibrium price is p_1 and is less than the original price of p. Individual firm output is x_1, at which both short-run and long-run marginal costs equal marginal revenue or price. The new industry output is X_1. The long-run supply curve LS will be downward-sloping to the right.

What are the circumstances that could conceivably give rise to decreasing costs? Suppose the industry in question is a young one growing up in a new territory.[9] Transportation facilities and the organization of markets, both for resources and the final product, may not be well developed. An increase in the number of firms in the industry and, consequently, in the size of the industry may make feasible the development of improved transportation and marketing facilities that will substantially reduce the costs of individual firms. For example, industrial growth of an area may stimulate development and improvement of railway, highway, and air transportation service into and out of the area. However, good explanations of decreasing costs are rather hard to find; whatever the explanations given for particular cases, they usually stem basically from improvements in the quality of resources furnished or from greater efficiencies developed in the resource-furnishing industries.

Decreasing costs, or *external economies* of increasing production, as discussed above, should not be confused with the *internal economies* of size

---

[9] In this case the chances of its being one of pure competition are small.

possible for a single firm with a size of plant smaller than the most efficient one. The individual firm has no influence over external economies. These result solely from expansion of the industry or from forces outside the control of the firm. Internal economies of size are under the control of the firm. The firm can secure them by enlarging its plant.

Probably, increasing cost industries are the most prevalent of the three cases analyzed. Decreasing costs are most unlikely to occur. Industries of constant cost and of decreasing cost are likely to become industries of increasing cost as they become older and more well established. If it is possible to have decreasing costs, once the decreasing costs or external economies of increasing production have been taken advantage of, the industry must surely become one of constant or increasing costs.

The disturbing force triggering these chains of adjustments was assumed to be an increase in demand for the product. It could just as well have been a decrease in demand, in which case losses would occur for individual firms and exit from the industry would have occurred until long-run equilibrium was again established. Or, in lieu of changes in demand, we could have assumed that major technological developments caused disequilibrium to occur, and these would induce new firms to enter the industry until long-run equilibrium was reestablished.

The welfare effects of pure competition

In a private enterprise economic system, what effects on welfare would be expected if the market structure in which producers and sellers operate were purely competitive? A complete assessment of the expected effects must wait until we have examined resource pricing and employment in detail; however, some tentative statements can be made at this point.

The welfare effects of purely competitive forces can be brought out by summarizing how the purely competitive mechanism operates. Suppose that initially disequilibrium exists; there is a random array of prices, outputs, and distribution of productive capacity (resources). There are two "givens" throughout the discussion: (1) pure competition exists in all markets, and (2) the distribution of purchasing power does not change. We shall focus attention on two goods, food (F) and clothing (C).

The very short run

In the very short run consumers, confronted with the initial prices of goods and services, attempt to allocate their incomes so as to maximize satisfaction. Since supplies are initially fixed, prices move to the levels that will just clear the markets and create no surpluses. All exchanges that are mutually beneficial occur as prices move toward their equilibrium levels. Since such exchanges benefit the exchanging parties without decreasing the welfare of anyone external to the exchanges, community welfare increases. Community welfare with fixed supplies is maximum when for each consumer

$$MRS_{fc} = \frac{p_f}{p_c} \;;$$

or, in marginal utility terms,

$$\frac{MU_f}{MU_c} = \frac{p_f}{p_c},$$

or

$$\frac{MU_f}{p_f} = \frac{MU_c}{p_c}.$$

All consumers are on their contract curves, and the distribution of goods is complete.

The short run

If the plant capacity in food and clothing production is fixed and outputs of both products are not at short-run profit-maximizing levels, will the consequent adjustments increase welfare? Suppose that firms producing food are operating at outputs such that $SMC_f < p_f$, and that clothing firms are producing outputs at which $SMC_c > p_c$. The production of clothing will be reduced, and the production of food will be increased. Community welfare will be increased in the process. Consumers value variable resources used in producing F more than they value them used in producing other goods. This differential valuation is the meaning of $SMC_f < p_f$. The price p_f is the value that consumers place on any one unit of F at the current supply level. At current production levels of F the short-run marginal cost of F is the value of the products that the resources used in producing the last one-unit increment in F can turn out in their best alternative uses. Consequently, consumer welfare can be increased by transfers of resources from those other uses into the production of F—that is, from uses in which those resources produce a smaller value of product into the use where their output is of greater value. Similarly, $SMC_c > p_c$ means that consumers value resources used in producing C less than they value them used in producing other goods. Consumer welfare can be increased by resource transfers from C into the production of other goods.

The purely competitive market mechanism induces producers to accomplish the output changes that consumers desire. To maximize profits or to minimize losses in the short run, producers of F want to increase their outputs to levels at which $SMC_f = p_f$. Producers of C desire to contract their outputs to levels at which $SMC_c = p_c$. Producers in industry F offer slightly higher prices for the necessary variable resources. In industry C output contraction decreases demand for variable resources used in that industry, which, in turn, depresses the prices offered for those variable resources. To the extent that F and C use the same kinds of variable resources, voluntary reallocation by resource owners, from the lower-paying to the higher-paying uses sufficient to equalize their remuneration in the two uses, will occur. If the two industries use different kinds of variable resources, a general reallocation of variable resources may occur throughout the economy. Reallocation may occur from industry C to other industries that can use the kinds of variable resources used in producing C. In turn, reallocation of the kinds of resources used in industry F from other industries to industry F may occur. The overall short-run resource reallocation that occurs will be limited, however, by the existing plant capacity in the two industries. Short-run equilibrium exists in the two industries when $SMC_f = p_f$ and $SMC_c = p_c$.

The long run

Although the short-run reorganization of production increases the welfare of consumers, it stops short of maximizing it because of fixed plant capacity in each industry. In the long run there is ample time for productive capacity to move, that is, for firms to enter and to exit whenever incentives to do so occur.

Suppose that short-run equilibrium exists and that firms in industry F show profits while those in C incur losses. The profits in F and the losses in C mean that consumers value investment in plant and equipment more in industry F and less in industry C than they value it in other uses; their welfare will be increased by transfers of investment out of C, where they value it less, and into F, where they value it more. The incentives motivating producers bring about this result.

The short-run losses in C bring about rates of return on investment in that industry below what investment elsewhere in the economy will earn. Consequently, disinvestment in C will occur—through failure to take care of depreciation on plant and equipment and through the eventual liquidation of some existing firms. As firms leave industry C, the supply of C decreases, causing its price to rise. The decreased demands for resources in industry C lower their prices, decreasing costs of production for individual firms. The exit of firms will cease when the decreasing supply has increased the price and lowered costs enough so that losses are no longer being incurred. A smaller number of firms in C will be producing with plants of most efficient size and most efficient rates of output, but in total they will produce a smaller combined output at a higher price than in the short run.

At the same time short-run profits in industry F will be attracting resources (productive capacity) into that industry. The profits indicate a higher return on investment than investors can earn elsewhere in the economy. This is a lucrative field in which to invest. New firms are established in the industry. Increasing demands for resources raise resource prices and the cost curves of both entering firms and firms already in the industry. The entry of new firms increases industry supply, driving the price down. New firms enter until the increasing supply lowers the price of F to the level of the higher average costs. Entry stops when profits no longer appear to be obtainable to entering firms. Firms are forced to use most efficient plant sizes and operate them at most efficient rates of output to avoid losses. More firms are in the industry; their combined outputs are greater; and the product price is lower than it was in the short run.

The reallocation of resources may be direct or indirect. If the plant capacity of firms in industry C can be easily converted to the production of product F, firms in industry C may simply switch over to producing the more profitable F. Or, if the production processes of the two industries are unrelated, reallocations will be of the indirect nature described above, with firms folding in industry C and new firms emerging in industry F. In either case profits and losses, and differential prices for resources in the two industries, bring about the desirable reallocation of resources or productive capacity.

With the establishment of long-run equilibrium the economy is operating at maximum economic efficiency. Individual firms in each industry operate most efficient plant sizes at most efficient rates of output. Consumers receive units of each product at prices equal to the minimum obtainable average cost per unit. Each consumer is induced to consume those quantities of goods at which the marginal rate of substitution between any two is equal to the price ratio of the two. Thus, the marginal rate of substitution between any two goods is the same for all consumers. Producers are induced to produce quantities of each good at which long-run marginal costs are equal to their respective prices. Marginal rates of transformation between any two goods are thus equal to their price ratios and, in turn, are equal to consumer marginal rates of substitution between the goods.

The achievement of long-run equilibrium conditions in purely competitive markets appears to lead to maximum consumer welfare. As we examine the other market structures, we shall find that they fall short of reaching the summit; one of our tasks is to assess the extent to which they fall short. The purely competitive model provides an excellent bench mark for this purpose, and several conditions resulting from long-run purely competitive equilibrium that have welfare implications are worth noting.

First, pure competition leads to that organization of productive capacity at which *prices of products are equal to their per unit costs—marginal and average.* There are no profits or losses. Productive capacity (resources) is so allocated that it is valued equally by consumers in all its alternative uses, and no reallocation can increase welfare.

Second, *each firm operates at peak efficiency,* producing its product output at the least possible cost per unit. In long-run equilibrium the firm is induced to operate a most efficient plant size at the most efficient rate of output in order to avoid losses. It takes advantage of all possible economies of size as well as using the most efficient resource combination for the output level it produces.

Third, *resources are not diverted into sales promotion efforts.* No necessity exists for individual firms to engage in aggressive activities to promote sales when they sell in purely competitive markets. One firm alone cannot influence product price, and the products produced by all firms in the industry are homogeneous. Since the individual firm can sell all it wishes to sell at the going market price, sales promotion to increase its volume is unnecessary. The homogeneity of the product produced by all sellers largely precludes sales promotional activities on the part of one to raise his price. Buyers have so many alternative sources of supply that price increases on the part of one seller cause his sales to drop to zero.

Summary

This chapter draws together the analysis of demand and the analysis of costs to show how the price system organizes production under the special conditions of pure competition. Pricing and output are discussed from the time viewpoints of the very short run, the short run, and the long run.

Supplies of goods are fixed in amount in the very short run. Price serves to ration existing supplies among consumers. Additionally, price rations the fixed supply over the duration of the period of the very short run.

Individual firm outputs can be varied within the limits of their fixed sizes of plant in the short run. In order to maximize profits, individual firms produce the outputs at which their short-run marginal costs equal marginal revenue or product price. Industry price of a product is determined by the interactions of all consumers and all producers of the product. Individual firms may make profits or incur losses in the short run.

In the long run additional firms will enter industries that make profits, and some existing firms will leave industries in which losses occur. Thus, productive capacity expands in the former industries and contracts in the latter. Expansion of productive capacity lowers market price of the product and decreases individual firm profits. Contraction of productive capacity increases market price and reduces losses. Long-run equilibrium exists in each industry when the number of firms in the industry is just sufficient for profits not to be made nor losses incurred. When an industry is in long-run equilibrium, product price equals average cost of production. Each firm must be operating a most efficient size of plant at the most efficient rate of output if losses are to be avoided.

Industries may be characterized as increasing cost, constant cost, or decreasing cost industries. Increasing costs occur when the entrance of new firms into an industry increases the price of resources used to produce the product. The resulting higher costs are called external diseconomies. In constant cost industries the entrance of new firms does not increase demand for resources enough to raise their prices. Consequently, no changes in the costs of existing firms occur. Decreasing costs, which must be rare in the real world, occur when the entrance of new firms causes resource prices and costs of production to fall. These are termed external economies.

Pure competition has certain welfare effects or implications that are important. First, consumers get products at prices equal to their per unit costs of production. Second, pure competition, where pure competition can exist, results in the greatest economic efficiency. Third, there is little motivation for sales promotion efforts on the part of individual firms.

Suggested readings

Friedman, Milton, *Price Theory*. Chicago: Aldine Publishing Co., 1976. Chap. 5.

Marshall, Alfred, *Principles of Economics,* 8th ed. London: Macmillan & Co., Ltd., 1920. Bk. V, Chaps. IV–V.

Viner, Jacob, "Cost Curves and Supply Curves." *Zeitschrift für Nationalökonomie,* Vol. III (1931), pp. 23–46.

Questions and exercises

1. A corporation's managers, contemplating a substantial increase in the corporation's plant and equipment, are puzzling over means of financing the new investment. The problem is whether they should float a bond issue to raise the money or sell additional shares of common stock. How will the corporation income tax affect the decision that they make on this issue?

2. In order to maximize profits, the firm produces an output level at which total revenue exceeds total costs by the greatest possible amount. At the same time profits are maximized at the output level at which marginal cost equals marginal revenue. Can you reconcile these two statements?

3. The Flight School at State University has offered to lease an individually owned Cessna 150 on a part-time basis for flight instruction purposes. The individual is free to use the airplane whenever she so desires. The

Flight School proposes to pay a rate of $10 per hour for the use of the plane, plus the gasoline and oil that it uses. The costs to the individual of owning and operating the airplane are as follows:

Depreciation:	$1,000 per year
Insurance:	$600 per year if she leases to the Flight School
	$350 per year if she does not lease to the Flight School
Tiedown:	$150 per year
Annual Inspection:	$150 per year
Maintenance and Repair:	$5 per flight hour
Gasoline and Oil:	$4.50 per flight hour

    a. If the owner does not lease the airplane to the Flight School and flies the airplane 100 hours per year, what is her hourly cost?

    b. Should she lease it to the Flight School at the proposed rate

        (1) if she flies the airplane 100 hours per year and the Flight School flies it 100 hours per year? Explain.

        (2) if she flies it 100 hours per year and the Flight School flies it 50 hours per year? Explain.

        (3) if she flies it 100 hours per year and the Flight School flies it 25 hours per year? Explain.

4. Explain why the long-run supply curve of a purely competitive industry is more elastic at each price level than the short-run supply curve.

Chapter 11

Chapter contents		Key concepts
Costs and revenues under monopoly	Costs of production Revenues	Pure monopoly Marginal cost
The short run	Profit maximization: total curves Profit maximization: per unit curves Two common misconceptions Short-run supply	Marginal revenue Price elasticity of demand Short run Long run Most efficient size of plant
The long run	Entry into the industry Size of plant adjustments Less than most efficient size of plant Most efficient size of plant Greater than most efficient size of plant	Most efficient rate of output Economies of size Diseconomies of size Price discrimination Welfare Excise tax
Price discrimination	Distribution of sales Profit maximization Examples of price discrimination	
The welfare effects of pure monopoly	Short-run output restriction Long-run output restriction Inefficiency of the firm Sales promotion activities	
Regulation of monopoly	Price regulation Taxation A specific tax A lump-sum tax	
Summary	Suggested readings Questions and exercises	

Appendix I to Chapter 11

Derivation of the marginal revenue curve	Straight-line curves Nonlinear curves

Appendix II to Chapter 11

Price, marginal revenue, and elasticity of demand

Pricing and output under pure monopoly

The nature of pure monopoly was explained in Chapter 7; but we shall review briefly its essential characteristics before examining pricing and output in a pure monopoly situation. Pure monopoly is a market situation in which there is a single seller of a product for which there are no good substitutes. The product sold by the monopolist is clearly different from other products sold in the economy. Changes in the prices and outputs of other goods leave the monopolist unaffected. Conversely, changes in the monopolist's price and output leave the other producers in the economy unaffected.

Pure monopoly in the real world is rare. Local public utility industries approximate it. Other industries that approach this type of market structure include the manufacturing of locomotives, telephone equipment, and shoe machinery as well as the production of magnesium and nickel.[1] But monopoly is not pure unless substitutes are nonexistent. Even in the public utility field, gas and electricity are to some extent substitutes. Aluminum also has substitutes, as do the metal alloys produced with the aid of molybdenum and magnesium.

Nevertheless, the pure monopoly model provides tools of analysis that are indispensable for the study of prices, outputs, resource allocation, and economic welfare. We shall discuss in turn basic monopoly concepts, short-run and long-run pricing and output, price discrimination, effects of monopoly on welfare, and the control of monopoly pricing.

Costs and revenues under monopoly

Costs of production

The cost concepts that we developed in Chapter 9 are as applicable to pure monopoly as they are to pure competition. The difference between pure

---

[1] F. M. Scherer, *Industrial Market Structure and Economic Performance* (Chicago: Rand McNally & Company, 1970), p. 59.

Table 11–1   Demand, total revenue and marginal revenue schedules

(1) Price	(2) Quantity per Unit Time	(3) Total Revenue	(4) Marginal Revenue
$10	1	$10	$10
9	2	18	8
8	3	24	6
7	4	28	4
6	5	30	2
5	6	30	0
4	7	28	(−)2
3	8	24	(−)4
2	9	18	(−)6
1	10	10	(−)8

monopoly and pure competition lies in the conditions under which goods and services are *sold,* not in the conditions under which resources are purchased. In this chapter we assume that the monopolistic seller of a product is a purely competitive buyer of resources and has no effect on resource prices.[2] The monopolist can get as much of any resource as is desired without affecting its price per unit.

Revenues

What is the difference between the purely competitive firm and the monopolistic firm on the selling side? A purely competitive firm faces a horizontal demand curve and a marginal revenue curve that coincides with it since the firm can sell any desired amount at the market price. However, the monopolist faces the market demand curve. With that demand curve the price must be decreased in order to increase sales. The downward slope of the demand curve facing the firm has important implications for the monopolist's marginal revenue in relation to the price.

Marginal revenue at different levels of sales per unit of time for the monopolist will be less than the price per unit at those sales levels. Consider Table 11–1. A typical demand schedule faced by a monopolist is shown by columns (1) and (2). Total revenue at different levels of sales is listed in column (3) and at any given level of sales equals the price multiplied by the quantity sold. The marginal revenue column shows the changes in total receipts resulting from one-unit changes in the sales level. With the excep-

---

[2] Modifications of cost curves to take account of a single firm's influence on resource prices are deferred to Chapter 15. If used here, the modifications would make no essential difference in the development of the chapter.

tion of the first unit, marginal revenue is less than the price at each level of sales. Suppose that the firm's current level of sales is 3 units of X. Price per unit is $8 and total receipts are $24. If the firm desires to increase sales per unit of time to 4 units of X, it must reduce the price per unit to $7 in order to expand sales. The fourth unit sells for $7. However, the firm takes a $1 loss per unit on its previous sales volume of 3 units. The total loss of $3 must be deducted from the selling price of the fourth unit in order to compute the net increase in total receipts resulting from the 1-unit increase in sales. Thus, marginal revenue at a sales volume of 4 units is $7 − $3 = $4 (the difference between $28 and $24).[3]

When the demand schedule and marginal revenue schedule of Table 11–1 are plotted on the same diagram, the marginal revenue curve lies below the demand curve. In fact, the marginal revenue curve bears the same relationship to the demand curve as does any marginal curve to its corresponding average curve. The demand curve is the firm's average revenue curve. When any average curve—average product, average cost, or average revenue—decreases as the firm's output increases, the corresponding marginal curve lies below it.

The relationship of a firm's marginal revenue and price is stated in a convenient form by

$$MR = p - \frac{p}{\epsilon};$$

that is, marginal revenue is equal to price minus the ratio of price to the elasticity of demand at any given level of sales.[4] Consider the demand curve

---

[3] Let the demand curve be

$$p = f(x).$$

Then

$$TR = xp = xf(x)$$

and

$$MR = \frac{d(TR)}{dx} = p + x\frac{dp}{dx} = f(x) + xf'(x).$$

A geometric method of finding the marginal revenue curve for a given demand curve is developed in Appendix I of this chapter.

[4] From Footnote 3

$$MR = \frac{d(TR)}{dx} = p + x\frac{dp}{dx} = p + \frac{p}{\dfrac{dx}{dp} \times \dfrac{p}{x}} = p - \frac{p}{\epsilon}$$

since

$$\epsilon = -\frac{dx}{dp} \times \frac{p}{x}.$$

This proposition is proved geometrically in Appendix II of this chapter.

Figure 11–1   Implications of demand elasticity for marginal revenue

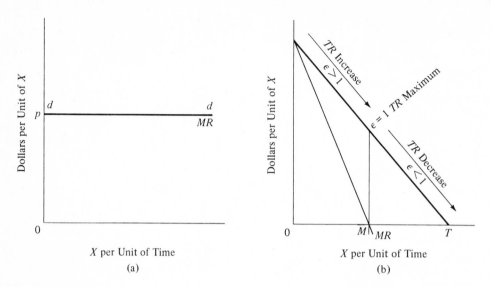

(a)

(b)

faced by a purely competitive firm as is shown in Figure 11–1(a). Elasticity of demand at all outputs approaches infinity (∞). Because $MR = p - p/\epsilon$ and because $\epsilon \to \infty$, p/ϵ approaches zero and MR approaches p; that is, for all practical purposes $MR = p$ at all outputs. Now consider a monopolist faced by the straight-line demand curve of Figure 11–1(b). At output M, halfway between zero and T, $\epsilon = 1$. At smaller outputs $\epsilon > 1$ and at larger outputs $\epsilon < 1$.[5]

We noted in Chapter 3 that an increase in sales when $\epsilon > 1$ causes TR to increase. This means that when $\epsilon > 1$, MR must be positive. The equation $MR = p - p/\epsilon$ states the same thing. If $\epsilon > 1$, then p/ϵ must be less than p and MR must be positive. The greater ϵ is, the smaller p/ϵ will be, and the smaller will be the difference between p and MR. At the output where $\epsilon = 1$, TR is maximum and MR should be zero. The formula supports this point. If $MR = p - p/\epsilon$ and $\epsilon = 1$, then $MR = p - p = 0$.

In Chapter 3 we also learned that increases in sales when $\epsilon < 1$ cause TR to decrease. MR must be negative in this case. If $MR = p - p/\epsilon$ and $\epsilon < 1$, then $p/\epsilon > p$ and MR is negative. The formula is consistent with our earlier observations regarding the relationships between elasticity and total revenue when sales are increased.

[5] See pp. 47–48.

The short run

Profit maximization: total curves

The rules for profit maximization are the same for a pure monopolist as they are for a pure competitor. When plotted, the total receipts schedule of Table 11–1 becomes a total receipts curve like that of Figure 11–2. Note the

Figure 11–2   Short-run profit maximization: total curves

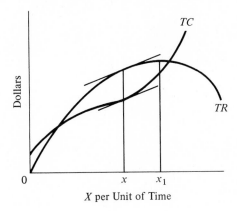

difference between the monopolist's *TR* curve and that of a purely competitive firm. The difference results from the fact that to sell greater outputs the monopolist must charge lower prices. Therefore, total receipts increase at a decreasing rate and at some output level, such as x_1, they reach a maximum. Still larger sales cause total receipts to decrease rather than increase. The monopolist maximizes profits at output x, where the difference between *TR* and *TC* is greatest. The output at which the difference between the *TR* and *TC* curves is greatest is that at which their slopes are equal (tangents to the curves at this output are parallel). Since the slope of the *TC* curve is marginal cost and the slope of the *TR* curve is marginal revenue, profits are maximum at the output at which marginal revenue equals marginal cost.[6]

---

[6] The mathematics of profit maximization for a monopolist are the same as for a purely competitive firm (see p. 236).

Profit maximization: per unit curves

Diagrammatic representation of short-run profit maximization by a monopolist in terms of per unit costs and receipts is presented in Figure 11–3. Profits are maximum at output x, at which SMC equals MR. The

---

Figure 11–3   Short-run profit maximization: per unit curves

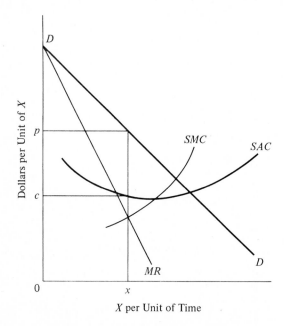

price per unit that the monopolist can get for that output is p. Average cost is c, and profits are equal to cp multiplied by x. At smaller outputs MR is greater than SMC; thus, larger outputs up to x add more to total receipts than to total costs and increase profits. At larger outputs MR is less than SMC; hence, increases beyond x add more to total costs than to total receipts and cause profits to decrease.[7]

Two common misconceptions

There is a common misconception that a monopolist always makes profits. Whether or not this is so always depends on the relationship between the

---

[7] The intersection of MR and SMC tells us nothing other than that profits are maximum or losses are minimum at that output. The price is shown by the demand curve at that output and not by the MR curve. Profits are determined by the price and *average cost*, not by the price and *marginal cost*.

market demand curve faced by the monopolist and the conditions of cost. The monopolist may incur losses in the short run and, like the purely competitive firm, continue to produce if the price more than covers average variable costs. In Figure 11–4 the monopolist's costs are so high and the

---

Figure 11–4   Short-run loss minimization: per unit curves

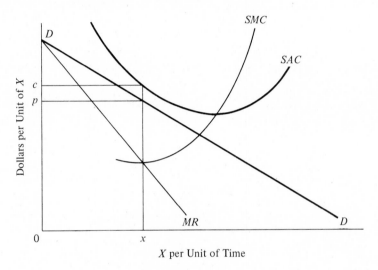

market is so small that at no output will the price cover average costs. Losses are minimum, provided the price is greater than the average variable costs, at output x, at which SMC equals MR. Losses are equal to $pc \times x$.

Another common misconception is that the demand curve faced by a monopolist is inelastic. Most demand curves, with the exception of those faced by firms under conditions of pure competition, range from highly elastic toward their upper ends to highly inelastic toward their lower ends[8] and cannot be said to be either elastic or inelastic. They are usually both, depending on the sector of the demand curve under consideration. The output that maximizes a monopolist's profits will always be within the elastic sector of the demand curve if there are any costs of production. Marginal cost is always positive; therefore, at the output at which marginal cost equals marginal revenue, marginal revenue must also be positive. If marginal revenue is positive, then the elasticity of demand must be greater than one.

---

[8] The situation could conceivably be reversed, but such an occurrence would be unusual. A demand curve that is inelastic toward the upper end and elastic toward the lower end would necessarily be one with a greater degree of curvature than that of a rectangular hyperbola.

Short-run supply

A monopolistic firm has no short-run supply curve. That part of the *SMC* curve lying above the average variable cost curve does *not* show the quantities that the monopolist would place on the market at the various alternative prices above minimum *AVC*. Instead, it shows the quantities that would be placed on the market at alternative levels of *marginal revenue* for the monopolist. Any given level of marginal revenue at the profit-maximizing output level is consistent with several alternative demand and price possibilities.

By way of illustration, suppose that a monopolist faces demand curve D_1D_1 in Figure 11–5. Profits are maximum at output x; product price is p_1;

Figure 11–5   Absence of the supply curve in monopoly

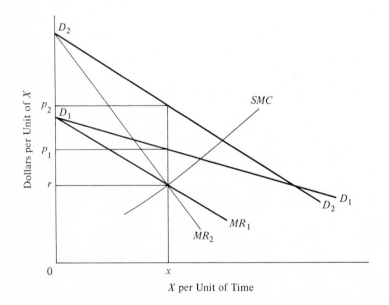

and the level of marginal revenue at that output level is r. Now suppose that the demand curve is D_2D_2, such that the marginal revenue curve MR_2 for the new demand curve also is equal to *SMC* at output level x and marginal revenue level r. The price at which output x will be sold is now p_2 instead of p_1. Thus, the monopolist's output is not determined by marginal cost and price. Instead, it is determined by marginal cost and marginal revenue. For purposes of comparison consider again the discussion of a purely competitive firm's short-run supply on page 242.

The long run

Entry into the industry

Whereas the entry of new firms into an industry of pure competition is easy in the long run, entry into a monopolistic industry is blocked. The monopolist must be able to forestall the entry of new firms when profits are being made or the firm does not remain a monopoly. Entry into the industry will change the market situation in which the firm operates.

The monopolist may block entry in several ways. It may be possible to control the sources of raw materials necessary for the production of the product. The Aluminum Company of America, for example, prior to World War II was reputed to own or control over 90 percent of the available supplies of bauxite, the basic raw material used in the making of aluminum.[9] Or patents held by the monopolist prevent other firms from duplicating the product. In the manufacture of shoe machinery a single company has held patents simultaneously on virtually all equipment used in the manufacture of shoes. Instead of selling machinery outright to shoe manufacturers, the company leased it to them and collected royalties. The shoe manufacturer who obtained any equipment from another source would then find it impossible to obtain key equipment from the company.[10] The market of a monopolist may be so limited relative to its most efficient size of plant that even though one firm makes profits, the entry of another would drive prices so low that both would incur losses. Thus, entry is blocked. Still other methods of blocking entry are possible. In the public utility field exclusive franchises granted by the governmental unit concerned will do the job. These are some of the more important monopolizing devices.[11]

The requirement that entry be completely blocked if pure monopoly is to remain pure monopoly helps explain why it is rare. Except in cases where the government blocks entry, it is extremely difficult for a monopolist to suppress the rise of substitutes when profits can be made in the field. Patents similar to those of the monopolist can be secured, although putting them to use in producing substitute products may be difficult in some cases. Some patents may become obsolete as new ideas and processes supersede those of the past. Where sole ownership of raw materials is the monopolizing device used, substitute raw materials frequently can be developed to make a product that is a reasonably good substitute for the original.

[9] Clair Wilcox, *Competition and Monopoly in American Industry,* Temporary National Economic Committee Monograph No. 21 (Washington, D.C.: Government Printing Office, 1940), pp. 69–72.

[10] *Ibid.,* pp. 72–73.

[11] A more complete list of devices for restricting entry into particular industries is discussed on pp. 316–318.

Size of plant adjustments

Since entry into the industry is blocked, the monopolist adjusts the long-run output by means of size of plant adjustments. Three possibilities exist. First, the relationship between the monopolist's market and long-run average costs may be such that a plant smaller than the most efficient size will be built. Second, the relationship may be such that a most efficient size of plant will be appropriate. Third, the monopolist may, under certain circumstances, be induced to build a plant larger than the most efficient size.

Less than most efficient size of plant Suppose the monopolist's market is so limited that the marginal revenue curve cuts the long-run average cost curve to the left of its minimum point. Figure 11–6 illustrates this situation.

Figure 11–6 Long-run profit maximization: less than most efficient plant size

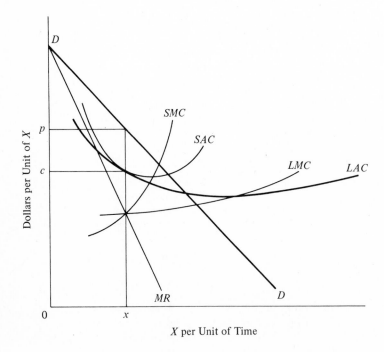

Long-run profits are maximum at the output at which LMC equals MR. The output is x and the price is p. The monopolist should build the size of plant that will produce output x at the least possible average cost for that output; that is, its short-run average cost curve SAC should be tangent to the LAC at output x. If SAC is tangent to LAC at output x, SMC is necessarily equal to *LMC* at that output.[12] Also, because output *x* is the output at which *LMC* equals *MR*, *SMC* is equal to *MR* at the same output. Thus, a monopolistic firm in long-run equilibrium is necessarily in short-run equilibrium, too. Profits are equal to $cp \times x$. Any change in the size of plant or in the rate of output of *SAC* will decrease profits.

In this case the monopolist will build a less than most efficient size of plant and operate it at a less than most efficient rate of output. The market is not large enough to expand the plant sufficiently to take advantage of all economies of size. The size of plant used will have some excess capacity. If it were made smaller than *SAC*, so that no excess capacity occurs, there would be a loss of some of the economies of size that *SAC* offers. The loss would more than offset any ''gains'' from fuller utilization of a smaller plant size.

Local power companies in small- and medium-sized towns often operate plants smaller than the most efficient size at less than the most efficient rates of output. The relatively small local market for electricity limits the generating plant to a size too small to use the most efficient generating equipment and techniques. Yet, the well-planned plant will have some excess capacity—both to take advantage of economies of size and to meet peak output requirements.

Most efficient size of plant   Suppose that the monopolist's market and cost curves are such that the marginal revenue curve hits the minimum point of the *LAC* curve as in Figure 11–7. The long-run profit-maximizing output is *x*, at which *LMC* = *MR;* this will necessarily be the output at which *LAC* is minimum. The monopolist, to produce *x* at the least possible cost per unit for that output, should build plant *SAC*, the most efficient size of plant. In this case *SMC* = *LMC* = *MR* = *SAC* = *LAC* at output *x*. The firm is in both short-run and long-run equilibrium. The price is *p;* the average cost is *c;* and profits are equal to $cp \times x$. Under the assumed conditions the firm operates a most efficient size of plant at the most efficient rate of output.

Greater than most efficient size of plant   Suppose that the monopolist's market is large enough for the marginal revenue curve to cut the *LAC* curve to the right of its minimum point. This situation is diagrammed in Figure 11–8. The long-run profit-maximizing output is *x*. The proper plant to build is *SAC*, which is tangent to *LAC* at output *x*. At output *x*, *LMC* = *SMC* = *MR;* hence, the monopolist is in short-run equilibrium as well as long-run equilibrium.

Under the assumed conditions the monopolist builds a plant larger than the most efficient size and operates it at more than the most efficient rate

[12] See Chapter 9, pp. 218–220.

Figure 11–7   Long-run profit maximization: most efficient size of plant

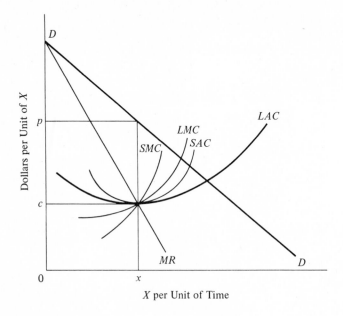

Figure 11–8   Long-run profit maximization: greater than most efficient plant size

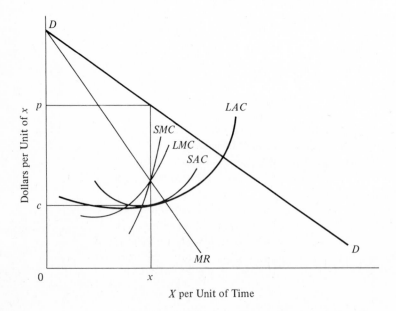

of output if profits are maximized. The plant is so large that diseconomies of size occur. It pays to use a plant a little smaller than the one that would produce output x at its most efficient rate of output. By operating SAC at more than its most efficient rate of output a lower per unit cost can be attained than would be possible with a larger plant. The diseconomies of size of a still larger plant are of a greater cost magnitude than is the operation of SAC beyond its most efficient rate of output.

Price discrimination

In some cases a monopolist may find it possible and profitable to separate and keep separate two or more markets for its product and to charge a different price for the product in each of the markets. Two conditions are necessary for such *price discrimination* to occur. First, the monopolist must be able to keep the markets apart. Otherwise, the product will be purchased in the market with the lower price and resold in the market with the higher price, thus ironing out the price differential that the monopolist attempts to establish. Second, as we shall soon discuss, for price discrimination to be profitable the elasticities of demand at each price level must differ among the markets.

Distribution of sales

Consider first the way in which a discriminating monopolist would distribute sales between two (or more) markets. Up to any given volume of sales (we shall ignore costs for the moment) it pays always to sell in the market in which an additional unit of sales per unit of time adds most to total receipts. This amounts to saying that sales should be distributed among the markets in such a way that marginal revenue in each market is equal to marginal revenue in the other market(s). This distribution yields the greatest total receipts from a given volume of sales.

Diagrammatically, suppose that the monopolist can sell in the two separate markets of Figure 11–9. The demand curves are D_1D_1 and D_2D_2, respectively. For convenience the quantity axis of Market II is reversed, with units of X measured from right to left instead of from the usual left to right. If the volume of sales is less than x_0, the entire amount should be sold in Market I, since the additions to total receipts from sales in that market will exceed any addition to total receipts made from selling in Market II. If the total volume of sales equals x_1 plus x_2, the monopolist should sell x_1 in Market I and x_2 in Market II so that marginal revenue in Market I equals marginal revenue in Market II. The level of marginal revenue will be r in each market. To show that this distribution brings in the greatest possible

Figure 11–9   Distribution of sales among markets: price discrimination

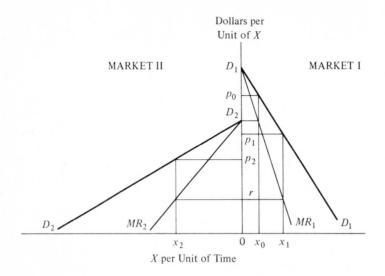

total receipts, suppose that the sales volume in one market is cut by one unit and that in the other market it is increased by one unit. Cutting sales by one unit in either market reduces total receipts from that market by an amount equal to r. Increasing sales by one unit in the other market will add less to total receipts than r, since marginal revenue from an additional unit of sales per unit of time in that market will be less than r. With the proper distribution of sales the price in Market I will be p_1 and the price in Market II will be p_2.

The reasons why elasticity of demand at each possible price must differ between the two markets now becomes clear. Since $MR = p - p/\epsilon$, if elasticities were the same in the two markets at equal prices, the corresponding marginal revenues would also be the same. The distribution of sales that makes marginal revenue in Market I equal to marginal revenue in Market II would make the price in Market I equal to the price in Market II. If such were the case, there would be neither point nor profit in separating the markets.

Profit maximization

The monopolist's cost curves, together with the marginal revenue curve for the total sales volume, are needed to solve the profit-maximizing problem. Let the average cost curve and the marginal cost curve be those of Figure 11–10. They depend in no way on how the monopolist's output is distributed among markets. The marginal revenue curve for the monopolist's total

Figure 11–10   Profit maximization: price discrimination

sales volumes when sales are properly distributed among markets is ΣMR in Figure 11–10. The demand curve and the marginal revenue curve for Market II have been drawn in the usual way. Then MR_1 and MR_2 are summed horizontally to obtain ΣMR.

The profit-maximizing problem is now reduced to a simple monopoly problem. The total output of the monopolist should be x, at which $MC = \Sigma MR$. The distribution of sales and the prices charged should be x_1, sold at price p_1 in Market I, and x_2, sold at price p_2 in Market II. Marginal revenue in Market I equals marginal revenue in Market II equals r with this distribution of sales. If total output and sales were less than x, marginal revenue in one market or the other (or both) would be greater than r, and marginal cost would be less than r. Increases in production up to x would, therefore, add more to total receipts than to total costs and would increase profits. If total output and sales were expanded beyond x, marginal cost would exceed r and marginal revenue in one market or the other (or both) would be less than r. Such increases in production would add more to total costs than to total receipts and would decrease profits. With output x properly distributed between the two markets, profits in Market I will equal

$cp_1 \times x_1$ and profits in Market II will equal $cp_2 \times x_2$. Total profits will be $cp_1 \times x_1$ plus $cp_2 \times x_2$.[13]

Examples of price discrimination

Price discrimination is frequently encountered in public utility industries. Electric power companies usually separate commercial from domestic users of electricity. Having a separate meter for each user enables the company to keep the markets apart. Elasticity of commercial users' demand for electricity is higher than that of domestic users; consequently, a lower rate is charged commercial users. This discrimination stems from the greater possibilities of commercial users adopting substitutes for the power company's product. Large commercial users may find it possible not only to find substitute sources of power but to generate their own electric power. Although domestic users may, and sometimes do, generate their own electric power, generating plants for their power needs are so small that costs per unit tend to be prohibitive.

Another example of price discrimination occurs in the field of foreign trade in the classic case of "dumping." Goods are sold abroad for a lower price than the domestic or home price. The markets are separated by transportation costs and tariff barriers. Elasticity of the demand curve facing the seller in the foreign market is usually higher than that in the domes-

---

[13] Let the monopolist's total receipts for both markets be

$$R = R_I + R_{II},$$

in which

$$R_I = R_I(x_I)$$

and

$$R_{II} = R_{II}(x_{II}).$$

Let the total cost equation be

$$C = C(x),$$

in which

$$x = x_I + x_{II}.$$

The profit equation is

$$\pi = R - C = R_I(x_I) + R_{II}(x_{II}) - C(x_I + x_{II}).$$

To maximize profits

$$\frac{\delta\pi}{\delta x_I} = R_I'(x_I) - C'(x) = 0$$

$$\frac{\delta\pi}{\delta x_{II}} = R_{II}'(x_{II}) - C'(x) = 0,$$

or

$$R_I'(x_I) = R_{II}'(x_{II}) = C'(x),$$

which means that marginal revenue in Market I equals marginal revenue in Market II equals marginal cost for the monopolist's entire output.

tic market. Although the seller may be a monopolist in the domestic market, he may find himself confronted abroad with competitors from other countries. Substitutes for his product on the world market increase the elasticity of the foreign demand curve he faces.

The welfare effects of pure monopoly

What impact would the introduction of pure monopoly into the purely competitive world discussed in the last chapter have on consumer welfare? The effects appear most striking when we assume that some markets are characterized by pure competition while others are characterized by pure monopoly. As in the purely competitive case, a complete statement of the welfare effects of pure monopoly must wait until resource pricing and employment have been discussed.

Short-run output restriction

If all industries were initially purely competitive and were in long-run equilibrium, monopolization of one or more of them would reduce consumer welfare. Suppose, for example, that X in Figure 11–11 represents one industry in a purely competitive economy. The market demand curve is DD and the market short-run supply curve (the sum of the individual firm

Figure 11–11   Monopolistic output restriction

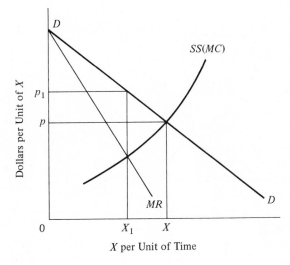

marginal cost curves) is SS. The market price is p, and the industry output level is X. Although the average cost curves are not drawn, suppose that the industry is in long-run equilibrium and that Pareto optimality exists throughout the economy.

What would be the short-run impact of monopolization of industry X? If the productive capacity of the industry were brought under the control of a single firm, demand would look different to the monopolist than it did to the individual firms making up the industry when it was purely competitive. The purely competitive firms each saw a horizontal demand curve at the market price p. Each firm saw a marginal revenue curve that coincided with that demand curve and produced an output level at which short-run marginal cost was equal to marginal revenue or price p. The monopolist sees the market demand curve sloping downward to the right and a marginal revenue curve that lies below the demand curve like MR in Figure 11–11. When we assume that the monopolist takes over intact the physical facilities of the industry and that no diseconomies of size are thereby engendered, SS (the industry supply curve or marginal cost curve under pure competition) is also the marginal cost curve of the monopolist. To maximize profits, the monopolist would reduce the industry's output level to X_1 and raise the price to p_1. The reduction in the output of X would release some of the resources used in the industry, and these would be used to increase the outputs of other goods, reducing their prices in the process.

As resources are transferred out of X into other uses, welfare is reduced. The marginal cost of X at any output level is the value in other uses that consumers attach to the resources used to produce a unit of X. The price of X at that output level is the value they attach to the same resource bundle used to produce X. We note, in Figure 11–11, that as the output level of X is reduced from X toward X_1 the marginal cost of X falls below its price, indicating that resources are being transferred from uses where their values to consumers are greater to uses where their values to consumers are less. This change must necessarily reduce the level of well-being of at least some members of the society.

Long-run output restriction

Welfare will also be held below its optimum level in the long run by blocked entry into an industry in which profits are being made. Where long-run profits occur, the product price exceeds average costs, indicating that productive capacity in the industry is too small relative to productive capacity elsewhere in the economy. Consumers value those resources making up plant capacity more when they are used in the profit-making industry than when they are used elsewhere—therefore, welfare is less than it could be.

A major problem posed by monopoly in a private enterprise economy, then, is that it prevents the price mechanism from organizing production in a Pareto optimal way. The monopolized industries are induced to produce output levels that are too small—marginal costs are less than the respective product prices—and the monopolies prevent productive capacity itself from expanding where consumers desire expansion, that is, where profits are made. The use of too few resources in the monopolized industries necessarily means the use of too large quantities in competitive industries if full employment of resources exists.

Inefficiency of the firm

In addition to the welfare impact of output restriction, the monopolistic firm ordinarily will not use resources at their peak potential efficiency. The purely competitive firm in long-run equilibrium uses the most efficient size of plant at the most efficient rate of output. The size of plant and the output that maximize the monopolist's long-run profits are not necessarily the most efficient ones.[14] However, if monopoly is to be compared with pure competition on this point, the comparison is legitimate only for industries in which pure competition can exist. In an industry with a limited market relative to the most efficient rate of output of the most efficient size of plant, monopoly may result in lower costs or greater efficiency than would occur if there were many firms, each with a considerably less than most efficient size of plant. In such a case even though monopoly may result in greater efficiency than any other type of market organization, resources still are not used at peak potential efficiency.

Sales promotion activities

It may be to the advantage of the monopolist to engage in some sales promotion activities, whereas under pure competition there is little point to activities of this kind. The monopolist may use sales promotion to enlarge his market, that is, to shift his demand curve to the right. Also, if he can convince the public that consumption of his product is highly desirable or even indispensable, elasticity of demand at various prices may be decreased. Additionally, such activities may be used to shield him from potential competition and to protect his monopoly position. His objective in this case will be to get his firm name so closely tied to his product that potential competitors will find it futile to attempt to enter the market. At this point it is difficult to assess the impact of sales promotion activities on welfare. We shall be in a better position to analyze these effects when we have completed the chapter on oligopoly.

---

[14] See pp. 270–273.

Regulation of monopoly

The tools of monopoly analysis so far discussed provide some indications of how monopoly might be regulated to offset, at least in part, the adverse effects of monopoly on welfare. Two possible governmental regulatory devices are (1) direct regulation of monopoly price and (2) regulation through taxation.

Price regulation

Authority is frequently invested in state regulatory commissions to govern the rates or prices charged by public utilities, such as gas and electric power companies. The economic problem involved is determination of the rate that will induce the monopolist to furnish the greatest amount of product consistent with his costs and with consumer demand.[15]

The profit-maximizing output of a monopolist in the absence of price regulation is shown in Figure 11–12.[16] The monopolist maximizes profits at output level x, where marginal cost equals marginal revenue. The price will be p, and profits are $cp \times x$. Since entry into the industry is blocked, the profits may persist over time.

By establishing a maximum price below p but greater than r, the regulatory commission can induce the monopolist to increase output. Suppose a maximum price of p_1 is established—at the level at which the marginal cost curve cuts the demand curve. The demand curve faced by the monopolist becomes $p_1 AD$. Between output levels of zero and x_1, sales will be made at p_1 per unit. The monopolist cannot charge more, but the public will take his entire output at that price. For output levels greater than x_1 the monopolist must lower the price below p_1 to clear the market; hence, the market demand curve is relevant.

The change in the demand curve faced by the firm alters the marginal revenue curve as well. From zero to x_1 the new demand curve is infinitely elastic—it is the same as the demand curve faced by a firm under pure competition—and marginal revenue equals p_1. Beyond output x_1 the market demand curve and the original marginal revenue curve are relevant. After the maximum price is established, the marginal revenue curve of the monopolist is $p_1 ABC$.

The monopolist's profit-maximizing position must be reexamined in view of the altered demand and marginal revenue situation. With the establishment of the maximum price, x is no longer the profit-maximizing output.

---

[15] Economic aspects of the problem frequently are subordinated to political aspects, but we shall omit the latter.

[16] The analysis can be presented in either long-run or short-run terms. A short-run explanation has the virtue of being less complex.

Figure 11–12   Regulation of monopoly by price control

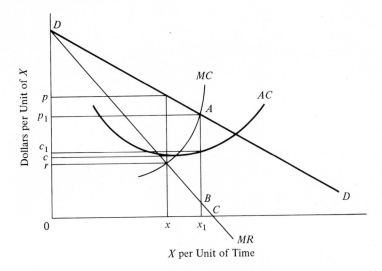

Profits will be maximized at the level of output at which the marginal cost curve cuts the new marginal revenue curve. At x marginal revenue exceeds marginal cost; consequently, increases in output up to x_1 increase profits. At outputs beyond x_1 marginal cost would exceed marginal revenue—which drops off sharply, or is said to be "discontinuous" at x_1—causing profits to decrease. The new profit-maximizing output is x_1, a larger output than before. Even though profits $c_1 p_1 \times x_1$ occur, welfare has been increased.

Taxation

Taxes levied on monopolists are often thought to be appropriate regulatory devices to prevent them from reaping the full benefits of their monopolistic positions. We shall consider two types: (1) a specific tax or a fixed tax per unit on the monopolist's output[17] and (2) a lump-sum tax levied without regard to output.[18]

A specific tax   Suppose that a specific tax is levied on the monopolist firm of Figure 11–13. Its original average cost and marginal cost curves are AC and MC, respectively. The original price and output are p and x. The tax is a variable cost and shifts the average and marginal costs upward by the

---

[17] The general effects would be the same if an *ad valorem* tax, a fixed percentage of the product price, were levied.

[18] The general effects would be the same if the tax were a fixed percentage of the monopolist's profits.

Figure 11– 13   Regulation of monopoly by a specific tax

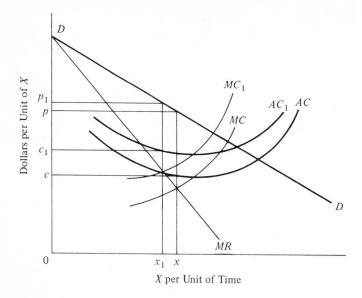

amount of the tax. Faced with the new cost curves, AC_1 and MC_1, the monopolist cuts output to x_1 and raises price to p_1 in order to maximize profits.

The monopolist is able to pass a part of the specific tax to the consumer through a higher price and a smaller output. At the same time the monopolist's profits will be smaller after the tax than before. Before-tax profits were $cp \times x$. After-tax profits are $c_1p_1 \times x_1$. To make certain that after-tax profits are smaller than before-tax profits, think for a moment of the firm's total revenue and total cost curves. Total receipts of the monopolist at various outputs are unchanged by the tax, but total costs at all outputs will be greater. Profits at all possible outputs will be smaller than before, and maximum profits after the tax necessarily will be smaller than they were before. If all the monopolist's profits were taxed away through specific taxes, prices still higher and outputs still smaller than those shown in Figure 11–13 would result. It appears that a specific tax on the monopolist's product would reduce welfare rather than increase it.[19]

A lump-sum tax   Suppose that a lump-sum tax is imposed on the monopolist of Figure 11–14—for example, a license fee imposed by a city

---

[19] Consider, however, the possible effects of specific taxes levied on the outputs of pure competitors in the economy, which would induce them to reduce their output levels, releasing resources to the monopolized industries and inducing the latter to expand their outputs. Or consider the impact of per unit subsidies paid to monopolists.

Figure 11–14   Regulation of monopoly by a lump-sum tax

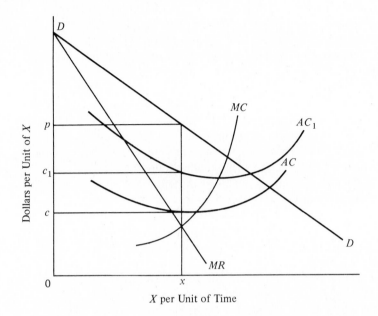

on its only swimming pool. The original average and marginal cost curves are AC and MC. The original price and output are p and x. Since the lump-sum tax is independent of output, it is a fixed cost to the monopolist. It shifts the average cost curve to AC_1, but it has no effect on the marginal cost curve. Consequently, the profit-maximizing price and output remain at p and x, but profits fall from $cp \times x$ to $c_1p \times x$.

The lump-sum tax must be borne by the monopolist alone. It is not possible to pass any part of it on to the consumer through higher prices and smaller outputs. Attempts to do so will decrease profits even more. All of the monopolist's profits may be taxed away in this manner with no effect whatsoever on output and price. The lump-sum tax by itself has no impact on welfare.

Summary

Pure monopoly is rare in the real world; however, the theory of pure monopoly is applicable to those industries in which it is approximated and to firms that act as though they were monopolists. Additionally, the theory furnishes necessary tools of analysis for the study of oligopoly and monopolistic competition.

The differences between the theory of pure monopoly and the theory of pure competition rest on the demand and revenue situations faced by the firm and on the conditions of entry into industries in which profits are made. Marginal revenue is less than price for the monopolist. The firm's marginal revenue curve lies below the demand curve that it faces. Entry into monopolistic industries is blocked.

The monopolist maximizes short-run profits or minimizes short-run losses by producing the output and charging the price at which marginal revenue equals short-run marginal cost. A monopolist may incur losses and, if so, continue to produce if price exceeds average variable cost. The monopolist operates within the elastic sector of its demand curve.

In the long run the monopolist maximizes profits at the output at which long-run marginal cost equals marginal revenue. The size of plant to be used will be the one with its short-run average cost curve tangent to the long-run average cost curve at the profit-maximizing output. Short-run marginal cost will equal long-run marginal cost and marginal revenue at that output.

A monopolistic firm finds it profitable to practice price discrimination when the firm can keep markets for its product separate and when elasticity of demand for each market is different at each possible price. The price-discriminating monopolist produces an output and distributes it among markets in such a way that marginal revenue in each market equals marginal revenue in every other market and is also equal to marginal cost.

Monopoly has important implications for welfare in a private enterprise economy. Where it exists along with competitive industries, it leads to output restriction and prices that are higher than marginal costs. The possibility of long-run profits under monopoly exists because of blocked entry into monopolized industries. Where profits occur, consumers are willing to pay more for a product than is necessary to hold the resources making that product in the industry concerned. Blocked entry limits transfer of resources into and expansion of output of a monopolized profit-making industry, and thus reduces welfare. A monopolistic firm is not likely to operate most efficient sized plants at most efficient rates of output. Some sales promotion efforts may be made to enlarge the market, to decrease elasticity of demand for the monopolist's product, and to discourage potential competition.

The theory of monopoly sheds some light on effective means of monopoly regulation. A maximum price set below the monopoly price will benefit consumers through both the lower price and an increased product output. A specific tax levied on the monopolist's product will be shifted partly to consumers through output restriction and higher prices. A lump-sum tax must be borne entirely out of the monopolist's profits.

Suggested readings

Dewey, Donald, *Monopoly in Economics and Law*. Chicago: Rand McNally & Company, 1959.

Harrod, R. F., "Doctrines of Imperfect Competition." *Quarterly Journal of Economics*, Vol. XLVIII (May 1934), pp. 442–470.

Irwin, Manley R., "The Telephone Industry," in Walter Adams, ed., *The Structure of American Industry*, 5th ed. New York: Macmillan Publishing Co., Inc., 1977. Pp. 312–333.

Marshall, Alfred, *Principles of Economics*, 8th ed. London: Macmillan & Co., Ltd., 1920. Bk. V, Chap. XIV.

Robinson, Joan, *The Economics of Imperfect Competition*. London: Macmillan & Co., Ltd., 1933. Chaps. 2–3, 15–16.

Questions and exercises

1. Suppose that there is a single supplier of natural gas in a community and that a regulatory commission is contemplating a ceiling price for the product. The commission decides to use "average cost pricing" methods, that is, to set the ceiling at the level at which the firm's average cost curve intersects the demand curve. If there is more than one such intersection, the one occurring at the largest output level will be used. What can you say about (1) the regulated price and output versus the unregulated price and output and (2) the shortages or surpluses resulting from the price regulation under each of the following circumstances?
    a. The average cost curve is falling at its point of intersection with the demand curve
    b. The average cost curve is rising at its point of intersection with the demand curve
    c. The average cost curve is minimum at its point of intersection with the demand curve.

2. Consider the transformation curve for a two-product world in which product X is produced and sold by a monopolist while product Y is produced and sold by pure competitors. If firms in each industry maximize profits, what, if anything, can we say about the output mix in the economic system?

3. In Hometown, U.S.A., the motion picture theater charges higher prices for the movie in the evening than in the afternoon. Explain why the management would want to do so and the circumstances that make it possible to do so. Illustrate your discussion diagrammatically.

4. Are there any circumstances under which a single firm in an industry would be expected to sell at a lower price than would be possible if there were many smaller firms, each of the same size, in the industry? If so, give examples and explain the circumstances fully.

5. Would you expect a monopolist to engage in extensive advertising of its product? Why or why not? What would determine the size of the monopolist's advertising budget?

6. What effect do you think monopoly has on the distribution of income? Explain.

Appendix I to Chapter 11
Derivation of the marginal revenue curve

The marginal revenue curve can be derived geometrically from a given demand curve. A straight-line demand curve will be used to develop the method that will then be modified to cover the case of a nonlinear demand curve.

Straight-line curves

Consider first what a marginal revenue curve is. In Figure 11–15 the quantity units are purposely large. Suppose a single unit of sales adds an amount

Figure 11–15 Marginal and total revenue

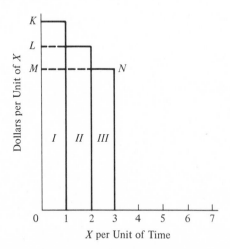

$0K$ to the firm's total receipts. Both total receipts and marginal revenue are equal to area I, or $0K \times 1$. When sales are increased to 2 units of X per unit of time, suppose total receipts increase by an amount $0L$. Marginal revenue of a unit now equals area II, or $0L \times 1$. Area II does not overlap area I but lies entirely to the right of it. The dotted line from the top of area *II* to point *L* is a reference line only, to assist in reading marginal revenue from the dollar axis. Total revenue from the 2 units equals marginal revenue when sales are 1 unit, plus marginal revenue when sales are increased to 2 units; in other words, total revenue equals area *I* plus area *II*. Marginal revenue when sales are increased to 3 units per unit of time equals $0M$, or, what amounts to the same thing, equals area *III*. Total revenue is now equal to area *I* plus area *II* plus area *III*. The stairstep curve from *K* to *N* is the marginal revenue curve for the firm through 3 units of sales.

For a typical firm a single unit of output is measured by an infinitesimal distance along the *X* axis. If the distance measuring a single unit of output is infinitesimal, the marginal revenue curve no longer looks like the discontinuous or stairstep curve of Figure 11–15 but looks as smooth as the *MR* curve in Figure 11–16. The point to be made from Figure 11–15 is that at any

Figure 11– 16   Derivation of the marginal revenue curve from the demand curve

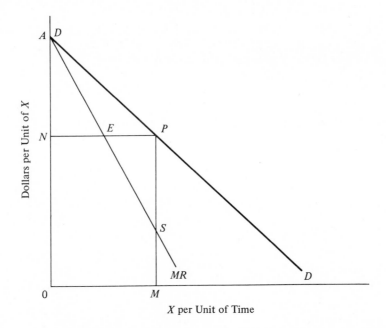

given level of sales total receipts are equal to the area under the marginal revenue curve up to that quantity. In Figure 11–15 total receipts from 3 units of sales equal the sum of areas *I*, *II*, and *III* as we have said. The same is true in Figure 11–16 where total receipts when sales are $0M$ are equal to area $0ASM$.

Assume that the demand curve faced by a monopolist is the straight line *DD* of Figure 11–16, and that we want to determine marginal revenue at sales level $0M$. Ignore the *MR* curve of the diagram temporarily. Price at quantity $0M$ will be *MP* or $0N$. Suppose now that *MR* is drawn in Figure 11–16 as a tentative marginal revenue curve. It should start from the vertical axis at a common point with the demand curve.[20] Reference to Table 11–1 shows that the marginal revenue curve for a straight-line demand curve also will be a straight line spreading away from the demand curve as the sales level increases.

What conditions must be fulfilled if marginal revenue is to be correctly measured at sales level $0M$? If *MR* were the marginal revenue curve, area $0ASM$ would equal total receipts. Also, area $0NPM$ (that is, price times quantity) equals total receipts. Hence, area $0NPM$ must equal area $0ASM$. Area $0NESM$ is common to both the larger areas, and if subtracted from each, the area of triangle *ANE* must be equal to the area of triangle *EPS*. Angle *NEA* equals angle *SEP* because the opposite angles formed by two intersecting straight lines are equal. Since triangles *ANE* and *EPS* are right triangles, with an additional angle of one equal to the corresponding angle of the other, they are also similar triangles. If *MR* is correctly drawn, triangles *ANE* and *EPS* are equal in area as well as similar and thus will be congruent. If they are congruent, *SP* must equal *NA* since the corresponding sides of congruent triangles are equal. Therefore, to locate correctly marginal revenue at sales level $0M$, we must measure the distance *NA* and set point *S* below point *P* so that *SP* equals *NA*. Marginal revenue at $0M$ will be *MS*.

Use of the geometric method for deriving marginal revenue from a given demand curve is much simpler than the proof. Suppose that we locate the marginal revenue curve for demand curve *DD* in Figure 11–17. Select several points such as P, P_1, and P_2 at random on the demand curve. The corresponding levels of sales are $0M$, $0M_1$, and $0M_2$. Corresponding prices will be $0N$, $0N_1$, and $0N_2$. Now drop below P by an amount equal to *NA* and call the newly located point S. Marginal revenue at sales level $0M$ is *MS*. Drop below P_1 by an amount equal to N_1A. Call this point S_1. Marginal revenue at $0M_1$ equals M_1S_1. Repeat the process at P_2 so that S_2P_2 equals N_2A. A line joining the S points is the marginal revenue curve.[21]

---

[20] Actually, it coincides with the demand curve at a sales level of one unit. However, if the distance measuring a unit of sales on the quantity axis is infinitesimal, we can assume that both curves start from a common point on the vertical axis.

[21] Mathematical determination of the marginal revenue function from a linear demand function is a simple calculus exercise. Let the demand equation be

$$p = a - bx.$$

Then

$$TR = xp = ax - bx^2$$

Figure 11–17   Location of the MR curve for a linear demand curve

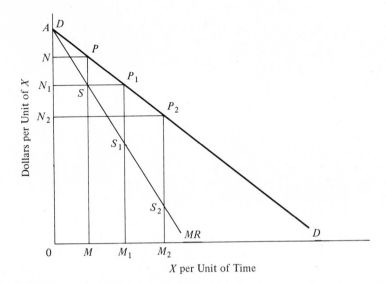

Nonlinear curves

The procedure with a slight modification can be used to locate the marginal revenue curve for a nonlinear demand curve. Suppose that the demand curve is DD in Figure 11–18. The demand curve and the marginal revenue curve start from a common point on the vertical axis, and we should locate marginal revenue at several different sales quantities, say $0M$, $0M_1$, and $0M_2$. The corresponding points on the demand curve are P, P_1, and P_2. The corresponding prices are $0N$, $0N_1$, and $0N_2$. Draw a tangent to the demand curve at point P so that the tangent cuts the vertical axis. Call this point A. If the tangent were the demand curve, we could easily find marginal revenue for it at sales level $0M$. We would drop below P by an amount equal to NA and set point S so that SP equals NA. Actually the tangent and demand curve DD are the same curve and have the same slope at the point of tangency. Therefore, MS will be marginal revenue for DD at sales level

and

$$MR = \frac{dTR}{dx} = a - 2bx.$$

Thus, for a linear demand function the marginal revenue function is also linear, has the same intercept a on the price axis, and has twice the slope b of the demand function.

Figure 11–18 Location of the MR curve for a nonlinear demand curve

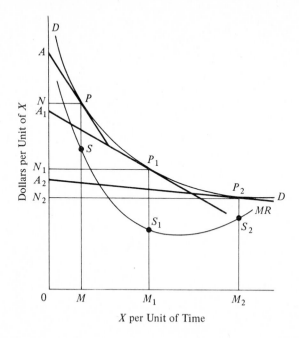

X per Unit of Time

$0M$, as well as being marginal revenue for the tangent when the tangent is thought of as being the demand curve. Marginal revenue at sales $0M_1$ can be found by drawing a tangent to DD at P_1. The tangent intersects the vertical axis at A_1. Drop below P_1 by an amount equal to N_1A_1 and marginal revenue at $0M_1$ is M_1S_1. Repeat the procedure at P_2, so that S_2P_2 equals N_2A_2. Marginal revenue at $0M_2$ is M_2S_2. A line joining the S points is the marginal revenue curve for DD. Note that when the demand curve is not a straight line, the A points on the vertical axis shift as different levels of sales are considered.[22]

---

[22] A common mistake in locating the marginal revenue curve for a given demand curve is that of merely drawing the marginal revenue curve so that it bisects the distance between the demand curve and the vertical axis. This procedure will locate the marginal revenue curve accurately for a linear demand curve only. If the demand curve has any curvature to it—that is, if it is convex or concave when viewed from below—such a procedure is not valid. If the demand curve is convex from below, the marginal revenue curve will lie to the left of a line bisecting the distance between the vertical axis and the demand curve. If the demand curve is concave from below, the marginal revenue curve will lie to the right of such a line.

Even in the case of a linear demand curve the procedure described here is correct in a mathematical sense only. It is not sound logically from the point of view of economics. For example, in Figure 11–16

Appendix II to Chapter 11
Price, marginal revenue, and elasticity of demand

The proposition that marginal revenue equals price minus the ratio of price to elasticity of demand at that price is proved geometrically with the aid of Figure 11–19. Suppose that the sales level is $0M$. The demand curve is

Figure 11–19 Price, elasticity of demand, and marginal revenue

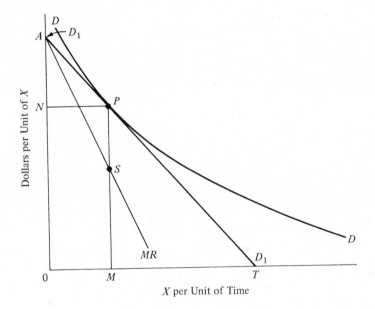

either DD or D_1D_1—which are tangent at that level of sales. At sales level $0M$ the elasticity of both curves is the same, and the corresponding marginal revenues will also be the same. For convenience, draw the marginal revenue curve corresponding to D_1D_1. Elasticity of demand at $0M$ equals $MT/0M$. However, $MT/0M$ is equal to PT/AP, since a line (PM) parallel to one side of a triangle $(A\,0)$ cuts the other two sides into proportional segments. Likewise, $PT/AP = 0N/NA$. Because $0N = MP$ and $NA = SP$,

---

point E lies on the marginal revenue curve for demand curve DD. Sales level $0M$ (or NP) and price $0N$ (or MP) are used in locating point E. However, there is no economic reason why sales level $0M$ or price $0N$ (or MP) should have any connection at all with marginal revenue at one half of sales level $0M$. The connection is purely a mathematical one stemming from the fact that DD is a straight line. With regard to sales level $0M$ and price $0N$, the only marginal revenue value which could be derived from them logically is marginal revenue at that sales level and that price.

$0N/NA = MP/SP$. Elasticity of demand at $0M$ is equal to $MT/0M = PT/AP = 0N/NA = MP/SP$, or $\epsilon = MP/SP$. Dividing through by ϵ and multiplying through by SP, $SP = MP/\epsilon$. From the diagram it can be seen that $MS = MP - SP$. Because $SP = MP/\epsilon$, then $MS = MP - MP/\epsilon$, or:

marginal revenue = price − price/elasticity.

Chapter 12

Chapter contents

		Key concepts
Costs and demand	**Costs of production** **Demand**	Pure oligopoly Differentiated oligopoly
Pure and differentiated oligopoly		Centralized cartel Market-sharing cartel Price leadership
Collusion versus independent action	**Perfect collusion** **Imperfect collusion** **Independent action** **Classification limitations**	Price wars "Kinked" demand curve Nonprice competition
The short run	**Perfect collusion** The centralized cartel The market-sharing cartel	
	Imperfect collusion Price leadership by a low-cost firm Price leadership by a dominant firm	
	Independent action Price wars and price rigidity The "kinked" demand curve	
The long run	**Size of plant adjustments** **Entry into the industry** Entry and existence of oligopoly Entry and collusion Barriers to entry	
Nonprice competition	**Advertising** **Differences in quality and design**	
The welfare effects of oligopoly	**Output restriction** **Efficiency of the firm** **Sales promotion wastes** **Range of products**	
Summary	**Suggested readings** **Questions and exercises**	

Pricing and output under oligopoly

Market situations in which there are few enough sellers of a particular product for the activities of one to be of importance to the others are called *oligopoly* situations. A single seller occupies a position of sufficient importance in the product market for changes in the firm's market activities to have repercussions on the others in that market. Other sellers react to the market activities of the one, and their reactions in turn have repercussions on it. The individual seller is aware of this interdependence; and when changing price, output, sales promotional activity, or quality of product, the reactions of others must be taken into account.

The analysis of pricing and output under oligopoly lacks the neatness and precision of the theories of pure competition and of monopoly. The imprecision is partly because of oligopolistic uncertainty—in many cases an oligopolistic firm cannot be sure what rivals' reactions will be to various kinds of activities on its part—and partly because oligopoly covers a wide range of cases, each with its own unique characteristics. There is not now, nor is there likely to be in the foreseeable future, a general theory of oligopoly. Consequently, in this chapter we try to develop a sense of the problems and principles involved in analysis of oligopolistic industries. Several selected models are examined with this objective in mind.

First, we shall briefly discuss costs and demand as they are to be used in the analysis. Next, we shall consider collusion versus independent action by oligopolists. Then we shall examine short-run pricing and output, long-run pricing and output, and nonprice competition. Finally, we shall consider the effects of oligopolistic market structures on the operation of the economy.

Costs and demand

Costs of production

We continue to assume in this chapter that the oligopolistic firm buys its resources competitively. Its cost curves are like those of the purely competitive firm and the pure monopolist.

Demand

Differences in the conditions of demand as seen by the individual firm constitute the main feature setting oligopoly apart from the other types of market structure. Since what one firm is able to do in the market is conditioned by the ways in which other firms react to the market activities of the one, the extent of this oligopolistic uncertainty is highly variable from case to case. In some situations the firm is quite knowledgeable as to the reactions it can expect from other firms, and so it can determine the demand curve it faces with some confidence. In other situations the firm does not possess this knowledge, and the position and shape of the demand curve it faces are highly conjectural. Interdependence of demand among the firms of an industry and oligopolistic uncertainty give rise to a whole host of problems and strategies for firms that we do not find in the other market classifications.

Pure and differentiated oligopoly

The distinction between differentiated oligopoly and pure oligopoly will not play a prominent role in our analysis. As a practical matter, sellers in most oligopolistic industries sell differentiated products.[1] Nevertheless, some of the fundamental principles of differentiated oligopoly, as well as of pure oligopoly, are seen most clearly when we assume that pure oligopoly exists. For example, instead of a single market price for a product produced under differentiated oligopoly, a cluster of prices may occur. Automatic toasters may range in price from $19.95 to $29.95. The various price levels reflect consumers' views regarding the respective qualities of the different sellers' wares and the availabilities of different makes. Analysis may be simplified and basic pricing principles not distorted seriously if we assume that pure oligopoly exists, thus reducing the cluster of prices to a single market price for the product.[2] Wherever necessary, we shall specify whether conditions of differentiated or pure oligopoly are assumed.

---

[1] Industries approaching pure oligopoly include cement, basic steel, and most of the other basic metal-producing industries. Even here there are elements of differentiation among the products sold in a particular industry. Locational factors, service, and personal friendships may differentiate the products of the various sellers in an industry.

[2] One such distortion is that product differentiation may affect control of the individual seller over price. Attachment of consumers to the products of single sellers will reduce the changes in quantities sold for price adjustments upward or downward within a certain price range; that is, it will make the demand curve faced by the individual seller less elastic within that price range.

Collusion versus independent action

An oligopolistic market structure in an industry invites collusion among the industry's firms, but collusive arrangements are seldom perfect and are usually difficult to maintain over time. There are at least three major incentives leading oligopolistic firms toward collusion. (1) They can increase their profits if they can decrease the amount of competition among themselves and act monopolistically. (2) Collusion can decrease oligopolistic uncertainty. If the firms act in concert, they reduce the likelihood of any one firm's taking actions detrimental to the interests of the others. (3) Collusion among the firms already in an industry will facilitate blocking newcomers from that industry. However, once a collusive arrangement is in existence, any single firm has a profit incentive to break away from the group and act independently, thus destroying the collusive arrangement. We shall distinguish among cases of perfect collusion, imperfect collusion, and cases characterized by independent action on the part of individual firms.[3]

Perfect collusion

Cartel arrangements may approach perfect collusion among the sellers in an industry. A *cartel* is a formal organization of the producers within a given industry. Its purpose is to transfer certain management decisions and functions of individual firms to a central association in order to improve the profit positions of the firms. Overt formal cartel organizations are generally illegal in the United States, but they have existed extensively in countries outside the United States and on an international basis. In the United States covert collusion may result in cartel-like arrangements. The electrical equipment case of the 1960s provides an example.[4] In addition, the aid of the government itself may be enlisted to support what are essentially cartel arrangements. Oil prorationing by state commissions in the major petroleum-producing states has served this purpose.[5]

The extent of the functions transferred to the central association varies in different cartel situations. We shall consider two representative cartel types. The first, selected to illustrate almost complete cartel control over member firms, will be called *the centralized cartel*. The second illustrates

---

[3] *See* Fritz Machlup, *The Economics of Sellers' Competition* (Baltimore: The Johns Hopkins Press, 1952), pp. 363–365.

[4] *See* F. M. Scherer, *Industrial Market Structure and Economic Performance* (Chicago: Rand, McNally & Company, 1970), pp. 158–161.

[5] Walter S. Measday, "The Petroleum Industry," in Walter Adams, ed. *The Structure of American Industry,* 5th ed. (New York: Macmillan Publishing Company, Inc., 1977), pp. 144–145.

cases in which fewer functions are transferred to the central association. It will be designated as *the market-sharing cartel.*

In the centralized cartel the decision making with regard to pricing, output, sales, and distribution of profits is accomplished by the central association, which markets the product, determines prices, determines the amount that each firm is to produce, and divides profits among member firms. Member firms are represented in the central association, and cartel policies presumably result from exchanges of ideas, negotiation, and compromise. However, a firm's power to influence cartel policies is not necessarily proportional to its representation in the central association. Its economic power in the industry may significantly influence cartel policies.

The market-sharing cartel is a somewhat looser form of organization. The firms forming the cartel agree on market shares with or without an understanding regarding prices. Member firms do their own marketing but observe the cartel agreement.

Imperfect collusion

Imperfectly collusive cases are made up mostly of tacit informal arrangements under which the firms of an industry seek to establish prices and outputs and yet escape prosecution under the United States antitrust laws. The price leadership arrangements that have existed in a number of industries—steel, tobacco, oil, and others—are typical of this class. However, tacit unorganized collusion can occur in many other ways. Gentlemen's agreements of various sorts with regard to pricing, output, market sharing, and other activities of the firms within the industry can be worked out on the golf course and on "social" occasions of different kinds.

Independent action

Cases of independent action are just what the name implies. The individual firms of an industry each go it alone. In some industries independent action often touches off price wars when the reactions of rivals to the actions of one firm are retaliatory in nature. In other industries independent action may be consistent with industry stability over time. Firms may have learned by experience what the reactions of rivals will be to actions on their part and may voluntarily avoid any activity that will rock the boat. Or it may be that the management of each firm is reasonably well satisfied with present prices, outputs, and profits, and is content to let things continue as they are rather than chance the start of a chain reaction.

Classification limitations

Collusion is a matter of degree, with cases of perfect collusion and cases of independent action at the polar limits. We cannot with certainty say that all price leadership cases or all gentlemen's agreements fall under the heading of imperfect collusion. Ordinarily we would expect that to be the case, but in some instances the terms of agreement and adherence to those terms may be strict enough to present a case of perfect collusion. Similarly, cartel arrangements may not always be enforced strictly enough to warrant calling them perfect collusion, but rather they may fall in the category of imperfect collusion.

Reference to the number of firms in an industry is conspicuously absent from the classification that we have made. Yet the degree of collusion achieved is not entirely divorced from the number of firms involved. The greater the number of firms in a given industry, the harder it will be ordinarily to achieve a high degree of collusion. The smaller the number of firms involved, the easier it is for the activities of individual firms to come under the scrutiny of the others. Small numbers are more easily policed by the group as a whole; hence, collusive arrangements are less likely to be violated by individual firms.

The short run

We turn now to outputs and pricing in specific oligopoly cases in the short run. Typical examples under each of the three classifications of the preceding section will be examined so that a general grasp of the fundamental problems and principles involved in oligopolistic situations can be obtained. In the short-run analysis of the present section we should keep in mind that individual firms do not have time to change their plant sizes nor is it possible for new firms to enter the industry. The number of firms in the industry under consideration is fixed.

Perfect collusion

The centralized cartel   Collusion in its most complete form is exemplified by the centralized cartel. Its purpose is the joint or monopolistic maximization of industry profits by the several firms of the industry. "Ideal" or complete monopolistic price and output determination by a cartel will rarely be achieved in the real world—although it may be approached in some instances.

Suppose that the firms of an industry have surrendered the power to make price and output decisions to a central association. Quotas to be produced are determined by the association, as is the distribution of industry profits. Policies adopted are to be those that will contribute most to total industry profits. To simplify the analysis, we shall assume that the firms of the industry produce a homogeneous product.

Maximization of the cartel's profits is essentially a monopoly problem, since a single agency is making decisions for the industry as a whole. Profits are maximum where the industry output and price are such that industry marginal revenue equals industry marginal cost. These two concepts need explanation.

The association is faced with the industry demand curve for the product; the industry marginal revenue curve is derived from it in the usual manner. The industry marginal revenue curve shows how much each one-unit increase in the volume of sales per unit of time will increase industry total receipts. The industry demand curve and the industry marginal revenue curve are shown by DD and MR, respectively, in Figure 12–1.

Figure 12–1   The centralized cartel

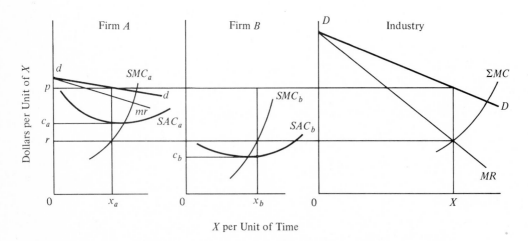

X per Unit of Time

The industry marginal cost curve is constructed from the short-run marginal cost curves of individual firms in the industry. The two-firm case in Figure 12–1 shows how this construction is done. For any given output level the central agency should minimize industry costs. This goal can be accomplished by allocating quotas to the member firms in such a way that the marginal cost of each firm when producing its quota is equal to the marginal cost of every other firm when each is producing its respective quota. If quotas are allocated to individual firms in any other way, industry costs for the given output will not be minimized. Suppose, for example, that the quota of firm A with respect to the quota of firm B is such that firm A's marginal cost is greater than that of firm B. Industry costs could be decreased by reducing firm A's quota and by increasing firm B's. Reducing firm A's production rate by one unit will reduce industry total cost by an amount equal to firm A's (higher) marginal cost. Increasing the production rate of firm B by one unit will increase industry total cost by an amount equal to firm B's (lower) marginal cost. Thus, the reduction of firm A's quota will reduce total cost by more than the increase in firm B's quota will increase it. When quotas are correctly allocated for each possible industry output, the industry marginal cost curve will be the horizontal summation of the individual firm's short-run marginal cost curves. The industry marginal cost curve is ΣMC in Figure 12–1.[6]

The profit-maximizing price for the cartel will be p, and the industry output will be X. Each individual firm should produce the quota at which its short-run marginal cost is equal to industry marginal revenue r. The quota of firm A will be x_a and that of firm B will be x_b. Ignore dd and mr in the firm A diagram for the present. If industry output exceeds X, marginal costs of one or more firms will be greater than r and industry marginal revenue will be smaller. More will be added to industry total costs by these outputs than to industry total receipts; hence, profits will decrease. If industry output is less than X, some or all firms' short-run marginal costs will be less than r, while industry marginal revenue will exceed r. Larger outputs up to X will add more to industry total receipts than to industry total costs, and profits will increase.[7]

Profits can be computed on a firm-by-firm basis and totaled for the industry. Profit per unit of output for a single firm will equal the industry price minus the firm's average cost at the output that the firm produces. Profit per unit multiplied by the firm's output equals the profit that the firm contributes to total industry profits. Profit of firm A is $c_a p \times x_a$, while that of firm B is $c_b p \times x_b$. Total industry profits are the sum of the profits con-

---

[6] *Cf.* the multiple-plant case discussed on pp. 221–223.

[7] Let π = profits:

$$R = f(x_a + x_b) = \text{total revenue of the cartel}$$
$$C_a = g(x_a) = \text{total cost for firm } A$$
$$C_b = h(x_b) = \text{total cost for firm } B.$$

Then,

$$\pi = R - (C_a + C_b) = f(x_a + x_b) - g(x_a) - h(x_b).$$

To maximize profits

$$\frac{\delta \pi}{\delta x_a} = f'(x_a + x_b) - g'(x_a) = 0$$

$$\frac{\delta \pi}{\delta x_b} = f'(x_a + x_b) - h'(x_b) = 0$$

and

$$f'(x_a + x_b) = g'(x_a) = h'(x_b),$$

or MR from cartel sales must equal the marginal cost of firm A's output and the marginal cost of firm B's output.

tributed by all individual firms. Industry profits may be distributed among firms on an "as earned" basis or according to any other scheme deemed appropriate.

The "ideal" monopolistic determination of industry output and price just described is seldom achieved in practice. Decisions made by an association result from negotiation, give-and-take, and compromise among the points of view and interests of cartel members. Therefore, it is not probable that the association would be able to act precisely as would a monopolist. Profits, for example, may be distributed according to production quotas assigned to individual firms. Some firms, able to exert great pressure on the central association, may receive quotas that run their marginal costs above those of other firms, thus increasing industry costs and decreasing industry profits. In addition, pressure on the central association to increase the quotas of some firms may result in decisions to increase industry output beyond the profit-maximizing level. Prices and profits below the full monopolistic level would result. Inefficient high-cost firms may be assigned quotas that run their marginal costs above industry marginal revenue, even though principles of economy may indicate that such firms should be shut down completely. These possibilities by no means exhaust the field, but they do serve to illustrate the point that political decisions on the part of the association, made to placate certain member firms, may sometimes take precedence over economic considerations.[8]

In a cartel composed of several firms there exists an incentive for individual firms to leave the cartel and operate independently. With the larger part of the industry adhering to the cartel price, an individual firm operating independently would be faced with a demand curve for its output that is much more elastic than the industry demand curve in price ranges around the cartel price.

Consider firm A in Figure 12–1, for example. If firm A could break away from the cartel, it would be faced with a demand curve such as dd, provided other firms in the cartel adhere to price p. The demand curve facing any one individual firm under these circumstances would be much more elastic than the industry demand curve at the cartel price, since a cut in price by the individual firm would attract buyers away from the rest of the cartel. Consequently, marginal revenue for firm A, operating independently at output level x_a, would be higher than marginal revenue for the cartel at output level X. Firm A's marginal revenue would exceed its marginal costs at output x_a, and the firm could increase its own profits by expanding its output beyond x_a. The firm that can break away from a cartel successfully can increase its profit possibilities if other firms do not try the same strategy. If all try it, the cartel falls apart, industry output increases, the price falls, and all end up with smaller profits.

[8] *See* Machlup, *op. cit.*, pp. 476–480.

The market-sharing cartel Market sharing of one type or another is characteristic of many cartel arrangements. Under certain conditions it can result in "ideal" monopoly price and output for the industry, that is, the industry profit-maximizing level of price and output. In practice it is likely to deviate from the monopoly position.

Suppose that the firms of the industry produce a homogeneous product and agree on the share of the market that each is to receive at each possible price. Homogeneity of the product will establish the rule of a single price in the product market. To simplify the analysis, assume further that there are only two firms in the industry. The two firms have equal costs and agree to share the market half and half.

Under the assumed conditions the two firms will have identical views regarding the price to charge and the output to produce. The industry demand curve for the product is *DD* in Figure 12–2. Each firm faces de-

Figure 12–2   The market-sharing cartel

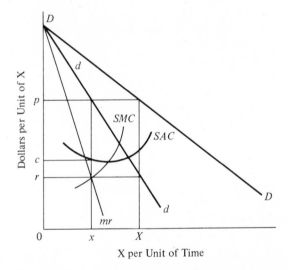

mand curve *dd* for its own output. Each has a short-run average cost curve and a short-run marginal cost curve of *SAC* and *SMC*, respectively. The marginal revenue curve faced by each firm is *mr*. The profit-maximizing output for each firm will be *x*, at which *SMC* is equal to *mr*. Each firm will want to charge price *p*. Profits for each firm will equal *cp* × *x*. Together the firms will produce an industry output of *X* that will fill the market at price *p*. Such will be the case since *dd* lies halfway between the market demand curve and the price axis.

Under the assumed conditions the market-sharing cartel, like the centralized cartel, will determine price and output at the levels that a monopolist would set if the monopolist were in complete control of the producing facilities of the industry. Such a monopolist's marginal cost curve would be the horizontal summation of the two SMC curves of the two plants—it would lie twice as far to the right at each price level as the SMC curve of Figure 12–2 does. The monopolist would face the industry demand curve DD, and at output X industry marginal revenue would be at level r—the same level as individual firm marginal revenue at output x. Such would be the case because DD has the same elasticity at price p as does dd.[9]

At output X industry marginal cost would be at level r. Output X would be the profit-maximizing output for the monopolist, since industry marginal revenue and industry marginal cost are equal at that output. The monopolist would sell output X at price p per unit.

Several factors, however, may stand in the way of the achievement of an "ideal" monopolistic price and output. Costs of production for the individual firms are likely to differ rather than being identical as we assumed that they were. Market sharing largely precludes the transferring of output quotas from firms with higher marginal costs to those with lower marginal costs at the outputs produced by each. Differing points of view and differing interests of the firms comprising the cartel may result in compromises that prevent maximization of industry profits. Individual firms, assigned market shares and given a product price, may deliberately or in good faith overestimate the quantities of product that constitute their respective proportions of the total market, and thus they may encroach on the markets of others.[10] Additionally, the degree of independent action left to individual firms may whet their desires to break away from the cartel and may increase the possibilities of their doing so.

Under a market-sharing cartel arrangement markets need not be shared equally. High-capacity firms may receive larger market shares than low-capacity firms. Market sharing may be accomplished on a regional basis, with each firm allocated a particular geographic area instead of sharing a common market. A whole host of difficulties may arise as a result of different demand elasticities at particular prices: different costs, inferior territories, encroachment upon each other's territories, and so on—all of

---

[9] Two demand curves with equal elasticities at each of various price levels are said to be isoelastic. Demand curves are isoelastic when the quantities taken at each of various prices form a constant ratio to each other. [*See* Joan Robinson, *The Economics of Imperfect Competition* (London: Macmillan & Co., Ltd., 1933), p. 61.] Because dd lies halfway between DD and the price axis at different prices, the quantities taken as shown by dd are in constant ratio to the quantities taken as shown by DD. The ratio is one-half.

[10] To minimize sales in excess of market shares or quotas, most cartels exact penalties from the member that exceeds its quota.

which make pricing and output problems much more uncertain than they appear to be in the model.

Imperfect collusion

Price leadership by a low-cost firm   In the absence of formal cartel arrangements price leadership by one firm in the industry frequently provides the means of colluding. Suppose that there are two firms in the industry, that a tacit market-sharing arrangement has been established with each firm assigned half the market, that the product is undifferentiated, and that one firm has lower costs than the other.

A conflict of interest will occur with regard to the price to charge. The market demand curve is DD in Figure 12–3. Each firm faces demand curve

Figure 12–3   Price leadership by a low-cost firm

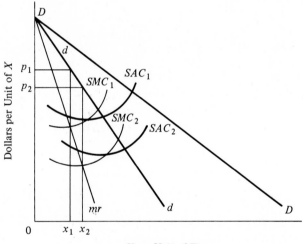

dd. The cost curves of the high-cost firm are SAC_1 and SMC_1. Those of the low-cost firm are SAC_2 and SMC_2. The marginal revenue curve of each firm is mr. The high-cost firm will want to produce an output of x_1 and charge a price of p_1, whereas the low-cost firm will want to produce an output of x_2 and charge a price of p_2.

Since the low-cost firm can afford to sell at a lower price than the high-cost firm can, the latter will have no recourse other than to sell at the price set by the low-cost firm. Thus, the low-cost firm becomes the price leader.

This type of situation has several ramifications, depending on the comparative costs of the firms, the number of firms in the industry, the shape and position of the market demand curve, and the share of the market that each firm is to receive.[11]

Price leadership by a dominant firm   Many oligopolistic industries are made up of one or more large firms, together with a number of small firms. To avoid large-scale price cutting, tacit collusion may occur in the form of price leadership by one or more of the large firms.[12] To simplify the analysis, assume that there is a single large dominant firm in the industry and a number of small firms. Suppose that the dominant firm sets the price for the industry and allows the small firms to sell all that they desire at that price. The dominant firm then fills out the market.

Each small firm tends to behave as though it were in a competitive atmosphere. It can sell all that it wants to sell at the price set by the dominant firm; it faces a perfectly elastic demand curve at the level of the established price. The marginal revenue curve of the small firm coincides with the demand curve faced by it; hence, to maximize profits, the small firm should produce the output at which its marginal cost equals marginal revenue and the price set by the dominant firm.

A supply curve for all small firms combined is obtained by summing the marginal cost curves of all the small firms horizontally. It shows how much all small firms together will place on the market at each possible price. This curve is labeled ΣMC in Figure 12–4.

The demand curve faced by the dominant firm can be derived from this information. The market demand curve DD shows how much of the product consumers will take off the market at each possible price, whereas the ΣMC curve shows how much the small firms combined will sell at each possible price. The horizontal differences between the two curves at all possible prices show how much the dominant firm can sell at those prices. The demand curve faced by the dominant firm is dd and is obtained by subtracting the ΣMC curve from the DD curve horizontally. To show in detail how dd is obtained, suppose that the dominant firm sets the price at p'. At this price, or any higher price, the small firms would fill the market, leaving no sales for the dominant firm. At a price of p'' the small firms would sell quantity $p''A''$, leaving $A''B''$ for the dominant firm to sell. In order to place the demand curve for the dominant firm's product in proper relationship to the quantity and dollar axes of the diagram, we can set point C'' so that $p''C''$ equals $A''B''$. This process can be repeated at various assumed

[11] *See* Kenneth E. Boulding, *Economic Analysis,* Vol. I, *Microeconomics,* 4th ed. (New York: Harper & Row, Publishers, Inc., 1966), pp. 475–482.

[12] Price leadership has been common in the fabrication of nonferrous alloys, steel, agricultural implements, newsprint paper, and other industries. *See* Scherer, *op. cit.,* pp. 164–173.

Figure 12–4   Price leadership by a dominant firm

X per Unit of Time

prices. A line joining all points thus established will be dd, the demand curve faced by the dominant firm. At any price below their respective average variable costs the smaller firms will drop out of the market, leaving the entire market to the dominant firm.

The profit-maximizing price and outputs are determined in the usual way. The marginal revenue curve of the dominant firm is MR_d, and its marginal cost curve is SMC_d. Profits are maximum for the dominant firm at an output level of x_d at which SMC_d equals MR_d. The price charged by the dominant firm is p. Each small firm maximizes profits by producing the output at which its marginal cost is equal to its marginal revenue, and marginal revenue for each small firm is equal to price p. Total output for the small firms combined is x_s, the output at whch ΣMC equals p. Total industry output is x_d plus x_s and equals X. Profit for the dominant firm is x_d times the difference between price p and the dominant firm's average cost at output x_d. Profit for each small firm is equal to its output times the difference between price p and its average cost at that output. Average cost curves are omitted from Figure 12–4 to avoid cluttering the diagram.

Many variations of the dominant-firm model are possible. For example, if there are two or more large firms surrounded by a cluster of small firms, the small firms may look to one or to a group of the large firms for price leadership. The large firms collectively may estimate the amounts that the small firms will sell at various prices and proceed to share or divide the remaining market in any one of various possible ways. The present analysis assumes no product differentiation. But product differentiation may occur in similar price leadership cases, causing price differentials for the products of the various firms. The gasoline industry furnishes a case in point. Retail prices of the major companies—one or more of which often serve as the price leader—will be very close together in a given locality, while those of small independents will tend to be a few cents per gallon below that of the majors.

Independent action

It would be a mistake to characterize all oligopolistic industries as collusive. In many such industries collusion has never existed. In others collusive arrangements, when effected, have broken down. It appears, too, that the antitrust laws may have deterred firms in some industries from engaging in collusion and may have forced firms in other industries to cease doing so. Empirical data on the extent to which collusion occurs in oligopolistic industries is not available, for this is the kind of information that colluding firms want to suppress rather than publicize. In any case, a very substantial segment of oligopolistic market structures is likely to contain firms that act independently of others.

Price wars and price rigidity   A persistent danger of price wars exists in oligopolistic industries characterized by independent action on the part of individual firms. Little of a precise analytical nature can be said about these. One seller may lower the price to increase sales. But this move takes customers away from rivals, and the rivals may retaliate with a vengeance. The price war may spread throughout the industry, with each firm trying to undercut others. The end result may well be disastrous for some individual firms.

The specific causes of price wars are varied, but they originate from the interdependence of sellers. A new filling station opening up in a given locality or an existing one attempting to revive lagging sales may be the initiating factor. Surplus stocks at existing prices and limited storage facilities have touched off price wars in the sale of crude oil in the petroleum industry. In a young industry sellers may not have learned what to expect of rivals, or they may be scrambling to secure an established place in the industry and may inadvertently start a price war.

Maturity on the part of an industry may substantially lessen the likelihood of price wars. Individual firms may have learned what not to do and may carefully avoid activities that could touch off price wars. They may have established a price or a cluster of prices that is tolerable to all from the point of view of profits. Such prices are thought by many to be rather rigid over time, although there is no clear-cut evidence that this is the case. Individual firms are thought to engage in nonprice competition rather than in price rivalry in order to increase their respective shares of the market and profits. Soft drinks and cigarettes are often cited as examples of mature rigid-price industries.

The "kinked" demand curve   An analytical device frequently used to explain oligopolistic price rigidity is the kinked demand curve. This case is thought to occur when certain assumptions concerning the industry and the firms in the industry are fulfilled. First, the industry is a mature one, either with or without product differentiation. A price or a cluster of prices fairly satisfactory to all has been established. Second, if one firm lowers its price, other firms will follow or undercut it in order to retain their shares of the market. For price decreases the individual firm cannot hope to do more than hold its former share of the market—and it may not succeed in doing that much. Third, if one firm increases its price, other firms will not follow the price increase. The customers of the price-raising firm will shift to the other, now relatively lower-priced firms, and the price-raising firm will lose a part of its share of the market.

The demand curve faced by a single firm in such a situation is pictured diagrammatically in Figure 12–5 as FDE. The firm is selling quantity x at price p. If it decreases the price below p, other firms follow, and it retains only its share of the market. For price decreases, then, the demand curve faced by the firm is DE, and it will have about the same elasticity at different prices as the market demand curve. Should the firm increase the

---

Figure 12–5   The kinked demand curve: cost changes

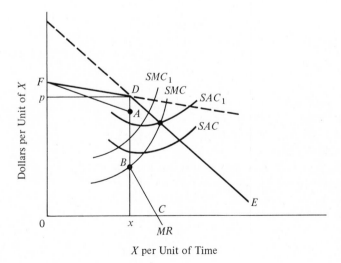

price above p, other firms will not follow, and it loses a part or all of its share of the market to the other firms. The demand curve faced by the firm for price increases is FD, and at each possible price it will have a considerably greater elasticity than the market demand curve. The demand curve FDE is not a smooth one; it has a "kink" in it at the established price p.

The kinked demand curve has important implications for the marginal revenue curve of the firm. The marginal revenue curve is discontinuous at output x; that is, it has a gap in it at that point. This gap can be visualized by imagining, first, that only the FD portion of the demand curve exists and by drawing the appropriate marginal revenue curve for it. Second, imagine that the DE portion of the demand curve extends smoothly on up to the price axis, and draw the appropriate marginal revenue curve for it. Since the imagined part of the DE curve does not exist, no marginal revenue curve exists for it at outputs less than x. Since the FD part of the demand curve does not go beyond x, neither does its marginal revenue curve. The two nonvertical sections of the marginal revenue curve can be thought of as the appropriate marginal revenue curves for two distinct continuous demand curves, and there would be no reason to expect them to be equal to each other at output x.

The discontinuous marginal revenue curve can be thought of also in terms of elasticity of demand. If the demand curve were continuous, its elasticity would be changing continuously as we move from higher to lower prices. Since $MR = p - p/\epsilon$, the marginal revenue curve would also be continuous as we move down the demand curve. However, the demand curve breaks at D. Elasticity at an output infinitesimally below x is substantially greater than elasticity at an output infinitesimally above x. Thus, marginal revenue must drop sharply at output x.

Cost curves SAC and SMC show a situation such that at price p some profit can be made. The marginal cost curve cuts the marginal revenue curve within its discontinuous part. Output x and price p are, in fact, the firm's profit-maximizing output and price. If the output level were less than x, marginal revenue would exceed marginal cost, and the firm's profits would be increased by expanding output to x. For output increases above x marginal cost exceeds marginal revenue, and profits will decrease.

Discontinuous marginal revenue curves may result in rigid pricing policies on the part of individual firms in the industry. Suppose that one firm's costs increase because of increases in the prices it must pay for resources. The cost curves will shift upward to positions such as SAC_1 and SMC_1. As long as the marginal cost curve continues to cut the discontinuous part of the marginal revenue curve, there is no incentive for the oligopolist to change either price or output. The reverse situation also holds. Resource price decreases will shift the cost curves downward, but as long as the marginal cost curve cuts the marginal revenue curve in its discontinuous part, no price-output changes will occur. If costs should go up enough for the marginal cost curve to cut the *FA* segment of the marginal revenue curve, the oligopolist will restrict output to the point at which marginal cost equals marginal revenue and will raise the price. Likewise, if costs decrease enough for the marginal cost curve to cut the *BC* segment of the marginal revenue curve, the oligopolist will lower the price and increase output up to the level at which marginal cost equals marginal revenue. Thus, there is room for the cost curves to shift up or down without changing the oligopolist's profit-maximizing price and output. Such will be the case as long as the marginal cost curve cuts the marginal revenue curve in its discontinuous part.

Price rigidity may also persist when demand changes. The initial position of the oligopolistic firm is pictured by Figure 12–6(a). Assume its costs do not change and market demand for the product increases. The demand curve faced by the oligopolist shifts to the right to $F_1 D_1 E_1$, as is shown in Figure 12–6(b), but it remains kinked at price p. The marginal revenue curve moves to the right also, with its discontinuous segment always occurring at the output at which the demand curve is kinked. If the increase in demand is limited enough so that the marginal cost curve still cuts the marginal revenue curve in the discontinuous segment $B_1 A_1$, the firm will continue to maximize profits at price p but at a larger output x_1. If the increase in market demand should shift the firm's demand curve farther to the right than $F_1 D_1 E_1$, the marginal cost curve would cut the marginal revenue curve's $F_1 A_1$ segment; and to maximize profits the firm should increase the price as well as the output. A decrease in market demand shifts the firm's demand curve to the left to $F_2 D_2 E_2$, as is shown in Figure 12–6(c). Here there is no incentive to change the price, although output decreases, until the demand curve shifts far enough to the left for the marginal cost curve to intersect the $B_2 C_2$ segment of the marginal revenue curve. This amount of shift would induce the firm to lower the price as well as to decrease output.

The case of the kinked demand curve is only one of many possible oligopolistic situations, and it rests on a special set of assumptions regarding the behavior of rivals when confronted with certain actions on the part of the firm under analysis. Often students (and some professors) become intrigued with the case and tend to think of it and the term "oligopoly" as being synonymous. We should avoid this inaccuracy in our thinking.

The long run

Two types of adjustment are possible in oligopolistic industries in the long run. Individual firms are free to build any desired size of plant; thus, the relevant cost curves for the firm are the long-run average cost curve and the

Figure 12–6   The kinked demand curve: changes in demand

(a)

(b)

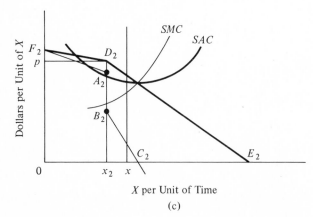

(c)

long-run marginal cost curve. Second, some industry adjustments may be possible in the form of entry of new firms into the industry or exit of old firms from the industry. These types of adjustment will be considered in turn.

Size of plant adjustments

The size of plant that the individual firm should build depends on its expected rate of output. For any given rate of output we can say as a first approximation that the firm attempts to produce that output at the least possible average cost; that is, it builds the plant size that makes its short-run average cost curve tangent to the long-run average cost curve at that output.

Under perfect collusion, and often under imperfect collusion, quotas, market shares, and outputs of individual firms may be predictable with some degree of accuracy. In such cases the firm would be expected to adjust its size of plant accordingly. Not much can be said with regard to whether the size of plant would be of most efficient size, less than most efficient size, or greater than most efficient size. It may be any one of the three, depending on the nature of the oligopolistic situation involved. Certainly, there is no reason to expect that the firm would tend to construct a most efficient size of plant.

For a firm in an industry characterized by independent action there will be no more certainty regarding the size of plant to build than there is regarding the output to produce and the price to charge. Growth possibilities of the industry may influence the decisions of the firm to a large extent. The existence of a large growth potential would make the individual firm optimistic with respect to anticipated sales and would result in plant enlargements. "Live-and-let-live" policies or fear of "rocking the boat" on the part of individual firms may lead to fairly determinate outputs and, consequently, to some degree of certainty as to the sizes of plant to build. Again, there is no reason for believing that most efficient sizes would be built.

Entry into the industry

When individual firms in an industry make profits or when they incur losses, incentives exist for new firms to enter the industry or for old firms to leave. Exit from an oligopolistic industry will usually be much easier than entry and need not detain us. Ease or difficulties of entry are much more important. The very existence of oligopolistic markets depends to some extent on whether or not entry into the industry can be partially or completely blocked. In addition, the degree of collusion that can be attained or maintained within the industry tends to be an inverse function of the ease of entry.

Entry and the existence of oligopoly If entry into an oligopolistic industry is comparatively easy, it may not remain oligopolistic in the long run. Whether it does or not will depend on the extent of the market for the product, as compared with the most efficient size of plant for an individual firm. Profits will attract new firms, lowering the market price or the cluster of prices as industry output increases. When the price no longer exceeds long-run average costs for individual firms, entry will cease. If the market is limited, the number of firms may still be small enough to make it necessary for each firm to take account of the actions of the others. If so, the market situation remains one of oligopoly. If the market is extensive enough so that the number of firms can increase to the point at which each firm no longer considers that its activities affect the other firms or that the activities of other firms affect it, the market situation will have become one of either pure or monopolistic competition.

Entry and collusion Easy entry tends to break down collusive arrangements. We have seen already that in a collusive arrangement a strong incentive exists for any one individual firm to break away from the group. The same sort of incentive operates to attract new firms into a cartelized industry and to induce those entering firms to remain outside the cartel. The entering firm, if it remains outside the group, will face a demand curve more elastic at various price levels than that of the group and, consequently, will be confronted with higher marginal revenue possibilities. At prices slightly below the cartel price it can pick up many of the cartel's customers. At prices slightly above the cartel price it can sell little or nothing. Entering firms that remain outside the collusive group will encroach more and more on the profits of that group or will cause the group to incur losses and force its eventual dissolution.

Even when the entering firms are taken into the cartel, a strong presumption exists that dissolution of the cartel will follow eventually. Refer to Figure 12–7. Suppose the ΣMC is the horizontal summation of individual firm short-run marginal cost curves. The price will be p, and industry output will be X. The entry of new firms will move the ΣMC curve to the right,[13] increasing the industry profit-maximizing output and lowering the profit-maximizing price. When enough firms have entered to shift the industry marginal cost curve to ΣMC_1, forcing the price down to p_1 and increasing the level of output to X_1, profits for the industry may still exist. More firms will enter, shifting the industry marginal cost curve to some position

---

[13] Assume that M is the minimum price at which any firm will enter the industry.

Figure 12–7   Long-run cartel equilibrium and the effects of entry

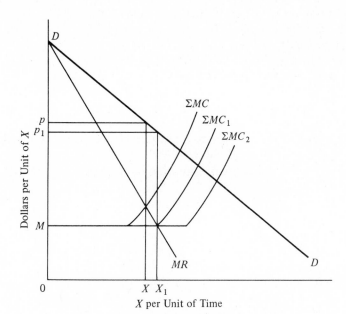

ΣMC_2; however, industry profits will decrease if output is expanded beyond X_1. Industry marginal revenue for the additional output will be less than the industry's marginal cost. The more profitable course of action for the cartel is to keep the additional firms idle and simply cut them in on the industry's profits. Plant costs of additional firms augment industry total costs, and, eventually, enough firms will have entered the industry to cause all profit to be eliminated. A strong incentive now exists for individual firms to break away from the cartel. Any single firm, if it markets its own output, faces a more elastic demand curve in the neighborhood of the cartel price than does the cartel. Marginal revenue for the firm exceeds marginal revenue for the cartel. Also, average cost for the firm is lower than average cost for the cartel.[14] The firm that can break away can make profits, provided others remain in the cartel and the cartel price is maintained. The temptations facing each individual firm are likely to result in a breakup of the cartel.[15]

[14] The individual firm's cost is lower since the cartel is holding the plant capacity of a number of firms idle, thus adding to cartel average costs.

[15] *See* Don Patinkin, "Multiple-Plant Firms, Cartels, and Imperfect Competition," *Quarterly Journal of Economics,* Vol. LXI (February 1947), pp. 173–205.

Barriers to entry   Since ease of entry into an industry tends to be the nemesis of collusive oligopoly, collusion usually can be maintained only when entry is restricted; collusion has as one of its purposes the erection of barriers to potential entrants. Barriers to the entry of new firms may be inherent in the nature of the industry, or they may be established by the existing firms of the industry. These will be called "natural" barriers and "artificial" barriers, respectively. Natural barriers to entry may be inevitable in particular industries. Artificial barriers conceivably can be removed.

Probably the most important natural barrier to entry is the smallness of the product market in relation to the most efficient size of plant for a firm in the industry. Suppose, for example, that there are two firms in the industry, and each is operating with a plant size somewhere near the most efficient size. Price exceeds average costs for each, and some profit exists. Heretofore we have considered the existence of profit as the signal for the entrance of new firms. Prospective entrants eye the profit and consider the possibility of entering. They discover that if a new firm enters with a less than most efficient plant size, average costs of the entrant will be so high that no profit could be made. Further, if a new firm enters with a most efficient size of plant, industry output will be increased to the extent that price will be below average costs both for existing firms in the industry and for the entrant. Therefore, no new firms will enter.

Another natural barrier to entry consists of the difficulty of putting together a large and complex plant and of obtaining funds to build it. The automobile industry is a case in point. The initial investment outlay for a potential entrant is extremely high. Large amounts of space, several buildings, and specialized heavy equipment must be obtained. Highly skilled and well-paid personnel are necessary. A nationwide organization of dealership, maintenance, and repair facilities must be established. The difficulties of entry are so great that only a few firms have had the financial backing to try it since World War II, despite record profits in the industry. This barrier to entry is not the only one for the automobile industry, but it has been major.

Among the artificial barriers to entry those enforced or supported by the state loom large. Patent rights to key machines or technological processes may be obtained by certain firms of an industry. Those firms may then maintain control of the machines or processes by leasing them to a limited number of other firms.[16] Or the firms of an industry, through cross-licensing arrangements, may give each other access to the patents of each but refuse to allow any new firms to use them.[17]

Government-supported barriers to entry exist extensively in the field of

[16] Entry into the glass-container industry has been controlled in this manner. *See* Wilcox, *op. cit.*, pp. 73–78.

[17] *See* Joe S. Bain, *Industrial Organization*, 2nd ed. (New York: John Wiley & Sons, Inc., 1968), pp. 335–337.

transportation. On a local basis taxicab and bus companies operate under franchises guaranteeing limited "competition" in the industry. Entry into the interstate public transportation field, with the exception of air carriers, is regulated by the Interstate Commerce Commission. The Civil Aeronautics Board regulates entry into the air transportation field.

Local governments regulate entry into a host of local oligopolistic industries. Building codes in many cities prevent the entrance of firms producing prefabricated houses or parts of houses. Local licensing laws are frequently used to limit the number of barbers, taverns, plumbers, morticians, and others in service trades. Entry-restricting devices are usually rationalized as maintaining standards of competency, keeping undesirables out of the trades, and protecting the public in other ways.

A second artificial barrier to prospective entrants is the control by the firms already in the field of strategic sources of raw materials necessary for producing the product. This barrier will be of greatest importance where raw material sources are highly concentrated geographically, or, at least, where the better sources are highly concentrated. Concentration of raw material sources facilitates concentration of ownership. Magnesium, nickel, molybdenum, and aluminum provide examples.

Third, so-called limit pricing policies of established firms in an industry may be used to bar the door. Established firms may deliberately produce outputs greater than those that maximize profits, lowering price sufficiently so that it is not profitable for a potential newcomer to enter.[18] Or, similar tactics may be used by large financially powerful firms to drive smaller firms out of an industry. The classic example is the Standard Oil case of the late 1800s. Additionally, recurrent price wars may create such an atmosphere of uncertainty about the profit possibilities of an industry that new firms will steer clear of it.

Fourth, product differentiation may form an artificial barrier to entry. The industry's product may have become so closely identified with particular sellers' names that consumers will refuse to buy "off brands." Even though standard brands are differentiated from each other, the standard brands are well known to almost all consumers. What consumers fear and refuse to consume are the new, unknown, and, consequently, "inferior" brands. This reluctance is an important barrier to entry into the automobile industry.

Restricted entry into an oligopolistic industry makes it possible for profits to exist in the long run for the firms in the industry. This is not to say that pure profits will always exist in oligopolistic industries. Losses can and do occur. Or, the firms of an industry may be just covering average costs, showing neither profit nor loss. When no profits are being made, entry will

---

[18] *See* Donald Dewey, *Microeconomics* (New York: Oxford University Press, 1975), pp. 114–119, 141–151.

not be desired regardless of whether it is restricted or open. The possibility of profits provides the motivation for entry, and when entry is restricted, profits may persist over time. Restricted entry prevents profits from playing their essential role in the organization of productive capacity in a private enterprise economy.

Nonprice competition

Although oligopolists may be reluctant to encroach upon each other's market shares by lowering the product price, they appear to have little hesitancy in using other means to accomplish the same results. While open undercutting of the price(s) of rivals raises the specter of price wars that may be disastrous to some firms, product differentiation offers a more subtle and a much safer way of accomplishing approximately the same results. Product differentiation occurs in two major forms: (1) advertising and (2) variation in design and quality of product. Both forms may and do occur simultaneously, but, for purposes of analysis, we shall treat them separately.

Advertising

The primary purpose of advertising is to shift the demand curve faced by the single seller to the right and to make it less elastic. Thus, the seller can sell a larger volume at the same or a higher price without the danger of touching off a price war. Each seller tries to encroach on the markets of others through advertising. When one firm launches an ingenious and successful advertising program, ordinarily there will be a time lag before rivals can embark on similar programs, and profits can result during the time-lag interval.

Frequently the products of sellers in an industry can be differentiated effectively by advertising alone. Each seller attempts to attract customers to its particular brand name, although basically the product of each seller may be the same as that of other sellers in the industry. The success of sellers in this respect is especially evident in the aspirin industry. All 5-grain aspirin tablets conform to certain United States pharmacopoeia specifications, and one is as effective for the patient as another; nevertheless, some nationally known sellers are able to attract and hold customers at prices far greater than those of other sellers in the same industry.

In some instances rival advertising campaigns succeed only in increasing the costs of individual sellers. Attempts on the part of a single seller to encroach on the markets of others may be anticipated by the other sellers. They launch counteradvertising campaigns of their own, and all sellers succeed only in holding their original places in the market. The overall market for the product may not be expanded at all by advertising activity—

the present-day cigarette industry is a case in point. Once rival advertising is started, however, no single seller can withdraw without losing its place in the market. The advertising outlays become "built in" to the cost structures of individual firms and lead to higher product prices than would otherwise prevail.

How far should nonprice competition through advertising be carried by the individual seller seeking to maximize profits? The same principles that have guided us thus far in profit maximization apply in this case. Advertising outlays are expected to add to the seller's total receipts, but successively larger outlays per unit of time beyond some point will add successively less to total revenues. That is, marginal revenue from advertising will decrease as outlays increase. Similarly, larger advertising outlays add to the seller's total costs; that is, marginal costs of advertising are positive. The profit-maximizing outlay on advertising will be that outlay at which the marginal cost of advertising is equal to the marginal revenue received from it.[19]

Differences in quality and design

Variations in quality and design of particular products are usually used, along with advertising, to differentiate the product of one seller from another. The objective of variations on the part of one seller is that of causing consumers to prefer its product over the products of others—that is, to shift its demand curve to the right (or to enlarge its share of the total market) and to make its demand curve less elastic. Additionally, quality variation may be used to extend the market vertically—different qualities to appeal to different classes or groups of buyers.

When quality and design variations are used to increase an individual firms's market shares, rival firms would not be expected to sit by idly while their markets shrink. Retaliation by rivals will occur. Successful innovations will be imitated and improved on. Individual firms may succeed in increasing their market shares temporarily, but if a permanent increase is to be obtained, such firms must be able to keep ahead of their rivals.

The automobile industry furnishes an excellent example of product variation to increase market shares of particular firms. One producer initiates power steering. Consumers take to the innovation, and other producers follow in order to regain their market positions. Another mounts the motor on rubber, and the process is repeated. Low-pressure tires, automatic transmissions, high horsepower, and many other improvements, both real and fancied, are introduced initially to enlarge the market share of one

---

[19] In practice, probably less is known about the effects of advertising outlays than about the effects of any other cost outlays made by the firm. Nevertheless, any intelligent approach by management to the "correct" magnitude of the advertising budget must be made on the basis of estimated marginal revenue and estimated marginal cost resulting from its contraction or expansion.

producer, and are in turn copied by other producers to regain or hold their shares of the market.

When quality differences are introduced to extend the market vertically for a product, we may find the same firm producing different product qualities to sell to different groups of buyers at different prices or we may find different firms specializing in particular qualities of the product. Initially a product, say deluxe garbage disposals, may be produced for middle-income group markets. Sellers find that by producing "super deluxe" models the market can be expanded into upper-income levels. Likewise, by stripping the deluxe model of fancy gadgets, a standard model can be sold to lower-income groups at a lower price. When different firms specialize in a particular quality of the product, quality differences may become the basis for market sharing.

Product variation often operates in the best interests of consumers. When it passes along the fruits of industrial research in the form of an improved product to the consuming public, consumer desires may be more adequately met than before. The electric mixer in lieu of the old hand-driven egg beater, the more portable and more versatile tank type of vacuum cleaner in lieu of the upright model, the no-frost refrigerator, the high-fidelity stereo sound system, the self-starter on the automobile, and many other variations in product probably represent improved fulfillment of consumer wants.

Some product variation falls in the same class as retaliatory advertising. It adds to costs but adds little to the fulfillment of consumer desires. Design changes adding nothing to the quality of the product may occur. The purpose of the design change may simply be to differentiate last year's from this year's model. Each seller believes that other sellers will make some changes and decides it should do the same to hold its share of the market.

The principles of profit maximization with respect to design and quality changes are the familiar ones. Any changes that will add more to total receipts than to total costs will increase profits (or reduce losses), or any changes that will reduce total costs more than total receipts will increase profits (or reduce losses). To maximize profits with respect to changes in the product, the firm should carry out changes to the point at which the marginal revenue from the changes is equal to the marginal cost of making them.

The welfare effects of oligopoly

Oligopolistic market structures, as compared with purely competitive market structures, would be expected to have adverse effects on consumer welfare. The problems are essentially the same as those brought about by pure monopoly. There is output restriction, internal inefficiency of the firm, and resource waste in sales promotion activities. There may, however, be some welfare gains from product differentiation.

Output restriction

An oligopolistic firm ordinarily faces a demand curve for its output that is downward-sloping to the right, or that is less than perfectly elastic. As a consequence, marginal revenue at each level of sales is less than the price; and since the profit-maximizing firm produces the output level at which marginal revenue equals marginal cost, marginal cost will be less than the product price. The important point is that resources used in producing this product are more valuable to consumers in this use than in alternative uses. Welfare would be increased by transfers of resources into the product and expansion of its output to the point at which marginal cost is equal to the product price.

In addition, an oligopolistic firm may make profits in the long run because entry into the industry is restricted. The price of the product exceeds the average costs of production, indicating that an expansion of the productive capacity of the industry would increase welfare. However, restricted entry keeps this desirable reallocation of resources from taking place.

Efficiency of the firm

The maximum potential economic efficiency for individual firms in the production of particular products is realized when those firms are induced to build most efficient sizes of plant and operate them at most efficient rates of output. As we have observed, there is no automatic tendency for this state of affairs to occur in the long run under oligopoly. The firm's output depends upon its quota, its market share, or its anticipations with regard to its marginal revenue and its long-run marginal costs. Once a long-run output is decided on, the firm will want to produce that output as cheaply as possible; that is, it will build the size of plant whose short-run average cost curve is tangent to the long-run average cost curve at that output. Coincidence of the desired output with the output of a most efficient size of plant, operated at the most efficient rate of output, would be sheer accident.

It should be emphasized that firms in an oligopolistic type of market, even though they do not use most efficient plant sizes, operated at most efficient rates of output, may provide more efficiency in producing a certain product than would firms of any other type of market organization. The most efficient size of plant may be so large in comparison with the market for the product that not enough firms can exist to make the market one of pure competition. If the firms of the industry were broken up or atomized so that no one firm could appreciably influence market price, each might have a much smaller than most efficient size of plant. Consequently, costs and price(s) of the product might be higher, and output levels smaller, with such an arrangement than they would be with the oligopolistic market structure.

Sales promotion wastes

Firms in oligopolistic markets engage in extensive sales promotion activities designed to extend their own markets at the expense of the markets of rivals. As we have seen, the major forms of such activities are advertising and changes in product quality and design. To the extent that they add nothing to consumer satisfaction, resources used in these activities are obviously wasted. Often, however, they yield certain satisfactions to consumers in the forms of entertainment and improved product quality. In these instances the important question with regard to economic efficiency and welfare is whether or not the values of the additional satisfactions obtained from resources used in sales promotion activities are equal to their marginal costs, that is, equal to the satisfactions that the resources could have produced in alternative employments. A strong case can be made that since decisions regarding entertainment and product quality variations are made by business firms rather than by consumers in the market places of the economy, expenditures on resources so used will be too large and will be misdirected. The value of the additional consumer satisfaction obtained will consequently be less than the marginal costs of providing it. To the extent that this phenomenon occurs, economic waste will be the result—welfare will be less than optimum.

Range of products

Differentiated oligopoly provides each consumer with a broader range of products among which to choose than does either pure competition or pure monopoly. Rather than being limited to a single kind and quality of automobile, each consumer can choose the kind and quality that best suits individual needs and income. The same observations apply to television receivers, washing machines, refrigerators, or even entertainment. Gradations in product qualities, with each lower quality selling at a correspondingly lower price, increase the divisibility of the consumer's purchases of particular items. Consequently, the opportunities for allocating income among different products may be so enhanced that the consumer can achieve a higher level of want satisfaction than would otherwise be possible. Additionally, product differentiation enables a consumer to give vent to individual tastes and preferences with regard to alternative designs for a particular product. The range of products available under differentiated oligopoly appears to work in the consumer's favor or to increase individual welfare over what it would otherwise be.

Summary

In oligopolistic market structures there are few enough firms in the industry for the activities of a single firm to influence and evoke reactions from others. The demand curve faced by a single firm will be determinate when the firm can predict with accuracy what the reactions of rivals will be to market activities on its part. Otherwise it will be indeterminate.

We classified oligopolistic industries according to the degree of collusion that exists among firms of each of the industries. Under perfect collusion we included groups of firms such as cartels. Under imperfect collusion we included situations typified by price leadership and gentlemen's agreements. Under independent action we included noncollusive cases.

In the short run perfectly collusive oligopolistic cases approximate the establishment of monopoly price and monopoly output for the industry as a whole. The less the degree of collusion, usually, the lower the price and the greater the output. In industries characterized by independent action on the part of individual firms, price wars are likely to be common occurrences. As the industry matures, the situation may become collusive, or it may develop into a "live-and-let-live" attitude on the part of the firms in the industry. In the latter case price rigidity may occur. Firms may be afraid to change price for fear of touching off a price war.

In the long run the firm can adjust its plant size as desired and new firms can enter the industry, unless entry is blocked. The size of plant chosen by the firm will be the one that will produce its anticipated output at the least possible average cost for that output. Easy entry into the industry is largely incompatible with a high degree of collusion. Collusion exists partly to block entry. Barriers to entry may be classified as "natural" and "artificial." Restricted entry may enable firms in the industry to make long-run pure profits.

The firms of particular oligopolistic industries frequently engage in nonprice competition through product differentiation to avoid touching off price wars. Nonprice competition takes two major forms: advertising and quality and design variation. To the extent that firms using them succeed only in holding their respective market shares, costs of production and product prices will tend to be higher than they would otherwise be. The firm desiring to maximize profits will use each to the point at which the marginal revenue from it equals the marginal cost of extending its use.

Some of the welfare effects of oligopolistic markets on the economy are these:

1. Outputs are restricted below and prices are increased above the levels that will yield Pareto optimality, since product price tends to be higher than marginal cost. With entry partially or completely blocked, pure profits and additional output restrictions occur.

2. Individual firms are not induced to produce at their maximum efficiency plant sizes, although in many cases they produce more efficiently than they would if the industry were atomized.
3. Some sales promotion wastes occur.
4. The range of products available to consumers is broader under differentiated oligopoly than it would be under pure competition or pure monopoly.

Suggested readings

Bain, Joe S., *Industrial Organization,* 2nd ed. New York: John Wiley & Sons, Inc., 1968.

Machlup, Fritz, *The Economics of Sellers' Competition.* Baltimore: The Johns Hopkins Press, 1952. Chaps. 4, 11–16.

Scherer, F. M., *Industrial Market Structure and Economic Performance.* Chicago: Rand, McNally & Company, 1970.

White, Lawrence J., "The Automobile Industry," in Walter Adams, ed., *The Structure of American Industry,* 5th ed. New York: Macmillan Publishing Co., Inc., 1977. Chap. 5.

Wilcox, Clair, *Competition and Monopoly in American Industry.* Temporary National Economic Committee Monograph No. 21. Washington, D.C.: U.S. Government Printing Office, 1940.

Questions and exercises

1. Suppose that the auto repair shops in Universityville form an association. They agree to, and post, a schedule of minimum hourly labor charges for shop work.
    a. How, if at all, could this action be advantageous to them as a group?
    b. If it is advantageous to them as a group, why may it be necessary for them to police the arrangement; that is, why may some shops want to "chisel"?
2. In many states barber shops must be licensed by the state to "protect the public from incompetent barbers." In some states county organizations of barbers determine the minimum prices to be charged for various barbering services. These minimum prices then have the force of law—it is illegal to charge less. The rationale of these laws is that minimum prices must be set at a level that will enable individual shops to be kept clean and sanitary.
    a. Do you believe that licensing is necessary to protect the public? Why or why not? Can you think of any other reason why licensing laws might be effected?
    b. Would you expect minimum prices to be set with the stated rationale

in mind? Why or why not? Can you think of alternative ways of insuring sanitation that may lead toward higher consumer welfare?

3. Since World War II no new automobile-manufacturing firms have been able to enter the industry and survive. What possible explanations can be offered in view of the fact that established firms in the industry, except for Chrysler and American Motors in some years, have been generally profitable?

4. Would you favor breaking General Motors into several companies, each producing a specific line of automobile—for example, Chevrolets? Why or why not?

5. Outline in some detail the set of policies that you think the government should pursue with respect to oligopolistic market structures. State and explain what you would expect each policy to accomplish.

Chapter 13

Chapter contents

Some special characteristics	
The short run	
The long run	**Adjustments with entry blocked**
	Adjustments with entry open
Welfare effects of monopolistic competition	**Output restriction**
	Efficiency of individual firms
	Sales promotion wastes
	Range of products available
Summary	**Suggested readings**
	Questions and exercises

Key concepts

Monopolistic competition
Short run
Long run
Welfare
Most efficient size of plant
Most efficient rate of output

Pricing and output under monopolistic competition

There are many sellers of the product in an industry characterized by monopolistic competition, and the product of each seller is in some way differentiated from the product of every other seller. Several questions arise. What does "many sellers" mean? How can we distinguish between differentiated oligopoly and monopolistic competition? How many sellers must there be in an industry to warrant calling the case one of monopolistic competition? These questions cannot be answered objectively in terms of numbers alone. When the number of sellers is large enough so that the actions of any one seller have no perceptible effect upon other sellers, and their actions have no perceptible effect upon the one seller, the industry becomes one of monopolistic competition.

The theory of monopolistic competition provides few new analytical tools; it is very similar to that of pure competition. It furnishes a better description of those competitive industries in which product differentiation occurs—food processing, men's clothing, cotton textiles, and the service trades in large cities, for instance—in that it recognizes small monopoly elements and the consequent different prices charged by different sellers of a particular type of product.

Some special characteristics

The conditions of demand faced by the firm set monopolistic competition apart from the three market situations discussed previously. Product differentiation leads some consumers to prefer the products of one seller in an industry over those of others. Consequently, the demand curve faced by an individual seller has some downward slope to it and enables the seller to exercise a small degree of control over its product price. Ordinarily the demand curve faced by the firm will be very elastic within its relevant range of prices because of the numerous good substitutes available for the product.

Product differentiation by the sellers in an industry increases the complexity of presenting the analysis in graphic terms. For example, in the analysis of pure competition, market demand and supply curves create no graphic problems. Under monopolistic competition, the construction of market curves is rather unsatisfactory. Product differentiation makes the product units sold by one seller somewhat different from the product units sold by another. Tubes of toothpaste differ from cans of tooth powder. Bottles of liquid dentifrice are still different. Unless all of these can be converted into terms of a common denominator, difficulty in constructing the quantity axis for the industry curves will be encountered.

An additional difficulty arises. No single price prevails for the differentiated products of the industry. Different sellers receive somewhat different prices, depending on consumers' judgments with regard to the comparative qualities of the differentiated products. These problems make it appear preferable to confine diagrammatic analysis to the individual firm. The market as a whole is there, but it is best discussed in linguistic rather than in graphic terms.

The short run

Short-run output and pricing analysis in an industry of monopolistic competition is very similar to that of other market situations. It is primarily an analysis of the adjustment of the individual firm to the conditions each faces. A firm does not have time to change its plant size; therefore, there is insufficient time for new firms to enter the industry. Individual firms can make price and output adjustments. Additionally, they may be able to bring about small changes in demand for their individual outputs through advertising and slight variations of product quality and design.

Profit maximization with respect to output and price by the individual firm follows the rules set out in earlier chapters and is shown graphically in Figure 13–1. The firm's short-run average cost curve and short-run marginal cost curve are SAC and SMC, respectively. The demand curve faced by the firm is dd. Since dd is less than perfectly elastic, marginal revenue for each possible level of sales is less than the product price, and the marginal revenue curve lies below the demand curve. The firm maximizes profits (or minimizes losses if the SAC curve lies above dd for all possible outputs) by producing output x at which marginal cost equals marginal revenue. Profits per unit are cp. Total profits are $cp \times x$.

The firm may also attempt to maximize profits with respect to advertising outlays and outlays on product variation; however, since there are many good substitutes for the product of the individual firm, neither strategy will be carried very far. To the extent that the firm does make advertising and product variation outlays, the principles involved are the familiar ones. Each should be carried to the point at which its marginal revenue is equated to its marginal cost, if profit maximization is the firm's objective.

Figure 13–1 Short-run profit maximization

Short-run equilibrium does not imply that all firms charge identical prices. Identity of prices is not expected since the firms of the industry do not produce homogeneous outputs. Each firm seeks its own profit-maximizing position. Each equates its own marginal cost to its own marginal revenue. Yet the prices charged by different producers will not be far apart. In short-run equilibrium we would expect prices to be clustered but not necessarily equal. Although each producer has some discretion in setting its own price, each one is subjected to the restrictive effects of the competition from many close substitutes for the product that the particular firm produces.

The long run

All resources used by the firm are variable in the long run; consequently, two types of adjustment are possible: (1) the firm can build any desired size of plant; (2) unless entry into the industry is blocked, it will be possible for new firms to enter when profits are being made by existing firms. In the event losses are being incurred, existing firms can exit from the industry.

Adjustments with entry blocked

Blocked entry into an industry characterized by monopolistic competition clearly will not be the usual case; still it may, and sometimes does, occur. Where it occurs, it is usually the result of legislative activity of one kind or another. Owners or operators of the firms in a particular industry may belong to a trade association that has some political influence on a local, statewide, or perhaps even a nationwide basis. The industry may be fairly profitable, and the trade association may foresee the possibility of wholesale entry into the industry. Therefore, it may use its influence to secure the enactment of legislation that is rationalized as insuring an adequate supply of the commodity at prices allowing those in the trade to make fair and reasonable profits. In the service trades in a particular city or state one can easily find licensing laws that tend to block entry.[1]

In such situations individual firms seek to adjust their respective plant sizes to those required for long-run profit maximization. The long-run average cost curve and the long-run marginal cost curve are the relevant ones for the firm. These are shown as *LAC* and *LMC* in Figure 13–2. The

Figure 13–2   Long-run profit maximization: entry blocked

X per Unit of Time

demand curve faced by the firm is *dd*, and the marginal revenue curve is *MR*. Profits will be maximum at output *x*, at which long-run marginal cost equals marginal revenue. Output *x* can be sold for price *p* per unit. To produce output *x* at the least possible cost per unit, the firm should build the plant size that has its short-run average cost curve tangent to the long-run average cost curve at that output. Since *SAC* is tangent to *LAC* at output *x*, short-run marginal cost is equal to long-run marginal cost and to marginal revenue at that output. Profits are equal to $cp \times x$.

[1] *See* Milton Friedman, *Capitalism and Freedom* (Chicago: University of Chicago Press, 1962), Chap. IX.

If the firm should deviate from output x by increasing or decreasing its rate of output with the given size of plant, SMC would be greater than or less than MR, and profits would decline. If it should increase or decrease its rate of output by increasing or decreasing the size of plant, LMC would be greater than or less than MR, and profits would decline. Long-run equilibrium for the firm when entry into the industry is blocked means that the firm produces the output at which SMC equals LMC equals MR and at which SAC equals LAC.

Adjustments with entry open

Ordinarily we would expect entry into or exit from a monopolistically competitive industry to be easy. Existing firms without the benefit of a trade association are likely to feel unconcerned about a few firms more or less in the industry; or, in the event they are concerned about the entry of new firms, they feel powerless to do anything about it. The mere fact that a large number of firms exists in the industry suggests that the size of each firm is something less than gigantic and that effective collusion without government support would be extremely difficult. Thus, most of the bars to entry that exist in oligopolistic markets are not effective in markets of monopolistic competition.

When pure profits exist for firms in the industry and potential entrants believe that they, too, can make pure profits, entry will be attempted. As new firms enter, they encroach on the markets of existing firms, causing the demand curve and the marginal revenue curve faced by each to shift downward. The downward shift of each firm's demand curve results from the increase in industry supply of the product as new firms enter. The increase in supply (and in the number of suppliers) pushes the whole cluster of price ranges for individual firms downward.[2]

The entry of new firms into the industry will affect costs of production for existing firms. As in pure competition (and in oligopoly to the extent that entry is possible), an industry classification of increasing cost, constant cost, and decreasing cost can be used. If the industry were one of increasing costs, the entry of new firms would cause resource prices to rise, which would shift the cost curves of existing firms upward and would raise the level of costs of entering firms. Under constant costs the entry of new firms would have no effects on resource prices or on the cost curves of individual firms. In the unlikely case of decreasing costs the entry of new firms would cause resource prices to decrease and the cost curves to shift downward. We shall examine only the case of increasing costs.

The entry of new firms will shift the demand curves faced by individual

---

[2] This analysis parallels that of pure competition. Larger market supply under pure competition shifts demand curves faced by individual firms downward.

firms downward and cost curves of the firms upward. These shifts will cause profits to decrease, but new firms will continue to enter as long as profit possibilities remain. Eventually, enough firms will have entered to squeeze out pure profits.

This situation for the individual firm is pictured graphically in Figure 13–3. Compared with Figure 13–2, the demand curve faced by the firm has

Figure 13–3   Long-run profit maximization: entry open

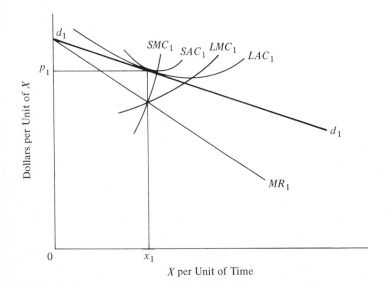

shifted downward as new firms enter, from dd in Figure 13–2 to $d_1 d_1$ in Figure 13–3. The long-run cost curves have shifted upward to LAC_1 and LMC_1. The short-run cost curves have also shifted upward, and adjustments in the size of plant have occurred. When enough firms have entered to cause the demand curve faced by each firm to be just tangent to its long-run average cost curve, firms of the industry will no longer be making profits, and entry will stop.

Long-run equilibrium will be achieved by individual firms and by the industry as a whole when each firm in the industry is in the position shown in Figure 13–3. For each individual firm long-run marginal cost and short-run marginal cost equals marginal revenue at some output such as x_1. Any deviation from that output with size of plant SAC_1 will cause losses to be incurred. Any change in the size of plant will cause losses to be incurred. Short-run average cost equals long-run average cost at that output, and both are equal to the price per unit received by the firm for its product. The industry as a whole will be in equilibrium since no profits or losses occur to provide the incentive for entry into or exit from the industry.

Welfare effects of monopolistic competition

Output restriction

If one of the industries of a purely competitive economy in long-run equilibrium were to become monopolistically competitive, welfare would tend to be reduced by a slight restriction of output and a slight increase in the prices charged for the product. The demand curve faced by the monopolistic competitor, though very elastic, is less than perfectly elastic. Marginal revenue for the individual firm is less than price, and the rate of output is stopped short of that at which marginal cost equals the product price. The more elastic the demand curve faced by the firm, the less will be the deviation from purely competitive price and output.

In the long run the price will equal the average costs of production unless entry into the industry is blocked. When entry is free and easy—as appears to be the usual case—new firms enter the profit-making industries and reduce profits to zero. Consumers pay just enough to enable firms to hold the desired quantities of resources in the production of the product. Organization of the economy's productive capacity can follow consumers' tastes and preferences with a high degree of accuracy.

When entry into profit-making industries is blocked, the consequences with respect to prices and average costs are much the same as they are under pure monopoly and oligopoly. Productive capacity of the economy cannot be organized to conform accurately to consumers' tastes and preferences. Additional quantities of resources are prohibited from moving into the profit-making industries where they would be more productive than they are in alternative employments.

Efficiency of individual firms

There will be some inefficiency of individual firms in the long run when entry into the industry is easy; that is, the firm will not be induced to build the most efficient size of plant nor to operate the one it does build at the most efficient rate of output. This point can be seen best by reference to Figure 13–3. A most efficient size of plant would involve the firm in losses since average cost at such an output would be greater than price. If the long-run average cost curve lies below the demand curve for any range of outputs, pure profits can be made by any firm that builds the correct size of plant for any one of those outputs. New firms will enter until profits are eliminated. Profit possibilities are eliminated when individual firm long-run average cost curves are tangent to the demand curves faced by them. Losses are incurred when the long-run average cost curve lies above the demand curve for all outputs. Exit of firms from the industry will continue until the long-run average cost curve for each firm is again tangent to the demand curve faced by it.

In long-run equilibrium the output at which losses are avoided by the firm ($SMC = LMC = MR$) is the output at which the average cost curves are tangent to the demand curve. Since the demand curve faced by the firm is downward-sloping, the average cost curves must be downward-sloping, also, at their point of tangency with the demand curve. Thus, with easy entry into the industry, individual firms will build a less than most efficient size of plant, such as SAC_1 in Figure 13–3, and they will operate at less than the most efficient rate of output.

Some overcrowding with regard to the number of firms in the industry and some excess plant capacity may occur when entry is easy. Since each firm builds a less than most efficient size of plant, there is room for more firms to exist than there would be if all were building plants of most efficient size. Also, since each firm tends to operate the plant that it does build at less than the most efficient rate of output, it follows that excess plant capacity may exist. Empirical examples of both situations are not hard to find. The various textile industries illustrate both an excess of firms in an industry and excess capacity for individual firms.

The inefficiencies of the firm pointed out above should not be overemphasized, nor is the foregoing paragraph an argument for restriction of entry into monopolistically competitive industries. The demand curve faced by the firm is highly elastic; and the more elastic it is, the nearer the firm will come to building an optimum size of plant to operate near the optimum rate of output. Free entry into the industry will cause the total industry output to be greater than it would be if entry were restricted, and it will cause prices to be correspondingly lower.

When entry is restricted, the firm will build the appropriate size of plant to produce the output at which long-run marginal cost equals marginal revenue. There is no inducement for the firm to build an optimum size of plant. The plant built will be optimum only in the event that the firm's marginal revenue curve passes through the minimum point on its long-run average cost curve. Such an occurrence would be purely accidental.

Sales promotion wastes

Some waste advertising or design changes may occur under monopolistic competition. Efforts on the part of individual firms to expand their markets in this way may be counteracted by similar efforts on the part of the others, and the resources so used merely add to costs of production. Any such waste of resources will be much smaller under monopolistic competition than under oligopoly, where efforts on the part of one firm to expand its share of the market induces others to put forth similar efforts to prevent such expansion. Such rivalries do not exist under monopolistic competition. Advertising done by one firm induces no retaliatory action by others. When the advertising done by one is counteracted by that of others, this is simply the result of all firms trying to do the same thing—expand their own markets. None are reacting to encroachments of other firms on their particular markets.

Range of products available

Consumers will have a broad range of types, styles, and brands of particular products from which to choose in market situations of monopolistic competition. The consumer can choose the type, style, or color of package that most nearly suits his or her fancy and pocketbook.

The different kinds of a specific product may be so numerous that they prove confusing to the consumer, and problems of choice may become very complicated. Ignorance with regard to actual differences of quality results in a willingness by the consumer to pay higher prices for particular brands, which in reality are not superior to lower-priced brands of the same product. What shopper can possibly be familiar with the comparative qualities of all the many different brands of soaps and detergents, floor waxes, electric irons, and so on?

Summary

In a market situation of monopolistic competition there are enough sellers of differentiated products so that the activities of each have no effect on others and their activities in turn have no effect on one. The demand curve faced by a firm in the market has some downward slope because of product differentiation and the attachment of consumers to particular brand names. However, it is highly elastic within the relevant price-output range.

Short-run profit maximization by the firms in the industry will occur at the prices and outputs at which each is equating its marginal cost to its marginal revenue. There is no single industry price. There will be a cluster of market prices reflecting consumer opinions of comparative qualities of the product.

In the long run the nature of the adjustment of firms and the industry to a position of equilibrium will depend on whether entry into the industry is blocked or easy. With entry blocked individual firms will produce the output and sell at the price at which long-run marginal cost equals marginal revenue. The firm will build the appropriate size of plant for that output, and, with the appropriate size of plant, short-run marginal cost will also equal marginal revenue.

With entry easy the existence of profits will induce new firms to enter, decreasing the demand curve faced by the firm and shifting the cost curves upward, if the industry is one of increasing costs. Entry will continue until profits are squeezed out. The long-run average cost curve and the short-run average cost curve for each firm will be tangent to the demand curve faced by it at the appropriate output. Long-run marginal costs and short-run marginal costs will equal marginal revenue.

Monopolistic competition existing along with pure competition tends to reduce welfare through (1) output restriction and price increases, (2) inefficient plant size, and (3) some advertising wastes. There will also be a broader range of products among which consumers may choose than will occur in the other three market situations, a condition that may or may not affect welfare.

Suggested readings

Chamberlin, Edward H., *The Theory of Monopolistic Competition,* 8th ed. Cambridge: Harvard University Press, 1962. Chaps. IV–V.

Machlup, Fritz, *The Economics of Sellers' Competition.* Baltimore: The Johns Hopkins Press, 1952. Chaps. 5–7, 10.

Stigler, George J., "Monopolistic Competition in Retrospect," *Five Lectures on Economic Problems.* New York: The Macmillan Company, 1947. Pp. 12–24. Reprinted in George J. Stigler, *The Organization of Industry.* Homewood, Ill.: Richard D. Irwin, Inc., 1968.

Questions and exercises

1. University City boasts 35 barber shops. In each shop there are three barbers of equal ability, and the barbers in any one shop are as technically competent as those in any other. Would you expect the demand curve for the services of each barber to be horizontal, or would you expect it to slope downward to the right? Catalogue completely the reasons for your answer.

2. Check the licensing laws of your state, and compile a list of all the occupations, trades, and businesses for which licenses are required. What reasons are cited in the statutes for requiring licenses? Do you agree that these are the actual reasons for licensing? Why or why not?

3. Casual observations in most cities and towns often show new automobile service stations being built. At such occurrences we hear people say time and again, "We don't really need all those stations." In

terms of the theory of monopolistic competition, can you put analytical content into observations and comments of this type?

4. Assume that firms of industry X sell under conditions of monopolistic competition and that the industry is in long-run equilibrium. Assume that firms in industry Y sell under conditions of pure competition and that the industry is also in long-run equilibrium. Each is an industry of increasing costs. An increase in demand now occurs in each. Using diagrams, compare and contrast between the two industries

   a. the short-run effects on prices and outputs of the demand increases
   b. the long-run effects on prices and outputs of the demand increases.

Part 5

The determination of and the functions of resource prices

For the analysis of the markets for goods and services we assumed that resource prices were given without much concern for how those prices were determined or for the functions they perform in a market economy. The purpose of Part 5 is to fill the void by examining resource markets in detail. It may be useful to review Chapter 8, "The Principles of Production," since Part 5 builds on the foundation established in that chapter.

Resource prices play a key role in guiding and directing a private enterprise economy. They are an essential element in determining the levels of employment of different kinds of labor and capital. They serve to allocate resources among different uses. They provide the inducements or incentives for individual firms to use efficient resource combinations. And, as the farmers' demonstrations of 1978 and the coal miner's strike of the winter of 1977 to 1978 illustrate, they are important to us personally. Since all of us are resource owners, the prices we get for the resources that we own affect our income and how we share in the economy's output.

Chapter 14

Chapter contents

		Key concepts

Simultaneous employment of several variable resources
Profit maximization and least cost combination
Marginal physical products and marginal cost

Pricing and employment of a given variable resource
The demand curve of the firm: one resource variable
Marginal revenue product
Value of marginal product
Level of employment
The demand curve

The demand curve of the firm: several resources variable
The market demand curve
The market supply curve
Resource pricing and the level of employment
Alternative costs reconsidered

Economic rent

Summary
Suggested readings
Questions and exercises

Key concepts
Pure competition
Least cost combination
Marginal physical product
Marginal cost
Marginal revenue
Marginal revenue product
Value of marginal product
Internal effects of a resource price change
External effects of a resource price change
Demand curve for a resource
Supply curve for a resource
Alternative costs
Economic rent

Pricing and employment of resources: pure competition

How are resource prices and employment levels determined when pure competition in both product markets and resource markets prevails?[1] Pure competition in resource markets implies several things. No one firm takes enough of any given resource to be able to influence its price. No one resource supplier can place enough of a given resource on the market to be able to influence its price. Variable resources are mobile among different employments, and their market prices are flexible. On the basis of these conditions we shall analyze the simultaneous employment of several variable resources by the firm; next, we shall consider the pricing and employment of any given variable resource.

Simultaneous employment of several variable resources

Up to this point profit maximization by the firm has been considered in terms of product outputs and sales, with little specific attention given to resource inputs. In this section profit maximization will be viewed in terms of resource inputs and least cost resource combinations.

Profit maximization and least cost combination

The least cost combination of variable resources for a given output was discussed in Chapter 8.[2] Resources must be so combined that the marginal physical product per dollar's worth of one is equal to the marginal physical product per dollar's worth of each of the other resources used if such a combination is to be achieved. The given output is not necessarily the profit-maximizing output of the firm. Suppose, in Figure 14–1, that the firm produces an output of x_0 and uses two variable resources, A and B. To

---

[1] A simple definition of the market for a resource will suffice for most purposes. The market for a resource is the area within which the resource is free to move (or is mobile) among alternative employments. The extent of the market for a given resource will vary, depending on the time span under consideration. The longer the period of time, the broader the market will be.

[2] See pp. 158–190.

Figure 14–1   Least cost combinations and profit maximization

produce output x_0, resources A and B must be combined so that MPP_a/p_a equals MPP_b/p_b, if average variable costs are to be kept down to v_0. If the product price is p_x, the firm's output is too small for profit maximization. Although A and B are used in proper proportions, not enough of either is being used.

To maximize profits the firm's output must be increased to x. Additional output can be obtained by using more of both resource A and resource B. To keep average variable costs as low as possible as output is increased, increases in the quantities of resources A and B must be in proportions such that the marginal physical product per dollar's worth of A continues to equal the marginal physical product per dollar's worth of B. When output x is reached, the firm will be using the resources not only in the least cost combination but also in correct absolute quantities.

Marginal physical products and marginal cost

The least cost combination conditions for resources A and B—MPP_a/p_a equals MPP_b/p_b—are the reciprocal of the marginal cost of product X. Consider resource A first. Any one unit of resource A contributes an amount to the firm's total cost equal to p_a. It adds an amount to the firm's total product equal to MPP_a. Thus, the fraction p_a/MPP_a should be read as "the change in the firm's total costs per unit change in the product." This is the same thing as the marginal cost of product X; hence, we can state that MC_x equals p_a/MPP_a. Likewise, MC_x equals p_b/MPP_b. Since MPP_a/p_a equals MPP_b/p_b, when the firm is using a least cost combination of A and B, we can state that

$$\frac{MPP_a}{p_a} = \frac{MPP_b}{p_b} = \frac{1}{MC_x}. \tag{14.1}$$

Or we can consider the reciprocals of the foregoing terms and state that

$$\frac{p_a}{MPP_a} = \frac{p_b}{MPP_b} = MC_x. \tag{14.2}$$

The last statement means that at whatever output the firm is producing, if it uses the least cost combination of resources, the amount of A or the amount of B or the combined amounts of both necessary to add a single unit to the firm's output brings about the same addition to the firm's total costs. Suppose that the product is men's suits and the variable resources used are labor, machines, and materials. The last one-unit increment in quantity produced per unit of time should increase total costs of the firm by the same amount, regardless of whether the increment in product is obtained by increasing the ratio of labor to materials and machines, materials to labor and machines, or machines to labor and materials. Total costs should be increased by the same amount if the increment in product is obtained by simultaneous increases in the quantities of all three resources. When resources are used in the correct combination, they are equally efficient at the margin. The last dollar outlay on one resource adds the same amount to total product as the last dollar outlay on any other resource. The increment in cost necessary to bring about the last unit increase in product output per unit of time is the marginal cost of the product.

Suppose that we again consider profit maximization by the firm in terms of the quantities of resources that should be used. With reference to Figure 14–1 at output x_0, MC_x is less than MR_x or

$$\frac{MPP_a}{p_a} = \frac{MPP_b}{p_b} = \frac{1}{MC_x} > \frac{1}{MR_x} = \frac{1}{p_x}. \tag{14.3}$$

The firm is using the resources in correct proportions to produce output x_0; however, output x_0 is too small for profit maximization since MC_x is less than MR_x. In the pursuit of maximum profits the firm will increase output by increasing the inputs of A and B. Additional quantities of A and B used with the constant quantities of fixed resources cause the marginal physical product of each to decrease. The prices of A and B remain constant since the firm purchases them under conditions of pure competition; consequently, MPP_a/p_a and MPP_b/p_b decrease as does $1/MC_x$.

Decreases in $1/MC_x$ mean increases in MC_x. Thus, decreases in the marginal physical products of A and B are the same as increases in the marginal cost of product X. Larger quantities of A and B will be employed to expand the firm's output up to the point at which

$$\frac{MPP_a}{p_a} = \frac{MPP_b}{p_b} = \frac{1}{MC_x} = \frac{1}{MR_x} = \frac{1}{p_x}, \tag{14.4}$$

or up to the point at which the firm's marginal cost equals its marginal revenue or product price. At the profit-maximizing output the firm will be using its variable resources both in the correct combination and in the correct absolute amounts.

Pricing and employment of a given variable resource

Demand and supply analysis is used to show how the market price and employment level of a given resource are determined. First, the individual firm demand curve, the market demand curve, and the market supply curve for the resource must be constructed. Once we have accomplished these objectives, we can then determine the market price, the firm's employment level, and the market level of employment of the resource.

The demand curve of the firm: one resource variable

The demand curve of a firm for a given variable resource should show the different quantities of it that the firm will take at various possible prices. But the factors influencing the quantities that a firm will take when confronted by various alternative prices of the resource differ when the given resource is the only variable resource used by the firm from the factors that prevail when the given resource is one of several variable resources used by the firm. Assume for the present that the given resource is the only variable one used; that is, the quantities of all other resources employed remain constant.[3] Assume also that the firm's objective is to maximize its profits.

The firm considers different quantities of the resource—for example, resource A—with regard to their effects on its total receipts and total costs. If larger quantities of A per unit of time will add more to the firm's total receipts than to its total costs, those quantities will increase profits (or decrease losses). On the other hand, if larger quantities of A will add more to the firm's total costs than to its total receipts, they will cause profits to decrease (or losses to increase). The firm should employ that quantity of the resource at which a one-unit increase in its employment level increases both total receipts and total costs by the same amount.

Marginal revenue product   The change in a firm's total receipts when it changes the employment level of some resource A by one unit is called the *marginal revenue product* of the resource to the firm, or MRP_a. To compute it, note first that the change in the output of the firm caused by a one-unit change in the employment level of A is the marginal physical product of resource A, or MPP_a. This change in output changes the firm's

---

[3] The assumption is the same as that made in defining the law of diminishing returns.

total receipts by an amount per unit equal to the marginal revenue the firm receives from its sale. Thus, a one-unit change in the employment level of A changes the firm's total receipts by the marginal physical product of A multiplied by the marginal revenue received from the sale of the product. If X is the product and A is the resource under consideration, then

$$MRP_a = MPP_a \times MR_x.$$

Value of marginal product   When the employment level of some resource A is changed by a firm producing some product X, it is often important to consider the *market's* valuation of the change as well as the impact of the change on the firm's total receipts. Again, a one-unit change in the employment level of A changes the output level of X by MPP_a. The change in the output of X is valued by the market or by buyers of the product at p_x per unit. The market's valuation of the employment level change, or the *value of the marginal product of A*, is the marginal physical product of A multiplied by the product price. Symbolically,

$$VMP_a = MPP_a \times p_x.$$

For the purely competitive seller of product X the marginal revenue product of a resource is equal to its value of marginal product. Such must be the case since $MR_x = p_x$. Consequently, VMP_a and MRP_a can be used interchangeably for the purely competitive seller; however, we shall note in the next chapter that the distinction between the two concepts becomes very important in analyzing resource pricing and employment by monopolistic sellers of product X.

In Table 14–1, which represents Stage II for resource A, column (2) lists the marginal physical product of A when various quantities of it are used with constant quantities of other resources. The price per unit and the marginal revenue of the final product of the firm is shown in column (3). The

Table 14–1   Value of marginal product, resource price, and profit maximization

(1) Quantity of A	(2) Marginal Physical Product (MPP_a)	(3) Product Price and Marginal Revenue ($p_x = MR_x$)	(4) Marginal Revenue Product and Value of Marginal Product ($VMP_a = MRP_a$)	(5) Resource Price (p_a)
4	7	$2	$14	$4
5	6	2	12	4
6	5	2	10	4
7	4	2	8	4
8	3	2	6	4
9	2	2	4	4
10	0	2	0	4

marginal revenue product and the value of marginal product of resource A are shown in column (4).

In Stage II for resource A the marginal revenue product decreases as larger amounts of A per unit of time are employed. This decrease is caused by the operation of the law of diminishing returns—in Stage II for resource A the marginal physical product of A declines as larger quantities of it are employed. Thus, A's marginal revenue product declines even though the price at which the final product is sold and its marginal revenue remain constant.

Level of employment   A one-unit increase in the employment level of a resource adds an amount equal to its price to the firm's total costs when resources are purchased under conditions of pure competition. One firm takes such a small proportion of the total supply of the resource that by itself it cannot affect the resource price. If the price of the resource (p_a) is $4 per unit, each one-unit increase in the amount of A employed adds $4 to the firm's total cost. These amounts are shown in column (5) of Table 14–1.

The profit-maximizing level of employment of A by the firm is that level at which the marginal revenue product of A is equal to the price per unit of the resource. Refer to Table 14–1. A fourth unit of A per unit of time adds $14 to the firm's total receipts but adds only $4 to the firm's total costs; therefore, it adds $10 to the firm's profits. A fifth, sixth, seventh, and eighth unit of A each add more to total receipts than to total costs and, consequently, make a net addition to profits. A ninth unit of A adds the same amount to both total receipts and total costs. A tenth unit of A, if employed, will decrease profits by $4. Hence, when p_a is $4, profits are maximized with respect to resource A at an employment level of 9 units. We can write the profit-maximizing condition in either of the following forms:

$$MRP_a = p_a$$

or

$$MPP_a \times MR_x = p_a. \tag{14.5}$$

The second form is simply an elaboration of the first.

The demand curve   The marginal revenue product schedule for resource A, as listed in columns (1) and (4) of Table 14–1, is the firm's demand schedule for A if A is the only variable resource employed. It shows the different quantities that the firm will take at different possible prices. If p_a were $10 per unit, 6 units would be employed. If p_a were $14 per unit, 4 units would be employed.

The demand curve of the firm for the resource is the marginal revenue product schedule plotted. Figure 14–2 shows such a curve. With reference

Figure 14–2   Marginal revenue product curve

to the quantity axis, it occupies Stage II for resource A. With reference to the dollars per unit axis, the marginal revenue product at each quantity of A is found by multiplying the marginal physical product at that level of employment by the marginal revenue at the corresponding level of product sales.

It may be instructive to consider profit maximization by the firm with respect to resource A again—this time in terms of the demand curve or the marginal revenue product curve. If the price of A in Figure 14–2 were p_{a2}, the firm would maximize profits by using quantity a_2. If the firm were to use quantity a_0, the a_0 unit would add a_0A_0 to the firm's total costs but would add a_0B_0 to the firm's total receipts. It would add A_0B_0 to the firm's profits. Increasing the employment level of A up to a_2 adds more to total receipts than to total costs, and, therefore, increases profits. Beyond a_2 larger quantities add more to the firm's total costs than to its total receipts and cause profits to decrease. If the price of A were p_{a1}, the firm would maximize profits by using that quantity at which the marginal revenue product of A equals its price per unit.

The demand curve of the firm: several resources variable

When a firm uses several variable resources, its demand curve for any one of them is no longer the marginal revenue product curve of the resource. When several variable resources are used by the firm, a change in the price of one, assuming the prices of the others remain constant, will bring about changes in the quantities used of the other resources; these changes will, in turn, affect the utilization of the one as the firm attempts to maximize profits and to reestablish a least cost combination of resources. Suppose we call such changes the *firm* or *internal effects* of a change in the price of a resource.

To illustrate the internal effects, suppose that we want to derive the firm's demand curve for resource A, which is one of several variable resources. Suppose that initially the firm is producing the profit-maximizing output of product X and is using the appropriate least cost combination of variable resources. As shown in Figure 14–3, the price of A is p_{a1} and the quantity

Figure 14–3   The firm's demand curve for one of several variable resources

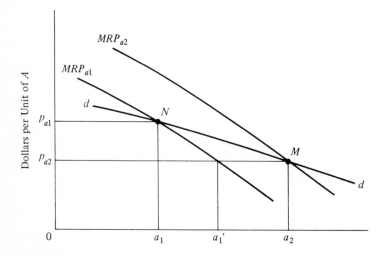

employed is a_1. The MRP_{a1} curve shows the marginal revenue product of A when the quantity of A only is varied.

Suppose that for some reason the price of A falls to p_{a2}. Since $MRP_a > p_a$, the firm will tend to expand employment of A toward $a_1{}'$. This increased utilization of A will shift the marginal physical product and the marginal revenue product curves of variable resources complementary to A to the right. The corresponding curves of substitute resources will be shifted to the left. Since the prices of other resources remain constant, the utilization of complementary resources will increase while that of substitute resources will decrease. Such changes in the utilization of other resources will shift the marginal physical product and the marginal revenue product curves of A to the right. Each different level of utilization of each other variable resource will result in a different marginal physical product curve and marginal revenue product curve for A.

When these and higher-order complementary and substitute effects have worked themselves out, the firm will be on some such marginal revenue product curve as MRP_{a2} and will be employing that quantity of A at which its marginal revenue product equals its price—that is, quantity a_2.[4] The employment levels of other variable resources will also be such that for each one its value of marginal product equals its price when the firm is again maximizing profits and using the appropriate least cost combination.

Points N and M are on the firm's demand curve for resource A. They show the quantities of A that the firm would take at alternative prices of A when the prices of other resources are held constant and the quantities of all other resources are adjusted appropriately for each price of A. Other points on the firm's demand curve for A can be established in a similar fashion and would trace out a curve such as dd. Ordinarily the firm's demand curve for a resource will be more elastic than will any single marginal revenue product curve of the resource. The better the substitutes available for a resource, the more elastic its demand curve will be.

The market demand curve

A first approximation to the market demand curve for a resource is the horizontal summation of individual firm demand curves for it. However, a straightforward horizontal summation leaves out what we shall call the *market* or *external effects* of changes in the price of a resource.

In a purely competitive world an individual firm is small enough relative to the markets in which it operates to anticipate that its actions will have no effect on the price of anything it buys or sells. Consequently, the firm's demand curve for a resource should show the different quantities that the firm would take at various alternative resource prices when the firm anticipates that its actions will have no effect on the price of whatever product the firm sells. The firm considers only the firm or internal effects of resource price changes.

The market or external effects come about as a result of simultaneous expansion or contraction of industry outputs of products by all firms using a given resource as the price of the resource changes. If industry X is one of the industries using resource A, a decrease in the price of resource A will cause all firms using A to increase their employment of it. Although no one firm's increase in output is sufficient to cause a decrease in the price of X, the simultaneous increases in output of all firms may cause such a price decrease to come about. Each such decrease in the price of X and the marginal revenue from X will cause shifts to the left or decreases in the whole family of individual firm marginal revenue product curves and con-

---

[4] The increasing ratios of resource A to fixed resources of the firm will insure that the marginal physical product and the marginal revenue product of A decline, even though the changing utilization of other variable resources tends to shift the curves for A to the right.

sequent shifts to the left or decreases in individual firm demand curves for resource A.

The external effects of changes in the price of a resource and the construction of the market demand curve for the resource are illustrated in Figure 14–4. Suppose that the firm of the diagram, and every other firm that

Figure 14–4   The market demand curve for a resource

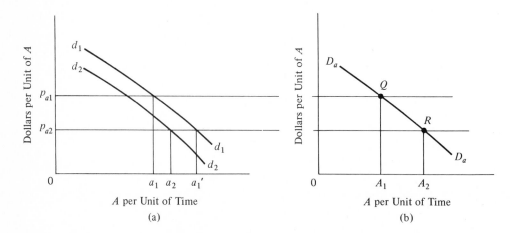

uses resource A, is in equilibrium and that the price of A is p_{a1}. The firm's demand curve for A is $d_1 d_1$; the firm is employing a_1 of A. By summing the amounts that all firms employ at price p_{a1}, we determine the total amount taken off the market at that price, A_1. Thus, Q is a point on the market demand curve for A.

Suppose next that the price of A falls to p_{a2}. Each firm will expand its employment of A; but as the firms in each industry that uses A expand employment of it and, consequently, the industry outputs of product, market prices of products decrease. Individual firm demand curves for resource A shift to the left toward positions such as $d_2 d_2$. Thus, the individual firm employment levels of A will increase toward such quantities as a_2 rather than toward a_1'.

Restricted expansion in the employment of A results from the market or external effect of the decrease in the resource price. When each individual firm has made the necessary adjustments to achieve a least cost combination of resources and a profit-maximizing product output, and when each firm's level of employment is some such level as a_2, the amounts that all firms together employ at price p_{a2} can be totaled to obtain quantity A_2. Then R is a second point on the market demand curve for A. Other points on the market demand curve can be found in a similar way; they trace out the market demand curve D_aD_a.

The market supply curve

The market supply curve for resource A, or for any other resource, shows the different quantities per unit of time that its owners will place on the market at different possible prices. Generally it will be upward-sloping to the right, indicating that at higher prices more of it will be placed on the market than at lower prices. If resource A is a certain kind of labor, there are several forces that may cause the quantity supplied to be greater at higher than at lower wage rates. First, as we noted in Chapter 5, individual workers will be induced to provide more hours of work if substitution effects are not outweighed by income effects.[5] Second, higher wage rates tend to induce more workers to enter the occupation. Third, higher wage rates in a given occupation tend to induce workers qualified for that occupation who have been working in other jobs to reenter it.

Nonhuman resources used in any one industry are in general the outputs of other industries. Their supply curves, then, will be the appropriate industry or market supply curves. Except in cases of constant cost and decreasing cost they will slope upward to the right. In the petroleum industry, for example, increases in crude oil prices lead to a more rapid rate of recovery and vice-versa. The precise shapes of resource supply curves are not of paramount importance for our purposes, although for certain types of economic problems they will be. They may be upward-sloping to the right, they may be absolutely vertical, or they may bend back on themselves at high prices. The basic analysis will be the same in each case.

Resource pricing and the level of employment

The conditions of market demand and market supply, as summed up in the market demand curve and the market supply curve, determine the market price of the resource. Its equilibrium price will be that at which resource buyers are willing to take the same quantity per unit of time that sellers want to sell.

In Figure 14–5(b) the market demand curve and the market supply curve are D_aD_a and S_aS_a, respectively. Resource A will be priced at p_a. At a higher price sellers will want to sell more than buyers will want to employ at that price. Some unemployment will occur, and the owners of unemployed units will undercut each other to secure full employment of their particular supplies. Thus, the price will be driven down to the equilibrium

[5] *See* pp. 107–109.

Figure 14–5   Determination of market price, market level of employment, and firm level of employment of a resource

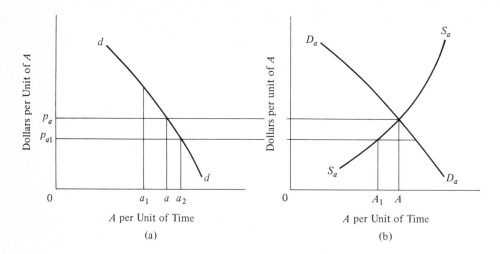

(a)   (b)

level of p_a. At prices lower than p_a there will be a shortage of the resource. Resource buyers will bid against each other for the available supply, driving the price up to the equilibrium level.

An individual firm, purchasing resource A competitively, can get as much as it wants at a price of p_a per unit. A single construction firm in Chicago will not be able to influence the market price of steel. The supply curve of the resource from a single firm's point of view is shown in Figure 14–5(a) as a horizontal line at the equilibrium market price. The dollars per unit axes on the firm and market diagrams are identical. The scale of the quantity axis of the market diagram is greatly compressed, as compared with that of the single firm. The level of employment of the resource by the single firm is quantity a, assuming that dd is the demand curve of the firm associated with price p_a; and at that quantity marginal revenue product is equal to its price per unit. The market level of employment of the resource is the summation of the quantities employed by the individual firms and is shown as quantity A in the market diagram.

The belief that resources are often paid lower than equilibrium prices is widespread enough to warrant its consideration in some detail. Suppose in Figure 14–5 that resource A is priced at p_{a1}. At that price individual firms want quantities, such as a_2, in order to maximize their profits with respect to the resource. All firms cannot get as much as they desire, since the entire quantity placed on the market at that price is only A_1. Some firms will necessarily get quantities even less than a, say a_1. For such firms the marginal revenue product of A is greater than the resource price. If these firms expand their employments of the resource, they will increase their profits. Each firm believes that by offering a price slightly higher than p_{a_1} it will be able to get as much of the resource as it desires. In the absence of collusion among the firms employing the resource—and in pure competition there is no collusion—each attempts the same strategy. No firm succeeds in getting as much as it wants until the price has been driven up to p_a. Under pure competition in resource buying, independent action on the part of each firm together with the incentive to maximize profits preclude the permanent location of a resource price below its equilibrium level.

It is worth noting that under pure competition, a particular resource receives a price per unit equal to both its marginal revenue product and its value of marginal product. Thus, a unit of resource A is paid just what it contributes to the value of the economy's product. The market demand curve for A shows the value of marginal product for A in all its uses combined. The market demand curve and the market supply curve determine the price; hence, the resource price is equal to its value of marginal product in any one or in all of the firms that use the resource. Any one firm takes the market price as given and adjusts the quantity of the resource employed in such a way that the marginal revenue product and the value of its marginal product in that firm is equal to the market price of the resource.[6]

The conditions set out in the first part of the chapter for employing the correct amounts and correct proportions of several resources simultaneously to maximize the firm's profits can also be established considering resources one by one. Suppose the firm uses two resources, A and B. To maximize profits with respect to A, it should employ A up to the point at which

$$MPP_a \times MR_x = p_a, \text{ or } \frac{MPP_a}{p_a} = \frac{1}{MR_x} = \frac{1}{p_x}. \quad (14.6)$$

Likewise, B should be employed up to the point at which

$$MPP_b \times MR_x = p_b, \text{ or } \frac{MPP_b}{p_b} = \frac{1}{MR_x} = \frac{1}{p_x}. \quad (14.7)$$

Equations (14.6) and (14.7) can then be combined as follows:

$$\frac{MPP_a}{p_a} = \frac{MPP_b}{p_b} = \frac{1}{MR_x} = \frac{1}{p_x}. \quad (14.8)$$

---

[6] This point is frequently misconstrued. A firm is said to pay a resource a price equal to its marginal revenue product—implying that the firm determines the marginal revenue product of the resource, then pays it accordingly. This implication misrepresents the nature of marginal productivity theory under pure competition. The firm has nothing to say about the price. It must pay the market price, but it adjusts the quantity taken to the point at which the marginal revenue product equals that price.

Since MPP_a/p_a and MPP_b/p_b are the same as $1/MC_x$, then

$$\frac{MPP_a}{p_a} = \frac{MPP_b}{p_b} = \frac{1}{MC_x} = \frac{1}{MR_x} = \frac{1}{p_x}. \tag{14.9}$$

When the firm employs each of its variable resources in the correct absolute amount for profit maximization, it necessarily will be using them in the correct combination.

Alternative costs reconsidered

The alternative cost doctrine, which we discussed in Chapter 9, can be stated in terms of the value of marginal product of any given resource. Under pure competition, each firm using a given resource employs that quantity of it at which its marginal revenue product and its value of marginal product equals its price. Any discrepancy in resource prices offered by different firms induces units of the resource to move from the lower-paying to the higher-paying uses until a single price prevails throughout the market. The resource price, or its cost to any firm, will be equal to the value of its marginal product in its alternative employments.

Economic rent

Perfect mobility of all resources does not occur in the short run even under conditions of pure competition. Those resources constituting the firm's size of plant are not mobile—they are fixed in quantity for particular uses or users. The longer the time period under consideration, the fewer will be the fixed resources.

   The returns received by fixed resources are not determined according to the principles set out above. Since those resources are not free to move into alternative employments, their short-run remuneration will be whatever is left over after the mobile resources have been paid whatever it takes to hold them to the particular firm. The mobile resources must be paid amounts equal to what they can earn in alternative employments—that is, amounts equal to the values of their marginal product in alternative employments. The residual left for the fixed resources is called *economic rent*.[7]

   A short-run cost-price diagram for an individual firm should help make clear the concept of economic rent. The short-run average cost curve, average variable cost curve, and marginal cost curve are drawn in Figure 14–6. Suppose that the market price of the product is p. The firm's output

---

[7] These returns are sometimes called *quasi rents*. This term, introduced by Alfred Marshall, is used so ambiguously in economic literature that we shall avoid it altogether.

Figure 14–6   Economic rent

will be x. Total cost of the variable (mobile) resources is $0vAx$. This is the outlay necessary if the firm is to hold its variable resources.

Should the firm attempt to reduce the payments made to variable resources, some or all of them would move into alternative uses where their marginal revenue products and remunerations are greater. Thus, the average variable cost curve shows the necessary outlays per unit of product output that the firm must make for variable resources. The fixed resources get whatever is left from the firm's total receipts; that is, they receive economic rent. Total rent for the fixed resources is $vpBA$. The lower the market price of the product, the less the rent will be. The higher the market price of the product, the higher the economic rent will be.

A problem now arises with regard to the nature of the SAC curve. What does it show? To get at the problem, suppose that we consider the firm's investment in the fixed resources. The rent represents the return on investment in the firm's fixed resources. Only that part of the rent, which represents a return on investment equal to what that amount of investment could earn elsewhere in the economy (or in alternative uses), constitutes fixed costs for the firm. Thus, letting the part of rent represented by $vcDA$ be the fixed costs for the firm, the rest of the rent is what we have defined previously as pure profits. Average cost at any output is equal to average fixed cost plus average variable cost at that output.

Economic rent may be equal to, greater than, or less than enough to cover the firm's fixed costs. When investment in the firm yields a higher rate of return than investment on the average elsewhere in the economy, rents are greater than total fixed costs; we then say that the firm is making pure profits. The firm's profits are zero when rents equal total fixed cost, that is, when investment in the firm yields the same rate of return as investment elsewhere. When product price is not sufficient for rents to equal total fixed costs or when investment elsewhere in the economy yields a higher rate of return than it does with the firm, we say that the firm is incurring losses.

Summary

This chapter applies the principles of production to the pricing and employment of resources under conditions of pure competition both in product selling and resource buying. First, the principles underlying the employment of several variable resources by a firm were established. Second, the principles underlying pricing and employment of any given variable resource were determined.

When several variable resources are used by the firm, two problems are solved simultaneously by the firm in the process of maximizing its profits. It must use resources in the correct (least cost) combination; and it must use the absolute amounts necessary to produce the quantity of the product that maximizes profits. Use of resources in the correct absolute amounts means that they are used in the correct combination also. The firm should employ those amounts of resources and produce that amount of product at which

$$\frac{MPP_a}{p_a} = \frac{MPP_b}{p_b} = \cdots = \frac{MPP_n}{p_n} = \frac{1}{MC_x} = \frac{1}{MR_x} = \frac{1}{p_x}.$$

The individual firm demand curve, the market demand curve, and the market supply curve for a resource are necessary for determining the market price, the individual firm level of employment, and the market level of employment of the resource. When the firm employs one variable resource only, the marginal revenue product curve for the resource is the firm's demand curve for it. If the firm employs several variable resources, the firm's demand curve for a given resource shows the different quantities that the firm would take at various alternative prices when prices of other resources are held constant. At each price of the given resource the firm makes all the adjustment necessary in the quantities of all resources used in order to maximize its profits. The market demand curve is obtained by summing the quantities that all firms in all industries using the resource will take at each possible resource price. The market supply curve shows the quantities of the resource that its owners will place on the market at various possible prices. Once the market price is established, the firm will employ a quantity of the resource at which its marginal revenue product is equal to its market price. The market level of employment is the summation of individual firm levels of employment.

Suggested readings

Hicks, John R., *Value and Capital,* 2nd ed. Oxford, Eng.: The Clarendon Press, 1946. Chaps. VI, VII.

Scitovsky, Tibor, *Welfare and Competition,* rev. ed. Homewood, Ill.: Richard D. Irwin, Inc., 1971. Chap. 7.

Stigler, George J., *The Theory of Price,* 3rd ed. New York: Crowell-Collier and Macmillan, Inc., 1966. Chap. 14, pp. 239–244.

Questions and exercises

1. ''Rising marginal costs result from the operation of the law of diminishing returns.'' Analyze this statement in detail.

2. Suppose that bricklayers' labor is purchased competitively and that the bricklayers' union is able to push wage rates above the equilibrium level. Show and explain the effects on
   a. the market level of employment
   b. the individual firm's level of employment
   c. the total wage bill for bricklayers
   d. the cost of housing.

3. The relationship between a commercially mixed feed for dairy cows and the quantity of milk produced per day by a cow, holding all other inputs constant, is as follows:

Feed	Milk
2	1.0
4	2.0
6	2.8
8	3.5
10	4.0
12	3.9

The price of milk is $1 per gallon. The price of the feed is $0.35 per pound. Determine the most profitable quantity of feed to use. Explain your reasoning.

4. A purely competitive producer of product X uses two variable resources, A and B, to produce its product. State and explain the complete set of conditions, both with respect to the level of product output and the levels of resource inputs, that must be met if profits are to be maximized.

5. Would you expect that price ceilings placed on crude oil would help solve the energy problem? Explain your answer in detail.

Chapter 15

Chapter contents

Key concepts

Monopoly in the selling of products

Simultaneous employment of several variable resources

Pricing and employment of a given variable resource

The demand curve of the firm: one resource variable

The demand curve of the firm: several resources variable

The market demand curve and resource pricing

Monopolistic exploitation of a resource

Monopsony in the buying of resources

Resource supply curves and marginal resource costs

Pricing and employment of a single resource

Simultaneous employment of several variable resources

Conditions giving rise to monopsony

Monopsonistic exploitation of a resource

Measures to counteract monopsony

Minimum resource prices

Measures to increase mobility

The concept of mobility

Summary

Suggested readings

Questions and exercises

Monopoly

Least cost combination of resources

Marginal revenue product

Demand curve for a resource

Exploitation

Monopsony

Supply curve of a resource

Marginal resource costs

Mobility

Pricing and employment of resources: monopoly and monopsony

For markets other than pure competition, some additions to and modifications of the principles of resource pricing and employment are in order. We shall examine how they work (1) when firms sell products as monopolists while buying resources under conditions of pure competition and (2) when firms buy resources as monopsonists while selling products either as pure competitors or as monopolists. For product monopoly the relationship between the value of marginal product and the marginal revenue product of a resource must be examined further. To take monopsony into account, a modified view of the resource supply curve facing the firm is necessary. Monopoly and monopsony will be considered in turn.

Monopoly in the selling of products

Simultaneous employment of several variable resources

A monopolist that uses several variable resources must determine the combinations of resources necessary to produce alternative outputs at the least possible costs. If it purchases resources under purely competitive conditions, its least cost conditions are the same as those faced by a pure competitor. The least cost combination for a given output is that at which the marginal physical product per dollar's worth of one variable resource is equal to the marginal physical product per dollar's worth of every other variable resource used. If A and B are two such resources, they should be combined so that

$$\frac{MPP_a}{p_a} = \frac{MPP_b}{p_b}. \tag{15.1}$$

To maximize profits, however, the monopolist must do more than determine least cost combinations of variable resources. It must use enough of each to produce the product output at which marginal revenue from its product sales and marginal cost of its product output are equal. With reference to Figure 15–1, suppose that he uses the least cost combination for the production of x_0 units of product. The marginal cost of the product, $0c$, is

Figure 15-1   Least cost combinations and profit maximization

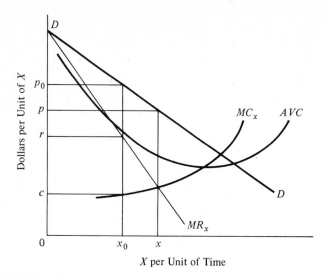

less than the marginal revenue, $0r$, from it. The output level of X and the quantities used of resources A and B are all too small. These conditions can be summarized as follows:

$$\frac{MPP_a}{p_a} = \frac{MPP_b}{p_b} = \frac{1}{MC_x} > \frac{1}{MR_x}. \qquad (15.2)$$

The monopolist can increase output by increasing the quantities of A and B used in combination with its fixed resources. The marginal physical product of both A and B will decrease, causing the marginal cost of the product to rise. The larger output and sales of the monopolist cause marginal revenue from the product to fall. The quantities of A and B, together with the firm's output, will be increased until the marginal cost and the marginal revenue are equal. At output x and price p profits will be maximized. Variable resources will be used in the least cost combination, as well as in the correct absolute quantities. The profit-maximizing conditions with respect to resource purchases, resource combinations, and product output can be summarized as follows:

$$\frac{MPP_a}{p_a} = \frac{MPP_b}{p_b} = \frac{1}{MC_x} = \frac{1}{MR_x}. \qquad (15.3)$$

These principles of profit maximization apply to all types of sellers' markets—pure competition, pure monopoly, oligopoly, and monopolistic competition—as long as pure competition prevails in the buying of resources.

Pricing and employment of a given variable resource

The price and employment level of a given variable resource are determined in much the same way when resource purchasers are monopolistic sellers of product as when they are purely competitive product sellers. The monopolist's demand curve for a resource, while defined in the same way as that of the pure competitor, is slightly more difficult to compute. As in the purely competitive market, we differentiate between the case in which the given resource is the only variable one employed by the firm and the case in which it is one of several variable resources employed.

The demand curve of the firm: one resource variable   To maximize profits with respect to a single variable resource, the monopolist must employ that quantity at which a one-unit change in the quantity employed per unit of time changes total revenue and total cost in the same direction by the same amount. The effects on total receipts and on total costs of one-unit changes in the quantities employed are determined in the same way as they were for the pure competitor.

Changes in the firm's total receipts and the causes of those changes are shown in Table 15–1. Columns (1) and (2) show a portion of the marginal

Table 15–1   The computation of the marginal revenue product of a resource

(1) Quantity of A	(2) Marginal Physical Product (MPP_a)	(3) Total Product	(4) Product Price (p_x)	(5) Total Revenue	(6) Marginal Revenue Product (MRP_a)
4	8	28	$10.00	$280.00	—
5	7	35	9.80	343.00	$63.00
6	6	41	9.60	393.60	50.60
7	5	46	9.50	437.00	43.40
8	4	50	9.40	470.00	33.00

physical product schedule for resource A lying in Stage II for that resource. Resource A is the only variable resource used by the firm; the quantities of all other resources are fixed. Columns (3) and (4) show the portion of the product demand schedule of the monopolist corresponding to the quantities of A shown in column (1).

Column (6) is the important one for the present. It shows the additions to the firm's total receipts made by one-unit increments in the quantity of A employed per unit of time, that is, the *marginal revenue product* of resource A. The marginal revenue product of a given quantity of A can be computed directly from column (5), but in a fundamental sense it is the marginal physical product of A at that quantity multiplied by the marginal revenue obtained from sale to the final product. Marginal revenue product of A or MRP_a when, say, 5 units are employed, equals marginal physical product of A at that point multiplied by the marginal revenue from each of the additional units of sales.[1]

Increases in the level of employment of A by the monopolist cause the marginal revenue product of A to decrease for two reasons. First, they cause the marginal physical product of A to decline because of the operation of the law of diminishing returns. Second, marginal revenue for the monopolistic firm ordinarily will decrease as it markets larger quantities of product.

The marginal revenue product curve is the monopolistic firm's demand curve for A when it buys the resource competitively and when resource A is the only variable resource used by the firm. The monopolist will buy that quantity of A at which the addition made to total receipts by a one-unit increment is equal to the addition made to total cost by the increment. Since the resource is purchased competitively, the addition to total cost made by each additional unit of A purchased per unit of time is the same as the price per unit of A. Thus, in Figure 15–2 if MRP_a is the monopolist's marginal revenue product curve for A and p_a is the price per unit of A, the monopolist will use quantity a. The profit-maximizing conditions can be written as

$$MRP_a = p_a$$

or

$$MPP_a \times MR_x = p_a \qquad (15.4)$$

At different possible prices of A the marginal revenue product curve shows the different quantities that the monopolist will purchase per unit of time.

---

[1] A fifth unit of A per unit of time increases output and sales of X from 28 units to 35 units, and total receipts of the firm from \$280 to \$343. The increment in revenue per unit increment in sales, or MR_x, equals \$63 ÷ 7 or \$9 per unit for each of the 7 units. Marginal revenue product of A, then, when 5 units are employed, must equal $MPP_a \times MR_x$; that is, $7 \times \$9 = \$63$.

In terms of calculus,

$$x = f(a) = \text{the firm's production function}$$

and

$$p_x = h(x) = \text{the demand curve facing the firm.}$$

Thus,

$$R = x \times p_x = x \times h(x) = \text{the firm's total revenue}$$

and

$$\frac{dR}{dx} = p_x + x \times h'(x) = \text{marginal revenue.}$$

Therefore,

$$MRP_a = \left(\frac{dR}{dx}\right)\left(\frac{dx}{da}\right) = [p_x + x \times h'(x)]f'(a).$$

Figure 15–2   The marginal revenue product curve for a resource

The demand curve of the firm: several resources variable   The procedure for establishing the monopolist's demand curve for a given resource
when several variable resources are employed is the same as that used in
the purely competitive case. Assuming that the prices of all other resources
remain constant, changes in the price of the given resource will give rise to
the same sort of firm or internal effects.

These effects are shown in Figure 15–3, in which A is the given variable
resource. Suppose that the initial price of A is p_{a1}; the firm is using a least
cost combination of variable resources and is producing the profit-

Figure 15–3   The firm's demand curve for a resource

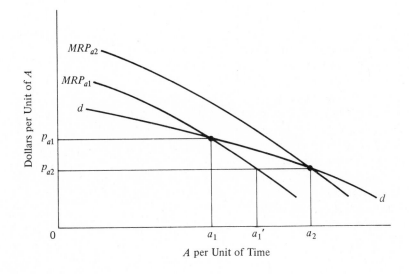

maximizing quantity of product X. The quantity of A employed is a_1. The curve MRP_{a1} is valid for changes in the quantity of A only.

A decrease in the price of A to p_{a2} will provide an incentive for the monopolist to increase employment of the resource toward a_1'. But, as the employment of A is expanded, the marginal physical product curves and marginal revenue product curves of complementary resources will be shifted to the right, causing larger quantities of these resources to be used at their given prices. The corresponding curves of substitute resources will be shifted to the left by the greater utilization of A, and smaller quantities of substitute resources will be employed at their given prices by the monopolist. Both effects will shift the marginal physical product curve and the marginal revenue product curve of resource A to the right. When the monopolist has again established a least-cost profit-maximizing combination of variable resources, the marginal revenue product curve for A will be in some position such as MRP_{a2}, and the quantity of A employed will be a_2. Thus, the firm's demand curve for resource A will consist of points tracing out a curve such as dd.

The market demand curve and resource pricing   If all purchasers of resource A were purely monopolistic sellers of product, the market demand curve for A would be the horizontal summation of all individual firm demand curves for it. There would be no external or industry effects resulting from a decrease in the price of A, for each monopolist is the sole supplier of product for his industry. The effect of a decrease in the price of A on the quantity of product produced in any given industry and, consequently, on the price of the product has already been taken into account in the marginal revenue product curves and in that monopolist's demand curve for the resource.

If the purchasers of resource A are oligopolists or monopolistic competitors, the market demand curve for the resource is no longer the horizontal summation of individual firm demand curves for it. A change in the resource price changes not only the output that any single firm in a given industry will produce but the outputs of all other firms in the industry as well. These changes will occur in every such industry that uses the resource. As in the purely competitive case of Chapter 14, changes in product outputs of other firms in the industry will shift the product demand curve facing any given firm and, consequently, the firm's demand curve for resource A. Thus, at any given price the quantities employed by all firms in all industries using A, when each firm is maximizing its profits, must be totaled to locate a point on the market demand curve for A. Other points on the market demand curve can be obtained in the same fashion.

The procedure just outlined is applicable for establishing the market demand curve for a resource regardless of the type of product market in which the firms using the resource sell. The usual case will be that some of the firms using resource A will sell in one type of product market and some will sell in other types. The only market structure requirement to be met is that all firms purchase the resource competitively.

With regard to market supply, resource pricing, and resource employment, monopoly in the product market adds nothing new to the analysis presented in the preceding chapter. The market supply curve for resource A again shows the different quantities of it that its owners will place on the market at various alternative prices. The market price of the resource moves toward the level at which firms are willing to employ the quantity per unit of time that its owners are willing to place on the market.

The market price of A determines its level of employment. The monopolist, like a firm selling under conditions of pure competition, is faced with a horizontal supply curve for resource A at a level equal to its market price. The monopolist will employ the resource up to the point at which it is maximizing profits with respect to it. At this point the marginal revenue product of the resource is equal to its price. The market level of employment of the resource is the summation of all individual firm employment levels, whether those firms be monopolists, pure competitors, oligopolists, or monopolistic competitors.

When the monopolist is maximizing profits with respect to each variable resource used, those resources will necessarily be used in a least cost combination. Suppose that A and B are the only two variable resources used by a monopolist producing product X. When profits are maximized with respect to A, then

$$MPP_a \times MR_x = p_a. \tag{15.5}$$

Similarly, maximization of profits with respect to B means that

$$MPP_b \times MR_x = p_b. \tag{15.6}$$

Consequently,

$$\frac{MPP_a}{p_a} = \frac{MPP_b}{p_b} = \frac{1}{MC_x} = \frac{1}{MR_x}. \tag{15.7}$$

Monopolistic exploitation of a resource

Monopoly in a product market is said to result in exploitation of resources used by the monopolist. In this respect *exploitation* means that units of a resource are paid less than the value of the product that any one of them adds to the economy's output. A monopolist employs that quantity of a resource at which its price equals its marginal revenue product—marginal physical product multiplied by marginal revenue from the sale of the product. But the value of product added to the economy's output by a unit of the resource is its value of marginal product—marginal physical product multiplied by price per unit at which the product is sold. The marginal revenue product of the resource to a particular firm facing a downward-sloping product demand curve is less than the value of marginal product of the resource, since marginal revenue is less than product price in such cases. Hence, the prices paid resources used by monopolistic firms are less than the values of the products that they add to the economy's output.

Nevertheless, the price paid a resource must be equal to what it can earn in its alternative employments. Exploitation does not mean that the monopolist pays units of the resource less than do competitive firms hiring units of the same resource. Exploitation under monopoly occurs because the monopolist, faced by the market price of the resource, stops short of the employment level at which the value of marginal product of the resource equals the resource price. Units of the resource contribute more to the value of the economy's output when employed by the monopolist than they do when employed by the purely competitive firm, but they are paid the same price in each market situation. Thus, market forces will not induce resources to move into their more valuable uses.

Monopsony in the buying of resources

A resource market situation in which there is a single buyer of a particular resource is called one of *monopsony*.[2] A monopsonistic situation is the opposite extreme to pure competition among resource buyers—the situation that we have heretofore assumed exists. Two additional resource market situations can be distinguished. The first is oligopsony, in which there are a few buyers of a particular resource that may or may not be differentiated. One buyer takes a large enough proportion of the total supply of the resource to influence the market price of the resource. The other situation is one of monopsonistic competition. Here there are many buyers of a particular kind of resource, but there is differentiation within the resource category that causes specific buyers to prefer the resource of one seller to that of another. Our analysis will center around monopsony—one buyer of the resource—but it may also be applied to oligopsony and monopsonistic competition.

Resource supply curves and marginal resource costs

As the only buyer of a resource, the monopsonist faces the market supply curve for it. Ordinarily that supply curve is upward-sloping to the right. A

---

[2] The term *monopsony* is applied, also, to cases in which there is a single buyer of a particular product; however, our discussion will be confined to monopsony in resource markets.

producer who furnishes virtually the entire source of employment in an isolated area would be in this position, in the short run at least. Contrast the supply curve faced by a monopsonist with that faced by the firm that buys a resource under conditions of pure competition. Under pure competition the firm can get as many units of the resource per unit of time as it desires at the going market price; hence, it is faced with a horizontal or perfectly elastic resource supply curve even though the market supply curve may be upward-sloping to the right or less than perfectly elastic.

The upward slope of the resource supply curve faced by the monopsonist gives monopsony the characteristics that distinguish it from pure competition. To obtain larger quantities of the resource per unit of time, the monopsonist must pay higher prices. Columns (1) and (2) of Table 15–2

Table 15–2   The computation of marginal resource cost

(1) Quantity of A	(2) Resource Price (p_a)	(3) Total Resource Cost (TC_a)	(4) Marginal Resource Cost (MRC_a)
10	$0.60	$6.00	—
11	0.65	7.15	$1.15
12	0.70	8.40	1.25
13	0.75	9.75	1.35

present a portion of a typical resource supply schedule illustrating this situation. Column (3) shows the total cost of resource A to the firm for different quantities purchased. Column (4) shows marginal resource cost of A to the firm.

Marginal resource cost is defined as the change in the firm's total costs resulting from a one-unit change in the purchase of the resource per unit of time. When the resource supply curve faced by the firm is upward-sloping to the right, marginal resource cost will be greater than the resource price for any quantity purchased by the firm. This relationship can be explained with reference to Table 15–2.

Suppose that the firm increases the quantity of A that it purchases from 10 units to 11 units. The eleventh unit costs the firm $0.65. However, in order to obtain 11 units per unit of time, the firm must pay $0.65 per unit for *all 11 units*. Therefore, the cost of obtaining the other 10 units has increased from $0.60 to $0.65 per unit. An additional cost of $0.50 is incurred on the 10. Add this to the $0.65 that the eleventh unit costs, and the increase

Figure 15–4   Marginal revenue product, marginal resource cost, and profit maximization for a monopsonist

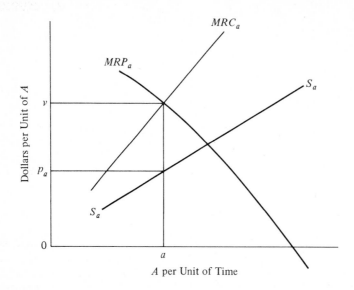

in the firm's total cost is $1.15. The marginal resource cost of the twelfth and thirteenth units can be computed in a similar way.[3]

A graphic illustration of the resource supply curve and the marginal resource cost curve faced by a monopsonist is shown in Figure 15–4. The market supply curve for resource A is $S_a S_a$. The marginal resource cost curve is MRC_a and lies above the supply curve. The marginal resource cost curve bears the same relationship to the supply curve that a marginal cost curve bears to an average cost curve. In fact, the market supply curve of

---

[3] Let the supply curve for resource A be

$$p_a = \phi(a).$$

Then

$$TC_a = a \times \phi(a)$$

and

$$MRC_a = \frac{dTC_a}{da} = \phi(a) + a \times \phi'(a) = p_a + a \times \phi'(a);$$

that is, marginal resource cost of A at the a level of employment is equal to the price of A at that level of employment plus the incremental cost of A for the entire a units of the resource.

If the firm buys resource A under conditions of pure competition, the supply curve of A to the firm is horizontal,

$$\phi'(a) = 0,$$

and

$$MRC_a = p_a.$$

resource A is the average cost curve of resource A alone; and the marginal resource cost curve is the marginal cost curve of resource A alone. Obviously then, if the supply (average cost) curve of A is increasing, the marginal resource cost (marginal cost) curve must lie above it.[4]

Pricing and employment of a single resource

Profit maximization with respect to resource A is governed by the same general principles for the monopsonist as for firms buying resources competitively. Larger quantities of A per unit of time will be purchased if they add more to the firm's total receipts than to its total costs. Additions to the monopsonist's total receipts as more A is employed are shown by the curve MRP_a in Figure 15–4. Additions to total costs are shown by the marginal resource cost curve. Profits are maximized when quantity a of the resource is employed. Larger quantities would add more to total costs than to total receipts and would cause profits to decline. We can state the profit-maximizing conditions in equation form. When the monopsonist's profits are maximized, that quantity of A is employed at which

$$MRP_a = MRC_a$$

or

$$MPP_a \times MR_x = MRC_a. \qquad (15.8)$$

The monopsonist differs from the competitive buyer of resources with respect to the price paid for the resource at the profit-maximizing level of employment. For quantity a of the resource it is necessary for the monopsonist to pay a price of only p_a, although the marginal revenue product of the resource at that level of employment is v. Should the monopsonist employ that quantity of A at which its marginal revenue product is equal to its price—as does the competitive resource buyer—less profit would be made. To maximize profits, the quantity of the resource used is restricted and it is paid a price per unit that is less than its marginal revenue product. The important consideration for profit maximization is the employment of that quantity at which the marginal resource cost equals the marginal revenue product—and for the monopsonist the resource price is less than the marginal resource cost. Monopsony profits, resulting from the excess of the marginal revenue product of the resource over its price per unit, are equal to $p_a v \times a$.

Simultaneous employment of several variable resources

The conditions that must be met by the monopsonist if he is to employ least cost combinations of variable resources for given outputs differ slightly

---

[4] *See* pp. 206–208.

from those that apply to purely competitive resource buyers. As before, the least cost combination for the monopsonist is that combination at which the marginal physical product per dollar's worth of one resource is equal to the marginal physical product per dollar's worth of every other resource. The difference between the monopsonistic and the competitive buyer rests on what constitutes the marginal physical product per dollar's worth of a resource.

An illustration will help make this difference clear. Suppose that a coal-mining firm buys miners' labor monopsonistically. At the current level of employment a single miner's labor adds a ton of coal per day to the firm's output. This is the marginal physical product of the miner's labor. It adds $20 to the firm's total costs. This is the marginal resource cost of the miner's labor, and it exceeds the daily wage rate. The addition made to the firm's total production per additional dollar's expenditure on labor is 1/20 of a ton of coal, or is equal to MPP_l/MRC_l. The same calculation applies to any other resource purchased monopsonistically. The marginal physical product per dollar's worth of any resource is found by dividing its marginal physical product by its marginal resource cost.

If a firm purchases variable resources A and B monopsonistically, to achieve the least cost combination for a given output it must use them in such proportions that

$$\frac{MPP_a}{MRC_a} = \frac{MPP_b}{MRC_b}. \tag{15.9}$$

The reciprocal of either or both of the fractions in the equation represents the marginal cost of the product at whatever output the firm is producing. A unit of A used adds an amount MRC_a to total costs and an amount MPP_a to total product. Therefore, the addition to total costs per unit increase in output is MRC_a/MPP_a. Similarly, the marginal cost of the product in terms of resource B is MRC_b/MPP_b.

Suppose that initially the monopsonistic firm is using too little of A and B for profit maximization, but it is using the least cost combination for the product output it is producing. Marginal cost of the product is less than marginal revenue from its sale. These conditions can be summed up as follows:

$$\frac{MPP_a}{MRC_a} = \frac{MPP_b}{MRC_b} = \frac{1}{MC_x} > \frac{1}{MR_x}. \tag{15.10}$$

Profit maximization requires the employment of greater quantities of the variable resources per unit of time. The additional resource units will increase the output and decrease the marginal revenue received from the product. Additional quantities of A and B cause the marginal physical products of both resources to decline. At the same time the marginal resource costs of A and B increase. Thus, the marginal cost of the product to the firm rises as a result of two forces working simultaneously—declining marginal physical products and rising marginal resource costs. Additional quantities of A and B will be employed per unit of time until the marginal cost equals the marginal revenue. At this point the resources are used in the correct absolute quantities, as well as in the least cost proportions. The conditions necessary for profit maximization can be stated as follows:

$$\frac{MPP_a}{MRC_a} = \frac{MPP_b}{MRC_b} = \frac{1}{MC_x} = \frac{1}{MR_x}. \qquad (15.11)$$

The conditions necessary for profit maximization by the monopsonist also can be established by considering resources A and B one at a time. Resource A should be used up to the point at which:

$$MPP_a \times MR_x = MRC_a \qquad \text{or} \qquad \frac{MPP_a}{MRC_a} = \frac{1}{MR_x}. \qquad (15.12)$$

Likewise, resource B should be used up to the point at which:

$$MPP_b \times MR_x = MRC_b \qquad \text{or} \qquad \frac{MPP_b}{MRC_b} = \frac{1}{MR_x}. \qquad (15.13)$$

From (15.12) and (15.13) we arrive again at the conditions expressed in (15.11).

The profit-maximizing conditions set forth above for the monopsonist are general enough to apply to all classifications of both product sellers' markets and resource buyers' markets. Under conditions of pure competition in resource buying, MRC_a and MRC_b become p_a and p_b, respectively. Under conditions of pure competition in product selling, MR_x becomes p_x.[5]

---

[5] In terms of calculus, the general solution to the problem of profit maximization by a firm with respect to several variable resources is as follows:

$$x = f(a, b) = \text{the firm's production function}$$

$$p_x = h(x) = \text{the product demand curve facing the firm}$$

$$p_a = \phi(a) = \text{the supply curve facing the firm for resource } A$$

$$p_b = \psi(b) = \text{the supply curve facing the firm for resource } B.$$

On the revenue side,

$$R = x \times p_x = \text{total revenue of the firm}$$

$$\frac{dR}{dx} = p_x - x \times h'(x) = \text{marginal revenue of the firm}$$

and

$$\frac{\delta R}{\delta a} = \left(\frac{dR}{dx}\right)\left(\frac{\delta x}{\delta a}\right) = [p_x - x \times h'(x)]\frac{\delta x}{\delta a}$$
$$= \text{marginal revenue product of } A \text{ to the firm.}$$

Similarly,

$$\frac{\delta R}{\delta b} = \left(\frac{dR}{dx}\right)\left(\frac{\delta x}{\delta b}\right) = [p_x - x \times h'(x)]\frac{\delta x}{\delta b}$$
$$= \text{marginal revenue product of } B \text{ to the firm.}$$

On the cost side,

$$C = k + a \times p_a + b \times p_b = \text{total costs of the firm}$$

Conditions giving rise to monopsony

Monopsony results from either or both of two basic conditions. First, monopsonistic purchases of a resource may occur when units of the resource are specialized to a particular user. This statement means that the marginal revenue product of the resource in the specialized use is enough higher than it is in any alternative employments in which it conceivably can be used to eliminate the alternative employments from the consideration of resource suppliers. Thus, the resource supply curve facing the monopsonist will be the market supply curve of the resource and usually will be upward-sloping to the right. The more the user is willing to pay for the resource, the greater will be the quantity placed on the market.

A situation of the kind described may occur when a special type of skilled labor is developed to meet certain needs of a specific firm. The higher the wage rate offered for the special category of labor, the more individuals there will be who are willing to undergo the necessary training to develop it. No other firm utilizes labor with this or similar skills; consequently, once trained, the workers' only options are to work for this firm or to work elsewhere at jobs where their marginal revenue products and their wage rates are significantly lower.

$$\frac{\delta C}{\delta a} = p_a + a \times \phi'(a) = \text{marginal resource cost of } A$$

$$\frac{\delta C}{\delta b} = p_b + b \times \psi'(b) = \text{marginal resource cost of } B.$$

To maximize profits,

$$\pi = R - C = x \times p_x - (k + a \times p_a + b \times p_b)$$

$$\frac{\delta \pi}{\delta a} = [p_x - x \times h'(x)]\frac{\delta x}{\delta a} - [p_a + a \times \phi'(a)] = 0$$

$$\frac{\delta \pi}{\delta b} = [p_x - x \times h'(x)]\frac{\delta x}{\delta b} - [p_b + b \times \psi'(b)] = 0$$

$$[p_x - x h'(x)]\frac{\delta x}{\delta a} = p_a + a \phi'(a)$$

$$[p_x - x h'(x)]\frac{\delta x}{\delta b} = p_b + b \psi'(b)$$

$$MRP_a = MRC_a \quad \text{and} \quad MRP_b = MRC_b.$$

If the firm is a purely competitive seller of product, then

$$p_x = h(x) = k \quad \text{and} \quad h'(x) = 0.$$

If it is a purely competitive purchaser of A, the supply curves of A and B are horizontal; so

$$\phi'(a) = 0 \quad \text{and} \quad \psi'(b) = 0.$$

Thus, the profit-maximizing conditions can be stated as

$$p_x \times \frac{\delta x}{\delta a} = p_a \quad \text{and} \quad p_x \times \frac{\delta x}{\delta b} = p_b$$

or

$$VMP_a = p_a \quad \text{and} \quad VMP_b = p_b.$$

Specialization of resources to a particular user is not confined to the labor field. A large aircraft or automobile manufacturer may depend on a number of suppliers to furnish certain parts used by no other manufacturer. In the tightest possible case such suppliers sell their entire outputs to the manufacturer, and complete monopsony by the manufacturer exists. Given time, the suppliers may be able to convert production facilities to supply other types of parts to other manufacturers, and the degree of monopsony enjoyed by the one may be decreased correspondingly.

Special monopsonistic cases occur in the field of entertainment. Performers are placed under contract by specific employers and are then no longer free to work for alternative employers. Major league baseball players fall in this category, also. Under the well-known reserve clause, once a player is signed to play for a given team, a player either accepts the best salary terms he can get from that employer or else is forbidden to play in the major leagues at all. He cannot transfer from one major league team to another of his own volition, although his contract can be sold to another team by his employer.

The second condition from which monopsony may stem is the immobility of certain resources. It is not necessary that resources in general be immobile. It is only necessary that mobility out of certain areas or away from certain firms be lacking, thus creating unique monopsonistic situations. Various forces may hold workers in a given community or to a given firm. Among these are emotional ties to the community together with a fear of the unknown. Ignorance regarding alternative employment opportunities may exist. Funds may not be sufficient to permit job seeking in and movement to alternative job areas. Seniority and pension rights accumulated with a firm may make workers reluctant to leave. Specific cases of immobility among firms within a given geographic area may result from agreements among employers not to "pirate" each other's work forces.

Monopsonistic exploitation of a resource

Monopsony in the purchase of a resource also is said to result in exploitation of that resource. Monopsonistic exploitation can be understood best by comparing monopsony with pure competition in resource buying. In a purely competitive situation each firm will add to its profits by taking larger quantities of the resource up to the point at which the marginal revenue product of the resource is equal to the resource price. The resource receives a price per unit equal to what any one unit of it contributes to the firm's total receipts.[6]

---

[6] Monopolistic exploitation will occur if the resource-buying firms face downward-sloping product demand curves, but there is no monopsonistic exploitation.

In contrast, the monopsonist maximizes profits by stopping short of the resource employment level at which marginal revenue product of the resource is equal to its price per unit. This situation is shown in Figure 15–4. The profit-maximizing level of employment is that at which the marginal revenue product equals the marginal resource cost. Since the marginal resource cost exceeds the resource price, the marginal revenue product of the resource does also. Hence, units of the resource are paid less than what any one of them contributes to the total receipts of the firm. This situation is called monopsonistic exploitation of the resource. The monopsonist restricts the quantity of the resource used and holds down its price.

Measures to counteract monopsony

What can be done to counteract monopsonistic exploitation of resources? Two alternatives will be considered. First, administered or fixed minimum resource prices can be used. Second, measures successful in increasing resource mobility will reduce the monopsonistic power of particular resource users.

Minimum resource prices   Minimum resource prices can be established by the government or by organized groups of resource suppliers. The typical monopsonistic situation is pictured in Figure 15–5. The level of employment of resource A is quantity a. Its price per unit is p_a; however,

---

Figure 15–5   Control of monopsony by minimum resource prices marginal revenue product is v, and the resource is being exploited. Suppose that a minimum price is set at p_{a1} and that the firm must pay a price of at least p_{a1} per unit for all units purchased. Should the firm want more than a_1 units, it faces the mn sector of the resource supply curve. The entire supply curve now faced by the firm will be $p_{a1}mn$.

The alteration in the resource supply curve facing the firm also alters the marginal resource cost curve. For quantities between zero and a_1, each additional unit of A employed per unit of time adds an amount equal to p_{a1} to the firm's total costs. The new marginal resource cost curve coincides with $p_{a1}m$, the new supply curve, out to quantity a_1. For quantities greater than a_1, the regular supply curve mn is the relevant one, and the corresponding sector of the marginal resource cost curve becomes lk. The altered marginal resource cost curve is $p_{a1}mlk$. At quantity a_1 it is discontinuous between m and l.

The quantity of A that the firm should now use to maximize profits will differ from the quantity used before the minimum price was set. The firm should use quantity a_1, at which the new marginal resource cost is equal to the marginal revenue product of A. The minimum price not only eliminates monopsonistic exploitation of the resource, but also it increases the level of employment in the process.

This analysis assumes that the minimum price of resource A is set at just the correct level to counteract monopsony completely. Such precision may or may not be achieved in fact. However, any minimum price between p_a and p_{a1} will counteract monopsony to some extent. The nearer to p_{a1} the price is set, the more nearly will exploitation be eliminated. Prices set between p_{a1} and v will counteract exploitation also, but at the expense of employment. Unemployment will occur, since at any price level above p_{a1} resource sellers will want to put more on the market than buyers are willing to buy.

Countering of monopsony by price regulation is at best a difficult job. The precise price level at which monopsony is offset completely is hard to determine. In the labor field—where monopsony is most publicized—minimum wage laws may be the counteracting device used. However, different degrees of monopsony for different kinds of labor and for different situations make blanket price fixing of this type impractical as an overall monopsonistic offset. Collective bargaining on a firm-by-firm basis could more nearly meet and offset individual monopsonistic cases. But even here the problem of determining—leaving aside the difficulty of obtaining—the "correct" minimum price for the resource remains.

Measures to increase mobility   Measures to increase resource mobility among alternative employments get directly at the causes of monopsony. Immobility of resources is thought by many economists to be most serious in labor markets; hence, our discussion will be centered on the labor resource. We shall present a few general lines of approach rather than specific and detailed programs. With regard to the labor resource, mobility among geographic areas and firms, horizontal mobility among occupations at the same skill level, and vertical occupational mobility to higher skill classifications will be of value in counteracting monopsony.

An efficient system of federal employment exchanges should provide one avenue of attack on labor immobility. An important function of such a system is the collection and dissemination of information regarding alternative employment opportunities. It should make data available to the entire labor force—including those in now isolated communities—with regard to high-wage, scarce-labor-supply areas and give descriptions of the requisite skills for obtaining employment in such areas. In addition, the system should perform the more common function of bringing together job opportunities and workers seeking alternative jobs.

The educational system offers a second avenue of attack. It can increase both the vertical and horizontal mobility of labor resources. With regard to vertical mobility, the availability and use of educational opportunities can channel larger numbers of the younger generation toward higher-paying, higher-level occupations. By means of vocational and trade schools the educational system can provide older workers with training for upward movement through skill classifications. With regard to horizontal mobility, vocational guidance can assist in steering the potential labor force away from lower-paying occupations toward those providing higher remuneration. Additionally, adult education programs can furnish the retraining necessary to escape from particularly low-paying occupations.

Still a third line of attack is that of a limited amount of subsidization of worker migration out of areas characterized by monopsony, since one of the causes of immobility is lack of funds needed by workers to move into alternative employment areas. Subsidization of migration may occur in the form of government loans or outright grants of funds to assist in worker relocation.

The concept of mobility

A few observations regarding the meaning of mobility are in order so that no wrong impression be given. To some people a mobile labor force may imply a drifting one with a high job turnover rate—an undesirable social situation. Mobility, as the term is used in economics, does not mean a complete lack of ties to particular communities and social institutions; nor does it mean that all workers must be ready to pack up and move at the slightest provocation. The amount of actual movement necessary to prevent monopsony from occurring usually will be quite small. The possibility or likelihood of migration is the important factor. Also, there is at all times considerable change and turnover of the labor force—workers changing jobs, new workers entering the labor force, and old workers retiring. This constant change constitutes mobility. The primary problem is that of directing the mobility that already exists into economically desirable channels.

Summary

The principles of resource pricing and employment in situations other than pure competition are a modification of the principles established in the preceding chapter. Monopoly in product markets alters the nature of individual firm demand curves for resources. Monopsony in the purchase of resources alters the nature of the resource supply curve faced by the firm.

The monopolistic firm employing several variable resources must determine the least-cost resource combinations for various possible outputs and also the profit-maximizing quantities of variable resources to use. The least cost combination for a given product output is the one at which the marginal physical product per dollar's worth of one resource is equal to the marginal physical product per dollar's worth of every other resource used. To maximize profits, the firm must use both a least cost combination and the correct absolute amounts of each resource. Resources must be used so that

$$\frac{MPP_a}{p_a} = \frac{MPP_b}{p_b} = \cdots = \frac{MPP_n}{p_n} = \frac{1}{MC_x} = \frac{1}{MR_x}.$$

Monopoly in product markets is said to result in monopolistic exploitation of resources, since the resource price equals its marginal revenue product for the firm and is less than the value of its marginal product for the economy as a whole.

The market price and the employment level of a resource are determined simultaneously. Where monopoly occurs in product markets, marginal revenue product of each variable resource used must be equal to its price if profits are to be maximized. If the monopolist uses only one variable resource, the marginal revenue product curve of the resource is the firm's demand curve for it. If several variable resources are used, internal or firm effects of price changes in any given resource must be taken into account in determining the firm's demand curve for it.

The market demand curve for a resource is obtained by summing the quantities of it that all firms will employ at each possible price, whether those firms operate as monopolists or as pure competitors in selling products. Resource price is determined by the conditions of market demand and market supply. As the market price is established, the firm adjusts its employment of the resource to the level at which the marginal revenue product equals the resource price. The market employment level is the summation of individual firm employment levels.

Monopsony means a single buyer of a particular resource; hence, the monopsonistic firm faces a resource supply curve that slopes upward to the right. It also faces a marginal resource cost curve that lies above the supply curve. The firm maximizes profits by employing the quantity of the resource that equates its marginal revenue product to its marginal resource cost. The marginal resource cost and the marginal revenue product of the resource exceed the resource price at the profit-maximizing level of employment, thus resulting in monopsonistic exploitation of the resource.

Suggested readings

Cartter, A. M., and Marshall, F. R., *Labor Economics*. Homewood, Ill.: Richard D. Irwin, Inc., 1967. Chap. 10.

Fellner, William, *Modern Economic Analysis*. New York: McGraw-Hill, Inc., 1960. Chap. 19.

Rees, Albert, *The Economics of Work and Pay*. New York: Harper & Row, Publishers, 1973. Pt. II.

Robinson, Joan, *The Economics of Imperfect Competition*. London: Macmillan & Co., Ltd., 1933. Chaps. 25–26.

Questions and exercises

1. Would you expect a monopolist to use
   a. an efficient mix of variable resources? Why or why not?
   b. Pareto optimal quantities of resources? Why or why not?

2. Commutative justice is said to be attained when units of a resource are paid what they are worth to the society. Consider two of many purchasers of common labor. One sells the product as a monopolist. The other sells the product as a pure competitor. Explain the wage rate that each would pay, the level of employment in each firm, and whether or not commutative justice is attained. Illustrate your answer with a diagram.

3. a. Explain and illustrate with a diagram the following concepts:
      (1) monopolistic exploitation of a resource
      (2) monopsonistic exploitation of a resource.
   b. Explain and illustrate how price fixing may be used in each case to counteract exploitation. Would you expect such price fixing to be feasible? Why or why not?

4. Would you expect that there is much monopsony in the purchase of common (unskilled) labor in the United States? Why or why not?

5. What kinds of government policies other than price fixing might be used to counteract monopsonistic exploitation of resources?

Chapter 16

Chapter contents

**The conditions of
maximum welfare**

Resource markets

**Resource allocation
under pure
competition**
    Allocation within a given submarket
    Allocation among submarkets
    Allocation of labor
    Allocation of capital

**Conditions
preventing correct
allocation**
    Monopoly
    Monopsony
    Nonprice impediments
    Ignorance
    Sociological and psychological impediments
    Institutional factors

    Price fixing
    Case I
    Case II
    Case III

Summary
    Suggested readings
    Questions and exercises

Key concepts

Value of marginal product
Pure competition
Monopoly
Monopsony
Marginal revenue product
Marginal resource cost
Pareto optimality

Resource allocation

One of the most important functions performed by resource prices in a private enterprise economy is that of allocating resources among different uses and different geographic areas. If a high level of efficiency is to be attained in the economy, constant reallocation of resources must be in process in response to changes in human wants, in the kinds and quantities of resources available, and in the available techniques of production. In developing the principles of resource allocation, we shall first discuss the conditions of "correct" resource allocation, then consider the concept of resource markets and the allocation of resources among them leading to maximum efficiency in resource use, and finally examine certain circumstances that prevent resources from being correctly allocated.

The conditions of maximum welfare

What are the allocation conditions that must be met if units of any given resource are to make their maximum contributions to welfare? In general terms, the requirement is that the value of marginal product of the resource in any one of its uses must be the same as its value of marginal product in all of its other uses. Suppose that some other allocation prevails—for example, that a tractor used on a farm contributes at the margin $2,000 worth of farm products annually to the economy's output, and that an identical tractor used in construction can contribute $3,000 worth of products annually to the economy's output. If a tractor were switched from farming to construction, there would be a net gain to consumers of $1,000 worth of product. Obviously, some consumers can be made better off without making anyone worse off. Transfers of resources from lower value of marginal product uses to higher value of marginal product uses always yield a welfare increase; and maximum welfare results when these transfers have been carried to the point that for each resource its value of marginal product is the same in all its alternative uses.

Resource markets

When the price system is used to allocate resources, the concept of a resource market becomes important. The extent of a resource market depends on the nature of the resource under consideration and on the time span relevant to the problem at hand. Within a given time span some resources are more mobile than others, and, consequently, their markets tend to be larger. Mobility depends on a number of things—shipping costs, perishability, social forces, and the like—and resources differ with respect to these characteristics.

Ordinarily, the mobility of any given resource varies with the time span under consideration. Over a short period of time its mobility is more limited than it is over a longer period. Consider labor of a certain kind, say, machinists. Over a short time period of a few months, or perhaps a year, machinists in the United States will not move freely from one geographic area to another, although they may be fairly free to move from one employer to another within a single locality. The longer the period of time under consideration, the larger the geographic area within which they are free to move. Over a period of 25 years they will be fairly mobile over the entire economy.[1]

Over short periods of time all the machinists, or all the units of any other resource in the economy, do not necessarily operate in the same market. The economy can be divided into a number of submarkets, each submarket being the area within which units of a resource are mobile in the given time span. The longer the time span considered, the greater the interconnections among the submarkets. Over a sufficiently long period the submarkets tend to fuse into a single market.

The submarkets for a resource tend to be conceptual rather than real in the sense that boundaries between submarkets are blurred. Each submarket overlaps others. However, if we think of them as being separate and apart from each other, we can make better progress with the analysis of resource allocation. Also, in place of the whole continuum of time periods, only two need be considered: (1) a short period during which the submarkets for a given resource are separate and (2) the long period in which resources have sufficient time to move freely among the submarkets and create a fusion of these into a single market.

---

[1] Mobility does not require the physical transference of a machinist from one area to another or even from one employer to another. As old machinists retire from the work force and new machinists enter, mobility can exist; for in certain areas the retiring machinists may not be replaced, while in others the number of entries into the trade may exceed retirements.

Resource allocation under pure competition

Will the price system allocate resources among their various uses so that optimal welfare tends to be approached? If pure competition exists in both product markets and resource markets, and if there are no externalities in consumption and production, such an allocation will tend to occur; therefore, the competitive model with no externalities provides a convenient starting point. We shall begin with the short-period allocation of a resource within a given submarket. Then the analysis will be extended to include long-period allocation among submarkets or over the entire economy.

Allocation within a given submarket

When units of a resource are so allocated that the value of marginal product in one use is greater than it is in other uses, the allocation is incorrect from the point of view of economic efficiency and welfare. The resource units would be more valuable to the society in the higher value of marginal product use; and if they were transferred from the lower to the higher value of marginal product uses, the total value of the economy's output would be increased.

Resource prices furnish the mechanism for reallocation when resources are incorrectly allocated under a purely competitive system. Suppose that units of a given resource are allocated between two industries in such quantities that the value of marginal product of the resource is higher in one than in the other. Given this allocation, firms in the industry in which the value of marginal product is higher will also be willing to pay more per unit for the resource because in each industry the resource will be paid an amount equal to its value of marginal product. Consequently, resource owners, seeking maximum income, transfer resource units from the lower-paying to the higher-paying uses.[2] As units of the resource are transferred, its value of marginal product decreases in the employments to which it is transferred and increases in the employments from which it is transferred. The transfer continues until its value of marginal product is equalized in all its uses, and all firms in the submarket are paying a price per unit equal to that value of marginal product. At this point the resource is correctly allocated and, within the submarket, is making its maximum contribution to net national product.

---

[2] New resource units just entering the market, say, college graduates, may be attracted to the jobs offering higher pay. This attraction, together with the failure to replace resource units retired from the market in lower-paying employments, provides an important method of transfer.

To illustrate the technical economics of the allocation process, suppose that the firms in two different industries, X and Y, operate in the same submarket for resource A. Suppose also that, initially, units of A are correctly allocated among the firms of the two industries. The VMP_{ax}, or value of marginal product of A in firms of the industry producing X, is equal to VMP_{ay}, or the value of marginal product of A in firms of the industry producing Y. Suppose further that there is neither a surplus nor a shortage of A on the market, so that

$$VMP_{ax} = VMP_{ay} = p_a$$

or

$$MPP_{ax} \times p_x = MPP_{ay} \times p_y = p_a,$$

where p_a is the price per unit of resource A, and p_x and p_y are the respective prices of product X and product Y.

Suppose that an increase occurs in the market demand for commodity X, while demand for commodity Y remains unchanged. The level of aggregate demand remains constant, and the increase in demand for X is offset by decreases in demand for commodities other than X and Y. The price of X rises, thereby increasing VMP_{ax}. Resource A has become more valuable to society in the production of X than it is in the production of Y. The original allocation of A no longer maximizes welfare; that is, this allocation is no longer the correct one. At price p_a for the resource, employers in the industry producing X find that a shortage of A exists. Consequently, they will bid up the price of A enough to cause owners of A to transfer units of it from the industry producing Y to the industry producing X. As the quantity of A employed by firms in the industry producing X increases relative to the quantities of other resources used, MPP_{ax} declines. As the output of X increases, p_x declines. Thus, VMP_{ax} declines.

Changes within the industry producing Y will accompany changes in the industry producing X. As units of A are transferred from the production of Y to X, the proportions of A to other resources used by firms in the industry producing Y decrease, and MPP_{ay} increases. Smaller amounts of Y are produced and sold; consequently, p_y rises. Increases in MPP_{ay} and p_y increase VMP_{ay}.

Reallocation of A from the production of Y to X continues until units of the resource are again correctly distributed between the two industries. Units of A move from the industry producing Y to the industry producing X until the VMP_{ax} has gone down enough and the VMP_{ay} has gone up enough for the two to be equal. The new price per unit of A will be somewhat higher than the old price, for its value of marginal product is now higher in both industries than it was previously. In bidding against each other for the available supply of A, firms in both industries have raised the price of A to the level of its value of marginal product in both uses.

Resource A will again be making its maximum contribution to net national product. When VMP_{ax} was greater than VMP_{ay}, every movement of a unit of A from the industry producing Y to the industry producing X increased A's contribution to net national product. Withdrawal of a unit of A from the industry producing Y decreased A's contribution to net national product by an amount equal to VMP_{ay}. Putting the unit of A to work in the industry producing X increased A's contribution to net national product by VMP_{ax}. Hence, a net gain in A's contribution to net national product resulted from such transfers until A's value of marginal product was once more equalized among firms in the two industries.

Allocation among submarkets

We extend the analysis by increasing the time span under consideration, joining short-period with long-period analysis. Consider two resources: (1) a certain kind of labor and (2) capital. All units of labor are homogeneous. Capital is fixed in specific forms and is immobile for the short period; but over the long period it is mobile, can change its form, and can be reallocated from one use to others.[3]

Allocation of labor   Suppose that Area I and Area II initially constitute separate but identical short-period submarkets. The products produced in the two submarkets are the same; capital facilities are the same; and their labor demand curves, D_1D_1 and D_2D_2, as in Figure 16–1, are the same. However, labor supplies for the two areas differ. Area I has a larger labor supply than Area II; thus, the labor supply curve S_1S_1 of Area I lies farther to the right than S_2S_2 of Area II.

Labor is malallocated, and its maldistribution causes its value of marginal product and its price to differ between the two areas. The price of labor, or the wage rate, in Area I will be w_1, and in Area II it will be w_2. The level of employment in Area II is L_2, while that in Area I is higher at L_1. The higher ratio of labor to capital in Area I causes the marginal physical product and value of marginal product of labor to be lower in that area. The reverse holds in Area II. The ratio of labor to capital is smaller; consequently, the

---

[3] Capital is usually considered in two contexts: (1) as concrete agents of production and (2) as a fluid stock of productive capacity. The first context is a short-run concept, with capital taking such specific forms as buildings, machinery, wheatland, and so on. The second is a long-run concept. Concrete pieces of equipment have time to wear out and be replaced. But replacement of the same kind and in the same place does not necessarily occur. Replacement can be in the form of new and different kinds of concrete agents. In agriculture horse-drawn machinery was allowed to depreciate as the use of tractors became widespread and special machinery adapted to the tractor gradually came into use. Or capital may flow from one industry to another and from one location to another through depreciation in the one and the building of new equipment in the other. Thus, while capital may be almost completely immobile in the short run, in the long run it becomes quite mobile. *See* Frank H. Knight, *On the History and Method of Economics* (Chicago: University of Chicago Press, 1956), pp. 56–57.

Figure 16–1   Allocation of labor between submarkets

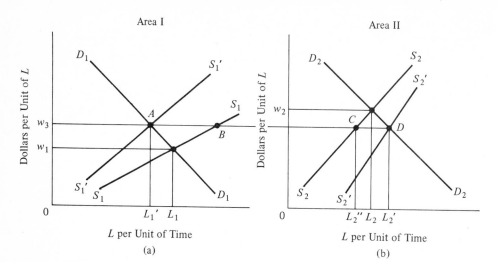

marginal physical product and value of marginal product of labor are higher.

The disparate submarket prices for labor furnish the incentive for long-period movement or reallocation of labor from Area I to Area II; and reallocation tends to eliminate the wage differential. As workers leave Area I, the short-period supply curve for that submarket shifts to the left. As they enter Area II, its short-period supply curve shifts to the right. As the ratio of labor to capital declines in Area I, labor's value of marginal product and the wage rate increase. In Area II the increasing ratio of labor to capital decreases labor's value of marginal product and the wage rate. Reallocation continues until wage rates of the two submarkets are equal at w_3. The labor supply curve of Area I is now $S_1'S_1'$, and that of Area II is $S_2'S_2'$.

The reallocation of labor between Areas I and II increases real net national product and welfare. Before the movement began, the value of marginal product of labor in Area I was w_1. In Area II it was substantially higher at w_2. The movement of a unit of labor from Area I to Area II causes a loss of w_1 dollars' worth of product in Area I and a gain of almost w_2 dollars' worth of product in Area II. This gain more than offsets the loss in Area I and creates a net increase in total value of product produced in the economy. Each transfer of a unit of labor from Area I to II brings about such a net increase until the values of marginal product and the wage rates of labor are the same in the two submarkets. Labor is then correctly allocated between the two areas—it is making its maximum contribution to welfare. No further transfer of labor in either direction can increase net national product; rather it will decrease it instead. Also, equalization of the wage rates will have removed the incentive for labor migration to occur.

Allocation of capital   The entire burden of adjustment will not be thrown on labor in the long period as the foregoing analysis suggests; it will be partly absorbed by reallocation of capital. The high ratio of labor to capital in Area I amounts to the same thing as a low ratio of capital to labor. Likewise, the low ratio of labor to capital in Area II means a high ratio of capital to labor. Therefore, we would expect the value of marginal product of capital in Area I to exceed that in Area II. Differing productivities of capital and returns on investment between the two areas furnish the incentive for capital to migrate from Area II to I.

Long-period capital migration affects the short-period labor demand curves and the wage rates of the two areas. As units of capital leave Area II, the demand curve (value of marginal product curve) for labor in that area shifts to the left, augmenting the decline in wage rates caused by the increasing labor supply. As units of capital enter Area I, the demand curve for labor in Area I increases. The increases in demand join the decreases in supply in raising the wage rates of Area I.

When the reverse migrations of labor and capital have been sufficient to equalize wage rates and the returns on investment between the two areas, both labor and capital will be correctly allocated. Further transfers of either resource in either direction will reduce the real net national product yielded by the two submarkets combined.

Conditions preventing correct allocation

A number of forces in the real world prevent the price system from allocating resources correctly. Even with the price system free to operate and with resource prices free to guide resource allocation, three important causes of incorrect allocation can be cited: (1) monopoly in product markets, (2) monopsony in resource markets, and (3) certain nonprice impediments to resource movements. Additionally, direct interference with the price mechanism by the government or by private groups of resource owners and resource purchasers constitutes a cause of incorrect allocation. We shall consider these causes in turn.

The term *monopoly* is used in a broad context to include pure monopoly, oligopoly, and monopolistic competition—all cases in which individual firms face downward-sloping product demand curves. Similarly, the term *monopsony* is used broadly. Complete monopsony in resource purchases precludes any reallocation whatsoever. With less than complete monopsony, units of a given resource may be free to move among a limited number of buyers, any one of which can influence market price of the resource.

Monopoly

Monopoly in product markets may not affect resource movements directly. Resources may be free to move among alternative employers even though the firms employing them enjoy a degree of product monopoly. Steel, common labor, certain raw materials, and other resources are employed by many firms and may be free to flow from one to another without regard to the types of product market in which individual firms sell. Where price discrepancies for any such resource exist within or among submarkets, long-period reallocation of the resource tends to occur to whatever extent necessary to eliminate the discrepancies. Every firm in every submarket tends to employ that quantity of the resource at which its marginal revenue product equals its marginal resource cost. Reallocation tends to occur until the price of the resource is the same in all its alternative employments.

When some degree of product monopoly exists, real net national product and welfare would not be maximized even if all resources were so allocated that the marginal revenue product of each is the same in all its alternative employments. Individual firms face downward-sloping product demand curves. For each firm marginal revenue is less than product price. Thus, for any given resource, value of marginal product in each of its uses would exceed marginal revenue product. But discrepancies would occur among the values of marginal products of the resource in its various uses even though its marginal revenue product were the same in all of them. This will be the case because of the differing demand elasticities of the various products that the resource aids in producing. Differing demand elasticities mean that product prices and corresponding marginal revenues are not proportional to each other among the different products. Hence, values of marginal products of the resource in its various uses are not proportional to its marginal revenue products. When the latter are equal, the former will be unequal. Inequalities among values of marginal product of a resource in its various uses show that net national product could be increased by transferring units of the resource from lower value of marginal product uses to higher value of marginal product uses.

It is *value of marginal product* of a resource that measures the contribution of a unit of it to the value of the economy's output—its marginal physical product multiplied by the price of the final product. *Marginal revenue product* shows the contribution that a unit of the resource makes to the total receipts of a single firm; but where monopoly exists, this is less than the value of the product added to the economy's output by the resource unit. Thus, when a resource is so allocated that its price is equalized in all alternative uses, the price system has done its job. Even though further reallocation from lower value of marginal product uses to higher value of marginal product uses will increase net national product, there is no automatic motivation to make it occur.

Suppose that machinists in Detroit work both for firms selling as oligopolists and those selling as pure competitors. An automobile manufacturer furnishes an example of the former type of firm, whereas any one of many small independent machine shops is an example of the latter. Suppose that an equilibrium allocation of machinists exists—they are paid $8 per hour in all alternative employments. The small machine shop hires that quantity at which the value of marginal product of machinists is $8 per hour. The automobile manufacturer hires that quantity at which marginal revenue product equals $8 per hour. Since the automobile manufacturer faces a downward-sloping product demand curve, value of marginal product of machinists employed by the firm exceeds their marginal revenue product. Value of marginal product may thus be $12 per hour. Society would gain in terms of net national product if some machinists would transfer from the small independent machine shops to automobile manufacturers. However, since both pay $8 per hour, the price system will not motivate the transfers.

In addition, partially or completely blocked entry into monopolistic industries may prevent other resources from being so allocated that their respective marginal revenue products and prices are equalized within and among submarkets. We can think of such resources as being inseparable from the existence of individual firms—they are short-run "fixed" resources. They can enter industries only in the form of plant for new firms. The existence of long-run profits for the firms in an industry indicates that the marginal revenue products of such resources are greater in that industry than they are elsewhere in the economy.

Monopsony

The existence of monopsony in resource purchases may also prevent the price system from allocating resources correctly. Where some degree of monopsony is present, an individual firm purchases that quantity of a resource at which its marginal revenue product equals its marginal resource cost. When the resource supply curve to the firm slopes upward to the right, marginal resource cost exceeds the price that the firm pays the resource. When equilibrium in the purchase of the resource is reached on the part of any single firm, the price paid the resource is below its marginal revenue product.

Differential prices of the resource guide its allocation among the few firms using it, just as they did in the previous analysis. Voluntary reallocation of the resource will cease when its price is the same in its alternative uses. Resource owners will have no incentive to transfer units of it from one employment to another, and an equilibrium allocation will have been achieved.

Even though an equilibrium allocation may be achieved and all firms may be paying the same price for the resource, it will not be making its maximum contribution to net national product. To the extent that the supply curves of the resource facing different firms having differing elasticities, marginal resource costs and marginal revenue products of the resource among different firms will not be equal. Some degree of monopoly in product markets will create further distortions in the pattern of values of marginal products. Hence, there is no reason for believing that the values of marginal products of the resource will be the same among its alternative employments even though it is everywhere paid the same price. About the most that we can say on this point is that resource transfers from lower value of marginal product uses to higher value of marginal product uses would increase real net national product. However, since the resource price is the same in its alternative employments, resource owners will not make such transfers voluntarily.

Nonprice impediments

Ignorance   Lack of knowledge on the part of resource owners may prevent resources from moving from lower-paying to higher-paying uses. In the most obvious case resource owners may lack information concerning the price patterns of the resources over the economy as a whole. Bricklayers may not be aware of the areas and firms paying the highest wages for bricklayers. Farmers may sell products in some areas at unnecessarily low prices when they are not aware of the higher prices that can be obtained elsewhere. Investors make mistakes when they lack knowledge of alternative investment opportunities throughout the economy.[4]

Lack of knowledge may also prevent potential resources from being channeled into the resource supply categories in which they will contribute most to net national product. Various kinds of labor resources illustrate the point. For what trade or profession should potential entrants to the labor force be trained? Do those responsible for influencing or selecting the vocation possess full knowledge of the future returns to be derived from alternative vocations? Usually they do not. Children may follow parents as sharecroppers or machine operators, when alternative occupations would be more lucrative. Or, where children do not follow parents' occupations, the information on which decisions are made is often sketchy. Frequently the potential entrant and his or her advisers do not discover until the training pro-

---

[4] The classic examples here are the many single proprietorships that fail in such fields as neighborhood grocery stores, eating and drinking establishments, and filling stations.

gram is well advanced or completed that the choice of occupation has been an unfortunate one economically—and at this point it may be too late to change.

Sociological and psychological impediments Sociological and psychological factors may throw blocks in the way of the allocation of resources that will maximize net national product.[5] They include those ties to particular communities, to friends, and to the family that restrict mobility regardless of the monetary incentives to move. Or, the virtues of a particular occupation, community, or way of living may be so extolled by various social groups that mobility is restricted. Glorification of the family farm, or of southern California, or of the teaching profession may be cases in point.

Institutional factors Various institutional barriers to reallocation of resources are evident in the economy. In the industrial world workers accumulate certain rights with particular firms. These include pension and seniority rights. In some cases labor unions may restrict entry directly into particular occupations. Patent rights held by one firm or a group of firms in an industry may block the entry of new firms into the industry and thus condemn quantities of certain resources to other occupations in which their values of marginal products and rates of pay are lower. The list can be extended considerably, but these cases illustrate the point.

Price fixing

Sometimes the price mechanism is not allowed to perform its function of signaling the spots where quantities of certain resources should be transferred in or out. Some resource prices are fixed or controlled by the government. Control may be exercised through such devices as minimum wage legislation, agricultural price supports, or the general price and wage controls that many advocate during inflation. Some resource prices may be partially or completely controlled by organized private groups of resource owners and resource purchasers. Some labor unions fall within this category, as do certain farm-marketing cooperatives and some employer associations. Three hypothetical examples will illustrate some of the effects of controlled resource prices on the equilibrium allocation of resources and on net national product. We shall assume that, in the absence of control, pure competition would exist; however, even if some degree of monopoly in product markets were to exist, the results would be approximately the same.

---

[5] We are not saying that such blocks constitute mistakes on the part of society. The "good life" is not necessarily achieved through maximization of net national product. It may be desirable to sacrifice some product, if necessary, for the achievement of other objectives or values.

Two submarkets for a given resource are shown in Figure 16–2. As a matter of convenience we shall call the resource labor. The two submarkets are alike except for the initial distribution of labor. They produce the same products and have identical supplies of capital. The demand curves for

Figure 16–2   The impact of minimum resource prices on labor allocation

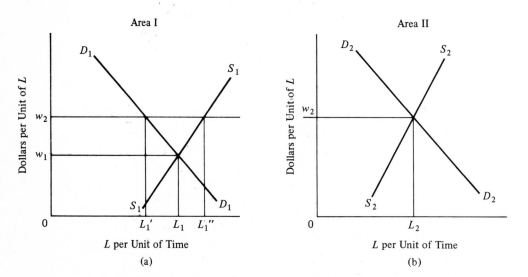

labor are the same for each submarket. Since Area I has a greater labor supply than Area II, the short-period price of labor will be lower in Area I and the employment level will be higher. We shall consider three possible cases.

Case I   Assume that the workers of Area II are organized and that those of Area I are not. The initial labor demand and labor supply situations are shown in Figure 16–2. The equilibrium wage rate and employment level in Area I are w_1 and L_1, respectively. In Area II they are w_2 and L_2, respectively. Assume further that organized workers, through collective bargaining, succeed in placing a floor of rate w_2 under Area II wage rates. The immediate or short-period effects of the minimum wage rate of w_2 in Area II will be nil. Since w_2 is initially the equilibrium wage rate in Area II, the union should have little difficulty in obtaining it. At that wage rate employers of Area II are willing to employ as much labor as is willing to go to work. The wage differential between the two areas continues to reflect the existence of the initial maldistribution of labor.

The effects of the minimum wage rate set in Area II are felt in the long period. The wage differential creates an incentive for workers to migrate from Area I to Area II. However, if additional workers were hired in Area II, the ratio of labor to capital would increase, the marginal physical product of labor would decrease, and the value of marginal product of labor would decrease. Since the wage rate of such additional workers would be w_2 and since this rate would exceed their values of marginal product, they would not be hired. Any workers migrating from Area I to Area II would find themselves unemployed, and this prospect would keep migration from occurring. Employment in Area I at the lower wage rate of w_1 would be preferable to no employment at all in Area II, regardless of how high wage rates are. Labor would remain poorly allocated between the two areas, and welfare would be permanently below its optimum level.

This situation sets the stage for interesting repercussions with regard to capital. An incentive for capital to migrate in the long period will be present in this case, also. In fact, capital migration is the only adjustment in resource allocation that can occur. As capital migrates from Area II to Area I, demand for labor will decrease in Area II and will increase in Area I. This demand change will increase wage rates and employment in Area I. However, unemployment will develop among the organized workers of Area II, and welfare will still be below its maximum potential level.[6]

Case II   Assume that the organized workers of Area II succeed in extending their organization to Area I. Once Area I is organized, assume that workers in both places can bring wage rates in Area I up to w_2 (Figure 16–2). Immediate short-period effects occur. There will be no initial effect on the employment level in Area II. In Area I unemployment amounting to $L_1'L_1''$ will occur. In Area I at the old wage level of w_1, employment level L_1 equates value of marginal product of labor to the wage rate. The minimum wage rate of w_2 makes the wage rate greater than the value of marginal product of labor at the old employment level of L_1. Employers find that a reduction in employment will decrease their total receipts by less than it reduces their total costs; hence, workers are laid off. The decreasing ratio of labor to capital increases the value of marginal product of labor until, when only L_1' workers are employed, their value of marginal product is again equal to the wage rate. Here the layoffs will stop.

The long-period effects of the minimum wage rate of w_2 will be approximately the same as the immediate effects. Since the wage differential is eliminated, there is no incentive for employed workers of Area I to migrate to Area II. Employers of Area II will not find it profitable to employ more

[6] The women's full-fashioned hosiery industry furnishes an excellent example of the migration of capital from high-cost union areas to low-cost nonunion areas. *See* Sumner H. Slichter, *Union Policies and Industrial Management* (Washington, D.C.: The Brookings Institution, 1941), pp. 353–360.

workers than L_2 at a wage rate of w_2; hence, unemployed workers of Area I will not find migration to Area II of any benefit.

With regard to capital, the minimum wage rate of w_2 in Area I and the reduced ratio of labor to capital (increased ratio of capital to labor) eliminate the incentive for capital to migrate to Area I in the long period. The ratio of capital to labor in Area I is increased sufficiently by the worker layoffs to make the value of marginal product of capital in Area I equal to that in Area II.[7] Thus, the minimum wage rate of w_2 extended to both areas prevents the effects of the initial malallocation of resources from being alleviated by either labor or capital migration; and, in addition, it creates unemployment.

Case III   A third possibility, in which controlled resource prices may not affect resource allocation adversely, deserves some consideration. Assume that both areas are organized or, alternatively, that the government sets a minimum wage rate applicable to both. The wage rate is set through collective bargaining or by the government at level w_3, as is shown in Figure 16–3—that is, at precisely the level that would prevail in free markets in the long period after workers had had sufficient time to migrate. The initial demand and supply relationships are D_1D_1 and S_1S_1, respectively, in Area I. In Area II they are D_2D_2 and S_2S_2, respectively. In Area I the minimum wage rate of w_3 will cause unemployment equal to AB. In Area II a labor shortage equal to CD will occur at wage rate w_3, and the wage rate in that submarket will rise to w_2.

Unemployment will assist the price system in reallocating labor from Area I to Area II in the long period. The unemployed and the lower-paid workers of Area I will seek the higher-paying jobs of Area II. The supply curve for labor in Area I will shift leftward to $S_1'S_1'$ and that of Area II will shift rightward to $S_2'S_2'$. Labor will be reallocated so that its value of marginal product is equalized between the two submarkets and so that labor is making its maximum contribution to net national product.

Again, some migration of capital from Area II to Area I may occur in the long period. At wage rate w_3 the initial employment level is L_1' in Area I and is greater than the initial employment level of L_2 in Area II. Therefore, the ratio of capital to labor is smaller, and the marginal revenue product of capital is greater, in Area I than in Area II. Capital migration will reduce the demand for labor in Area II and will increase the demand for labor in Area I, thus reducing the amount of labor migration necessary to secure full employment and maximum net national product.

---

[7] Since the initial capital facilities and products produced in the two areas were assumed to be the same, the labor demand curves are also the same. At wage rate w_2 each market employs the same quantity of labor; that is, L_1' units of labor equals L_2 units of labor in Figure 16–2. Consequently, ratios of labor to capital in the two areas, when the wage rate for both is w_2, will be the same; and the value of marginal product of capital will also be the same.

Figure 16–3   Job opportunities as incentives for labor migration

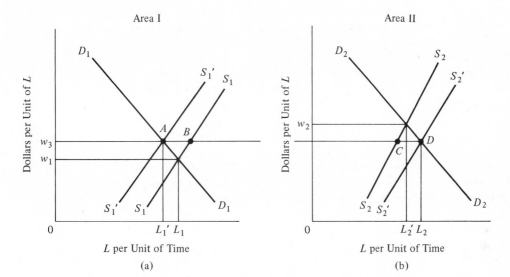

Summary

Any given resource is "correctly" allocated—makes its maximum contribution to economic welfare—when its value of marginal product is the same in all of its alternative uses. In a private enterprise economic system resource prices serve the function of directing the allocation of resources.

Only under pure competition in product markets and resource markets will resources automatically be allocated so that maximum real net national product or welfare will tend to be realized. Under pure competition a malallocation of any given resource causes its values of marginal products in different employments to differ from each other. Consequently, employers for whom its value of marginal product is higher bid resources away from those for whom its value of marginal product is lower. Transfers of resource units from lower to higher value of marginal product uses increase the contributions of the resource to welfare. Its maximum contribution occurs when value of marginal product of the resource is the same in all its possible uses. Price of the resource will also be the same in all its alternative uses; therefore, no incentive will exist for further transfers to be made.

With some degree of monopoly in product markets, a resource will be reallocated among its alternative uses until its price is the same in all of them. However, where employers are monopolists in some degree, they employ those quantities of the resource at which its marginal revenue product equals its price. Marginal revenue products of the resource will be the same in alternative employments. Differing product demand elasticities cause values of marginal products of the resource to differ in alternative employments. Thus, the resource does not make its maximum contribution to net national product.

Where employers have some degree of monopsony, but there is no resource differentiation, a resource will again be reallocated until its price is the same in alternative employments. But a monopsonist employs the resource up to the point at which marginal revenue product equals marginal resource cost. Different monopsonists may face resource supply curves of differing elasticities; and, if so, marginal resource cost will be different for each even though all pay the same price per unit for the resource. With equilibrium allocation of the resource achieved, marginal revenue products differ. The usual case will be that differences in values of marginal product also occur, and the resource will not be making its maximum contribution to net national product.

Nonprice impediments to correct allocation of resources include ignorance, sociological and psychological factors, and institutional restrictions. In some instances the achievement of noneconomic values may be of more importance to society than correct resource allocation.

Direct interferences with the price mechanism by the government and by private groups may prevent resources from being correctly allocated in some cases. In other cases they may not lead to adverse effects.

Suggested readings

Clark, John Bates, *The Distribution of Wealth*. New York: The Macmillan Company, 1923. Chap. XIX.

Pigou, A. C., *The Economics of Welfare*, 4th ed. London: Macmillan & Co., Ltd., 1932. Pt. III, Chap. IX.

Rees, Albert, *The Economics of Work and Pay*. New York: Harper & Row, Publishers, 1973. Pt. III.

Questions and exercises

1. Suppose that coal miners in Kentucky are initially unorganized and that an equilibrium wage rate w_1 prevails. Then suppose that a union is formed and succeeds in organizing approximately one-half of the miners. The rest of the miners are unorganized. The union succeeds in raising wage rates in unionized mines to w_2. Explain the effects on
   a. resource allocation
   b. national income.

2. Much of the nation's crude oil is produced in Louisiana, Texas, and Oklahoma. In an uncontrolled market the price per barrel of crude oil to

buyers in New York is typically greater than it is in one of the producing states—for example, Oklahoma.

    a. What explanation can you offer for the difference?

    b. Does the price difference (to users) mean that crude oil is misallocated? Why or why not?

    c. What would be the effect on the allocation of crude oil if a ceiling price equal to the initial Oklahoma market price is placed on the resource?

3. One of the traditional objectives of labor unions is to obtain "equal pay for equal work" for their members. Suppose that all carpenters belong to the Carpenters' Union and that initially this objective has been attained. Consider that initially at the union wage scale equilibrium exists in the market for carpenters in both Oldtown and Newcity. Over time Newcity grows and expands, while Oldtown deteriorates. What mechanism exists for reallocating carpenters.

    a. if the union wage scale is strictly maintained?

    b. if the union loses members and the wage scale is no longer enforced?

Chapter 17

Chapter contents

Key concepts

Individual income determination

Personal distribution of income — Distribution among spending units
Income equality and income differences

Causes of income differences — **Differences in labor resources owned**
Horizontal differences in labor resources
Vertical differences in labor resources

Differences in capital resources owned
Material inhertiance
Fortuitous circumstances
Propensities to accumulate

Price manipulations
Administered prices: pure competition
Supply restrictions: pure competition
Administered prices: monpoly
Administered prices: monopsony
Price increases accompanying demand increases

Movements toward less inequality — **Resource redistribution**
Labor resources
Capital resources

Administered prices
The negative income tax
Income redistribution and the price system

Summary — **Suggested readings**
Questions and exercises

Marginal productivity theory
Marginal revenue product
Value of marginal product
Marginal resource cost
Personal distribution of income
Lorenz curve
Functional distribution of income
Horizontal differences in labor resources
Vertical differences in labor resources
Administered prices
Negative income tax

Distribution of income and product

Of the four functions of an economic system with which we are concerned, we have yet to consider the distribution of the economy's product or income. Income distribution among the families and individuals of economic systems has been an age-old source of unrest and concern. A promise always extended by socialist economic systems is that they will improve the distribution of income. In recent years the governments of most private enterprise countries have been promising the same thing. In this chapter we examine the way in which a private enterprise system distributes income, the possibilities of redistribution, and the welfare implications of both.

Individual income determination

The principles of individual income determination and of income distribution in a private enterprise economic system are called *the marginal productivity theory*. These principles were set out in previous chapters; in this one we shall draw together and summarize them.

The principles of income determination where pure competition prevails, both in product markets and resource markets, were developed in Chapter 14. The owner of a given resource is paid a price per unit for the units employed equal to the marginal revenue product and the value of marginal product of the resource. The price of the resource is not determined by any single employer or by any single resource owner. It is determined by the interactions of all buyers and all sellers in the market for the resource.

If for some reason the price of a resource should be less than its marginal revenue product, a shortage will occur. Employers want more of it at that price than resource owners are willing to place on the market. Employers, bidding against each other for the available supply, will drive the price up until the shortage disappears and each is hiring (or buying) that quantity of the resource at which its marginal revenue product equals its price.

A price high enough to create a surplus of the resource will set forces in motion to eliminate the surplus. Employers take only those quantities sufficient to equate its marginal revenue product to its price. Resource owners undercut each other's prices to secure employment for their unemployed units. As price drops, employment expands. The undercutting continues until employers are willing to take the quantities that resource owners want to place on the market.

Where some degree of monopoly[1] exists in product markets, the determination of the equilibrium price of the resource occurs in the same way. Like the purely competitive firm, the monopolistic firm employs those quantities of the resource at which its marginal revenue product is equal to its price. However, the price per unit received by owners of the resource is less than its value of marginal product, and the resource is exploited monopolistically.

Some degree of monopsony in the purchase of a given resource will cause it to be paid still less than its marginal revenue product. The monopsonist, faced with a resource supply curve sloping upward to the right, employs that quantity of the resource at which its marginal revenue product is equal to its marginal resource cost. Marginal resource cost is greater than the price paid for the resource. Monopsonistic exploitation of the resource occurs to the extent that its marginal revenue product exceeds its price. If the resource purchaser is also a monopolist, marginal revenue product of the resource will in turn be less than its value of marginal product, and the resource will be exploited monopolistically as well as monopsonistically.

As we noted in Chapter 2, an individual's income per unit of time is the sum of the amounts earned per unit of time from the employment of the various resources which the person owns. If a single kind of resource is owned, the income will be equal to the number of units placed in employment multiplied by the price per unit which the individual receives. If the individual owns several kinds of resources, the income from each one can be computed in the same manner, and then all can be totaled to determine that person's entire income.

Personal distribution of income

The personal distribution of income refers to income distribution among spending units of the economy. We shall survey the distribution of income by size and then point up certain problems involved in discussing income differences and equality.

---

[1] Again, we use the term to refer to all cases in which the firm faces a downward-sloping product demand curve. They include cases of pure monopoly, oligopoly, and monopolistic competition.

Distribution among spending units

Some idea of the distribution of income in the United States is provided by Table 17–1. It is worth noting that 70 percent of the families had incomes of $10,000 or more per year in 1976. Note also that 10.4 percent of families fell

Table 17–1   Distribution of total money income in the United States before taxes, 1976

Total Money Income	Families		Unrelated Individuals	
	Number (Thousands)	Percent	Number (Thousands)	Percent
Under $5,000	5,842	10.4	10,146	47.2
$ 5,000 to $ 9,999	11,124	19.6	6,025	28.1
$10,000 to $14,999	11,481	20.2	3,109	19.5
$15,000 to $19,999	10,826	19.1	1,275	6.1
$20,000 to $24,999	7,326	12.9	459	2.1
$25,000 to $49,999	9,013	15.9	374	1.7
$50,000 and over	1,098	1.9	71	1.3
Total	$56,710	100.0	$21,459	100.0
Median Income	$14,958 (Families)		$ 5,375 (Individuals)	

Source   U.S. Department of Commerce, Bureau of the Census, *Consumer Income*, Series P–60, No. 107 (September 1977), p. 2.

below the $5,000 per year level. Among unrelated individuals—persons 14 years of age or over who are not living with any relatives—almost half had incomes under $5,000 per year. Using the poverty thresholds defined by the federal government for 1976—$5,815 for an urban family of four, with appropriate adjustments for other sizes of households—some 25 million persons lived in poverty in 1976. These constitute about 12 percent of the total population of the United States. Median family income was $14,958. The median income for unattached individuals was $5,515.

Income equality and income differences

Inequality in the distribution of income among households is of great concern to many people. The device usually used to indicate the extent of inequality is the Lorenz curve of Figure 17–1, in which we measure the percent of the total number of families and unattached individuals on the horizontal axis and the percent of total family and unattached individuals' income on the vertical axis. If income were equally distributed among families, the relation between the percent of families and the percent of income would form the straight diagonal line 0A—20 percent of the families would have 20 percent of the income; 50 percent of the families would have 50 percent of the income, and so on. But the actual distribution of income is

Figure 17—1   Inequality in the before-tax distribution of income, 1976

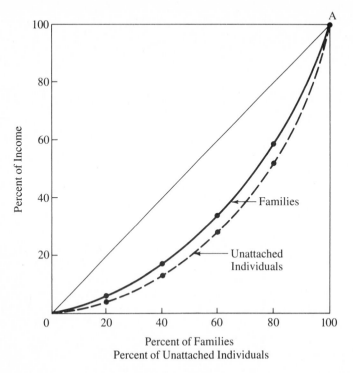

Source   U.S. Department of Commerce, Bureau of the Census, *Consumer Income*, Series P-60, No. 107 (September 1977), p. 11.

not an equal distribution. The actual distribution of family income is shown by the solid curved line. Note that the lower 20 percent of families received only 5.4 percent of total income and that the lower 60 percent of families received only 34.8 percent of total income. The extent to which the actual income distribution deviates from a perfectly equal distribution is reflected by the curvature of the Lorenz curve. The dotted line show the distribution of the total income of unattached individuals among those individuals. Note that unattached individual income was even more unequally distributed than was family income.

Even if the Lorenz curves show perfect equality in the distribution of income, there is no assurance that all spending units are treated equally by the economic system. Different unattached individuals vary in many ways. There are differences in ages, regional locations, cultural tastes, and the like. Therefore, equality of money income among them may lead to very different levels of fulfillment or of economic well-being. When we consider family spending units, the differences in family sizes and age distributions further compound the problem of lack of homogeneity among spending units.

The difficulties encountered in trying to define and measure income equality or income differences will not be of major importance for our purposes. We are interested in the causes of differences rather than in their ethical implications. We shall have occasion to refer to "movements toward greater equality," but this statement should be accepted for what it is—a loose statement meaning some mitigation of income differences among heterogeneous spending units. It means some lopping off of incomes at the top and some augmenting of incomes at the bottom. It does not mean that we can state with any precision the point at which income distribution is "equalized."

Causes of income differences

With reference to the determinants of individual[2] incomes, it becomes clear that differences in incomes arise from two basic sources: (1) differences in the kinds and quantities of resources owned by different individuals and (2) differences in prices paid in different employments for units of any given resource. The former are the more fundamental; the latter arise from various types of interference with the price system in the performance of its functions and from any resource immobility that may occur.

It will be convenient to discuss labor and capital resources separately. To enable us to see the importance of each in perspective, it is worthwhile to note the *functional distribution* of income in the United States; that is, distribution according to the resource classes into which resources are divided. In Table 17–2 compensation of employees represents income received by the owners of labor resources for the listed years, while corporate profits, interest, and rental income represent income received by capital owners. All are understated substantially because proprietors' income includes income both from labor and from capital. Since accounting records for such enterprises often do not differentiate between returns to labor and returns to capital, we cannot split this item into categories labeled capital and labor. We can guess roughly that labor resources account for 80 percent of national income and that capital resources account for some 20 percent.

In this section we shall first consider differences in the kinds and quantities of labor resources owned by different individuals. Next, differences in capital resources owned will be discussed. Finally, we shall examine the

---

[2] The term *individual* will be used throughout the rest of the chapter to refer to a spending unit, regardless of its size or composition.

Table 17-2   National income by type of income: 1939-1977

Type of Income	1939 Income (Billions of Dollars)	1939 Percent of Income	1949 Income (Billions of Dollars)	1949 Percent of Income	1959 Income (Billions of Dollars)	1959 Percent of Income	1969 Income (Billions of Dollars)	1969 Percent of Income	1977* Income (Billions of Dollars)	1977* Percent of Income
Compensation of Employees	48.1	66.3	140.8	64.7	278.5	69.6	565.5	72.8	1,155.8	76.0
Business and Professional Proprietors' Income	7.3	10.0	22.7	10.4	35.1	8.8	50.3	6.5	78.4	5.2
Farm Proprietors' Income	4.3	5.9	12.9	5.9	11.4	2.8	16.8	2.0	19.5	1.3
Rental Income	2.7	3.7	8.3	3.8	11.9	3.0	22.6	2.9	25.3	1.7
Net Interest	4.6	6.3	4.8	2.2	16.4	4.1	29.9	3.8	100.9	6.6
Corporate Profits	5.7	7.9	28.2	13.0	47.2	11.8	78.6	12.0	140.3	9.2
Total	72.8	100.0	217.7	100.0	400.5	100.0	763.7	100.0	1,520.2	100.0

* Provisional.
Sources   *Economic Report of the President* (Washington, D.C.: Government Printing Office, 1965), p. 203.
U.S. Department of Commerce, *Survey of Current Business* (May 1975), p. S-2, and (January 1978), p. 10.

effects on income distribution of certain manipulations of the price mechanism.

Differences in labor resources owned

The labor classification of resources is composed of many different kinds and qualities of labor. These have one common characteristic—they are human. Any single kind of labor is a combination or complex of both inherited and acquired characteristics. The acquired part of a worker's labor power is generally referred to as human capital. We shall make no attempt to separate inherited from acquired characteristics.

Labor can be subclassified horizontally and vertically into many, largely separate, resource groups. Vertical subclassification involves grading workers according to skill levels from the lowest kind of undifferentiated manual labor to the highest professional levels. Horizontal subclassification divides workers of a certain skill level into the various occupations requiring that particular degree of skill. An example would be the division of skilled construction workers into groups—carpenters, bricklayers, plumbers, and the like. Vertical mobility of labor refers to the possibility of moving upward through vertical skill levels. Horizontal mobility means the ability to move sideways among groups at a particular skill level.

Horizontal differences in labor resources   At any specific horizontal level individuals may receive different incomes because of differences in the demand and supply conditions for the kinds of labor that they own. A large demand for a certain kind of labor relative to the supply of it available will make its marginal revenue product and its price high. On the same skill level a small demand for another kind of labor relative to the supply available will make its marginal revenue product and its price low. The differences in prices tend to cause differences in income for owners of the kinds of labor concerned.

Suppose, for example, that bricklayers and carpenters initially earn approximately equal incomes. A shift in consumers' tastes occurs from wood to brick construction in residential units. The incomes of bricklayers will increase, while those of carpenters will decrease because of the altered conditions of demand. Over a long period of time horizontal mobility between the two groups tends to decrease the income differences thus arising, and welfare will be increased in the process.

Quantitative differences in the amount of work performed by individuals owning the same kind of labor resource may lead to income differences. Some occupations afford considerable leeway for individual choice of the number of hours to be worked per week or month. Examples include independent professionals, such as physicians, lawyers, and certified public accountants, along with independent proprietors, such as farmers, plumbing contractors, and garage owners. In other occupations hours of work are beyond the control of the individual. Yet in different employments of the same resource, differences in age, physical endurance, institutional restrictions, customs, and so on can lead to differences in hours worked and to income differences among owners of the resource.

Within a particular labor resource group, qualitative differences or differences in the abilities of the owners of the resource often create income differences. Wide variations occur in the public's evaluation of different dentists or physicians or lawyers or automobile mechanics. Consequently, within any one group variations in prices paid for services and variations in the quantities of services sold to the public will lead to income differences. Usually a correlation exists between the ages of the members of a resource group and their incomes. Quality tends to improve with accumulated experience up to a point. Data reported by Milton Friedman and Simon Kuznets suggest, for example, that the incomes of physicians tend to be highest between the tenth and twenty-fifth years of practice and that the incomes of lawyers tend to be highest between the twentieth and thirty-fifth years of practice.[3]

Vertical differences in labor resources   The different vertical strata themselves represent differences in labor resources owned and give rise to major labor income differences. Entry into high-level occupations, such as the professions or the ranks of business executives, is much more difficult than is entry into manual occupations. The relative scarcity of labor at top levels results from two basic factors: (1) individuals with the physical and mental characteristics necessary for the performance of high-level work are limited in number; (2) given the necessary physical and mental characteristics, many lack either the opportunities for training or the necessary social and cultural environment for movement into high-level positions. Thus, impediments to vertical mobility keep resource supplies low relative to demands for them at the top levels, and it keeps resource supplies abundant relative to demands for them at the low levels.

Differences in labor resources owned because of differences in innate physical and mental characteristics of individuals are accidents of birth. The individual has nothing to do with choosing them. Nevertheless, they account partly for restricted vertical mobility and for income differences. The opportunities for moving toward top positions and relatively large incomes are considerably enhanced by the inheritance of a strong physical constitution and a superior intellect; however, these by no means insure that individuals so endowed will make the most of their opportunities.

---

[3] Milton Friedman and Simon Kuznets, *Income from Independent Professional Practice* (New York: National Bureau of Economic Research, 1945), pp. 237–260.

Opportunities for training are more widely available to individuals born into wealthy families than to those born into families in lower-income groups. Some of the higher-paying professions require long and expensive university traning programs that are often beyond the reach of the latter groups. The medical profession is a case in point. However, we often see individuals who have had the initial ability, drive, and determination necessary to overcome economic obstacles thrown in the way of vertical mobility.

Differences in social inheritance constitute another cause of differences in labor resources owned. These are closely correlated with differences in material inheritance. Frequently, individuals born ''on the wrong side of the tracks'' face family and community attitudes that sharply curtail their opportunities and their desires for vertical mobility. Others, more fortunately situated, acquire the training necessary to be highly productive and to obtain large incomes because it is expected of them by the social group in which they move. The social position alone, apart from the training induced by it, may be quite effective in facilitating vertical mobility.

When vertical mobility would otherwise occur but is blocked, income differences persist and welfare is below its potential maximum. If those who are denied access to higher value of marginal product jobs and occupations were able to attain these, the result would be higher real net national product as well as greater equality in income distribution.

Differences in capital resources owned

In addition to inequalities in labor incomes, large differences occur in individual incomes from disparities in capital ownership. Different individuals own varying quantities of capital, such as corporation or other business assets, farmland, oil wells, or other property. We shall examine the fundamental causes of inequalities in capital holdings.

Material inheritance   Differences in the amounts of capital inherited or received as gifts by different individuals create disparities in incomes. The institution of private property on which private enterprise rests usually is coupled with inheritance laws allowing holdings of accumulated property rights to be passed from generation to generation. The individual fortunate enough to have a wealthy parent inherits large capital holdings; that person's resources contribute much to the productive process; and the individual is rewarded accordingly. The child of a southern sharecropper—who may be of equal innate intelligence with the child of a wealthy parent but inherits no capital—contributes less to the productive process and receives a correspondingly lower income.

Fortuitous circumstances   Chance, luck, or other fortuitous circumstances beyond the control of individuals constitute a further cause of differences in capital holdings. The discovery of oil, uranium, or gold on an otherwise undistinguished piece of land brings about a large appreciation in its value or its ability to yield income to its owner. Unforeseen shifts in consumer demand increase the values of certain capital holdings while decreasing the values of others. National emergencies, such as war, lead to changes in valuations of particular kinds of property and, hence, to differential incomes from capital. Fortuitous circumstances can work in reverse also, but, even so, their effects operate to creat differences in the ownership of capital.

Propensities to accumulate   Differing psychological propensities to accumulate and differing abilities to accumulate lead to differences in capital ownership among individuals. On the psychological side a number of factors influence the will to accumulate. Stories circulate of individuals determined to make a fortune before they reach middle age. Accumulation sometimes occurs for purposes of security and luxury in later life. It sometimes stems from the desire to make one's children secure. The power and the prestige accompanying wealth provide the motivating force in some cases. To others, accumulation and manipulation of capital holdings is a gigantic game—the activity involved fascinates them. Whatever the motives, some individuals have such propensities and others do not. In some instances the will to accumulate may be negative, and the opposite of accumulation occurs.

The ability of an individual to accumulate depends largely on the original holdings of both labor and capital resources. The higher the original income, the easier saving and accumulation tend to be. The individual possessing much in the way of labor resources initially is likely to accumulate capital with his or her income from labor; investments are made in stocks and bonds, real estate, a cattle ranch, or other property. Or the individual possessing substantial quantities of capital initially—and the ability to manage it—receives an income sufficient to allow saving and investment in additional capital. In the process of accumulation, labor and capital resources of an individual augment each other in providing the income from which further accumulation can be accomplished.

Price manipulations

Various groups of resource owners throughout the economy, dissatisfied with their current shares of national income, seek to modify income distribution through manipulation or fixing of the prices of resources that they own or the prices of products that they produce and sell. Groups of farmers—wheat, cotton, dairy, and others—have been able to obtain government-enforced minimum prices for the products that they sell. Groups of retailers have been able to secure state laws forbidding product-selling prices below a fixed percentage of markup over cost. Labor organizations seek to increase, or in some cases to maintain, their shares of national income by fixing wages through the collective bargaining process. People throughout the economy, concerned with the small distributive shares of low-paid workers, support minimum wage legislation. We shall examine typical cases of administered prices[4] in an attempt to assess their effects on income distribution.

Administered prices: pure competition   Suppose that owners of a given resource, dissatisfied with their shares of national income, seek and obtain an administered price above the equilibrium level for their resource. Will the incomes of the resource owners involved increase relative to the incomes of the owners of other resources? In other words, will the owners of the given resource receive a larger share of the economy's product? Equally important, what will happen to the share of total earnings of the resource received by each of its owners? What will be the effects on the efficiency of the economy's operation or on welfare?

If demand for the given resource remains constant,[5] the effect of the administered price on total income earned by the resource will depend on the elasticity of demand. If elasticity is less than one, total income will increase and owners of the resource as a group will have increased their distributive share. If elasticity equals one, no change in total income will occur. If elasticity is greater than one, total income and the distributive share of owners of the resource as a group will decline.

Reference to Figure 17–2 will help to answer the second problem—the effects of the administered price on the distribution among the owners of the resource of the total income earned by it. The demand curve and supply curve in the figure for resource A are DD and SS, respectively. The equilibrium price is p_a, and the level of employment is quantity A.

Suppose that an administered price of p_{a1} is set for the resource—none can be sold for less. Whether the administered price is set by the government, through bargaining between organized groups of buyers and sellers,

[4] *Administered prices* are prices fixed by law, by groups of sellers, by groups of buyers, or by collective action of buyers and sellers. They are the antithesis of free-market prices established by free interactions of buyers and sellers in the marketplaces.

[5] There seems to be no valid reason for assuming that a change in the price of the resource will change the demand for it, especially if the resource concerned constitutes a small proportion of the economy's total supplies of resources—and such is usually the case for any given resource. Even if the administered price raises the total income of the resource owners involved, it seems unlikely that demand for the products that the resource assists in producing will be increased to any significant degree. In a stationary economy, particularly, it seems logical to assume independence between resource price changes and consequent changes in demand for the resource.

Figure 17–2   Effects of administered prices on income distribution

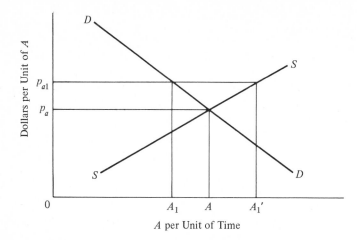

or through unilateral action on the part of either resource buyers or resource sellers is of no consequence. The effects will be the same. Confronted by the higher price, each firm using resource A finds that if it
employs the same quantity as before, marginal revenue product for the
resource will be less than its price. Consequently, each firm finds that
reductions in the quantity of the resource used will reduce total receipts less
than they decrease total costs and will increase the firm's profits. When all
firms have reduced employment sufficiently for the marginal revenue product of the resource in each to equal p_{a1}, they will again be maximizing
profits. The market level of employment will have dropped to A_1.

The administered price p_{a1} will create unemployment, thus causing income differences between those whose resources are employed and those
whose resources are unemployed.[6] At price p_{a1} employers will take quantity
A_1, but quantity A_1' of the resource seeks employment. Unemployment
amounts to A_1A_1'. Those whose units of the resource remain employed gain
greater distributive shares of the economy's product; however, those owning unemployed units now receive nothing for them. Units of the resource
still are paid according to their marginal contributions to the total receipts
of the firm. For the employed units marginal revenue product is greater
than formerly because of the reduction in the ratio of resource A to the
other resources used by individual firms. The marginal revenue product of
the unemployed units is zero.

The unemployed units of resource A may seek employment in another
resource classification. Suppose, for example, that units of resource A are

---

[6] Unless the unemployment is shared equally by all owners of the resource.

carpenters. Carpenters denied employment in that skill category, at a wage rate of p_{a_1}, may seek employment as common laborers rather than remain as unemployed carpenters. Their marginal revenue product and their wage rate will be lower in the lower skill classification. The administered wage rate increases income differences in two ways: (1) employed carpenters receive higher wage rates and incomes than they would otherwise receive; and (2) the wage rates and incomes of common labor are lower than they would otherwise be, as unemployed carpenters join their ranks and increase the supply of common labor.

The effects of the administered price on welfare are clear. The unemployed units of A contribute nothing to the value of the economy's output, or, to the extent that they shift into lower productivity classifications, they contribute less than they would otherwise have contributed. If the resource price were allowed to drop to its equilibrium level, greater employment in the higher value of marginal product uses would raise the real value of the economy's output—and at the same time would contribute toward greater income equality among owners of the resource.

Supply restrictions: pure competition   Resource prices in given employments may be increased indirectly through restriction of the resource supplies that can be used in those employments. Examples are furnished by governmental acreage restrictions placed on cotton and wheat farmers. Or the same result may be obtained by labor union activity. The milk-wagon drivers' union in a large city may succeed in making union membership a condition of employment, while at the same time it restricts entry into the union. The effects on income distribution and total output of the economy are about the same as those resulting from directly administered prices. The employment level of the resource in its restricted use is decreased, leaving some of the resource units either unemployed or seeking employment in alternative uses. Land excluded from cotton and wheat farming may be switched to the production of other products. Light-truck drivers excluded from driving milk wagons may secure such alternative employments as delivery-truck or taxi driving. Value of marginal product and price of resource units in the restricted use increase,[7] while value of marginal product

---

[7] In the case of wheatland or cottonland, the ratio of land to other resources is decreased both through decreased acreage allowances and through more intensive application of labor and fertilizer. Greater marginal physical product of the land and possibly higher prices for smaller crops increase the value of marginal product of land.

About the same thing happens with regard to milk-wagon drivers. Firms faced with restricted supplies attempt to make each driver as productive as possible. Slightly larger trucks may be used to minimize the number of trips back to the plant for reloading. Trucks may be made more convenient to get into, to get out of, and to operate. Idle truck time is avoided through better maintenance and repair facilities for trucks. Such measures increase the marginal physical product of the drivers. Additionally, the employment of fewer drivers may lead to smaller milk sales and higher milk prices. Thus, the value of marginal product of milk-wagon drivers will be higher than before.

and price of those placed in other employments decrease. These changes lead to differential prices for the resource and to greater income differences. At the same time they lead to net national product smaller than the economy is capable of producing.

Administered prices: monopoly   Do administered resource prices set above the equilibrium level offset the restrictive effects of monopoly when resource buyers sell a product as monopolists? The argument is frequently made that they do and that the advance in resource prices comes from the monopolists' profits. Suppose that initially the equilibrium price for a given resource prevails. Firms with some degree of monopoly in product markets are among those who buy the resource, and the resource is so allocated that its price is the same in its alternative uses. The resource price equals its marginal revenue product in its various employments, and those units of the resource employed by monopolistic sellers are exploited monopolistically—they receive less than they contribute to the value of the economy's output.

Will an administered resource price above the equilibrium price regain what is lost by resource owners from monopolistic exploitation? Suppose such an administered price is obtained. Marginal revenue product of the resource for individual firms will be less than the administered price if firms continue hiring the same quantities as before. Consequently, each firm reduces its employment of the resource to the level at which its marginal revenue product equals the administered price. But note that it is still marginal revenue product and not value of marginal product of the resource that is equal to its price. Despite the administered price, monopolistic exploitation of the resource continues to occur.[8]

In addition, the level of employment of the resource by monopolistic firms, already too low for maximum welfare, is reduced still further. At the higher price the firms employ fewer units of the resource. More units seek employment. Unemployment and even greater differences in income among owners of the resource occur. If the unemployed units then find employment in lower marginal revenue product resource classifications or uses, income differences are mitigated to some extent; but they still occur.

Administered prices: monopsony   In monopsonistic cases administered resource prices can offset monopsonistic exploitation of a resource. The employment level of the resource can be increased at the same time that its price is raised above the market level. The income and the distributive shares of the owners of the resource are increased relative to those of other

---

[8] Thus, measures to offset monopolistic exploitation of resources must attack the monopolistic product demand situation. They must eliminate the difference between marginal revenue and price for the monopolist and, hence, between marginal revenue product and value of marginal product of resources.

resource owners in the economy. At the same time the level of real net national product and welfare will be increased.

The detailed explanation of how an administered resource price offsets monopsonistic exploitation was presented in Chapter 15. To recapitulate the analysis, an administered price set above the market price makes the resource supply curve faced by the firm horizontal at that price. For prices higher than the administered price, the original supply curve is the relevant one. For the horizontal section of the resource supply curve, marginal resource cost and resource price will be equal. By judicious setting of the administered price the firm can be induced to employ that quantity of the resource at which marginal revenue product equals resource price. Without the administered price the firm restricts employment and pays units of the resource less than their marginal revenue product.

Price increases accompanying demand increases   The effects of administered resource price increases, when demand for the resource remains constant, are often confused with the effects of resource price increases that accompany increases in demand for the resource. Suppose that demand for a given resource is increasing while, simultaneously, resource owners organized as a group succeed in *bargaining out* a series of price increases with the buyers of the resource. Suppose further that the contract prices at no time exceed the rising equilibrium price. No adverse distributive effects for the owners of the resource arise. Their positions are continuously improving as individual resource owners and as a group. However, it is erroneous to conclude from situations of this kind that administered resource price increases will, in general, have no adverse effects on total income of the owners of the resource in question or on the distribution of income within the group. We must distinguish carefully between those administered price increases that are accompanied by increases in demand for the resource and those that are not. Although the former may have no adverse effects on total income of the owners of the resource or on the distribution of income among owners of the resource, adverse effects—except in the case of monopsony—are likely to arise from the latter.

Movements toward less inequality

In most societies that rely heavily on the market mechanism to organize economic activity, there is a general belief that some reduction of income differences is desirable. The result is a spate of antipoverty and income redistribution measures. What do we learn from microeconomics that will help us evaluate the effectiveness of alternative income-redistribution policies?

Resource redistribution

Since the market mechanism tends to reward households in proportion to their contributions to production processes, a major part of any redistribution program must consist of measures to improve the distribution of resource ownership. Some 80 percent of income is earned by labor resources, so it becomes apparent that differences in labor resources owned constitute the most important source of income differences. Differences in capital resources owned are also of some significance. How can these differences be reduced? In turn, we shall look at: (1) redistribution of labor resources and (2) redistribution of capital resources.

Labor resources   The ownership of labor resources can be redistributed through measures that increase vertical mobility. Greater vertical mobility will increase labor supplies at higher skill levels and decrease labor supplies at lower levels. Greater supplies at the higher levels will decrease values of marginal product or marginal revenue products, thereby reducing the top incomes. Smaller supplies at the lower levels will increase values of marginal product or marginal revenue products, thereby increasing incomes at the lower skill levels. The transfers from lower to higher skills will mitigate income differences and will increase net national product in the process.

At least two methods of increasing vertical mobility can be suggested. First, greater equality in educational and training opportunities for the poor and the rich can be provided. Second, measures may be taken to reduce the barriers to entry established by groups and associations of resource owners in many skilled and semiskilled occupations.[9]

Measures to increase horizontal mobility also can serve to decrease income differences. These include the operation of employment exchanges, perhaps some government subsidization of movement, vocational guidance, adult education and retraining programs, and other measures of a similar nature. The argument is really for a better allocation of labor resources, both among alternative jobs within a given labor resource category and among the labor resource categories themselves. Greater horizontal mobility, as well as greater vertical mobility, will increase net national product at the same time that it decreases income differences.

Capital resources   Policy measures to redistribute capital resources meet considerable opposition in a private enterprise economy. Many advocates of greater income equality will protest measures designed to redistribute capital ownership—and these measures are the ones that will contribute

---

[9] An example of such a barrier is provided by professional associations, which control the licensing standards that prospective entrants must meet in order to practice those professions.

most toward such an objective. The opposition centers around the rights of private property ownership and stems from a strong belief that the right to own property includes the right to accumulate it and to pass it on to one's heirs.

Nevertheless, if income differences are to be reduced, some means of providing greater equality in capital holdings among individuals must be employed. The economy's system of taxation may move in this direction. In the United States, for example, the personal income tax, the capital gains tax, and estate and gift taxes, both federal and state, are intended to operate in an equalizing manner.

The personal income tax by its progressive nature is supposed to reduce income differences directly; in so doing, it would reduce differences in abilities to accumulate capital. But the personal income tax alone is limited in the extent to which it can reduce income differences without seriously impairing incentives for efficient employment of resources and for reallocation of resources from less productive to more productive employments.

The capital gains tax constitutes either a loophole for escaping a part of the personal income tax or a plug for a loophole in the personal income tax, depending on one's definition of income. The capital gains tax is applied to realized appreciation and depreciation in the value of capital assets. Those who can convert a part of their income from capital resources into the form of capital gains have that part of their remuneration taxed as capital gains at a rate ordinarily below the personal income tax rate. For them the capital gains tax provides a loophole through which personal income taxes can be escaped. Yet if certain capital gains would escape taxation altogether under the personal income tax but are covered by the capital gains tax, the latter can be considered as a supplement to the personal income tax. In either case the capital gains tax allows some remuneration from capital resources to be taxed at rates below the personal income tax rates; if differences in opportunities to accumulate capital are to be mitigated, this tax must be revised to prevent individuals from taking advantage of its lower rates.

Estate and gift taxes will play major roles in any tax system designed to reduce differences in capital ownership. The estate taxes in such a system would border on the confiscatory side, above some maximum amount, in order to prevent the transmission of accumulated capital resources from generation to generation. Gift taxes would operate largely to plug estate tax loopholes. They would be designed to prevent transmission of estates by means of gifts from the original owner to heirs prior to the death of the original owner.

Administered prices

Widespread use is made of administered prices to accomplish the objectives of income redistribution. Examples include wage rates established through collective bargaining, legal minimum wage rates, price supports for farm products, rent controls, and crude oil price controls. Unfortunately many such measures miss their mark. We can seldom be certain that they will accomplish what they are intended to do. Wage rates set above equilibrium levels will generate unemployment. Price controls may deprive some (poor) consumers of goods they would like to have. As we have seen, administered prices in many cases add to rather than decrease income inequalities. In the process they often reduce economic efficiency.

The negative income tax

Measures that redistribute the ownership of labor and capital resources may fall short of accomplishing the desired reduction in income inequalities among households. Supplementary-income transfers from taxpayers to those at the bottom of the income distribution scale may be necessary. Negative income tax proposals provide a means of making supplementary transfers with minimal effects on economic incentives. No widespread use has been made of negative income tax ideas; however, they constitute an interesting possible alternative to such current transfer programs as public assistance, unemployment compensation, food stamps, subsidized housing, and even social security.

The essence of a negative income tax plan is presented in Table 17–3. Two essential elements of it are (1) the income base and (2) the negative tax

Table 17–3 A negative income tax plan

Income Base	Income Earned	Negative Tax (Base—50% of Income Earned)	Disposable Income (Income Earned + Negative Tax)
$5,000	0	$5,000	$5,000
5,000	1,000	4,500	5,500
5,000	2,000	4,000	6,000
5,000	9,000	500	9,500
$5,000	10,000	0	10,000

rate. The income base is the minimum level of income below which no household is allowed to fall. The negative tax rate is the percentage of income earned that is subtracted from the income base to determine the size of the subsidy or negative tax that is to be paid the household.

Suppose that the income base and the negative tax rate are set by the appropriate legislative body at $5,000 and 50 percent, respectively. There is nothing sacred about either of these figures—they can be whatever the society, acting through its legislature, wants them to be. If a household earns nothing at all during the year, this fact would be duly reported by an income tax return filed with the appropriate tax collection agency, say the Internal Revenue Service in the United States. The tax collection agency, acting for the government, would then send a $5,000 check to the household, this amount becoming the disposable income of the household. If the household reports an income earned of $1,000, the amount of the check mailed to it is $4,500, leaving it with a disposable income of $5,500. Similarly, an earned income of $2,000 results in a negative tax or subsidy of $4,000 and a disposable income of $6,000. At an earned income level of $10,000 or more per year, the household would receive no negative tax. Under the negative tax scheme a household can always have a larger disposable income if it earns income than it can have if it does not. In addition, the more income it earns, the larger its disposable income will be. Thus, positive incentives to earn are built into the plan. The larger the base and the smaller the negative tax rate, the larger will be the amount of income earned that the household will be allowed to keep, and the higher will be the income level at which the amount of the subsidy to the household becomes zero.

The negative income tax idea has several appealing features in addition to preserving incentives for resource owners to employ their resources productively. It is simple in concept and could be administered easily by the existing tax collection mechanism. It does not require a separate bureaucratic agency. It attacks the problem of poverty directly by making subsidy payments only to the poor. If it were used, it would eliminate the need for many of the special income-transfer programs now in existence.

Income redistribution and the price system

The foregoing discussion suggests that if a society that uses the price mechanism is not satisfied with the income distribution that the price mechanism generates, the most efficient way of redistributing income is to do it outside the operation of the price mechanism itself. Direct government intervention in the pricing of resources, goods, and services is likely to reduce the efficiency with which the economic system operates by distorting price signals and bringing about malallocations of resources. It may also generate unemployment and other surpluses, or, on the other hand, shortages. Redistributions of resource ownership and redistribution of money income by means of taxes and subsidies outside the price mechanism itself are less likely to have adverse effects on efficiency and can get directly at the heart of the problem—alleviation of poverty.

Summary

Individual claims to net national product depend on individual incomes; thus, the theory of product distribution is really the theory of income distribution. Marginal productivity theory provides the generally accepted principles of income determination and income distribution. Resource owners tend to be remunerated according to the marginal revenue products of the resources they own, except in cases where resources are purchased monopsonistically.

Incomes are unequally distributed among spending units in the United States. Income differences stem from three basic sources: (1) differences in labor resources owned, (2) differences in capital resources owned, and (3) restrictions placed on the operation of the price mechanism. With regard to the same general skill level, we call these horizontal differences in labor resources. Different individuals also own different kinds of labor graded vertically from undifferentiated manual labor to top-level professions. Differences in capital resources owned result from disparities in material inheritance, fortuitous circumstances, and propensities to accumulate.

Administered prices for a given resource often lead to unemployment or malallocation of some units of the resource and, hence, to differences in incomes among owners of the resource. The case of monopsony provides an exception. Under monopsony administered resource prices can offset monopsonistic exploitation of the resources involved.

Attacks on income differences, if society desires to mitigate those differences, should be made by way of redistribution of resources among resource owners. Attacks made by way of administered prices are not likely to accomplish this task. Redistribution of labor resources can be accomplished through measures designed to increase both horizontal and vertical mobility. These will, in turn, increase net national product. The tax system offers a means of effecting redistribution of capital resources. Estate and gift taxes will bear the major burden of effective redistribution and may be supplemented by personal income and capital gains taxes. In addition, a negative income tax plan can be used to accomplish supplemental, direct income transfers to the poor.

These measures can be accomplished within the framework of the price system and the private enterprise economy.

Suggested readings

Alkinson, A. B., *The Economics of Inequality*. Oxford: Oxford University Press, 1975.

Friedman, Milton, *Capitalism and Freedom*. Chicago: University of Chicago Press, 1960. Chaps. X–XII.

Okun, Arthur M., *Equality and Efficiency, the Big Tradeoff*. Washington, D.C.: The Brookings Institution, 1975.

Questions and exercises

1. In terms of economics only—discounting completely political feasibility—do you think it would be possible to eliminate poverty
   a. in the United States? Explain why and how.
   b. in Pakistan? Explain why and how.

2. To what extent would you expect each of the following to contribute to the poverty problem in the United States?
   a. monopolistic exploitation of resources
   b. monopsonistic exploitation of resources
   c. inequalities in labor resources owned
   d. inequalities in capital resources owned.

3. What impact would you expect licensing laws for particular occupations to have on
   a. income distribution
   b. economic welfare.

4. Price controls and rationing by the government are often suggested as a means of protecting the interests of the poor. Discuss the probable effects of this type of approach to redistribution of the economy's output on
   a. the efficiency of consumption (*Hint:* Consider a two-good, two-person case in which one person is initially rich and the other is initially poor.)
   b. the efficiency of production
   c. the efficiency of the product mix in the economy.

5. Outline a comprehensive income redistribution program that would have minimum adverse effects on economic efficiency.

Part 6   How the pieces fit together

We try to bring the many facets of microeconomics together in Part 6. It contains little that is new, but it provides a focus and a consistent logical framework that will help us understand what microeconomics is all about. It is especially important that the concepts of *welfare* and *general equilibrium* be kept separate. Maximum welfare is the most desirable state of affairs that we can define objectively, and the conditions that will yield maximum welfare are independent of the type of economic system that may exist. General equilibrium is the state of affairs that a price system will yield, and it may or may not be a maximum welfare situation. A major part of our task is to examine the price system in order to determine how well it performs in a welfare sense.

Chapter 18

Chapter contents   **Key concepts**

The concepts of equilibrium and welfare	**Welfare** **Equilibrium** Partial equilibrium General equilibrium
The conditions of optimum welfare	**Maximum consumer welfare: fixed supplies** **Maximum efficiency in production: given resource supplies** The conditions of maximum efficiency: no externalities The effects of externalities **Optimal outputs of goods and services** **Summary of optimum welfare conditions**
Private enterprise and general equilibrium	**Consumer equilibrium: fixed supplies** **Producer equilibrium: given resource supplies** Pure competition Monopoly and monopsony **Product output levels: given resource supplies** Pure competition Monopoly
Summary	**Suggested readings** **Questions and exercises**

Welfare
Pareto optimality
Equilibrium
Partial equilibrium
General equilibrium
Externalities in
  consumption
Externalities in production

Equilibrium and welfare

In this chapter we shall first review what is involved in the concepts of welfare and equilibrium. Then, we shall examine the conditions that must be met in order to maximize welfare, in the sense of Pareto optimality. Finally, we shall consider the conditions required for general equilibrium to exist in a private enterprise economic system, and the implications of these conditions for economic welfare.

The concepts of equilibrium and welfare

Welfare and equilibrium are different concepts, although they are frequently confused with one another. We have defined *welfare* as the state of well-being of the persons comprising an economic system. We have defined *equilibrium* as a state of rest, a position from which there is either no incentive or no opportunity to move. We shall look at some of the principal aspects of each of these concepts.

Welfare

Most economic analysis is concerned with the welfare aspects of economic activity—how to achieve maximum or optimum welfare for the population in the economic system. An objective definition of optimum welfare constitutes a major problem. As we noted in the introductory chapter, where only one person is being considered, the concept is straightforward and is synonymous with the well-being of that person. But when more than one person is being considered, an objective definition of a unique optimum welfare position for the group as a whole becomes impossible, since such a definition would require interpersonal comparisons of satisfaction. The Pareto optimum situation, in which no one can be made better off without making someone else worse off, is the best solution that we can attain.

Equilibrium

Equilibrium concepts are important, not because equilibrium positions are ever in fact attained but because these concepts show us the direction in which economic processes move. When equilibrium positions are *stable*—as they have been assumed to be throughout this book—economic units in disequilibrium move toward equilibrium positions. Even as they are doing so, however, changes in consumers' preference patterns, resource supplies, and technology alter the equilibrium positions themselves, thus redirecting the movements that are occurring. If equilibrium positions are *unstable,* disturbances will cause economic units to move farther away from rather than toward them.

Partial equilibrium   A large part of the analytical structure that we have built up is called *partial equilibrium analysis*. It has been concerned with the movements of individual economic units toward equilibrium positions in response to the given economic conditions confronting them. Thus, the consumer, with given tastes and preferences, is confronted with a given income and with given prices of goods and services. Each consumer adjusts his or her purchases accordingly to move toward equilibrium. The business firm—faced with given product demand situations, a given state of technology, and given resource supply situations—moves toward an equilibrium adjustment. The resource owner possesses given quantities of resources to place in employment. There are given alternative employment possibilities and resource price offers. The equilibrium adjustment is made on the basis of the given data. The conditions of demand and of cost in a particular industry cause profits or losses to be made, and these motivate the entry of new firms (if entry is possible) or the exit of existing firms, thus leading toward equilibrium for the industry. Changes in the given data facing economic units and industries alter the positions of equilibrium that each is attempting to reach and motivate movements toward the new positions.

Partial equilibrium is especially suitable for the analysis of two types of problems, both of which we met time and again throughout the book. Problems of the first type are those arising from economic disturbances that are not of sufficient magnitude to reach far beyond the confines of a given industry or sector of the economy. Problems of the second type are concerned with the first-order effects of an economic disturbance of any kind.

As an illustration of the first type of problem, suppose that the production workers of a small manufacturer of plastic products go on strike. Suppose further that the plant is located in a large city and that the workers are fairly well dispersed among the residential areas of the city. The effects of the strike will be limited largely to the company and the employees concerned. Partial equilibrium analysis will provide the relevant answers to most of the economic problems arising from the strike.

As an example of the second type of problem, suppose that a rearmament program increases the demand for steel suddenly and substantially. Partial equilibrium analysis will provide answers to the first-order effects on the steel industry—what happens to its prices, output, profits, demand for resources, the resource prices, and its resource employment levels. However, the first-order effects by no means end the repercussions from the initial disturbance.

General equilibrium   As individual economic units and industries seek equilibrium adjustments to what appear to be given facts, their total group actions change the facts that they face. If some units were in equilibrium and others were not, those in disequilibrium would move toward equilibrium. Their activities would change the facts faced by units in equilibrium and would throw the latter into disequilibrium. General equilibrium for the entire economy could exist only if all economic units were to achieve simultaneous partial, or particular, equilibrium adjustments. The concept of general equilibrium stresses the interdependence of all economic units and of all segments of the economy on each other.

A hard-and-fast line between partial equilibrium analysis and general equilibrium analysis is difficult to draw. Instead of establishing a dichotomy, it will be preferable to think in terms of moving along a continuum from partial to general equilibrium, or from first-order effects of a disturbance into second-, third-, and higher-order effects. For example, in discussing pricing and output under market conditions of pure competition, we were concerned, first, with partial equilibrium, or equilibrium of the individual firm. Next, we extended the analysis to an entire industry and observed the impact of individual firm actions on each other. Finally, we observed how productive capacity is organized in a purely competitive private enterprise economy according to consumers' tastes and preferences. This series of topics represents progressive movement from the application of partial equilibrium analysis to the application of general equilibrium analysis.

General equilibrium theory provides the analytical tools for accomplishing two objectives: (1) from the standpoint of pure theory it provides the means of viewing the economic system in its entirety—the means of seeing what holds it together, what makes it work, and how it operates; (2)—and this objective is really an application of the first one—the determination of the second-, third-, and higher-order effects of an economic disturbance. When the impact of an economic disturbance is of sufficient magnitude to have repercussions throughout most of the economy, general equilibrium analysis provides the more relevant answers regarding its ultimate effects. First comes the big splash from the disturbance. Partial equilibrium analysis handles this. But waves and then ripples are set up from it, affecting one another and affecting the area of the splash. The ripples run farther and farther out, becoming smaller and smaller, until eventually they dwindle away. The tools of general equilibrium are required for analysis of the entire series of readjustments.

Suppose that the higher-order repercussions from the increase in demand for steel are to be examined. The first-order, or partial, equilibrium effects are higher prices, larger outputs with given facilities, larger profits, and larger payments to the owners of resources used in making steel. These effects generate additional disturbances. Higher incomes for the resource owners increase demand for other products, setting off disturbances and adjustments in other industries. Demands also increase for steel substitutes, generating another series of disturbances and adjustments. Productive capacity will be diverted from other activities toward the making of steel. Eventually, effects will be felt over the entire economy. If the full impact of such a disturbance is to be determined, general equilibrium analysis must provide the tools to do so.

Since general equilibrium analysis covers the interrelationships of all parts of the economy, it necessarily becomes exceedingly complex. There are two principal variants of it. In the first one, following Walras, most economists find it convenient to discuss general equilibrium in mathematical terms. The interdependence of economic units is shown through a system of simultaneous equations relating the many economic variables to each other. It can be demonstrated that there are as many variables to be determined as there are equations relating them. Solving the system of equations establishes those values of the variables that are consistent with general equilibrium for the economic system. The Walrasian version of general equilibrium provides essentially the theoretical apparatus for understanding the interrelationships of the various sectors of the economy.

The second variant of general equilibrium analysis is Wassily W. Leontief's input-output analysis.[1] The input-output approach is an empirical descendant of the abstract Walrasian approach. It divides the economy into a number of sectors or industries, including households and the government, as "industries" of final demand. Each industry is viewed as selling its output to other industries; these outputs become inputs for the purchasing industries. Likewise, each industry is viewed as a purchaser of the outputs of other industries. Thus, the interdependence of each industry on the others is established. Statistical data gathered around the basic framework of the system provide an informative and useful picture of the interindustry flows of goods, services, and resources. The input-output approach has been used extensively by municipalities, states, and regions for economic development purposes.

The attainment of general equilibrium in an economic system does not imply that Pareto optimality is also attained. A price system tends to move the economy toward general equilibrium. Unless pure competition exists in

---

[1] For an excellent survey and analysis of this approach, *see* Robert Dorfman, "The Nature and Significance of Input-Output," *Review of Economics and Statistics,* Vol. XXXVI (May 1954), pp. 121–133.

both product and resource markets, however, Pareto optimality will not follow.

The conditions of optimum welfare

Optimum welfare conditions in an economy are usually grouped into three sets. The first consists of the set of conditions leading to maximum consumer welfare when supplies of goods and services are fixed. The second consists of the conditions of maximum efficiency in production, assuming that resource supplies are fixed. In the third the conditions of consumer welfare and maximum productive efficiency are brought together to determine conditions under which the outputs of different goods and services are optimal.

Maximum consumer welfare: fixed supplies

The conditions of maximum consumer welfare with fixed supplies of goods and services per time unit are illustrated in the two-good, two-person model of Figure 18–1. If the distribution of goods X and Y between the two consumers H and J is initially off the contract curve at some such point as D, exchanges can be made that will increase the welfare of either without

Figure 18–1   Optimum consumer welfare: fixed supplies

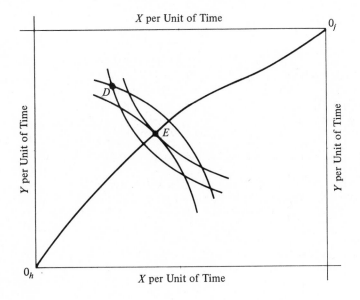

decreasing the welfare of the other. A movement from distribution D to distribution E increases the welfare of both. Once a contract curve distribution is achieved, any further exchanges can benefit only one consumer at the expense of the other. Any point on the contract curve represents a Pareto optimal distribution of X and Y between the two consumers. Each such point is defined by the condition that:

$$MRS_{xy}{}^h = MRS_{xy}{}^j. \qquad (18.1)$$

The condition can be extended to as many goods and services and as many consumers as there are in the economy.

Sometimes there are *externalities* involved in the consumption of a good or service. An externality occurs if the consumption of a good by someone else affects the level of satisfaction attained by any given consumer. Suppose, for example, that H and J are neighbors, that H increases her stereo capacity, and that J, whose musical tastes parallel those of H, can now hear and enjoy the music played by H. J receives an external benefit from H's consumption—his set of indifference curves between music and other goods and services is shifted inward toward the origin of his indifference map. On the other hand, the externality could have operated in the opposite direction. The music played by H could have annoyed J, shifting his set of indifference curves between music and other goods and services outward from the origin of his indifference map.[2]

When an externality in consumption occurs, we can no longer be sure that a point on the contract curve such as E in Figure 18–2 is Pareto optimal. Suppose that J's satisfaction is enhanced by H's increased purchase of music via an expansion of stereo capacity. An exchange of other goods and services for music that moves the consumers from distribution E to distribution F would not change H's level of satisfaction. Suppose that the external benefits that J receives from H's increased consumption of music shift J's indifference curves toward origin 0_j so that the satisfaction level formerly represented by I_j is now represented by I_j'. At point F, J will be at a higher level of satisfaction, represented by I_{j2}', than before; since H's satisfaction has not been lessened, the welfare of the two consumers combined is greater than it was at point E.

Maximum efficiency in production: given resource supplies

The conditions of efficiency: no externalities   Maximum efficiency in production refers to Pareto optimality in production processes. Given the

---

[2] The preference function of J takes the form of

$$U_j = f(x_j, y_j, x_h),$$

in which x_j and y_j represent J's consumption of two goods, X and Y, and x_h represents H's consumption of X.

Figure 18–2   Externalities in consumption

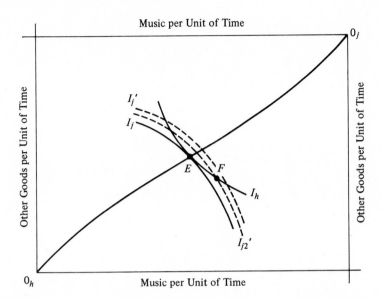

supplies of resources available, these must be allocated among the production of goods and services in such a way that the production of any one good cannot be increased unless the production of another is decreased.

The conditions of efficiency are illustrated in the two-resource, two-product model of Figure 18–3. Fixed supplies of resources A and B are used in the production of products X and Y. Any distribution of resources between the two products that lies on the contract curve, such as that at E, is more efficient than is any distribution not on the contract curve, such as that at N. Given any initial distribution such as N, the output of either product can be increased with no sacrifice of the other. It is also possible to increase the outputs of both products by allocating more A and less B to the output of X and less A and more B to the output of Y, thus moving from N to E. With any distribution such as E neither product's output can be increased unless some of the other is sacrificed. Any point on the contract curve represents a maximum efficiency allocation of resources. The condition that determines any such point is that

$$MRTS_{ab}{}^x = MRTS_{ab}{}^y. \qquad (18.2)$$

These conditions can be expanded to include as many resources and as many goods and services as exist in the economy.

The infinite number of efficiently produced combinations of X and Y shown by the contract curve of Figure 18–3 are also shown by the

Figure 18–3   Optimum productive efficiency

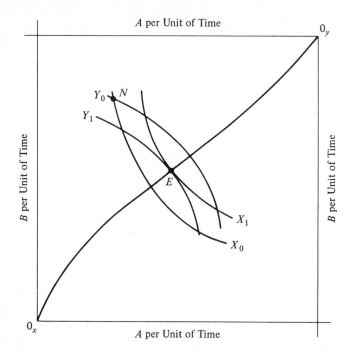

transformation curve of Figure 18–4. For every combination of X and Y on the transformation curve, resources are allocated to each product in the optimal combinations. The transformation curve is often appropriately called the production possibilities curve. Its slope at any point measures the rate at which one product must be given up to obtain an additional unit of the other, that is, the MRT_{xy}.

The effects of externalities   If externalities occur in the production of a product, the contract curve may no longer show the conditions of maximum efficiency. Congested facilities represent a very common type of externality. Suppose, for example, that highway facilities, along with other resources, are used by the producers of wheat and also by the producers of automobiles for getting their products to consumers. Initially, these two groups of users cause the highways to be congested to the extent that transportation delays result. In Figure 18–5 the marginal rate of technical substitution between highway facilities and other resources is the same for producers of wheat and producers of automobiles at point E. But this allocation of resources is not necessarily optimal. If highway congestion

Figure 18–4   A transformation curve

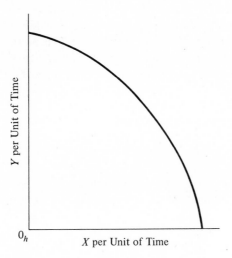

Figure 18–5   Externalities in production

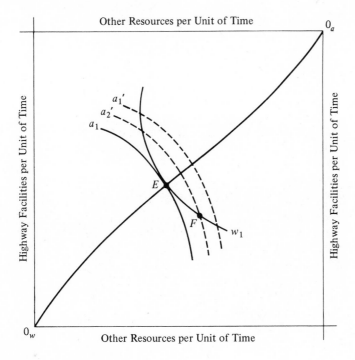

exists at E, a reduction in the use of the highways by firms in one industry will increase the productivity of highway facilities for those in the other.

Suppose that wheat producers reduce their use of the highways but maintain their output level at w_1 by increasing their use of alternative forms of noncongested transport, thus moving from point E to point F. This move shifts the set of isoquants of automobile producers toward the 0_a origin, and a_1 units of automobiles is now shown by the dashed line a_1'. At point F automobile production will be at a_2', a higher level than before. At the same time there will have been no change in total wheat production. The efficiency of production has been increased by the resource exchange.

Optimal outputs of goods and services

We have not yet determined which of the combinations of products represented by a transformation curve yield optimal welfare to consumers. If we assume that there are no externalities of production, the transformation curve of Figure 18–6 shows the combinations of X and Y that resources A and B can produce when those resources are used efficiently—that is, when $MRTS_{ab}{}^x = MRTS_{ab}{}^y$ for each combination. The slope of the transformation curve at any point, the MRT_{xy}, shows the rate at which it is possible technically to transform Y into X at that combination of goods.

For any combination of X and Y on the transformation curve an Edgeworth box for consumers can be constructed to show the optimal distributions of supplies making up the combination. For the combination at 0_{j1} in Figure 18–6 the Edgeworth box $0_h y_1 0_{j1} x_1$ is the appropriate one for a two-consumer, two-good model. For the combination at 0_{j2} the appropriate box is $0_h y_2 0_{j2} x_2$. Note that since the origin 0_h for consumer H remains in a fixed position, H's indifference curves, drawn with respect to the X and Y axes of the transformation diagram, are the same for all possible boxes. The origin of the indifference map for consumer J, however, is different for each different combination of X and Y shown on the transformation curve and for each different box. Consequently, J's set of indifference curves must be redrawn for each different box.

If the combination of X and Y being produced were 0_{j1}, would this be the optimal output of each product? Since it lies on the transformation curve, the outputs are being produced with maximum efficiency. Moreover, any distribution (such as K) of the output combination between consumers H and J that lies on the contract curve $0_h 0_{j1}$ is a welfare-maximizing distribution of the specific combination. Still, combination 0_{j1} of product outputs, together with distribution K of the products between consumers, does not result in maximum welfare. The slope of line $M_1 N_1$ through point K and tangent to the indifference curves of H and J measures the MRS_{xy} for both consumers at point K. It indicates the rate at which *both* consumers would be willing to give up Y for X. The slope of $R_1 S_1$ through point 0_{j1}, tangent to

Figure 18−6   The full conditions of maximum welfare

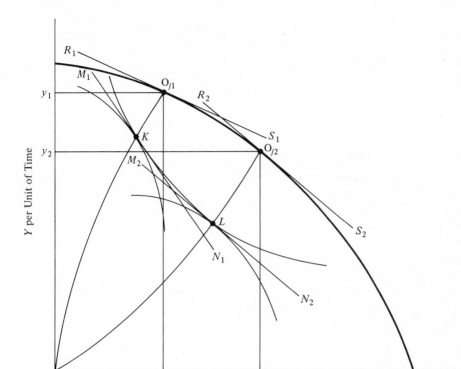

the transformation curve, measures the MRT_{xy} (the rate at which it is technically necessary to give up Y to produce more X). Since $MRS_{xy} > MRT_{xy}$ (that is, consumers are willing to give up more Y to obtain an additional unit of X than is necessary in the production processes), the welfare of both consumers can be increased by increasing the output of X and decreasing the output of Y.

The conditions for optimum welfare in terms of the output levels of X and Y and the distribution of that output between consumers H and J are that

$$MRS_{xy} = MRT_{xy}. \tag{18.3}$$

Consider combination 0_{j2} and distribution L. The lines M_2N_2 and R_2S_2 are parallel, indicating that $MRS_{xy} = MRT_{xy}$; therefore, this is an optimum welfare output combination and distribution. A small movement away from L or away from 0_{j2} will decrease the welfare of at least one of the consumers.

The optimum welfare combination of outputs and distribution of product among consumers is not a unique one, however. There may be an infinite number of output combination-product distribution possibilities at which the $MRS_{xy} = MRT_{xy}$. For output combination 0_{j_1}, even though at distribution K the $\mathrm{MRS}_{xy} \neq MRT_{xy}$, there may be other distributions on contract curve $0_h 0_{j_1}$ at which the $MRS_{xy} = MRT_{xy}$, although it is not certain that there are. The same thing can be said for other output combinations represented by the transformation curve.

Summary of optimum welfare conditions

In summary, then, for Pareto optimality to exist in an economic system three conditions must be met:

1. The distribution of product outputs must be such that the marginal rate of substitution of any one product for any other product is the same for all consumers.
2. The allocation of resources must be such that the marginal rate of technical substitution of any one resource for any other resource is the same in the production of all products for which those resources can be used.
3. The outputs of product and their distribution among consumers must be such that the marginal rate of substitution of any one product for any other product is equal to the marginal rate of transformation of the products.

The conditions of Pareto optimality leave us uninformed about which of the optimal distributions of product among consumers is the ''optimum'' optimum and about which of the optimal combinations of product output is the ''optimum'' optimum. We can eliminate those distributions of any output combination at which marginal rates of substitution are not equal to the corresponding marginal rates of transformation. After these deletions, however, we may still have a great many alternative possibilities.

Private enterprise and general equilibrium

Will a private enterprise economic system guided and directed by the price mechanism move toward optimum welfare positions as it moves toward general equilibrium positions? The optimum welfare conditions of the preceding subsection apply to any kind of economic system—socialist, private enterprise, or other. To evaluate the performance of a private enterprise system, then, it is necessary to examine the conditions of the equilibrium toward which it moves in order to determine whether these coincide with the conditions of optimum welfare or at least approach those conditions.

Toward this end we draw on, summarize, and extend the principles developed throughout the book.

Consumer equilibrium: fixed supplies

Consider first the problem of consumers' choice. Assume that the supplies of goods and services are fixed—they automatically come into being on the first of each month. The distribution among consumers may be any distribution, but it will not vary from month to month. Consumers' preference patterns are fixed. A monetary system exists. The price pattern is initially random. Each good or service is in the hands of many individuals, with the result that pure competition will exist in the event that exchange occurs. What happens at this point if individuals are free to buy and sell, that is, to exchange? Each consumer will seek to maximize satisfaction.

If for two goods—X and Y, priced initially at p_x and p_y—a consumer finds that $MRS_{xy} \neq p_x/p_y$, that individual will want to engage in exchange. Any consumer for whom $MRS_{xy} > p_x/p_y$ will want to sell Y and buy X in order to move to higher indifference curves. Any consumer for whom $MRS_{xy} < p_x/p_y$ will want to sell X and purchase Y in order to move to higher indifference curves.

At the initial price pattern the supplies of some items are likely to be exhausted before all consumers get as much as they desire. The prices of these items will rise, reducing the quantities that consumers want relative to the quantities of other goods. Prices will move to those levels at which consumers are just willing to ration themselves to the entire quantities available per month.

The supplies of other goods may be overabundant at their initial price levels. In order to reduce the quantities that they have on hand, those who hold surpluses will reduce the asking prices. Prices will fall to the levels at which consumers are just willing to take the entire quantities available per month.

General equilibrium exists when goods and services are so priced that each consumer gets the quantity of each of them that the consumer desires relative to the quantities of others and when there is neither a shortage nor a surplus of any item. Any one consumer H takes a combination of X and Y such that

$$MRS_{xy}{}^h = p_x/p_y.$$

Any other consumer J also takes a combination at which

$$MRS_{xy}{}^j = p_x/p_y.$$

It follows, since p_x/p_y is the same for all consumers, that

$$MRS_{xy}{}^h = MRS_{xy}{}^j. \tag{18.4}$$

All consumers are on the contract curve. Thus, under conditions of pure competition and in the absence of externalities, the conditions of general equilibrium with fixed supplies coincide with the conditions of optimum welfare with fixed supplies.

Producer equilibrium: given resource supplies

We turn now to the operation of the price mechanism in organizing production. To facilitate the discussion, several assumptions are useful. We shall assume that resource supplies are fixed quantities per month and that their initial prices are random. The range of production techniques is given. We shall start by considering the organization of production in terms of the purely competitive model. Then we shall modify the analysis to take monopoly and monopsony into account.

Pure competition Suppose that the fixed supplies that consumers receive are being produced by firms operating in purely competitive industries and that these firms seek to maximize their profits. Confronted with the initial resource prices, each firm attempts to acquire those quantities of different resources at which the marginal revenue product of each resource is equal to its marginal resource cost.

At the initial set of resource prices firms will find that they are not able to obtain enough of some resources to bring their marginal revenue products into line with their respective marginal resource costs; that is, shortages occur. The prices of these resources will rise, inducing firms to attempt to substitute other resources for them. Prices will reach equilibrium levels when each firm is just able to obtain the quantities that it desires.

Some other resources will not be fully employed when, at the initial prices, every firm takes the quantities at which their marginal revenue products equal their marginal resource costs. Surpluses of these resources will cause those who own them to cut the prices at which they are offered in order to induce firms to substitute them for now relatively more expensive resources. The prices will be in equilibrium when firms are just willing to absorb the entire quantities placed on the market.

General equilibrium exists when each resource is priced so that neither a surplus nor a shortage exists and when each firm is taking that quantity of each resource at which its marginal revenue product is equal to its marginal resource cost. These conditions, together with pure competition in both resource and product markets, lead to important additional consequences, as described below.

Since pure competition exists, the value of marginal product of each resource will be equal to the resource price. For any given resource, A, $MRP_a = MRC_a$ means also that $VMP_a = p_a$ because for any product, X, that A assists in producing, $MR_x = p_x$; and for any firm purchasing A, $MRC_a = p_a$.

When firms using several common resources to produce several products employ resources in profit-maximizing quantitites, they will also be employing them efficiently from a Pareto optimal point of view. Suppose that two resources, A and B, are employed by firms producing X and Y. Any firm in industry X employs those quantities of the resources at which

$$MPP_{ax} \times p_x = p_a$$

and

$$MPP_{bx} \times p_x = p_b.$$

Thus,

$$\frac{MPP_{ax}}{p_a} = \frac{1}{p_x} \quad \text{and} \quad \frac{MPP_{bx}}{p_b} = \frac{1}{p_x}.$$

Therefore,

$$\frac{MPP_{ax}}{p_a} = \frac{MPP_{bx}}{p_b} \quad \text{and} \quad \frac{MPP_{ax}}{MPP_{bx}} = \frac{p_a}{p_b},$$

or

$$MRTS_{ab}{}^x = \frac{p_a}{p_b}.$$

Similarly, we can show that

$$MRTS_{ab}{}^y = \frac{p_a}{p_b}.$$

Therefore,

$$MRTS_{ab}{}^x = MRTS_{ab}{}^y, \tag{18.5}$$

which is the condition for an efficient allocation of any two resources between any two products.

Monopoly and monopsony Monopoly in the sale of products will not deter the price system from allocating resources among different products so that they are used efficiently in the production of each product, but some degree of monopsony will act as a deterrent. If monopoly exists in the sale of products X and Y, but the firms in both industries purchase resources A and B competitively, we can show that when A and B are purchased in each industry in a manner such that the marginal revenue products of the resources equal their respective resource prices, then

$$MRTS_{ab}{}^x = MRTS_{ab}{}^y.$$

However, if some degree of monopsony exists in the purchase of A and B, then

$$MPP_{ax} \times MR_x = MRC_{ax}$$

and

$$MPP_{bx} \times MR_x = MRC_{bx}.$$

Therefore,

$$\frac{MPP_{ax}}{MRC_{ax}} = \frac{MPP_{bx}}{MRC_{bx}} \quad \text{and} \quad \frac{MPP_{ax}}{MPP_{bx}} = \frac{MRC_{ax}}{MRC_{bx}},$$

or

$$MRTS_{ab}{}^x = \frac{MRC_{ax}}{MRC_{bx}}.$$

We can show similarly that

$$MRTS_{ab}{}^y = \frac{MRC_{ay}}{MRC_{by}}.$$

The firm producing X must pay the same price for resource A as the firm producing Y.[3] But if the elasticity of the supply of A to the firm producing X differs from the elasticity of supply of A to the firm producing Y, at whatever the supply price of A to both firms may be, then

$$MRC_{ax} \neq MRC_{ay}.$$

Similarly, under the same set of circumstances

$$MRC_{bx} \neq MRC_{by}.$$

Consequently, it is not necessary that

$$MRTS_{ab}{}^x = MRTS_{ab}{}^y, \qquad (18.6)$$

and the price system will not necessarily bring about optimum efficiency in the use of the resources in the two industries.

Product output levels: given resource supplies

In this subsection we shall continue to trace the implications of the general equilibrium results brought about by the price mechanism. Equilibrium exists when (1) price levels of goods and services are such that there are no shortages and no surpluses, (2) price levels of resources are such that there are no shortages and no surpluses, and (3) firms purchase those quantities of

---

[3] Rather than assume pure monopsony, in which resource A would be specialized to one firm only, we assume a degree of monopsony in which units of the resource are mobile among a few firms, any one of which buys a sufficient proportion of the total available supply to have an effect on the resource price.

different resources at which their marginal revenue products equal their respective marginal resource costs. Again we shall consider purely competitive markets first and then turn to the effects of monopoly and monopsony.

Pure competition Under conditions of pure competition in both product and resource markets, and in the absence of externalities, the allocation of resources and the output levels of product determined by the price system will maximize welfare.

Consider first the allocation of resources between any two products, X and Y. When firms of industry X are using two resources, A and B, and are maximizing profits, then for each firm

$$\frac{MPP_{ax}}{p_a} = \frac{MPP_{bx}}{p_b} = \frac{1}{MC_x} = \frac{1}{p_x},$$

or

$$MC_x = p_x.$$

Similarly, for firms in industry Y,

$$\frac{MPP_{ay}}{p_a} = \frac{MPP_{by}}{p_b} = \frac{1}{MC_y} = \frac{1}{p_y},$$

or

$$MC_y = p_y.$$

The MRT_{xy}, at whatever combination of X and Y is being produced, is the measure of the amount of Y that must be given up by the economic system to produce an additional unit of X; MRT_{xy} can be expressed as $\Delta y/\Delta x$.

Since resources are used efficiently in the production of both X and Y, the cost of giving up Δy of Y must equal the cost of adding Δx of X to the economy's output;[4] that is,

$$\Delta y \times MC_y = \Delta x \times MC_x$$

and

$$\frac{\Delta y}{\Delta x} = \frac{MC_x}{MC_y}.$$

Since the price system leads to a product output combination at which

$$MC_x = p_x \text{ and } MC_y = p_y,$$

then

$$MRT_{xy} = \frac{\Delta y}{\Delta x} = \frac{MC_x}{MC_y} = \frac{p_x}{p_y}.$$

---

[4] This relationship must obtain since the identical quantities of resources released in giving up Δy of Y are used to produce Δx of X.

We can now put the pieces together. The price system induces consumers to establish a price ratio for the supplies of any two goods, X and Y, such that for each consumer

$$MRS_{xy} = \frac{p_x}{p_y}.$$

These prices in turn bring about an allocation of resources between the two goods such that

$$MC_x = p_x \quad \text{and} \quad MC_y = p_y,$$

or

$$\frac{MC_x}{MC_y} = \frac{p_x}{p_y}.$$

The ratio MC_x/MC_y in turn is the measure of the MRT_{xy}; thus, the price system leads to general equilibrium outputs of X and Y such that

$$MRS_{xy} = MRT_{xy}. \tag{18.7}$$

This condition for general equilibrium is also the condition for a set of optimum outputs of X and Y.

An output combination on the transformation curve, such that $MRS_{xy} \neq MRT_{xy}$, simply means that $MC_x \neq p_x$ and/or $MC_y \neq p_y$. For example, if $MRS_{xy} > MRT_{xy}$, as is the case at point K in Figure 18–6, it follows that $MC_x < p_x$ and $MC_y > p_y$. The price system will bring about an expansion in the output of X and a reduction in the output of Y. These changes will decrease MRS_{xy}, causing p_x to decrease and p_y to increase. At the same time they cause MRT_{xy} to increase, increasing MC_x and decreasing MC_y until $MC_x = p_x$, $MC_y = p_y$, and $MRS_{xy} = p_x/p_y = MC_x/MC_y = MRT_{xy}$.

Monopoly   The sale of a product under conditions of monopoly will prevent the attainment of optimal outputs by way of the price mechanism. Suppose that product X is sold monopolistically and product Y is sold competitively. The price system will lead to a set of outputs such that for each consumer

$$MRS_{xy} = \frac{p_x}{p_y}.$$

But profit maximization will induce the monopolist to produce the output at which $MC_x = MR_x < p_x$. Purely competitive producers of Y produce outputs at which $MC_y = p_y$. Thus,

$$MRT_{xy} = \frac{MC_x}{MC_y} = \frac{MR_x}{p_y} < \frac{p_x}{p_y} = MRS_{xy}. \tag{18.8}$$

The output level of X is too small and the output level of Y is too large for optimum welfare.

Summary

In this chapter we summarized the conditions that must be met in an economic system in order to achieve maximum welfare in the sense of a Pareto optimum. Then we summarized the operation of the price mechanism in a private enterprise type of economic system, examining it to see if its results are Pareto optimal. The price system will lead to Pareto optimality if all markets are purely competitive and if no externalities occur in consumption or production. Where selling markets are monopolized, outputs will be short of the optimal quantities. Monopsony in resource purchases has a further adverse effect, in that it leads to inefficiency in the use of resources by the purchasers.

Suggested readings

Bator, Francis M., "The Simple Analytics of Welfare Maximization," *American Economic Review,* Vol. XLVII (March 1957), pp. 22–59. Reprinted in William Breit and Harold M. Hochman, eds., *Readings in Microeconomics,* 2nd ed. New York: Holt, Rinehart and Winston, Inc., 1971. Chap. 32.

Baumol, William J., *Economic Theory and Operations Analysis,* 4th ed. Englewood Cliffs, N.J.: Prentice-Hall, Inc., 1977. Chap. 21.

Questions and exercises

1. It is frequently asserted that the market system underproduces medical services in relation to other goods and services. Two sets of causal factors are cited: (1) blocked entry into medical service professions and (2) externalities in the consumption of medical services. With "Medical Services" on one axis and "Other Goods and Services" on the other axis, show diagrammatically and explain each of these sets of causes. What evidence can you cite with regard to the validity or invalidity of each?

2. You are asked to render a reasoned opinion with regard to whether or not the government should subsidize housing. What will you use as analytical foundations for your opinions? List these and explain each.

3. Suppose that $MRS_{xy} > MRT_{xy}$ in a market economy. Is it possible that general equilibrium exists? Explain.

4. If a market economy in which $MRS_{xy} > MRT_{xy}$ is one of pure competition with no externalities, what can we expect to occur? Explain in detail and illustrate with a diagram.

5. Can you provide a justification solely on economic grounds for
   a. a progressive income tax?
   b. laws against gambling?
   c. state subsidization of education?

Appendix

Appendix contents

The assumptions	**The constraints**
	Constant prices
	Linear relations
Maximization problems	**One output, two inputs**
	Cost outlay constraints
	Input quantity constraints
	Multiple outputs, multiple inputs
The dual problem	
Summary	**Suggested readings**
	Questions and exercises

Key concepts

Process
Process ray
Linearly homogeneous
   production function
Isoquants
Isocosts
Optimal solution
Feasible solution
Objective function
Primal problem
Dual problem
Shadow prices

Linear programming is the simplest and most widely used of the mathematical programming techniques that have come into vogue since World War II. It is a technique for solving maximization and minimization problems confronting decision-making agencies subject to certain side conditions or constraints that limit what the agencies are able to do.

Linear programming techniques provide little information regarding the operation of the economy beyond that provided by the conventional theory of the firm. Their prime virtue is that they provide computational possibilities that are not present in conventional theory owing to the smooth, continuous, and frequently nonlinear nature of conventional theory's production, cost, and revenue functions. The observable data confronting decision-making agencies are ordinarily not continuous and may not be amenable to marginal analysis or calculus techniques. From an assumption that relations among observable data are linear, straightforward solutions to complex maximization and minimization problems can be obtained through linear programming. Sometimes the distortions resulting from the exclusive use of linear relationships may render worthless the solutions arrived at by means of the technique, but in many cases distortions of this kind may be more or less negligible. Like any other technique, if its results are to be useful, it must be applied with good judgment and common sense.

This chapter presents the nature and method of linear programming. After we establish the assumptions on which linear programming problems rest, we shall formulate and solve graphically a general maximization problem involving one output and two inputs. Then we shall formulate and solve a maximization problem involving multiple outputs and inputs. We shall conclude by considering the dual solution to a maximization problem.

The assumptions

The linear programming technique rests on several basic assumptions—in the decision making to which it is applied, there are constraints on the decision-making agency; input and output prices are assumed to be constant; and the firm's input-output, output-output, and input-input relations are presumed to be linear. These will be discussed in turn.

The constraints

In linear programming problems the firm faces various limitations on its activities.[1] There may be quantity limitations on particular kinds of inputs or facilities used by the firm. An automobile final assembly line, for example, can turn out some maximum number of automobiles per 24-hour period. A firm's warehouse space contains a fixed number of square feet. A candy factory can wrap only so many bars per day. The firm's access to credit may be restricted. And so on.

The firm also faces a limited number of alternative production processes. Any one process is defined in terms of a constant ratio of inputs. Suppose process A involves the use of one worker of a given skill and one machine of a given kind and size. Production carried on with process A can be increased or decreased until input quantity limitations are reached, but it always will involve one worker per machine regardless of the total number of machines used.

Constant prices

Linear programming techniques make use of the purely competitive approach to prices. Output prices and input prices are assumed to be unaffected by the actions of any one individual firm. Output prices are the same whether the firm's output is large or small; input prices are the same regardless of how much or how little of the inputs the firm uses. As sellers and buyers, firms are thought of as being price takers rather than price makers.

Linear relations

Linear programming techniques take advantage of the simplicity of linear relations. In many instances linear relations are found in fact. A firm purchasing an input at a constant price per unit faces a linear total resource cost curve for that input. The total revenue curve from the sale of a product will be linear when the product sells at a constant price per unit. An isocost curve for two inputs will be linear, given the prices of the inputs. An isorevenue curve for two outputs will be linear, given the prices of those outputs.

---

[1] As a matter of convenience, the decision-making agency will be designated as a firm throughout the chapter. Linear programming techniques can be and are used by agencies other than firms, for example, military procurement units.

In other cases, relations among variables that may not actually be linear can be represented usefully by a series of (different) discrete linear relationships or by a single linear relationship. An isoquant, for example, is ordinarily a nonlinear constant product curve for two resources. The linear programming counterpart is a series of connected linear relations. Similarly, actual production functions may very well show nonlinear relations between inputs and outputs. In linear programming problems, they are taken as being homogeneous of degree one.

Maximization problems

In this section two maximization problems will be considered. In the first we shall be concerned with the optimum use of inputs in the production of a single output. In the second we shall be concerned with the optimum output mix to be produced with particular inputs.

One output, two inputs

Cost outlay constraints   Suppose that a firm producing one output X and using inputs A and B seeks to maximize output subject to a given cost outlay. This problem is familiar from our previous study of the theory of production and serves as a good introduction to linear programming. However, suppose that the possibilities of continuous substitution between A and B that characterize the usual theoretical presentation of the problem are absent. Instead, suppose that there are only four processes—possible ratios of B to A—by which the firm can produce the product. The firm faces constant input prices and a constant output price.[2]

The nature of a process is illustrated in Figure A–1. Units of input A per unit of time are measured along the horizontal axis; units of input B per unit of time are shown on the vertical axis. If process C—one of the four processes available to the firm—requires 3 units of input B to every 1 unit of input A, the process can be represented by the linear ray $0C$. Ignore for the moment the scale numbers along $0C$. The various points making up the ray $0C$ show the fixed ratio of B to A, but at different levels of utilization. Similarly, process rays $0D$, $0E$, and $0F$ can be drawn for the other three processes available to the firm. Each process ray shows a given ratio of B to A throughout its length. The ratio of B to A is different for each of the process rays.

---

[2] The problem would not be changed if total revenue were stated as the quantity maximized. Since price per unit of output is given, maximization of output also maximizes total revenue.

Figure A–1   Process rays and isoquants

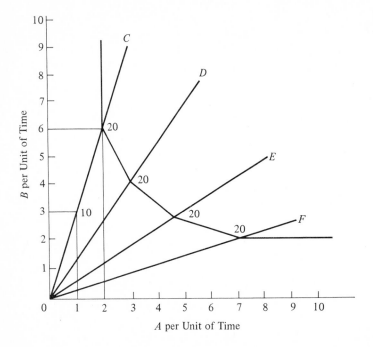

The assumption that the production function is homogeneous of degree one enables us to measure product output along each of the process rays. A production function is of this type if, when *all* inputs are increased in a given proportion, output is increased in the same proportion. Focusing for the moment on process ray 0*C*, suppose that 3 units of *B* used with 1 unit of *A* will produce 10 units of output *X*. The point on 0*C* representing this combination of *A* and *B* can be marked off as 10 units of *X*. Now if the inputs are doubled to 6 units of *B* and 2 units of *A*, output is doubled to 20 units of *X*. The point on 0*C* representing the new combination of *A* and *B* can be scaled as 20 units of *X* and will lie twice as far from the origin as the point representing 10 units of *X* does. The output scale along 0*C* is thus easily established.

Output scales can be established in a similar way along each of the other three process rays. However, the distance measuring 20 units of output (or any other given quantity of output) will not ordinarily be the same along one process ray as it will be along another. The technological efficiency of the other three processes is assumed to be such that the 20-unit output marks on their respective process rays are those indicated in Figure A–1.

The points on the various process rays representing any given quantity of output can be joined by a series of straight lines, as they are at the 20-unit level in Figure A–1. The resulting kinked curve can be called an isoquant, just as was its counterpart in traditional theory. A different isoquant can be drawn for each possible output level. The higher the output level, the farther from the origin the isoquant lies. The linear segment of an isoquant between any two process rays will always be parallel to the corresponding

Figure A–2   Simultaneous use of two processes

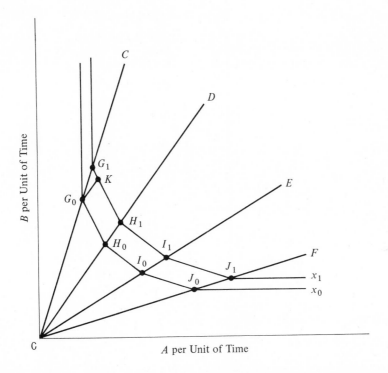

linear segment of any other isoquant. For example, in Figure A–2 the G_1H_1 segment of isoquant x_1 is parallel to the G_0H_0 segment of isoquant x_0.[3]

Any point (such as K) on isoquant x_1 represents the simultaneous use by the firm of two processes to produce a given amount of output. In this case the firm would be using processes C and D. The processes are assumed to

[3] This must be so because the sides $0G_1$ and $0H_1$ of triangle G_1H_10 are cut into proportional segments by line G_0H_0; that is, $0G_0/G_0G_1 = 0H_0/H_0H_1$.

be technologically independent of one another. The productivity of process C is unaffected by the level at which process D is used and vice-versa. Quantity $0G_0$ of X is produced by means of process C. Quantity G_0K $(= H_0H_1)$ of X is produced using process D. The output scale measuring G_0K (or H_0H_1) of X is different from that measuring $0G_0$ of X. The scale of process ray $0D$ is used for the former, while the scale of process ray $0C$ is used for the latter.

In general, we would expect isoquants to exhibit the shapes illustrated in Figures A–1 and A–2. In Figure A–2 suppose that B is capital and A is labor. Continuous substitution of one for the other is assumed to be impossible. Nevertheless, the same general type of reasoning as that used in discussing conventional isoquant shapes still applies. If the firm were using process F to produce a given amount of product, the ratio of labor to capital would be relatively high. Therefore, if the firm were to consider a process using smaller ratios of labor to capital, say, process E, it is likely that it could give up a rather large amount of labor to obtain the additional capital—the amount of output remaining constant. But as the firm moves to processes using relatively smaller ratios of labor to capital, say, processes D and C, the amounts of labor that could be given up to obtain additional units of capital, output remaining constant, would be expected to become smaller and smaller.

The cost constraint on the firm is represented by a conventional isocost curve. Its position and shape are determined by the fixed cost outlay and the fixed prices per unit of the firm's inputs. In Figure A–3 suppose that the cost outlay is T_1 while the prices of A and B are p_{a1} and p_{b1}, respectively. The cost outlay divided by the price of A, or T_1/p_{a1} establishes point S_1, which is the number of units of A that can be obtained if no B is purchased. Similarly, T_1/p_{b1} is the number of units of B that can be purchased if no A is taken; it is represented by point R_1. A straight line joining R_1 and S_1 is the isocost curve showing the combinations of A and B available with the cost outlay T_1. The isocost curve has a negative slope equal to

$$0R_1/0S_1 = T_1/p_{b1} \div T_1/p_{a1} = T_1/p_{b1} \times p_{a1}/T_1 = p_{a1}/p_{b1}.^4$$

The isocost curve and process rays $0C$ and $0F$ place limits on what the firm is able to do. Any point on or within the triangle $0M_1N_1$ is a possible combination of inputs A and B and will lie on some isoquant of the firm; that is, it will produce some specific level of output. The area bounded by

---

[4] The equation of the isocost curve will be

$$ap_{a1} + bp_{b1} = T_1,$$

or

$$b = \frac{T_1}{p_{b1}} - a\frac{p_{a1}}{p_{b1}},$$

for which T_1/p_{b1} is the B axis intercept and p_{a1}/p_{b1} is the slope.

Figure A-3   Output maximization, total cost constraint

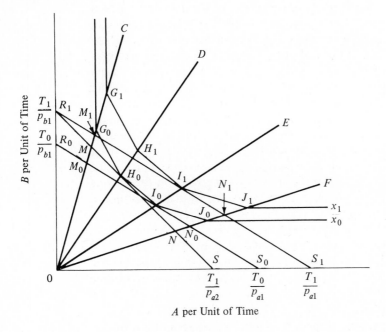

A per Unit of Time

$0M_1N_1$ is called the area of *feasible solutions* to the firm's problem. No production possibilities outside this area are open to the firm.

From the feasible solutions to the firm's problem the *optimal solution* must be found. This has already been postulated as the one that maximizes the firm's output subject to the cost outlay constraint. The optimal solution will occur at point I_1, at which the isocost curve touches the highest possible isoquant. Output x_1 is the highest output possible with the given cost outlay. The firm will use process E. Cost level T_1 expended on any of the other processes will not produce outputs as high as x_1.

A change in the cost constraint, with the prices of A and B remaining constant, will not affect the process used but will affect only the level at which it is used. Changes in T will shift the position of the isocost curve but will not affect its slope. A reduction in the cost outlay to T_0 shifts the isocost curve to the left parallel to itself to R_0S_0. The area of feasible solutions is now bounded by $0M_0N_0$. The firm maximizes output by using process E at level I_0. The maximum output is x_0. Isocosts parallel to R_1S_1 will always touch those isoquant corners falling along process ray $0E$. This will be so because, due to the assumption that the production function is homogeneous of degree one, the corresponding segments of the various isoquants are parallel to each other.

If the price of A relative to the price of B were to increase enough, the firm would shift to a different process. Suppose that the total cost outlay were to remain the same and that the price of A were to rise to p_{a2}. The restricting isocost curve now becomes $R_1 S$ and the area $0MN$ encloses the feasible solutions. To maximize output subject to the constraint, the firm would use process D at level H_0. It is possible, too, that the price of A relative to that of B could change just enough to make the isocost curve coincide with a linear segment of an isoquant, say, a segment corresponding to $G_1 H_1$. If this were the case, process C and process D would be equally efficient. It would make no difference which the firm uses; any combination of the two processes shown by the linear isoquant segment $G_1 H_1$ could be used.

Where the firm is faced by a single constraint, not more than one process is required to maximize whatever the firm is maximizing. In the case at hand the process to be used will be determined by the ratio of input prices. Once the output-maximizing process has been identified, it becomes apparent that a considerable change in input price ratios may occur without inducing the firm to switch from one process to another. The extent to which input price ratios must change to induce a change in the process used will depend on the number of processes available and the measures of the angles formed by linear segments of the isoquants.

Input quantity constraints   The optimal solution to the problem of output maximization is different if, instead of being faced with a total cost outlay constraint, the firm is faced with quantity limitations per time period on one or more of its inputs. Common examples of this are warehouse space, number of machines available, size of a drying kiln, and so on. We shall look first at a situation in which only one of two inputs is limited in quantity. Then we shall extend the constraint to include both of the inputs that the firm uses.

In Figure A–4 we assume first that not more than b_0 of B is available to the firm and that A is available in unlimited quantities. The area of feasible solutions would be on or within triangle $0PJ_2$—the area on or between process rays $0C$ and $0F$ and on or below the horizontal line extending to the right from b_0. There will be some isoquant, the horizontal segment of which coincides with the horizontal line. This isoquant is designated x_2 in the diagram and represents the highest output level available with quantity b_0 of B. Process F used at level $0J_2$ will maximize the firm's output.

If A were limited to a_0 while B were unlimited in quantity, the area of feasible solutions would lie between process rays $0C$ and $0F$ and on or to the left of a vertical line extending upward from a_0. Output would be maximized by using process C at level $0G_3$ and would be x_3. In each of the two cases output maximization requires but a single process. In neither case is the ratio of input prices a determinant of the process to be used.

Figure A–4   Output maximization, input quantity constraints

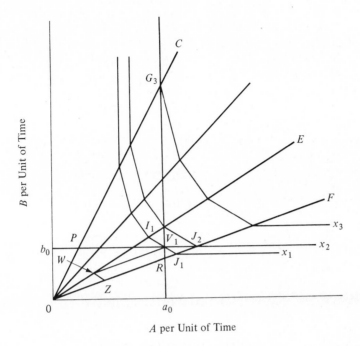

Turning now to the case in which both inputs are limited in quantity, assume in Figure A–4 that the availability of input A is limited to a_0 while that of B is limited to b_0. Subject to these limitations, the area of feasible solutions is on or within the polygon $0PV_1R$. The solution lies at point V_1, and the maximum output of the firm is x_1. In the case illustrated, process E and process F will both be used. Quantity $0W$ will be produced using process E, and quantity $WV_1 (= ZJ_1)$ will be produced using process F. Conceivably, if the available quantity of A were smaller and that of B were larger, the solution to the problem would fall at an isoquant corner such as I_1. If this were the case, process E only would be required. Again the ratio of the price of A to the price of B plays no part in determining the process or processes to be used.

The problems discussed illustrate a fundamental principle in linear programming techniques. No larger number of processes than the number of constraints placed on the firm will be required in whatever the firm is maximizing or minimizing. In the example in which total cost outlay was the only constraint, one process was required. In the example in which the constraint was the quantity of one input, no more than one process was required. When two inputs were limited in quantity, no more than two processes were required. Where there are more inputs limited in quantity, more processes may be required, but these will not exceed the number of inputs for which there are effective limitations.

Multiple outputs, multiple inputs

Moving now to a more complex problem, suppose that the objective of a firm is to maximize the excess of its total receipts over its total variable costs—that is, its total economic rent as defined in Chapter 14,[5] subject to limitations in the capacities of certain fixed facilities. Suppose the firm produces two kinds of output, X and Y. It has four kinds of facilities, each of which is fixed in capacity. We shall designate these as facilities M, N, R, and S. These could be such things as paint shop capacity, final assembly capacity, packaging capacity, and the like.

Rent yielded per unit of X and per unit of Y will depend on the prices received for each of the products and the average variable costs of each. We shall assume that given quantities of variable inputs are required per unit of X regardless of the amount of X produced; therefore, the average variable cost of X will be constant. The same assumption will be made for product Y. Rent yielded per unit of product X produced is equal to its price minus its average variable cost and thus will be a constant amount. Rent yielded per unit of product Y is computed in the same way. These can be designated as r_x and r_y, respectively.

If r_x and r_y were \$8 and \$6, respectively, the following *objective equation* could be established showing what it is that the firm wants to maximize:

$$8x + 6y = W. \qquad (A.1)$$

Rent yielded per unit of X multiplied by the total amount of X produced will be total rent received from the production of X. Rent yielded per unit of Y multiplied by the quantity of Y produced will show total rent obtained from the production of Y. The sum of the two will be W, or total rent received by the firm.

The objective equation is the equation for a family of *isorent curves*—one for every possible value of W. In Figure A–5 the line FG is the isorent curve for W equals \$120. It shows all combinations of X and Y that will yield that amount of rent. Its slope is r_x/r_y, or in this case, 8/6. Isorent curves for higher values of W lie farther to the right but have the same slope. Those for lower values of W also have the same slope but lie farther to the left.

The constraints on the firm's activities are the fixed facilities M, N, R, and S. Suppose that we designate the entire amount of each as unity. In

---

[5] Maximization of rent also means that profit will be maximized, since profit is equal to rent minus total fixed costs. In the problem being formulated the firm's fixed costs will not be known. Thus, rent can be computed but profit cannot.

Figure A–5   Multiple outputs, facility constraints

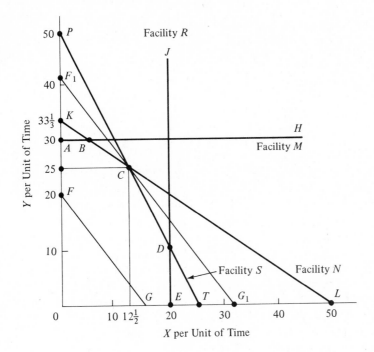

Table A–1 that part of each facility required in the production of one unit of X and that part of each required in the production of one unit of Y are shown.

Essentially, Table A–1 defines the processes involved in the problem. There will be two processes used if both outputs are produced. The production of X requires one process—fixed proportions of facilities M, N, S, and R. Similarly, the production of Y requires one process—fixed proportions of the four facilities, but proportions that are different from those required to produce X.

Table A–1   Multiple outputs, facility constraints

Facility	Facility Input per Unit of Output	
	X	Y
M	0.0	0.033
N	0.02	0.03
S	0.04	0.02
R	0.05	0.0

From Table A–1 we can construct a set of algebraic representations of the constraints placed on the production of X and Y by the fixed facilities. These are

$$0.033y \leq 1 \qquad\qquad\text{(A.2)}$$

$$0.05x \leq 1 \qquad\qquad\text{(A.3)}$$

$$0.02x + 0.03y \leq 1 \qquad\qquad\text{(A.4)}$$

and

$$0.04x + 0.02y \leq 1, \qquad\qquad\text{(A.5)}$$

in which

$$x \geq 0 \text{ and } y \geq 0.$$

Inequality (A.2) sums up the constraint exercised by facility M. This facility is useful in the production of Y only. It is not useful in the production of X. The amount required in the production of one unit of Y is 0.033 of the entire facility. If we consider (A.2) as an equation, solving for y, we find that the entire facility will permit the production of 30 units of Y per unit of time. It will also permit the production of smaller quantities. Graphically, the horizontal straight line AH in Figure A–5 at 30 units of Y represents the limitations on production inherent in facility M.

Similarly, inequality (A.3) sums up the constraint exercised by facility R, which is used only in the production of X. An amount 0.05 of the entire facility is required for each unit. The maximum quantity of X that facility R will permit is 20 units per time period. This is shown graphically by the vertical line EJ at that output level in Figure A–5.

The production possibilities of facility N are shown by inequality (A.4) and include both outputs. Because 0.03 of facility N are required for a unit of Y and 0.02 of it are required for a unit of X, (A.4) treated as an equation marks off possible combinations of outputs that the facility will allow from those it will not allow. If x were zero, 33⅓ units of Y could be handled by the facility. If y were zero, 50 units of X could be handled by it per time period. Locating these two points at K and L, respectively, the straight line joining them in Figure A–5 is the graphic representation of the equation.

Similarly, (A.5) treated as an equation separates the combinations of X and Y that facility S will permit from those it will not permit. If no X were produced, y could be 50 units per time period. If no Y were produced, x could be 25 units. The graphic representation of the equation is the line PT in Figure A–5.

The area of feasible solutions, showing all combinations of X and Y that can be turned out per unit of time by the firm, is $0ABCDE$. Facility M limits the firm to combinations equal to or smaller than those represented by AH; facilities M and N limit it to combinations equal to or smaller than those represented by *ABL;* facilities *M, N,* and *S* further limit it to combinations equal to or smaller than those represented by *ABCT;* facilities *N, S,* and *R* limit it to combinations equal to or smaller than those represented by *BCD;* facilities *S* and *R* limit it to combinations equal to or smaller than those represented by *DE;* and facility *R* limits it to combinations equal to or smaller than those represented by *EJ.*

The optimal solution to the firm's problem can be found graphically by moving to higher and higher isorent curves until the one just touched by the area of feasible solutions is reached. This will be isorent curve F_1G_1, which is just touched by point *C* in Figure A–5. No other point either within or on the boundary of the area of feasible solutions touches an isorent curve as high as F_1G_1. Every point other than *C* on the isorent curve F_1G_1 lies outside the area of feasible solutions. The firm would produce and sell 25 units of *Y* receiving rent of $6 per unit. It would produce and sell 12½ units of *X* receiving rent of $8 per unit. Thus, the maximum total rent obtainable would be $250 per time period.

The facilities' limitations are not all effective as constraints on the firm. At point *C* facility *M* is not used to capacity and, therefore, does not restrict the firm's output. Similarly, facility *R* is not used to capacity. To produce combination *C,* only facilities *N* and *S* are used to their full capacities. If more of these two facilities were available, the firm could move to a higher isorent curve.

Algebraically, the solution to the problem can be found by examining the "corners" of the area of feasible solutions. We need only to examine the corners since the number of processes involved in the problem will not exceed the number of effective constraints on the firm. Thus, the points at which both *X* and *Y* are positive (that is, where two processes are used) and that would be possible optimal solutions must lie at corners formed by two constraints (that is, where two constraints would be effective). A possible optimal solution in which only *X* is produced would require but one effective constraint and would be the corner at the intersection of the *X* axis and the constraint that exercises the greatest restriction when used exclusively in the production of *X.* Similarly, the corner on the *Y* axis represents the only possible optimal solution if *Y* alone were produced. If the optimal solution were a zero output for both *X* and *Y,* the necessity of a corner solution at the origin is obvious.

Suppose now that we start with the corner at the origin and proceed clockwise around the area of feasible solutions, attempting to find the one at which total rent to the fixed facilities is maximum; that is, at which the objective equation (A.1) yields the maximum *W.* At 0 we find that *W* equals zero. To find the coordinates of corner *A,* we solve the facility *M* equation (A.2). At this corner *x* equals zero and *y* equals 30. Plugging these values for *X* and *Y* into equation (A.1), we find that *W* equals $180. The simultaneous solutions of equations (A.2) and (A.4) for facilities *M* and *N* gives us corner B, at which y equals 30 and x equals 5. Thus, from equation (A.1), total rent is found to be $220. The simultaneous solution to equations (A.4) and (A.5) for facilities N and S is represented by corner C, where y equals 25 and x equals 12½. Substituting these values in equation (A.1), total rent is $250. When equations (A.5) and (A.3) for facilities S and R are solved simultaneously for the coordinates of corner D, x equals 20 and y equals 10. Substituting these values in equation (A.1), total rent is $220. The solution to (A.3) provides the coordinates of corner E with x equal to 20 and y equal to zero. Substituting in (A.1) we find that total rent would be $160.

Comparing the results obtained at the various corners shows that corner C provides maximum total rent. In problems where the number of outputs and constraints are too great for graphic analysis this sort of algebraic examination of the "corners" of the area of feasible solutions can be used to find the one that provides the optimal solution.[6]

Different ratios of r_x to r_y may result in different optimal solutions to rent maximization. The slope of an isorent curve $(-r_x/r_y)$ could conceivably be small enough so that the area of feasible solutions touches the highest isorent curve at point B. Or it could be great enough for the highest possible isorent curve to be touched at point D. If $-r_x/r_y$ were equal to the slope of the line segment CD in Figure A–5 [that is, if the highest attainable isorent curve were to coincide with the graphic representation of equation (A.5)], any combination of X and Y on line segment CD would be an optimal solution to maximization of total rent. In this case the limitations imposed by facility S would be the only effective constraint on the firm.

The dual problem

Every linear programming problem has a counterpart problem called its *dual*. The original problem is referred to as the *primal* problem. If the primal problem requires maximization, the dual problem is one of minimization; or if the primal is a minimization problem, the dual is a maximization problem. An illustration of the relationship between a primal problem and its dual is provided in the theory of production and costs. Suppose that the primal problem were that of maximizing output with a given cost outlay. The dual would be that of minimizing costs for the given product output. Whether or not a particular problem to be programmed should be set up for solution in its primal or its dual form depends on (1) which formulation

---

[6] The method used here is called the complete description method. An alternative is provided by the simplex method. *See* Robert Dorfman, Paul A. Samuelson, and Robert M. Solow, *Linear Programming and Economic Analysis* (New York: McGraw-Hill, Inc., 1958), Chap. 4.

yields the desired information more directly and (2) which formulation can be more easily solved.

In this section the dual of the primal problem of the preceding section will be formulated and solved. In the primal problem we sought the outputs of X and Y that would maximize total rent received by the firm, subject to capacity limitations of its fixed facilities M, N, R, and S. In the dual problem we seek to impute minimum values—sometimes called *shadow prices*—to the firm's fixed facilities just sufficient to absorb the firm's total rent.

The data available are those of the primal problem. Table A–1 shows the amount of each fixed facility available (one unit of each) and the portion of each fixed facility required in the production of a unit of X and a unit of Y. The contribution per unit of product X to total rent is given as \$8; that of a unit of product Y is given as \$6. The objective equation of the dual problem can be stated as

$$v_m + v_n + v_r + v_s = V. \tag{A.6}$$

The term v_m denotes the value to be imputed to facility M, while v_n, v_r, and v_s denote, respectively, the values to be imputed to facilities N, R, and S.[7] On the right side of the equation, V denotes the total valuation of the fixed facilities.

The constraints placed on the assigning of minimum values to the fixed facilities are summed up in the following inequalities:

$$0.0v_m + 0.02v_n + 0.04v_s + 0.05v_r \geq 8 \tag{A.7}$$

and

$$0.033v_m + 0.03v_n + 0.02v_s + 0.0v_r \geq 6, \tag{A.8}$$

in which

$$v_m \geq 0, v_n \geq 0, v_s \geq 0, \text{ and } v_r \geq 0.$$

Inequality (A.7) states that the values assigned to the various fixed facilities must be such that the values of productive capacity necessary for the production of one unit of X (*see* Table A–1) when added together must not be less than the value of a unit of X. Inequality (A.8) states the same thing with respect to the production of Y. Together and treated as equations, they state that the values assigned to each kind of productive capacity must be such that a dollar's worth of that productive capacity used in producing either X or Y must yield a dollar in rent.

---

[7] In the present problem the coefficient of each of the variables on the left side of the equation will be one since the entire capacity of each fixed facility is taken as being unity. If each fixed facility were to consist of some certain number of units, then the value per unit of each facility would have as its coefficient the number of units of the facility that are available.

We face the dilemma of having more unknowns than there are equations [treating (A.7) and (A.8) as equations] to solve for the unknowns. However, the linear programming principle cited earlier, together with conventional economic analysis, can rescue us. The linear programming principle tells us that the number of fixed facilities operating as effective constraints on the firm's output should not exceed the number of processes used. There are two processes used—one for producing X and one for producing Y. Consequently, only two of the fixed facilities can be effective constraints on the firm's output, and the other two must be underutilized.

Consider now an underutilized facility from the point of view of conventional economic analysis. A small increase—say, 1 percent—in such a facility would add nothing to the firm's output or total receipts. The marginal revenue product of such an increment would thus be zero and so would its imputed value. Every other 1 percent of the facility would also have an imputed value of zero and so would the whole underutilized facility. Since we must have two underutilized facilities, two of the variables of (A.7) and (A.8) should have values of zero and the other two will take on positive values.

The problem is to find which two of the variables—v_m, v_n, v_s, and v_r— have imputed values of zero and which two have positive values when the firm is minimizing total valuation of the fixed facilities. We can proceed by first assigning values of zero to any two of these, solving for the other two. Then we assign values of zero to another pair (one of the pair may be from the previous pair) and solve for the remaining pair. We proceed in this manner until every possible pair of the variables has been assigned zero values and the corresponding solutions in terms of the remaining variables have been obtained. Six solutions of this sort are possible. We shall examine them in turn.

Suppose, first of all, that v_m and v_n take on values of zero. Equations (A.7) and (A.8) become

$$0.04v_s + 0.05v_r = 8 \qquad\qquad (A.7a)$$

and

$$0.02v_s + 0.0v_r = 6. \qquad\qquad (A.8a)$$

Solving equation (A.8a) for v_s, we find that v_s equals \$300. Substituting this value of v_s in equation (A.7a), we find that v_r equals $-\$80$. This is recorded as solution (1) in Table A–2.

Second, suppose that v_m and v_s take on values of zero. Equations (A.7) and (A.8) become

$$0.02v_n + 0.05v_r = 8 \qquad\qquad (A.7b)$$

and

$$0.03v_n + 0.0v_r = 6. \qquad\qquad (A.8b)$$

Table A–2 Imputation of input values

Solution	Imputed Value in Dollars				Total Valuation in Dollars
	v_m	v_n	v_s	v_r	
(1)	0	0	300	−80	—
(2)	0	200	0	80	280
(3)	0	100	150	0	250
(4)	181.82	0	0	160	341.82
(5)	66.66	0	200	0	266.66
(6)	−181.82	400	0	0	—

Solving equation (A.8b) for v_n, we find that v_n is \$200. Substituting in equation (A.7b), v_r is found to be \$80. These values are recorded as solution (2) in Table A–2.

Third, let v_m and v_r assume zero values. Equations (A.7) and (A.8) become

$$0.02v_n + 0.04v_s = 8 \qquad \text{(A.7c)}$$

and

$$0.03v_n + 0.02v_s = 6. \qquad \text{(A.8c)}$$

Solving these simultaneously, we obtain v_n equal to \$100 and v_s equal to \$150. These are recorded as solution (3) in Table A–2.

Fourth, let v_n and v_s be zero. Equations (A.7) and (A.8) become

$$0.05v_r = 8 \qquad \text{(A.7d)}$$

and

$$0.033v_m = 6. \qquad \text{(A.8d)}$$

The solutions will be v_r equals \$160 and v_m equals \$181.82. These are shown as solution (4) in Table A–2.

Fifth, if v_n and v_r were zero, equations (A.7) and (A.8) would become

$$0.0v_m + 0.04v_s = 8 \qquad \text{(A.7e)}$$

and

$$0.033v_m + 0.02v_s = 6. \qquad \text{(A.8e)}$$

Solving equation (A.7e) for v_s yields a value of \$200. When we insert this value for v_s into equation (A.8e), v_m becomes \$66.66. These are listed as solution (5) in Table A–2.

Finally, when v_s and v_r take on values of zero, we will have exhausted the possibilities. In this case equations (A.7) and (A.8) become

$$0.0v_m + 0.02v_n = 8 \qquad \text{(A.7f)}$$

and

$$0.033v_m + 0.03v_n = 6. \qquad \text{(A.8f)}$$

In equation (A.7f) v_n is equal to \$400. Substituting this value for v_n in equation (A.8f), we find that v_m is $-\$181.82$. These are shown as solution (6) in Table A–2.

All six possible combinations of minimum values that may be assigned to the four facilities are shown in Table A–2. Of the six possible solutions, two can be ruled out immediately. Solutions (1) and (6) yield negative values for one variable, thus violating the requirement that imputed values must be zero or larger. To find which of the remaining four solutions will minimize V of the objective equation (A.6), we can evaluate (A.6) using each of the four in turn. The results are listed in Table A–2 in the last column. Thus, of the four solutions it appears that solution (3) is the one that we seek. Facilities M and R are assigned imputed values of zero. They are the ones that are not fully utilized. Facility N is assigned an imputed value of \$100. Facility S is assigned an imputed value of \$150. Thus the minimum possible valuation of the fully utilized fixed facilities is \$250 when the productive capacity of each of these is equally valuable in the production of either X or Y.

Alternatively, suppose that we look at the problem geometrically. Since facilities M and R have imputed values of zero, the objective equation (A.6) becomes

$$v_n + v_s = V. \qquad (A.6a)$$

This equation yields a family of isovalue curves, each having a slope of -1. If V were \$300, then F_1D in Figure A–6 would be the graphic representation of the objective equation. If V were \$250, then FG would be its graphic representation. For every different value assigned to V, a different isovalue curve is established. All such curves are parallel to each other.

Equations (A.7c) and (A.8c) are plotted in Figure A–6 as AB and CD, respectively. Curve AB shows the minimum possible combinations of values that could be assigned to facilities N and S, such that a dollar's worth of productive capacity would yield a dollar in rent in the production of X. Curve CD shows the minimum possible combinations of values that could be assigned to facilities N and S, such that a dollar's worth of productive capacity would yield a dollar in rent in the production of Y. Pairs of values represented by CE would undervalue the facilities in the production of X. Those represented by EB would undervalue the facilities in the production of Y. Thus, the lines joining A, E, and D represent the minimum possible combinations of values of facilities N and S at which a dollar's worth of productive capacity would produce a dollar's worth of either X or Y. The area above and to the right of AED is the area of feasible solutions to the imputation problem.

The optimal solution is approached geometrically by locating first the lowest isovalue curve touched by the area of feasible solutions. This is curve FG. The pair of values of facilities N and S represented by point E is the optimal solution with v_n equal to \$100 and v_s equal to \$250. At no other

Figure A–6 Imputation of input values

point on, above, or to the right of *AED* will the total imputed value, as shown by an isovalue line through that point, be as low. At point *E* a dollar's worth of productive capacity will produce a dollar's worth of either *X* or *Y* or both. It is worth noting that the optimal solution to the dual problem, like that of the primal problem, is a "corner" solution—the "corner" representing the simultaneous solution of two of the linear constraints on the firm.

A comparison of the dual solution with that of the primal problem shows that they provide the same information. In both we found that facilities *M* and *R* were underutilized and that only facilities *N* and *S* were utilized to capacity. We found that the minimum values that could be imputed to these two facilities total to an amount equal to the maximum rent that they can produce. Further, in the primal problem we found that maximum rent is obtained when 25 units of *Y* and 12½ units of *X* are produced. Twenty-five units of *Y*, yielding $6 in rent per unit, yield a total rent of $150. Twelve and one-half units of *X*, yielding $8 in rent per unit, provide a total rent of $100. From Table A–1 we can determine that the production of 25 units of *Y* requires 75 percent of the capacity of facility *N* and 50 percent of the capacity of facility *S*. The production of 12½ units of *X* requires 25 percent of the capacity of facility *N* and 50 percent of the capacity of facility *S*. From the dual problem, in which v_n and v_s were found to be $100 and $150, respectively, we find that the 75 percent of the facility *N* used in producing

Y is valued at \$75, while the 50 percent of facility S used in producing Y is valued at \$75. Thus, the total value imputed to that part of facilities N and S used in the production of Y is \$150—equal to the total rent that Y yields. Similarly, the 25 percent of facility N used in producing X is valued at \$25, while the 50 percent of facility S used in its production is valued at \$75. The total value of that part of the facilities used in the production of X is \$100—equal to the total rent yielded by product X.

Summary

Linear programming is a technique for solving maximization and minimization problems subject to certain side conditions or constraints. The technique is based on certain assumptions. Decision making is accomplished subject to certain constraints on the decision-making agency; input and output prices are assumed to be constant; and the firm's input-output, output-output, and input-input relationships are assumed to be linear.

The first problem considered was that of maximization of a firm's output (total revenue) subject to the constraint of a given cost outlay to be made by the firm. The production function of the firm was assumed to be linearly homogeneous, and the firm was limited to a choice among four different processes in producing its product output. Isoquants and isocosts were established for the firm. The area of feasible solutions to the problem was established, and then the optimal solution was found at the point where the isocost curve touched a corner of one of the firm's isoquants. Changes in cost outlay, given the prices of inputs, will not change which of the processes available is the optimal one but will affect only its level of use. Changes in the relative prices of inputs may result in changes in which of the processes available is the optimal one. If the constraints under which the firm maximizes output are quantity limitations on inputs, these rather than input prices determine the process or processes chosen. In general, the number of processes required to carry on its activities will be equal to the number of constraints under which the firm operates.

The second problem was that of maximizing the firm's total rents where multiple outputs are produced and several limited facilities are used to produce them. The processes for producing each output are specified. These, together with constraints, determine the area of feasible output solutions to the problem. If the amount of rent yielded by each output is known, isorent lines for the outputs can be established, and the optimal solution of the problem is that at which the area of feasible solutions just touches the highest possible isorent line. This will ordinarily be at a corner of the area of feasible solutions. Not all input or facility quantity limitations need be effective constraints on the firm. The number of effective constraints will generally be equal to the number of processes used. Changes in relative rents yielded by each output may change the optimal solution and, consequently, the input limitations that act as effective constraints.

Attention was then turned to the dual solution to a linear programming primal problem. For the primal linear programming problem summarized in the preceding paragraph, the dual problem consists of imputing values to the inputs that serve as effective constraints on the firm. The imputed values of the total amounts available of such inputs must be such that their sum will not exceed the firm's total rent. This involves finding the combination of minimum valuations at which a dollar's worth of any one input yields a dollar in rent in any one of the products it is used to produce.

Suggested readings

Baumol, William J., "Activity Analysis in One Lesson." *American Economic Review,* Vol. XLVIII (December 1958), pp. 837–873.

Dorfman, Robert, "Mathematical or 'Linear' Programming: A Nonmathematical Exposition." *American Economic Review,* Vol. XLIII (December 1953), pp. 797–825.

Liebhafsky, H. H., *The Nature of Price Theory,* rev. ed. Homewood, Ill.: The Dorsey Press, Inc., 1968. Chap. 17.

Wu, Yuan-Li, and Kwang, Ching-Wen, "An Analytical Comparison of Marginal Analysis and Mathematical Programming in the Theory of the Firm." Reprinted in Kenneth E. Boulding and W. Allen Spivey, eds., *Linear Programming and the Theory of the Firm.* New York: McGraw-Hill, Inc., 1960. Pp. 94–157.

Questions and exercises

1. In the production of concrete blocks a firm has three possible technological processes available to it. One of these requires 1 unit of labor for every unit of capital used. The second requires 2 units of labor per unit of capital. The third requires 5 units of labor per unit of capital. To produce 100 blocks per day, it takes 5 units of capital and 5 units of labor with Process One, 3 units of capital and 6 units of labor with Process Two, and 2 units of capital and 10 units of labor with Process Three.
   a. Draw the 100-, 200-, and 300-block isoquants.
   b. If the price of capital is $40 per unit and the price of labor is $20 per unit, which process will the firm use? Why?
   c. At the above prices of labor and capital, and with a cost constraint of $480 per day, how many blocks will be produced? Explain.
   d. If the price of labor rises to $32 and the price of capital falls to $16, how many blocks can be produced with a cost outlay of $480? Which process will the firm use?

e. Suppose that no cost constraint is imposed on the firm but that it is limited to the use of 11 units of capital and 17 units of labor per day. How many blocks per day can it produce and what process should it use?

2. A candy factory can use its facilities to produce 3-ounce candy bars, C, and 1-pound boxes of chocolates, B. The facilities available to it are a kitchen, K, for cooking candy ingredients; a packaging room, P; and a 10-person labor force, L.

   The kitchen will cook ingredients for a daily maximum of 600 candy bars, or 240 boxes of candy, or any combination between these limits with a tradeoff of 5 candy bars for 2 boxes of candy.

   In the packaging room the daily capacity is 800 bars or $106\frac{2}{3}$ boxes or any combination between these limits with a tradeoff of 15 bars for 2 boxes of candy.

   The labor force can cook and package a daily maximum of 1,000 bars or 100 boxes, or any intermediate combination with a tradeoff of 20 bars for 2 boxes of candy.

   a. If the firm's objective is to maximize its total revenue, R, set up and solve the objective function and the constraint inequalities. How many boxes of candy will be produced daily? How many candy bars? (*Hint:* You may find it helpful to plot the problem on squared paper.)

   b. What values can be imputed to K, P, and L?

Glossary

Alternative cost principle   the underlying basis of cost—the cost of producing a unit of any good or service—is the value of the resources needed to produce that good or service in their best alternative use.

Budget line or constraint   all combinations of goods and services available to the consumer when all of the consumer's income (purchasing power) is being utilized, given that income and the prices of the goods and services.

Capital   the nonhuman ingredients that contribute to the production of goods and services, including land, raw and semifinished materials, tools, buildings, machinery, and inventories.

Cartel   an organization of firms in an industry in which certain management decisions and functions that would otherwise be performed by individual firms are transferred to a group representing the firms.

Cartel, centralized   a cartel in which the central association or group makes decisions regarding pricing, outputs, sales, and distribution of profits.

Cartel, market-sharing   a cartel in which the market shares of the member firms are determined mutually.

Competition, monopolistic   *see* Monopolistic competition.

Competition, nonprice   *see* Nonprice competition.

Competition, perfect   pure competition plus an additional condition of perfect knowledge on the part of buyers and sellers which enables them to make instantaneous adjustments to disturbances.

Competition, pure   a market situation in which (1) individual buyers or sellers of an item are too small relative to the market as a whole to be able to influence its price, (2) units of the item are homogeneous, (3) the price of the item is free to move up or down, and (4) units of the item can be sold by any potential seller to any potential buyer.

Competitive goods   *see* Substitute goods.

Complementary goods   goods related in such a way that an increase in the consumption of one, holding the consumer's satisfaction level and the quantity consumed of the other constant, increases the marginal rate of substitution of the other for money.

Constant cost industry   an industry in which the entry of new firms causes no changes in resource prices or the cost curves of individual firms in the industry.

Constant returns to scale   *see* Linearly Homogeneous Production Function.

Contract curve   a curve generated in an Edgeworth box showing Pareto optimal distributions of goods (resources) between two consumers (producers).

Cross elasticity of demand   the responsiveness of the quantity taken of one item to a small change in the price of another. The elasticity coefficient or measure is computed as the percentage change in the quantity of one divided by the percentage change in the price of the other.

Decreasing cost industry   an industry in which the entry of new firms causes resource prices to fall, which, in turn, causes the cost curves of each individual firm to shift downward.

Demand   the various quantities per unit of time of an item that a buyer(s) is (are) willing to buy at all alternative prices, other things being equal. Demand for an item can be conveniently represented as either a demand schedule or a demand curve.

Diminishing returns, law of   the principle stating that if the input of one resource is increased by equal increments per unit of time while the quantities of other inputs are held constant, there will be some point beyond which the marginal physical product of the variable resource will decrease.

Diseconomies, external   forces outside the activities of any single firm causing resource prices to rise and cost curves of the firm to shift upward as new firms enter an industry.

Diseconomies of size   the forces causing a firm's long-run average costs to increase as the output level and the size of plant are increased. These are usually thought to be the increasing difficulties of coordinating and controlling the firm's activities as its size and output are increased.

Distribution, output   how the output, or net national product, of an economy (usually defined in terms of one-year time periods) is shared among individuals and/or families.

Distribution, personal income   how the income generated in an economy per time period (for example, one year) is shared among individuals and/or families.

Dual problem   the inverse counterpart statement of the primary or primal maximization or minimization problem in linear programming; if the primal problem is to maximize output for a given cost outlay, the dual problem is to minimize the costs of producing whatever that maximum (given) output is.

Economic activity   the interaction among economic units involved in the production, exchange, and consumption of goods and services.

Economic system   the institutional framework within which a society carries on its economic activities.

Economies, external   forces outside the activities of any single firm causing resource prices to fall and cost curves of the firm to shift downward as new firms enter an industry.

Economies of size   the forces causing a firm's long-run average costs to decrease as the output level and size of the plant are increased. These are usually thought to be (1) increasing possibilities of division and specialization of labor and (2) increasing possibilities of using more efficient technology.

Edgeworth box   an analytical device in which the indifference maps (isoquant maps) of the two consumers (producers) are placed over each other but with one turned 180 degrees from the other. The axes form a box, the sides of which measure the total quantities of two products (resources) available to the two consumers (producers).

Efficiency, economic   the ratio of the value of outputs obtained from an economic process to the value of inputs necessary to produce them. The higher the value of output per dollar's worth of resource input, the greater is the efficiency of the process.

Efficient distribution of goods   a distribution of goods among consumers such that the marginal rate of substitution between any two goods is the same for all consumers.

Efficient distribution of resources   a distribution of resources among products or uses such that the marginal rate of technical substitution between any two resources is the same for each of those products or uses.

Elastic demand   a situation in which the absolute value of the elasticity coefficient is greater than one.

Elasticity of demand, arc   the coefficient of price elasticity measured between two distinct points on a demand curve.

Elasticity of demand, cross   *see* Cross elasticity of demand.

Elasticity of demand, income   the responsiveness of quantity taken of a good to small changes in income, other things being equal. The elasticity coefficient or measure is computed as the percentage change in quantity divided by the percentage change in income.

Elasticity of demand, point   the coefficient of price elasticity measured at a point on a demand curve.

Elasticity of demand, price   the responsiveness of the quantity taken of an item to a small change in its price, given the demand curve. The elasticity coefficient or measure is computed as the percentage change in quantity divided by the percentage change in price.

Engel curve   a curve showing the various quantities of a good or service that a consumer (consumers) will take at all possible income levels, other things being equal.

Equilibrium   a state of rest from which there is either no incentive or no opportunity to move.

Equilibrium, general   simultaneous equilibrium of all individual economic units and subsections of the economy.

Equilibrium, partial   equilibrium of individual economic units and/or subsections of the economy with respect to given data or conditions external to the unit or subsection. Changes in those data or conditions will change the equilibrium position of the unit or subsection.

Equilibrium price   *see* Price, equilibrium.

Expansion path   a curve showing the least cost (maximum output) combinations of resources for all possible output levels of a firm.

Explicit costs of production   the costs of resources hired or purchased by a firm to use in the process of production.

Exploitation, monopolistic   the difference between what a resource is worth to a firm and what it is worth to consumers; that is, for resource A it is measured by $VMP_a - MRP_a$.

Exploitation, monopsonistic   the difference between what a unit of resource is worth to a firm and what it is paid; that is, for resource A it is measured by $MRP_a - p_a$.

Externalities in consumption   the effects that consumption of an item by one consumer may have on the welfare of others. Externalities may be positive as, for example, when flowers purchased by one person are enjoyed by others as well. They may also be negative as, for example, when one student in a class consumes garlic, making the classroom unpleasant for others.

Externalities in production   the effects that production of one product may have on the production possibilities of others. They may be positive as would be the case if an orchard of fruit trees is grown near a bee farm where honey is produced. They may be negative as would be the case if one producer pollutes water that another producer must then clean before using.

Feasible solutions   the set of possible solutions to a linear programming problem lying within the constraints under which the decision-making unit must operate.

Firms   single proprietorships, partnerships, and corporations engaged in the buying and hiring of resources and in the production and sale of consumer goods and services or of higher-order capital resources.

Fixed costs   the costs of the fixed resources used by a firm in the short run.

Fixed resources   those resources used by a firm that it cannot change in quantity in the short run.

Gentlemen's agreement   an informal or unwritten agreement among firms with regard to pricing, outputs, market sharing, and other activities of the firms.

Households   all unattached individuals and all family units of the economy.

Hypotheses   tentative statements of causal relations among variables.

Implicit costs of production   the costs of self-owned, self-employed resources used by a firm in the process of production.

Income consumption curve   a curve showing the various combinations of goods that a consumer will take at all possible income levels, given the prices of the goods.

Income distribution, functional   the distribution of income by kinds or classes of resources.

Income distribution, personal   the distribution of income among households of the economy.

Income effect of a price change   that part of a change in quantity taken of a good in response to a price change that results solely from the change in the real income of the consumer occasioned by the price change.

Increasing cost industry   an industry in which the entry of new firms causes resource prices to rise, which, in turn, causes the cost curves of each firm to shift upward.

Indifference curve   a curve showing the different combinations of two items among which a consumer is indifferent.

Indifference map   a family of indifference curves showing the complete set of a consumer's tastes and preferences—the individual's preference rankings of different combinations and sets of combinations—for two items.

Inelastic demand   a situation in which the absolute value of the price-elasticity coefficient is less than one.

Inferior goods   goods the consumption of which decreases as a consumer's (consumers') income(s) increase(s).

Isocost curve   a curve showing all combinations of two resources that a firm can purchase for a given cost outlay, given the prices of the resources.

Isoquant curve   a curve showing the combinations of resources required by a firm to produce a given level of product output.

Isoquant map   the family of isoquant curves of a firm describing the resource combinations required to produce all possible levels of output.

Kinked demand curve   the demand curve that a firm faces if other firms in the industry would follow price decreases but would not follow price increases. It would have a "kink" or corner in it at the initial price.

Labor   the capacity for human effort (both of mind and muscle) available for use in producing goods and services, ranging all the way from unskilled, undifferentiated to highly skilled, specialized labor power.

Least cost combination of resources   a combination of resources for a firm at which the marginal rate of technical substitution between the resources is equal to the ratio of the resource prices ($MRTS_{ab} = p_a/p_b$). It is also a combination at which the marginal physical product per dollar's worth of one resource is equal to the marginal physical product per dollar's worth of every other resource

$$\frac{MPP_a}{p_a} = \frac{MPP_b}{p_b}.$$

Limit pricing   price policies followed by the firms in an industry that are designed to discourage entry into the industry by new firms.

Linear programming   a technique for solving maximization and minimization problems where the function operated upon is linear and is subjected to linear constraints.

Linearly homogeneous production function   a production function with characteristics such that an increase of a given proportion in all resource inputs will increase output in the same proportion; that is, if $x = f(a,b)$, then $\lambda x = f(\lambda a, \lambda b)$.

Living standard   the level of well-being or welfare that an economic system provides for the members of a society, usually measured by per capita income.

Long run   a planning period long enough for the firm to be able to vary the quantities of all the resources it uses.

Losses   the difference between a firm's total costs and its total receipts when total receipts are less than total costs, including as costs the alternative costs of all resources used.

Macroeconomics   the economics of the economy as a whole—the forces causing recession, depression, and inflation together with the forces resulting in economic growth.

Marginal costs   the change in a firm's total costs per unit change in its output level.

Marginal physical product of a resource   the change in total output of a firm resulting from a one-unit change in the employment level of the resource, holding the quantities of other resources constant.

Marginal productivity theory   the theory that in a private enterprise economy, resource units are paid prices equal to either their values of marginal products or their marginal revenue products. Thus, income is distributed among households according to the relative contributions that the resources they own make to the productive processes.

Marginal rate of substitution   the amount of one good or service that a consumer is just willing to give up to obtain an additional unit of another, measured for any combination of goods and services by the slope of the indifference curve through the point representing that combination.

Marginal rate of technical substitution   the amount of one resource that a firm is just able to give up in return for an additional unit of another resource with no loss in output. For any given resource combination it is measured by the slope of the isoquant through the point representing that combination.

Marginal rate of transformation   the quantity of one product that must be given up in order to produce an additional unit of another. For any given combination of products on a transformation curve, it is measured by the slope of the curve.

Marginal resource cost   the change in a firm's total costs resulting from a one-unit change per unit of time in the purchase of a resource.

Marginal revenue   the change in a firm's total revenue per unit change in its sales level.

Marginal revenue product   the value to a firm of the change in output when the firm changes the level of employment of a resource by one unit. For resource A used in producing product X, it is computed as follows:

$$MRP_a = MPP_a \times MR_x.$$

Marginal utility   the change in the total utility of a consumer that results from a one-unit change in the consumption level of an item.

Microeconomics   the economics of interacting subunits of the economic system, such as individual consumers and groups of consumers, resource owners, firms, industries, individual government agencies, and the like.

Mobility   the capability of a seller to sell to any of various alternative buyers or of buyers to buy from any of various alternative sellers.

Monopolistic competition   a market situation in which there are many sellers with no one seller important enough to be able to influence any other seller and with each seller's product differentiated from that of the others.

Monopoly, pure   a market situation in which a single seller sells a product for which there are no good substitutes.

Monopsony   a market situation in which there is a single buyer of an item for which there are no good substitutes.

Most efficient rate of output   the output level at which a firm's short-run average costs are minimum—the most efficient of all possible short-run output levels, given the firm's size of plant.

Most efficient size of plant   that size of plant for which the short-run average cost curve forms the minimum point of the long-run average cost curve—the most efficient of all possible plant sizes for a firm.

Nonprice competition   activities by a firm intended to enlarge its market share without cutting the price of the product. Its major forms are (1) advertising and (2) variation in the design and quality of the product.

Normal goods   goods the consumption of which increases as a consumer's (consumers') income(s) increase(s).

Normative economics   study of the way that economic relationships ought to be. Value judgments play an integral part in the ranking of possible objectives and the choices to be made among them.

Objective function   in a linear programming problem the function defining what it is that the decision-making unit wants to maximize or minimize subject to the constraints that it encounters.

Oligopoly   a market situation in which the number of sellers is small enough for the activities of one to affect the others and for the activities of any or all of the others to affect the first.

Oligopoly, differentiated   an oligopolistic market situation in which the sellers sell differentiated products.

Oligopoly, pure   an oligopolistic market situation in which the sellers sell homogeneous or identical products.

Opportunity cost principle   *see* Alternative cost principle.

Optimal mix of goods and services   an output mix at which the marginal rate of substitution between any two goods is the same for all consumers and is equal to its marginal rate of transformation, given that all resources are fully employed and that there are no externalities in consumption or production.

Optimal solution   the best (for the decision-making unit) of the feasible solutions to a linear programming problem.

Pareto optimum   a situation in which no event can increase the well-being of one person without decreasing the well-being of someone else.

Plant, size of   *see* Most efficient size of plant.

Positive economics   study of the causal relationships that exist in economics; no value judgments are involved.

Postulates *see* Premises.

Premises the bedrock starting point for the construction of a theory, consisting of propositions or conditions that are taken as given or as being so without further investigation.

Price, administered a price fixed by law, by groups of sellers, by groups of buyers, or by collective actions of buyers and sellers. It is not completely free to move in response to changes in demand and supply.

Price ceiling an administered level above which the price of an item is not allowed to rise.

Price consumption curve a curve showing the various combinations of goods that a consumer will take at all possible prices of one, given the price of the others and the consumer's income.

Price discrimination the act of charging two or more buyers (sellers) different prices for the same product. It is possible and profitable if (1) buyers (sellers) can be separated into different markets that can be kept apart and (2) the elasticities of demand (supply) at each price level differ among the markets.

Price, equilibrium that price at which the quantity per unit of time that buyers want to buy is just equal to the quantity that sellers want to sell. It generates neither a surplus nor a shortage. There is no incentive for buyers or sellers to change it. If attained, it will be maintained.

Price floor an administered level below which the price of an item is not allowed to fall.

Price leadership a loose form of collusive arrangement in which one firm is identified as the price setter or leader and other firms follow the prices of the leader firm.

Price war a situation in which rival firms drive prices down through attempts to undercut each other's prices.

Primal problem in linear programming the original problem stated by the objective function and the constraints placed on the decision-making unit.

Principles statements of causal relations that have undergone and survived thorough testing.

Private enterprise system an economic system characterized by private property rights and voluntary private production and exchange of goods and services and of resources.

Process one of several resource proportion possibilities used in producing a good or service. The term is used in linear programming problems.

Process ray a linear line extending upward to the right from the origin of an isoquant diagram showing a given process at different levels of utilization of that process.

Product differentiation a situation in which sellers sell essentially the same product but that of each seller has, at least in the minds of the consumers, certain characteristics that distinguish it from the product of other sellers.

Production function   the physical relation between a firm's resource inputs and its output of goods and services per unit of time.

Profits   the difference between a firm's total receipts and its total costs when total receipts exceed total costs, including as costs the alternative costs of all resources used.

Rent, economic   the residual left for the fixed resources of a firm after the variable resources have been paid amounts equal to their alternative costs.

Resources   the ingredients available to go into the production of goods and services that are used to satisfy human wants. They consist of labor resources and capital resources.

Shadow prices   prices imputed to a good, service, or resource that is not priced by the marketplace or that is incorrectly priced by the market.

Shortage   a situation caused by a price below the equilibrium level in which buyers want to buy larger quantities than sellers want to sell.

Short run   a planning period so short that a firm is unable to vary the quantities of some of the resources that it uses—usually thought of as the time horizon during which the firm cannot change its size of plant.

Short-run supply curve, firm   a curve showing the different quantities per unit of time of a good that the firm will place on the market at all possible prices. It is that part of the firm's short-run marginal cost curve that lies above the average variable cost curve.

Short-run supply curve, market   a curve showing the different quantities per unit of time of a good that all firms together will place on the market in the short run at various possible prices.

Shut down price   the price below which the firm would cease to produce in the short run.

Socialistic system   an economic system characterized by governmental ownership or control of resources and of goods and services. Production is carried on by the government, which also specifies the terms or conditions under which exchange may take place.

Substitute goods   goods related in such a way that an increase in the consumption of one, holding the consumer's satisfaction level and quantity consumed of the other constant, decreases the marginal rate of substitution of the other for money.

Substitution effect of a price change   that part of a change in quantity taken of a good in response to a price change that results solely from the change in its price. The effects of the price change on the real income of the consumer, and the subsequent effect of the real income change on the quantity taken, have been eliminated.

Superior goods   *see* Normal goods.

Supply   the various quantities per unit of time of an item that a seller(s) is (are) willing to sell at all alternative prices, other things being equal. Supply of an item can be conveniently represented as a supply schedule or a supply curve.

Surplus   a situation caused by a price above the equilibrium level in which sellers want to sell larger quantities than buyers want to buy.

Tax, excise   a per unit tax on an item. It may be a specific tax based on the physical unit of the item or an *ad valorem* tax based on its price.

Tax incidence   The distribution of a tax among economic units.

Techniques of production   the know-how and the means available for combining and transforming resources into goods and services.

Theory   a set of related principles providing insight into the operation of some phenomenon.

Transformation curve   a curve showing the maximum production possibilities for two products, given the resources available to produce them.

Unitary elasticity of demand   a situation in which the absolute value of the elasticity coefficient is equal to one.

Utility   the satisfaction obtained from the goods and services that a consumer consumes.

Value of marginal product   the market value of the change in output when a firm changes the employment level of a resource by one unit. For resource A used in producing product X it is computed as follows:

$$VMP_a = MPP_a \times p_x.$$

Variable costs   the costs of the variable resources used by a firm in either the short run or the long run.

Variable resources   those resources used by a firm that it can change in quantity in either the short run or the long run.

Very short run   a time period with respect to a given good or service so short that the quantity of it placed on the market cannot be changed.

Wants   the varied and insatiable desires of human beings that provide the driving force of economic activity.

Welfare   the level of economic well-being or satisfaction attained by individuals and groups of individuals in the society.

Index

Administered prices and income distribution, 411–415
Advertising (*see* Nonprice competition)
Agricultural price supports, 61–63
Agricultural Adjustment Acts, 61–63
Allen, R. G. D., 77n
Allocation of resources (*see* Resource allocation)
Alternative cost principle, 193–194, 354
Atkinson, A. B., 420

Bain, Joe S., 316n, 324
Bator, Francis, 443
Baumol, William J., 57, 115, 188, 443, 467
Blocked entry
  effects on resource allocation, 389–397
  under oligopoly, 313–318
  under pure monopoly, 269
Boulding, Kenneth E., 132n, 141, 306n
Brozen, Yale, 73
Budget line, 85–87

Capital
  accumulation of, 25–26
  differences in ownership of, 409–410
  nature of, 6, 387n
  reallocation of, 389
  redistribution in ownership of, 416–417
Cartels
  centralized, 297, 299–302
  limitations to profit maximization by, 302, 304
  marginal cost curve of, 300–301
  market sharing, 297–298, 303–305
  nature of, 135, 297
  pricing and output by, 299–305
Cartter, A. M., 380
Cassels, John M., 188
Chamberlain, Edward H., 336
"Circular flow" model, 18–20
Clark, John Bates, 398
Collusion, incentives for, 297

Compensating variation in income, 99–100
Competitive goods (*see* Substitute goods)
Competition in the United States, 31–32
Complementary goods, 36, 83–85, 122–125
Constant cost industries, 250–251, 331
Constant returns to size, 169–170
Consumer behavior
  constraints on, 85–87, 128
  objectives of, 88–90, 128
Contract curve, 94, 182–186
Corner solutions, 92–93, 459–460, 465
Cost curves, assumptions underlying, 195
  long-run
    average, 211–213
    marginal, 218–220
      relation to short-run marginal, 218–220
    total, 209–211
  short-run
    average, 201–205, 227–228
      relation to long-run average, 211–218
    average fixed, 201–202, 225–226
    average variable, 202–204, 226–227
    marginal, 205–206
      derivation from total, 205–206
      relation to average and average variable, 206–209, 228
    total, 198, 200–201
    total fixed, 198–199
    total variable, 199–200
Costs of production
  alternative cost principle, 193–194
  explicit, 194
  fixed, 197–199
  implicit, 194–195
  variable, 197–200
  See also Cost curves
Cross elasticity of demand
  for complementary goods, 55
  industry definition in terms of, 55–56
  for substitute goods, 55

Decreasing cost industries, 251–253, 331
Deductive reasoning, 9
Demand curve faced by the firm
  definition of, 145
  under monopolistic competition, 151–
    153, 327–328
  under oligopoly, 148–151, 296
  under pure competition, 146–147
  under pure monopoly, 147–148, 262–264
  See also Kinked demand curve
Demand for goods and services
  changes in, 35–36, 41–43
  definition of, 32–35
  determination of market demand, 101–
    102
  See also Individual consumer demand
    curves
Demand for a resource
  assumptions underlying, 344
  market, 349–351
  under monopoly, 363–367
  under pure competition, 344–349
Dewey, Donald, 285, 317n
Differentiated products (*see* Product differentiation)
Diminishing marginal utility, 121–122
Diminishing returns
  definition of, 168–169
  and marginal cost, 342–344
Diseconomies of size, 215–216
Distribution of output, 23–24
Dorfman, Robert, 428n, 460n, 467

Economic activity, 3–8
Economic efficiency
  in allocation of resources, 182–186,
    430–434
  in distribution of final goods, 102–105,
    429–430
  under monopolistic competition, 333–334
  nature of, 22–23
  under oligopoly, 321–322
  under pure competition, long-run, 27
  under pure monopoly, 279
  in relation to resource combinations,
    169–181
Economic growth, requirements for, 26
Economic rent, 354–356
Economic system
  functions of, 20–26
  model of, 18–20
Economic theory, construction of, 9–10
  functions of, 10

  macroeconomics, 11–12
  microeconomics, 11–12
Economics, definition of, 3–4
Economies of size, 213–215
  division, and specialization of labor,
    214–215
  technological factors, 215
Edgeworth box, 102–105, 182–186, 429–436
Edgeworth, Francis Y., 77n
Efficiency (*see* Economic efficiency)
Einhorn, Henry A., 32
Elasticity, price
  of demand
    arc elasticity, 43–47
    definition of, 43–44
    factors influencing, 53–54
    measurement of, 43–48
    point elasticity, 47–48
    in relation to total money outlays,
      48–52
  of supply, 232–234, 243–244
Employment of resources
  competitive firm level of, 344–349
  market level of, 351–354
  monopolistic level of, 363–368
  monopsonistic level of, 368–379
Energy conservation, 139–140
Engel, Ernst, 90n
Engel curves, 90, 94–97
Entry into an industry
  barriers to, 316–318
  effects upon collusion, 314–315
  under monopolistic competition, 329–330
  under oligopoly, 313–318
  under pure competition, 245–253
  under pure monopoly, 269
Envelope curve, 211–218
Equilibrium, general
  importance of, in economic theory,
    427–429
  nature of, 425–429
  partial, 426–427
  See also General equilibrium theory
Equilibrium price, 39–41
Exchange, 102–105, 135–137
Expansion path of the firm, 181, 210–211
Explicit costs of production, 194
Exploitation of resources
  under monopoly, 367–368
  under monopsony, 375–376
External diseconomies, 249
External economies, 252–253
Externalities

in consumption, 430–431
in production, 432–434

Fair Labor Standards Act of 1938, 63
Fellner, William, 154, 380
Firm
    nature of, 18–19
    role in free enterprise system, 18–20
Fixed resources, 196–197
Friedman, Milton, 14, 27, 70–71, 258, 330n,
    408n, 420
Fringe benefits, 105–107
Functional distribution of income, 405–406
Functions of an economic system, 20–26

Gasoline price controls, 66–68
General equilibrium
    nature of, 427–429
    with constant product supplies, 437–438
    with constant resource supplies, 438–443
    monopoly impact on, 439
    monopsony impact on, 439–440
    and welfare, 436–443
General equilibrium theory
    objectives of, 427–429
    variants of, 427–429
Gentlemen's agreements, 298
Goods and services, valuation of, 20–21

Harrod, R. F., 285
Heady, Earl O., 188
Hicks, John R., 77n, 115, 357
Higher education costs, 220–221
Households
    nature of, 18
    role in free enterprise system, 18–20
Hypotheses, 9

Implicit costs of production, 194–195,
    220–221
Income-consumption curve, 94–97
Income determination, 23, 401–402
Income differences
    causes of, 405–415
    nature of, 402–405
    and resource allocation, 23–24, 385–389
Income distribution
    determinants of, 23–24
    effect of administered prices on, 411–
        415, 417–418
    effect of supply restrictions on, 413–414
    functional, 405–406

personal, 402–405
Income effects on a price change, 98–101
Income elasticity, 97–98
Income redistribution
    effects on free enterprise system, 415–
        419
    via administered prices, 417–418
    via resource redistribution, 416–417
Increasing cost industries, 247–250, 331
Increasing returns, 168–169
Index numbers
    Laspeyres, 109–111
    Paasche, 111–113
Indifference curves
    assumptions underlying, 78–79
    characteristics of, 79–82
    definition of, 78, 125–127
    from a utility surface, 125–127
Indifference map, 77–79
Individual consumer demand curves
    definition of, 90–93
    establishment of
        by indifference curve analysis, 90–93
        by utility analysis, 132–135
Inductive reasoning, 9
Inferior good, 96–97
Inflation control, 68–71
Input-output analysis, 428
Irwin, Manley R., 285
Isocosts, 179–181, 407–408
Isoquants
    characteristics of, 162–163
    nature of, 161–163, 177–179, 209–211
    in linear programming, 449–456
Isorent curves, 456–460
Isovalue curves, 464–466

Jevons, William S., 119

Kinked demand curve, 309–311
Knight, Frank H., 27, 57, 188, 387n
Knight, Wyllis R., 74
Koopmans, Tjalling C., 14
Kuznets, Simon, 408n
Kwang, Ching-Wen, 467

Labor resources
    allocation of, 387–389
    definition of, 6
    differences in ownership of, 407–409
    redistribution of, 416
Labor supply, 107–109
Lange, Oscar, 14

Least-cost resource combinations
  and average variable cost, 182, 341–344
  determination of, 179–181
  for a given product output, 179–181,
    341–344
  and long-run average cost, 213
  under monopsonistic buying, 371–373
  for profit-maximizing output, 341–344,
    361–362
Liebhafsky, H. H., 467
Leontief, Wassily W., 428
Levels of living, 5–6
Licensing laws, 317
Linear programming
  assumptions underlying, 447–449
  complete description method, 449–460
  constraints, 448
  dual problem, nature of, 460–466
  feasible solution defined, 453
  objective equation, 456, 461
  optimal solution defined, 453
  output maximization problems, 449–460
  primal problem, nature of, 449–460
  processes
    definition of, 449–452
    profit or rent maximization problems,
      456–460
    relation to constraints, 455–456
    shadow prices, 461–466
Living standards, 5–6
Long run, definition of, 197, 244–245
Lorenz curve, 403–405
Loss minimization
  under pure competition, 240–242
  under pure monopoly, 239–240

Machlup, Fritz, 154, 297n, 302n, 324, 336
Macroeconomic theory, 11–12
Marginal costs, as determined by resource
    inputs, 342–344
  nature of, 205–209
  See also Cost curves
Marginal productivity theory, 401–402
Marginal rate of substitution, 80–82, 125–
    127
Marginal rate of technical substitution, 163
Marginal rate of transformation, 184–186
Marginal resource costs
  discontinuous curves, 376–377
  nature of, 369
  relationship to resource supply curve,
    368–371

Marginal revenue
  derivation from demand curve, 262–264,
    286–290
  discontinuous curves, 309–311
  under monopoly, 262–264, 286–290
  under pure competition, 238–240
  relationship to price and to demand elas-
    ticity, 262–264, 291–292
Marginal revenue product
  definition of, 344–345
  as demand for a resource, 346–347,
    363–365
  relationship to value of marginal product,
    344–345, 367–368
Market price determination, 39–41
Markets
  consumer goods and services, 18–20
  resources, 18–20, 384
Marshall, Alfred, 14, 44, 44n, 57, 141, 258,
    285, 354n
Marshall, F. R., 380
Maximization of satisfaction
  in terms of indifference curves, 88–90
  in terms of utility, 128–132
Measday, Walter S., 297n
Menger, Karl, 119
Methodology, 8–10
Microeconomic theory, 11–12
Miller, James C., III, 74
Minimum wage rates, 63, 376–377, 393–397
Mobility of resources
  meaning of, 30, 378–379
  in relation to time, 384
Monopolistic competition
  characteristics of, 151–152, 327–328
  equilibrium under
    long-run
      entry blocked, 329–331
      entry open, 331–333
    short-run, 328–329
  long-run profits under, 329–333
  output restriction, 333
  pricing and output
    long-run, 329–333
    short-run, 328–329
  sales promotion under, 153–154, 334–335
  and welfare, 333–335
Monopoly
  effects on resource allocation, 390–391
  See also Pure monopoly
Monopsony
  conditions causing, 374–375
  counteraction

through aids to resource mobility, 377–378

by price fixing, 376–377

effects on resource allocation, 391–392

nature of, 368–371

profits, 371

Moore, Thomas G., 266

Most efficient rate of output, 209

Most efficient size of plant, 216–218

Multiple products, 182–186

Multiple-unit firm, 221–223

National income analysis, 11–12

Negative income tax, 418–419

Nonprice competition

advertising

effects of, 318–319

purposes of, 318

under monopolistic competition, 334–335

variations in quality and design

effects of, 319–320

purposes of, 319–320

Normal good, 96–97

Normative economics, 10

Nutter, G. Warren, 32

Okun, Arthur M., 420

Oligopoly

characteristics of, 148–149, 295

classification of types, 297–299

collusion under, 297–299, 299–308

differentiated, 148–149, 296

independent action under, 298, 308–311

long-run profits under, 311–318

output restriction under, 321

pricing and output under

long-run, 311–318

short-run, 299–311

pure, 148–149, 296–297

sales promotion under, 151, 318–320

and welfare, 320–322

Opportunity cost principle, 193–194

Optimal outputs of goods and services, 434–436

Optimum rate of output (*see* Most efficient rate of output)

Optimum size of plant (*see* Most efficient size of plant)

Organization of production, 21–23, 253–257

Output restriction

under monopolistic competition, 333

under oligopoly, 321

under pure monopoly, 277–279

Pareto optimum, 12–13, 104, 135–137, 182–186, 425, 429–436

Pareto, Vilfredo, 13n, 77n

Partial equilibrium, 426–427

Patents, 317

Patinkin, Don, 315n

Perfect competition, 30–31

Personal income

determinants of, 401–402

differences in, 402–405

distribution of, 402–405

Pigou, A. C., 398

Positive economics, 10

Postulates, 9

Premises, 9

Price ceilings, 66–71

Price-consumption curve

and elasticity of demand, 93–94

nature of, 91–92

Price discrimination

conditions necessary for, 273

distribution of sales under, 273–274

examples of, 276–277

profit maximization under, 274–276

Price elasticity (*see* Elasticity, price)

Price leadership

by dominant firm, 306–308

by low-cost firm, 305–306

Price rigidity, 308–311

Price supports, 61–65

Price wars, 308–309

Principles, nature of, 10

Product schedules and curves of a resource

average product, 164–167

and efficiency, 169–181

marginal physical product, 165–167

total product, 163–167

Product differentiation, 149, 296, 318–321

Product distribution (*see* Income distribution)

Product homogeneity, 29

Production, organization of, 21–23, 253–257

Production functions

nature of, 159–169

linearly homogeneous, 169–170, 405

Production surface, 160–163

Production techniques, 8, 160, 174

Profit

as incentive for efficiency, 21–23

measurement of, 235–240

nature of, 235–236

Profit maximization

under monopolistic competition, 328–333

Profit maximization (*continued*)
   under oligopoly, 299–318
   under pure competition, 236–240
   under pure monopoly, 265–273
   for resource inputs
      under monopoly, 361–362
      under monopsony, 371–373
      under pure competition, 341–344
Propensity to accumulate, 410
Pure competition
   adjustments to disturbances under,
      245–253
   firm and market
      long-run, 244–253, 255–257
      short-run, 235–244
   characteristics of, 29–31, 145–146, 231
   equilibrium under
      long-run, 245–253
      short-run, 235–244, 254–255
   marginal revenue under, 238–240
   as a "norm," 31–32
   price and average cost relationships
      under, long-run, 244–253
   pricing and output under
      long-run, 244–253, 255–256
      short-run, 228, 235–244
   total revenue under, 235
   use of, in economic analysis, 31–32
   very short-run pricing under, 231–234,
      253–254
   and welfare, 253–257
Pure monopoly, characteristics of, 147, 261
   elasticity of demand under, 263–264, 268
   equilibrium under
      long-run, 269–273
      short-run, 265–268
   examples of, 261
   long-run profits under, 269–273
   output restriction under, 277–279
   price discrimination under, 273–277
   pricing and output under
      long-run, 269–273
      short-run, 265–268
   regulation of, 280–283
   sales promotion under, 148, 279–280
   and welfare, 277–279

Quasi rent (*see* Economic rent)

Radford, R. A., 74
Rationing in the very short run, 25, 231–234
Rees, Albert, 380, 398
Regulation of monopoly, through maximum
   prices, 280–281

by taxation, 281–283
Rent (*see* Economic rent)
Resource allocation
   administered price distortions of, 393–
      397
   among different uses, 21–23, 385–389
   and economic efficiency, 385–389
   among industries, 385–387
   long-run, 387–389
   for maximum welfare, 383
   monopoly distortions of, 390–391
   monopsony distortions of, 391–392
   and net national product, 383–389
   nonprice distortions of, 392–393
   under pure competition, 385–389
   short-run, 385–387
Resource employment (*see* Employment of
   resources)
Resource exploitation (*see* Exploitation of
   resources)
Resource immobility, 374–375
Resource prices
   determination of
      under monopoly, 363–367
      under monopsony, 371–373
      under pure competition, 351–354
   functions of, 383–389
   and resource allocation, 384–389
Resource supply curve, 351, 368–371
Resources, characteristics of, 7–8
   classification of, 6–7
   economic, 7
   efficient combinations of, 22, 169–181
   fixed, 196–197
   free, 7
   nature of, 6–8
   scarcity of, 7–8
   variable, 196–197
   variations in proportions of, 7–8
   versatility of, 7–8
Revenue curves
   marginal
      under monopoly, 262–264, 286–292
      under pure competition, 236–242
   total
      under monopoly, 235–237, 262–264
      under pure competition, 236–242
Ridge lines, 179
Robinson, Joan, 285, 304n, 380

Sales promotion
   under monopolistic competition, 153–
      154, 334–335

under oligopoly, 151, 318–321, 322
under pure competition, 146–147, 257
under pure monopoly, 148–149, 279
Samuelson, Paul A., 460n
Scherer, F. M., 32n, 261n, 297n, 324
Scitovsky, Tibor, 357
Shortages, 39–40, 66–71
Short run, nature of, 196–197, 235
Size of plant, definition of, 197
and long-run output, 209–220
variability of, in long-run, 209–220
Size of plant adjustments
under monopolistic competition
with entry blocked, 329–331
with entry open, 331–333
under oligopoly, 313
under pure competition, 244–253
under pure monopoly, 270–273
Slichter, Sumner H., 395n
Smith, Adam, 214n
Solow, Robert M., 460n
Specialized resources, 374–375
Speculation, 25, 232–234
Standards of living (*see* Levels of living)
Stigler, George J., 27, 46n, 90n, 141, 224,
336, 357
Substitute goods, 36, 83–85, 122–125
Substitution effects of a price change,
98–101
Superior good, 96
Supply
changes in, 38–39, 41–43
long-run industry
under constant costs, 251
under decreasing costs, 251–252
under increasing costs, 250
nature of, 37–39
restriction of, 65–66, 413
short-run
firm, 242
market, 242–244
Surplus, 39–40, 61–63

Tangri, Om P., 188
Taxes
capital gains, 417
estate and gift, 417
excise tax incidence, 71–73
payroll, 73
personal income, 417

Techniques of production (*see* Production
techniques)
Transformation curves, 184–186, 433–436

Unemployment, 63–65, 393–397
Utility
marginal, and consumer tastes and preferences, 121–122
definition of, 119–122
diminishing, 121–122
for nonrelated goods, 119–122
for related goods, 122–125
maximization of, 128–132
measurement of, 121, 127
total, 119–121

Value
in exchange, 138–139
in use, 138–139
Value of marginal product
nature of, 345–346
relationship to marginal revenue product,
367–368, 390–391
Variable resources, 196–197
Very short run
nature of, 25, 231–234
pricing under, 231–234, 253–254
rationing among consumers, 231–232
rationing over time, 232–233
Viner, Jacob, 224, 258

Walras, Leon, 119, 132n
Wants
as ends of economic activity, 4
origins of, 4–6
Weintraub, Sidney, 145, 169
Welfare
effects of monopolistic competition on,
333–335
effects of pure competition on, 253–257
effects of pure monopoly on, 277–279
effects of pure oligopoly on, 320–322
exchange and, 102–105, 135–137
nature of, 12–13, 425
optimum, 429–436
resource allocation and, 383
White, Lawrence J., 324
Wilcox, Clair, 269n, 316n, 324
Wu, Yuan-Li, 467